Glbal
Movements
in the Asia Pacific

Glbal
Movements
in the Asia Pacific

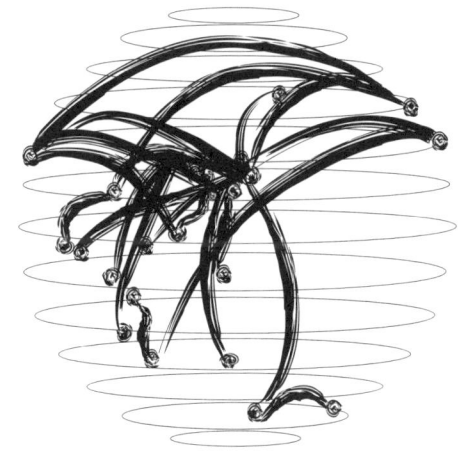

Editors

Pookong Kee
Hidetaka Yoshimatsu
Ritsumeikan Asia Pacific University, Japan

 **World Scientific**

NEW JERSEY · LONDON · SINGAPORE · BEIJING · SHANGHAI · HONG KONG · TAIPEI · CHENNAI

Published by

World Scientific Publishing Co. Pte. Ltd.

5 Toh Tuck Link, Singapore 596224

USA office: 27 Warren Street, Suite 401-402, Hackensack, NJ 07601

UK office: 57 Shelton Street, Covent Garden, London WC2H 9HE

Library of Congress Cataloging-in-Publication Data
Global movements in the Asia Pacific / edited by Pookong Kee & Hidetaka Yoshimatsu.
    p. cm.
   ISBN-13: 978-981-283-373-0
   ISBN-10: 981-283-373-0
   1. Globalization--Social aspects--Asia. 2. Globalization--Social aspects--Pacific Area.
3. Asia--Emigration and immigration. 4. Pacific Area--Emigration and immigration.
5. Asia--Foreign economic relations. 6. Pacific Area--Foreign economic relations.
I. Kee, Pookong. II. Yoshimatsu, Hidetaka.
   HN801.Z9G565 2009
   303.48'25--dc22

                            2009018243

British Library Cataloguing-in-Publication Data
A catalogue record for this book is available from the British Library.

Cover image with compliments from Mr Souno Shigeaki

Typeset by Stallion Press
Email: enquiries@stallionpress.com

Printed in Singapore by Mainland Press Pte Ltd

ACKNOWLEDGMENTS

In compiling this collection of papers we have received the help of a number of organizations and individuals. We would like to thank especially the Japan Society for the Promotion of Science (JSPS), an agency of the Ministry of Education, Culture, Sports, Science and Technology for its award of an International Scientific Meetings grant to Kee Pookong.

The competitive grant program encourages the participation of international researchers in meetings of scientific importance in Japan, and wider dissemination of scientific and practical knowledge to the international community. This volume comprises mainly papers selected or developed from the meeting.

The funding program's emphasis on younger researchers facilitated the participation of several graduate students in the final stage of their doctoral research and post-doctoral scholars who had recently completed their dissertations. The contributions of these younger scholars have enriched the content of this volume.

We would also like to acknowledge the role of the Ritsumeikan Center for Asia Pacific Studies (RCAPS), secretariat for this project, in hosting the meeting under its annual Ritsumeikan Asia Pacific Conference series. Established in 1998 at the Kyoto-based Ritsumeikan University, RCAPS has been a driving force in promoting research on the Asia Pacific within the Ritsumeikan Asia Pacific University (APU) since its opening in 2000 in Beppu, Oita.

As Director and Secretary-General respectively of RCAPS during this project, the co-editors would like to thank the RCAPS Steering Committee for its guidance and support at different stages of the project. We also acknowledge the administrative backing of the Research Office and assistance of several graduate students. We are grateful to the printer of the event poster for allowing us to use Mr Souno Shigeaki's artwork for the book cover design.

Pookong Kee and Hidetaka Yoshimatsu
Editors

We would like to thank Cindy Wachowski, Naomi Stenning and Emma Barber for their assistance with editing and proofreading, and especially to Jerry and Carla Eades, who were responsible for most of the text editing. Jerry Eades also compiled the index.

Malcolm Cooper
Vice President, Ritsumeikan
Asia Pacific University
Director, Ritsumeikan Center
for Asia Pacific Studies

CONTENTS

Acknowledgments   v

About the Authors and Editors   xi

Introduction   xv

Chapter 1:   Brain Drain, Brain Gain, and Brain Circulation
in a Half-Globalized World   1
Yuan T. Lee

Chapter 2:   Transnational Business and Diplomacy in the
Asia Pacific   9
Alfonso T. Yuchengco

Chapter 3:   International Mobility of the Highly Skilled:
The Role of the Global Knowledge Network   21
Yasuo Uchida

Chapter 4:   International Migration in Asia and the Pacific:
Key Features and the Role of the United Nations   27
Keiko Osaki

Chapter 5:   Globalizing Householding: Toward a
Multicultural Age in East Asia   37
Mike Douglass

Chapter 6:   Migration Policy: Major Issues for Japan and
Other OECD Countries   69
Susumu Yamagami

Chapter 7: The Occupational and Geographical Locations
of Transnational Immigrant Minorities in Japan 93
Tony Fielding

Chapter 8: Between Privilege and Prejudice: Chinese
Immigrants in Corporate Japan's
Transnational Economy 123
Gracia Liu-Farrer

Chapter 9: Multicultural Coexistence Policies: Responses
of Local Governments in the Tokyo
Metropolitan Area to the Pressures of
International Immigration 147
Stephen Robert Nagy

Chapter 10: Migration under the Japan–Philippines Free
Trade Agreement 181
Michael Angelo A. Cortez

Chapter 11: International Migration, Brain Drain, and the
Philippine Economy's Rocky Road to Development 201
Jose V. Camacho Jr.

Chapter 12: The Growing Role of International Remittances
in the Vietnamese Economy: Evidence from the
Vietnam (Household) Living Standard Surveys 225
Wade Donald Pfau and Thanh Long Giang

Chapter 13: Staying in the Global Economy: A Preliminary
View of Vietnam after the End of the Agreement
on Textiles and Clothing 249
John Thoburn

Chapter 14: Emergence of the Global Development
Network in the Personal Computer Industry 265
Yumiko Nakahara

Chapter 15: The Changing Global Environment of
            Logistics: The Cases of Hakata and Kitakyushu
            in Japan   285
            Hiroshi Hoshino

Chapter 16: The Development of China's International
            Shipping Industries   297
            Meilong Le

Chapter 17: The Future of the World's Number One Port —
            Hong Kong: A Case Study   309
            Sunny Ho

Chapter 18:   Impact of Port Security on Liquefied Natural
            Gas and Container Cargo Movements   323
            Paul T.-W. Lee and Young-Tae Chang

Chapter 19: Transnational Architectural Production in
            Downtown Beijing   341
            Xuefei Ren

Index   369

ABOUT THE AUTHORS AND EDITORS

Jose V. CAMACHO Jr. is Associate Professor and Associate Dean of the College of Economics and Management, University of the Philippines, Los Baños.

Young-Tae CHANG is Professor at the Global School of Logistics, Inha University and the past President of the Korea Port Economics Association and former Secretary-General of the Global U8 Consortium.

Michael Angelo A. CORTEZ is Assistant Professor in International Management, Ritsumeikan Asia Pacific University, Japan.

Mike DOUGLASS is Director of the Globalization Research Center and Professor of Urban and Regional Planning at the University of Hawai'i.

J.S. EADES is Dean of the College of Asia Pacific Studies, Ritsumeikan Asia Pacific University, and Senior Honorary Research Fellow in Anthropology, University of Kent, UK.

Tony FIELDING is Research Professor in Human Geography at the Sussex Centre for Migration Research at the University of Sussex, Brighton, UK.

Thanh Long GIANG is a lecturer at the National Economics University (NEU) and a researcher at the Vietnam Development Forum (VDF), both in Hanoi, Vietnam.

Sunny HO is Executive Director of The Hong Kong Shippers' Council and Chairman of the Hong Kong Logistics Management Staff Association, Fellow of CIM and Council Member of CILT.

Hiroshi HOSHINO is Professor of Business Administration at the Graduate School of Economics, Kyushu University and Head of Kyushu University Business School.

Pookong KEE is Professor of Asia Pacific Studies at Ritsumeikan Asia Pacific University, Japan.

Meilong LE is the Professor of Transportation and Logistics in Shanghai Jiao Tong University, and Vice Dean and co-founder of Sino-US Global Logistics Institute.

Paul T-W LEE is Professor and Director of the Shipping, Port and Logistics Research Center, Kainan University in Taiwan and Invited Research Fellow of JRI, Inha University, Korea.

Yuan T LEE is past President of Academia Sinica and winner of the 1986 Nobel Prize in Chemistry.

Gracia LIU-FARRER is Associate Professor at the Graduate School of Asia-Pacific Studies, Waseda University, Japan.

Stephen Robert NAGY is a Research Associate at Waseda University's Institute of Asia-Pacific Studies at time of going to press, and from December 2009 will be Assistant Professor, Department of Japanese Studies, Chinese University of Hong Kong, Hong Kong.

Yumiko NAKAHARA is a Lecturer in the Faculty of Management, Kyushu Sangyo University, Japan.

Keiko OSAKI is a Chief of the Demographic and Social Statistics Branch, Statistics Division, United Nations.

Wade Donald PFAU is an Associate Professor at the National Graduate Institute for Policy Studies (GRIPS) in Tokyo, Japan.

Xuefei REN is Assistant Professor in the Global Urban Studies Program and the Department of Sociology at Michigan State University, USA.

John THOBURN is Emeritus Reader and Senior Research Fellow in Economics at the School of Development Studies, University of East Anglia, UK, and was previously Professor of Development Economics at Ritsumeikan Asia Pacific University, Japan.

Yasuo UCHIDA is Dean of Planning and Development and Coordinator of the Graduate School, Ritsumeikan Asia Pacific University, Japan.

Susumu YAMAGAMI is Vice President of Student Affairs and Professor of Asia Pacific Studies, Ritsumeikan Asia Pacific University, Japan.

Hidetaka YOSHIMATSU is Professor of Asia Pacific Studies, Ritsumeikan Asia Pacific University, Japan.

Alfonso T YUCHENGCO is Presidential Advisor on Foreign Affairs with Cabinet rank of the Republic of the Philippines and Chairman of the Yuchengo Group of Companies.

INTRODUCTION

Hidetaka Yoshimatsu and J. S. Eades

Globalization is one of the most important phenomena in the current international arena. It can be defined as the processes and activities that promote interdependence and interconnectedness between peoples and societies throughout the world, together with their acceleration and intensification. Globalization is variously seen as a challenge (Sassen, 1998; Bhagwati, 2004), a result of technological change (Castells, 1996, 1997, 1998), or a largely inevitable process that we have to live with and make work (Stiglitz, 2006). For as Friedman has pointed out (2005), thanks to the new technology and patterns of innovation, the world is now becoming increasingly flat.

Even though waves of globalization took place long before the 20th century as Alfonso Yuchengco reminds us in Chapter 2 of this book, the current phase of globalization is different from those that preceded it in terms of its extent and pervasiveness: it is unique in its scope. In the current globalized world, events taking place in one place can have an increasingly direct and profound influence on events in geographically distant locations, and in an increasingly short time. This pervasive globalization has been produced by a combination of factors: the falling cost of transport, thanks to the deregulation of air transport, the arrival of wide-bodied jets, and the container revolution in the shipping industry since the 1970s; the global acceptance of liberal capitalism, leading to free movement of people, goods, capital, and services, especially since the end of the Cold War in the late 1980s; and the rapid evolution in information and communications technologies in the 1990s.

Globalization as a process therefore has a complex and multidimensional nature. Even though most attention has been devoted to the economic dimensions of globalization, with trade, investment and financial transactions regarded as both its major causes and consequences, the social, cultural, environmental and political dimensions are also very important. These may be linked directly to the economy, as is typically the case with the environmental problems resulting from the long-distance transport of materials either by sea or air. The social and cultural dimensions of globalization also have a long-term impact on both societies and individuals in them, through changing attitudes towards politics, social institutions, and people's sense of identity (Castells, 1997). The political dimension is reflected in the growth of intergovernmental organizations, and national governments seek to formulate new systems of governance and cooperation in the face of the forces that globalization has unleashed (Castells, 1998).

Globalization has had a significant influence on a wide range of state and non-state actors at the local, national, regional, and global levels. It presents a major challenge to the cohesion of both local communities and nation states. Communities are affected by migration and the spread of new technologies, goods and values, while national governments seek to respond to their increasing inability to control flows of information, capital and people through developing new forms of regionalism, as seen most dramatically in Europe (Castells, 1998: 330–354.). Meanwhile, transnational corporations, nongovernmental organizations (NGOs), and local governments are increasingly forming their own cross-border linkages and networks that have a significant influence on the interests and behavior of the state.

The multidimensionality and complexity of globalization require politicians, technical specialists, administrators and researchers to examine its causes, processes, and consequences from plural, multi-disciplinary perspectives. We need to pay attention both to the logic underpinning globalization, and its implications for key issues involving state and society such as inequality, state sovereignty, and the prospects for liberal democracy.

Globalization and Global Movements

The growing pace, volume and complexity of international movements of people, goods, capital, services, and knowledge are both causes and consequences of the latest round of globalization. In particular, the increasing movements of people, including migrants, tourists, students, and refugees, have an immense impact on society at many different levels (Castles and Miller, 1998). Intergovernmental organizations and national governments alike are forced to devise new institutions and administrative frameworks to manage the new forms of mobility. Inflows and outflows of people create new opportunities for people, but also result in new sorts of conflict in local communities. Moreover, the growing flows of trade, investment, technology, and knowledge have changed the world's industrial and economic maps. The diffusion of the latest technology and knowledge of production methods has shifted the location of value-added activities (Castells, 1996), away from the economically more developed nations to those like China and India currently experiencing their own waves of high-speed growth. Massive investment and the adoption of advanced technologies have enabled these countries to become major bases for manufacturing industries. Such a process of transformation has been accompanied by massive movements of skilled and unskilled laborers.

Whereas these movements often imply mobility of goods, people, capital, and knowledge on a global scale, they may also take place on the local or regional level, because of the lower transaction costs associated with geographic proximity. These regional movements are often effective responses to the challenges and opportunities brought about by global processes. This means that the extent, significance and consequences of global movements can be explored and understood by focusing on phenomena and processes taking place at the level of regions such as the Asia Pacific. Given that this region consists of nations with a range of cultures, political systems, and levels of development, investigation of the dynamics of movements within the region is all the more valuable for understanding the complex and multidimensional processes of globalization in relation to regional growth, stability and identity.

Human Movement and Technology

Many of the early chapters in this book deal with the varieties of human movement to be found in the contemporary Asia-Pacific region. The first paper by Nobel Prize winner Yuan T. Lee (Chapter 1) begins with an account of his own personal odyssey. In the early 1960s, he left Taiwan together with many other Chinese students to study in America, many of whom became successful in the companies and research institutes of the United States. However, instead of the conventional analysis of the "brain drain" and its impact on developing countries, Lee argues that the migrants' countries of origins may eventually benefit from the out-migration, as the migrants return with the technical knowledge acquired elsewhere and use it to build up high-technology industries back home. It is worth asking the conditions under which this can take place, given that it seems to be a more common phenomenon in the Asia-Pacific region than elsewhere. Clearly the new technologies brought back by the migrants can only take root where there is reasonable political stability, an institutional framework which is friendly to entrepreneurs, and a "developmental state" interested in fostering high-technology development (Woo-Cumings, 1999). The results, as Yuchengco reminds us in Chapter 2, can be seen in the rise of companies from the "dragon economies" (Hong Kong, Singapore, South Korea and Taiwan), as well as mainland China and India, becoming major players in the world market. Regional trade is also booming, with an increasing web of agreements between the ten ASEAN countries, China, Japan and South Korea, giving these countries an increasingly significant share of world trade. The other ingredient, discussed by Uchida in Chapter 3, is a population of highly skilled workers, able to help develop a knowledge economy and an environment for innovation. This may involve collaboration with the state, as in the development of science parks and silicon valleys around the region (Castells and Hall, 1994), including the Hsinchu Science-Based Industrial Park in Taiwan.

Dynamics of Migration: Households, Gender and Ethnicity

The main outlines of the contemporary migration system which has emerged in the Asia-Pacific region under the influence of globalization is described by Osaki in Chapter 4. She argues that two distinctive labor migration systems have developed in Asia. The first, centered on the Middle East, dates back to the rise in oil prices in the 1970s, which led to a massive construction boom and inflow of foreign workers in the Gulf states. The workers came initially from the surrounding states, but then increasingly from South Asia — at a time when the previous migration to Europe was slowing down. From the 1980s, the action moved to East and Southeast Asia with the rise of the dragon economies. Countries such as Japan, Taiwan, Korea, Singapore and Brunei have increasingly attracted labor from South Asia, the Philippines, and mainland China, as their economies expanded. Typically, these workers are short-term migrants, performing dirty, dangerous and demanding jobs which the local workers are no longer interested in taking up. Longer term settlement is difficult or impossible due to immigration regulations, making it possible for the governments of the region to lay off migrant labor first when economic recession strikes. Osaki also mentions the increasing "feminization" of migration, with an increasing number of women workers from the Philippines and elsewhere taking over domestic labor as local women become increasingly involved in the professional labor force. While the remittances from these workers provide welcome support for the local economy back home, there is increasing concern about the impact of their absence on their families, particularly their children as other relatives are forced to take over responsibility for them.

The relationship between households and migration is also a central theme of Chapter 5 by Mike Douglass, building on his earlier work on migration (Douglass and Roberts, 1999). He starts from the classic observation that the household is an essential component of the capitalist system because of its role in the reproduction of labor: raising children and supporting family members are functions which are difficult to carry out through the market. However, the family is starting to abandon many of its traditional functions, as seen most dramatically in the falling birth rate and rapidly aging populations of Japan (Traphagan and Knight, 2003) and the other highly-developed countries of the region. Global movements of people therefore play an important role in allowing the household to continue to play its role in social reproduction, despite the increasing strains and tensions to which it is subjected. Specific mechanisms include the recruitment of foreign spouses (usually wives) to offset the local shortage of partners; adoption and surrogate motherhood as new alternatives to traditional reproduction and child-rearing, sending children abroad for education rather than educating them locally; and the use of migrant domestic workers, usually women, to take over the chores of caring for children and the elderly. Meanwhile, the elderly are themselves on the move, taking their pensions and savings to countries where the cost of living is lower (e.g. Miyazaki, 2008; Ono, 2008), and where domestic help is cheaper, given the increasing lack of children either available or willing to look after their parents in old age.

Yamagami in Chapter 6 and Fielding in Chapter 7 focus specifically on migration to Japan as a case study of the general trends discussed in the earlier chapters. Yamagami notes that the proportions of women and skilled workers in the migrant labor force are both steadily increasing. He also points to the growing numbers of illegal and undocumented migrants, and increasing attempts by states to control them through sanctions against the employers for whom they work. Efforts to control the flow lead naturally to greater efforts by organized crime to help the migrants to cross borders, and thus an increase in human smuggling and trafficking. Finally, political instability in particular countries and regions usually results in an outflow of refugees and asylum seekers hoping to settle elsewhere, so that states constantly have to revise their laws and institutional arrangements for dealing with them. At the same time, countries suffering from aging populations and a shortage of labor in particular sectors of the market are actively encouraging migrants, especially highly skilled migrants to settle to fill these niches. Even in Japan, the numbers of skilled foreign workers being allowed to enter and settle is steadily rising, and the encouragement by the Japanese government of large numbers of foreign students to come to Japan for education will probably mean that this trend will continue in future.

Fielding's chapter deals in detail with the different waves of migrants coming to Japan and their locations within the country. Large-scale Korean and Chinese immigration to Japan dates back to Japan's colonial empire, which lasted from 1895 to 1945 (Weiner, 1994). Though many of these "oldcomer" migrants returned to China, Taiwan and Korea after the Second World War, some remained and became the nuclei of new waves of Chinese and Korean immigrants in the post-war period, as the Japanese economy revived (Ryang, 1997, 2000). They were also joined by an increasing number of "newcomers," including migrants from Thailand and the Philippines (often young women working as hostesses or entertainers), and South Americans claiming Japanese ancestry, most of them from Brazil and Peru (Tsuda, 2003). There are also differences in the location of different migrant groups, with the Chinese and Koreans largely concentrated in Kansai, and the more recent migrants more heavily concentrated in the Kanto and Chubu regions, around Tokyo and Nagoya. Finally, there are groups of assorted westerners, many of them working as professionals and teachers in Tokyo and the other major cities.

In Chapter 8, Liu-Farrer focuses on the Chinese community in contemporary Japan, particularly the skilled workers involved in information technology and related industries. A fascinating pattern emerges from her data: because they have Chinese workers fluent in Japanese working for them, some Japanese companies have found themselves able to expand their business to China. The bi-cultural immigrant workers thus become managers and specialists, occupying strategic positions in the companies that employ them. Clearly, many of the overseas workers trained in Japan are staying on in Japan to work for Japanese companies, many of which have been aggressively recruiting foreign talent. Unlike Japanese workers, however, they tend to change jobs regularly, moving generally between small- and medium-sized companies, partly because they find their progress into management positions blocked because they are still considered outsiders. In fact some workers do manage to get promoted, sometimes by demonstrating their ultimate commitment to Japan — by naturalizing and taking Japanese citizenship, in addition to permanent residence.

In contrast, Nagy (Chapter 9) focuses on the Japanese bureaucracy and its attempts to make life in modern Japan more bearable for foreigners. He presents case studies of multicultural policies in three areas of Tokyo: Shinjuku and Adachi Wards in central Tokyo, and Tachikawa City to the west. Shinjuku, in the commercial heart of the city, has the most diverse population, 10 percent of which are foreigners. While stopping at granting actual voting rights, Shinjuku tries hard to include the foreign population in its activities, by providing Japanese language programs, and information on topics such as disaster relief (given the danger of earthquakes) in foreign languages. Similar initiatives and problems are found in Adachi. However, rates of participation in these activities by foreigners remain low, partly because they have their own sources of information and support in the existing ethnic communities and church groups. The reasons for the lack of success are perhaps best summed up by Nagy's analysis of the problematic nature of the programs in Tachikawa. The events intended to include foreigners in fact emphasize the differences between foreign and Japanese residents and cultures. And in attempting to teach foreigners about Japanese culture, they focus on traditional elements such as tea ceremony and flower arrangement, which have little practical relevance to life in modern Japan.

Labor Markets and Remittances

A theme from Douglass' chapter, that of the regional demand for carers in aging societies, is the starting point of Cortez (Chapter 10). This chapter discusses recent developments in migration patterns between the Philippines and Japan. Until the beginning of the 21st century, the majority of male migrants from the Philippines to Japan were trainees, working in the automotive and electrical industries. Women migrants were divided between younger "entertainers," many of them actually working as hostesses in bars (Dizon, 2006), and domestic helpers, for which demand has been rising thanks to the rapidly aging Japanese population. The regional demand for nursing and care services throughout the region has led to a proliferation of training institutions in the Philippines, which the Philippine government has increasingly tried to bring under scrutiny and control. Under the terms of a free trade agreement between the two countries, Japan agreed to accept a quota of both nurses and caregivers from the Philippines from 2007, as a response to the increasing demand for care. These workers would be given a period of three years (for nurses) and four years (for caregivers) to pass Japanese licensing examinations, after which they could stay in Japan indefinitely. Even though the tough examination hurdle probably means that few Philippine workers will stay permanently under this agreement, the agreement does point to the possibility of freer legal movement of these categories of skilled workers in future, as the flows of labor increasingly reflect the demographic imbalances between the countries of the region.

Camacho, in contrast, traces the consequences of migration for the Philippines and its economy (Chapter 11). A feature of the Philippines is that supply of skilled labor produced by the education system has grown faster than the economy as a whole, where the rate of growth has been much more variable: industry has in fact declined along with agriculture over the years, while poverty has persisted, especially in the rural areas. Emigration has been a noticeable feature of the economy since the period of American colonization, but from the 1970s it became a labor export policy actively promoted by the Marcos regime. The flow of remittances from workers overseas has since become a mainstay of the national economy (Parrenas, 2001). Camacho argues that this outflow of skilled labor could eventually be problematic: the continued export of science teachers may already be having serious impact on levels of education in the Philippines, while the exodus of qualified nurses is also alarming, undermining the capacity of the country to expand its own medical services to meet the needs of the local population. Whether this situation will continue, or whether the global prospects of teachers and nurses will increase the flow of students into these professions, has yet to become clear.

Remittances are also the subject of Pfau and Giang (Chapter 12), this time in the context of Vietnam. Using data from successive surveys of household living standards, the authors find that the main source of remittances has been the United States, and that remittances have increasingly flowed to the rural areas and away from major cities. The proportion of households receiving remittances has held steady at around 5 to 7 percent, with a disproportionate amount going to households headed by elderly females or the unemployed. These findings suggest that overseas remittances are in fact slowly helping overcome income equalities in Vietnam.

Production and Trade

Thoburn (Chapter 13) also looks at Vietnam, though the focus is now on the flows of goods and services, rather than people. In discussing the case of the textile and clothing industry, Thoburn looks at the effects of the phasing out of the Multi-Fibre Arrangements, which restricted entry of goods from developing countries to major markets in the United States and Europe, and their replacement by a freer trade regime. This has in fact encouraged production of goods for exports by developing countries, making them in turn more vulnerable to competition from other low cost producers — and especially China. The chapter also addresses the question of how far Vietnam has been able to remain in the export game under the new trade regime. In the 1990s, Vietnam was able to increase its exports of clothing and textiles dramatically, despite restrictions on exports to the

United States. The situation here improved with the conclusion of a bilateral trade agreement in 2001, and Vietnamese imports to American markets rose rapidly. Thoburn argues that patterns buying in this industry are influenced by three sets of factors: distance and lead times, costs (particularly of labor), and trade distortions such as tariffs. The further away the suppliers are from the target market, the more likely they are to export standard goods which respond little to changes in fashion, such as tee-shirts, jeans, and men's suits. The Vietnamese industry concentrates more on production than product development, and thus adds less value to the Vietnamese economy than might otherwise be the case. Thoburn concludes that the industry thus remains vulnerable to competition — especially in markets which ease restrictions on the inflow of Chinese goods.

Nakahara (Chapter 14) also deals with production and networks of producers, this time in the personal computer industry. She argues that since the late 1980s, a new form of production has emerged in the industry, moving away from vertical integration in which the multinational company carries all the stages of production, to one where stages of the production process, such as marketing, planning, development, production and customer support, are increasingly subdivided and geographically dispersed. The main driver behind this dispersal is the difference in the cost of skilled labor between different countries and regions: Bangalore is much cheaper than Silicon Valley, and the skills have reached there through the process of the circulation of skilled labor, the brain circulation also described by Lee in Chapter 1. Flows of components and people are thus intimately linked. Nakahara also shows how the economy of Taiwan has benefited from the changes, by taking over the role of administering and supporting much of the production taking place throughout mainland China.

Logistics and Transport

Underpinning the changing location of production discussed by Thoburn and Nakahara is the global revolution in transport and logistics, and this is the subject of Hoshino (Chapter 15), Le (Chapter 16), Ho (Chapter 17), and Lee and Chang (Chapter 18).

Hoshino's chapter examines the cases of the two ports of Hakata and Kitakyushu, located in western Japan. Even though they are the largest ports in Kyushu, they suffer not only from competition with major regional hubs such as Shanghai and Busan, but also from exclusion by the Japanese government from its own "Super-Hub Port Initiative," involving major ports such as Kobe and Yokohama on Japan's Pacific coast. The increasing size of container ships and the economics of shipping means that larger ships tend to call at fewer ports, and increasingly these are located in China. Hakata and Kitakyushu still play a useful role in connecting Kyushu with other cities in the region, especially in relation to the automobile industry, but their role within the pattern of regional trade is relatively minor. One possibility for the future is to use Japan's excellent rail networks to speed the flow of goods from e.g. Shanghai to Tokyo, by offloading containers at Hakata and moving them to Tokyo by rail.

Le (Chapter 16) focuses directly on the development of international ports in China. As the economy surged ahead during the 1990s, the logistics industry also developed very fast, with the improvement of harbor facilities, rail networks and airports. Giant Chinese logistics companies also developed. Particularly spectacular was the investment in coastal ports, and Le notes that Chinese ports now occupy half of the top ten places in world container port rankings. The most ambitious construction projects are those at Shanghai, now the world's largest port in terms of total cargo throughput, and the second largest in terms of container traffic. Its dominance is due to its position at the mouth of the Yangtze River, where major East-West and North-South shipping routes intersect.

Shanghai's main rival within China is Hong Kong, and this is the focus of Ho (Chapter 17). Even though Hong Kong is still a dominant regional hub, it faces increasing competition from the neighboring ports of Shenzhen and Guangzhou, in addition to the looming presence of Shanghai further up the coast. It is still able to capture traffic arriving on smaller vessels from the Pearl River Delta, and it still has advantages over Shenzhen in terms of location, Chinese shipping regulations, and its status as a separate customs territory, though these are advantages which could eventually disappear. In air transport by contrast, Ho argues that Hong Kong is in a much stronger position, with much less competition from nearby cities in China. In general, Hong Kong benefits from the flexibility of its regulations and the efficiency of its operations, but it could generate considerable savings through reducing the red tape governing the movement of goods to and from the Chinese mainland, and the use of information technology to smooth the flow of goods.

Lee and Chang in Chapter 18 also deal with the logistics industry, and the specific problem of security in the wake of the 9/11 attacks in New York and Washington in September 2001. Movements of oil and liquefied natural gas are of particular strategic importance, not only in meeting energy requirements but also in keeping militaries on the move. The importance of the Asia-Pacific region for the US is that many of its imports originate from the major Asia-Pacific ports. Threats to international trade in the Asia-Pacific region include the vulnerability of strategic points such as the Straits of Malacca to piracy or terrorist attack. This chapter details the various measures taken by the US to monitor the movement of containers and their contents in order to reduce the risk of attack.

Architects and the Urban Landscape

At first sight, the final chapter in the book, Ren's study of architecture in Beijing (Chapter 19), looks separate from the others in the set, but in fact it brings together two of the major themes in the book: the creation of urban infrastructure under the influence of globalization, and the movement of people and ideas, in this case the stellar architects and their associates responsible for the grandiose buildings currently proliferating in the region's would-be global cities (Sassen, 1991; Yeung, 2000). She argues that this trend towards the use of "starchitects" to create high-tech buildings to brand and market cities through "megaprojects" has become commonplace, though Beijing provides a spectacular example thanks to its construction for the 2008 Olympics. These iconic buildings are important symbolic capital in the creation of a global city, even though the economic gains of such constructions are often far from clear. The Chinese case is interesting in that urban redevelopment is not a response to the de-industrialization of historic industrial cities as it often is in the West. Instead, it is driven by China's high-speed economic growth, and results from the collaboration of local investment capital, strong government, and prestigious international architectural partnerships specializing in the latest sleek, minimalist transnational designs. The Beijing city government is also driven by a desire to build a financial center which can rival Shanghai. The shaping of urban space thus takes place within the context of the globalization of capital, and the desire by cities and nations to establish a new global identity.

Conclusion

The chapters in this book thus form a cycle: they begin and end with the movement of highly-skilled migrants across the globe, leading the revolutions in technological development and mega-urbanization. In between, they take in the lives of ordinary people coping with the strains and tensions within households, trying to assimilate and adapt to often difficult migrant situations, and trying to keep things going at home as well as abroad through their remittances and investments. These movements have been made possible by the technological developments also taking place: the information technology which allows the global integration of production processes, and the technical advances and cost reductions in shipping and air transport. Mediating the flows are the nation states, increasingly powerless to control the flows of information, capital and people across their frontiers. They try hard to regulate migration, but their efforts are constantly circumvented by the desperate, the traffickers, and corruptable agents of the state. They try hard to regulate the movement of goods, but their efforts are frustrated both by the smugglers and the need to engage in free trade agreements and/or the World Trade Organization if they are to remain players in the global economy. And as the location of production shifts to the developing countries with their cheaper supplies of labor, they try to boost their economies by attracting investment through developing infrastructure and participating in the global competition for prestige and mega-events (Horne and Manzenreiter, 2006) such as the Olympics, World Expos, and the World Cup.

How long these trends will continue into the 21st century is an interesting question. As this book goes to press, the economic crash of the property bubble forecast by Yuchengco (Chapter 2) has already happened, and we are in the middle of a global economic recession. If the economic growth of China and India can bring the world economy back onto the rails, it is possible that these kinds of trends can continue for some time to come, though the spectres of climate change and rising energy costs also loom on the horizon. But whatever happens, people will still be on the move, their movements will be shaped by changes in technology and the location of capital, and states will still try to control their movements. These chapters play an important role both in describing the directions and extent of these changes in the last few decades, and providing insights into the possible shapes that they may take in the future.

References

Bhagwati, Jagdish (2004). *In Defense of Globalization.* New York: Oxford University Press.

Castells, Manuel (1996). *The Rise of the Network Society.* Oxford: Blackwell.

Castells, Manuel (1997). *The Power of Identity.* Oxford: Blackwell.

Castells, Manuel (1998). *End of Millennium.* Oxford: Blackwell.

Castells, Manuel and Peter Hall (1994). *Technopoles of the World.* London: Routledge.

Castles, Stephen and Mark. J. Miller (1998). *The Age of Migration: International Population Movements in the Modern World* (second edition). Basingstoke, UK: Palgrave.

Dizon, Jane (2006). "Revisiting the OPA Phenomenon: What's next for Filipino migrant workers to Japan?" *Ritsumeikan Journal of Asia Pacific Studies*, Vol. 20, pp. 69–84.

Douglass, Mike and Glenda Roberts (eds.) (1999). *Japan and Global Migration.* New York: Routledge.

Friedman, Thomas (2005). *The World Is Flat: A Brief History of the Globalized World in the Twenty-first Century.* London: Allen Lane.

Horne, John and Wolfram Manzenreiter (eds.) (2006). *Sports Mega-Events. Social Scientific Analyses of a Global Phenomenon.* Chichester, UK: Wiley.

Miyazaki, Koji (2008). "An Aging Society and Migration to Asia and Oceania." In Shinji Yamashita, Makito Minami, David W. Haines and J.S. Eade (eds.), *Transnational Migration in East Asia.* Osaka: National Museum of Ethnology, pp. 139–150.

Ono, Mayumi (2008). "Long-stay Tourism and International Retirement Migration. Japanese Retirees in Malaysia." In Shinji Yamashita, Makito Minami, David W. Haines and J.S. Eades (eds.), *Transnational Migration in East Asia.* Osaka: National Museum of Ethnology, pp. 151–162.

Parrenas, Rhacel (2001). *Servants of Globalization: Women, Migration and Domestic Work.* Stanford, CA: Stanford University Press.

Ryang, Sonia (1997). *North Koreans in Japan*. Boulder, CO: Westview.

Ryang, Sonia (2000). *Koreans in Japan*. New York: Routledge.

Sassen, Saskia (1991). *The Global City: New York, London, Tokyo*. Princeton, NJ: Princeton University Press.

Sassen, Saskia (1998). *Globalization and its Discontents*. New York: New Press.

Stiglitz, Joseph (2006). *Making Globalization Work*. London: Allen Lane.

Traphagan, John and John Knight (eds.) (2003). *Demographic Change and the Family in Japan's Aging Society*. Albany, NY: State University of New York Press.

Tsuda, Takayuki (2003). *Strangers in the Ethnic Homeland*. New York: Columbia University Press.

Weiner, Michael (1994). *Race and Migration in Imperial Japan*. London: Routledge.

Woo-Cumings, Meredith (ed.) (1999). *The Developmental State*. Ithaca, NY: Cornell University Press.

Yeung, Yue-man (2000). *Globalization and Networked Societies: Urban-Regional Change in Pacific Asia*. Honolulu: University of Hawaii Press.

CHAPTER 1

BRAIN DRAIN, BRAIN GAIN, AND BRAIN CIRCULATION IN A HALF-GLOBALIZED WORLD

Yuan T. Lee

At the end of the Second World War, as we entered the second half of the 20th century, the United States of America had become the most powerful country in the world, controlling about 50 percent of world economic activities. In addition to its wealth, the United States was the symbol of "democracy" and advocate of "liberty," "equality," and "justice." The United States was such a beautiful and perfect place that it was perceived by many people all around the world as a "dream land" or even as a "heaven on earth." On the other hand, in many war-torn countries in Asia, people were not only suffering from extreme poverty, miserable living conditions, and a low level of science and technology, but were also oppressed by repressive regimes. This drastic difference was the setting in which so-called "high-skill migration" started to take place.

There is a high correlation between education and legal migration. In the year 2000, for example, a person with a college or graduate school education was six times more likely to migrate legally than one with less than a high school education. Around 37 percent of the legal immigrant stock in OECD countries, more than 20 million people all told, fell into the high-skill category.

In 1962, I joined many young elite students in leaving my home country and becoming a graduate student in the United States. With a letter of admission to the graduate school, another letter offering a teaching assistantship, and carrying a small suitcase, I arrived at the University of California, Berkeley. The airfare took most of my parents' life savings.

My excitement at that time was beyond description. In the "land of opportunity," where people are the masters of the land, nothing seemed to be impossible. I arrived at a time when the free speech movement had just turned into an anti-war movement. The student movement at that time sent a tidal wave across the world. For several decades starting from the mid-1950s, the State of California was developing very rapidly, and was interested in attracting high-skill migrants. Higher education was essentially free at that time, in order to attract excellent out-of-state students to enter universities and eventually to become citizens of California.

With the arrival of a large number of foreign students, especially from India, Iran, Taiwan, Korea, the Philippines, and Japan, the student body became diversified. Hardworking foreign students, most of whom eventually became first-generation immigrants, made important contributions to the development of the society as a whole. Later, many of them became very successful, becoming movers and shakers in academic institutions and industry. In fact, foreign born and foreign educated workers in US science and engineering fields make disproportionately large and valuable contributions to knowledge. For example, they are over-represented, relative to their share of the science and technology work force, among authors of the most cited scientific papers and inventors of highly cited patents.

The consequence of this massive "brain gain" for the United States was of course a serious "brain drain" from other countries, especially developing ones. I remember about 20 years ago, when there was a serious accident in Taiwan involving the explosion of an electric transformer, engineers were blamed for their incompetence. However, it was pointed out immediately that more than 90 percent of the graduates of science and engineering departments of the National Taiwan University had left the country after receiving their PhDs and were residing in the United States. The consequences of the departure of a large number of competent scientists, engineers, and medical doctors could be vividly seen in every sector of the society. However, it seemed almost impossible to stop the "brain drain" at that time. For rural areas in Taiwan, the exodus was not exclusively to the United States. As the economy gradually picked up in Taiwan, centered on the capital Taipei, the city also became a destination for the "brain drain," thus creating a great disparity within the island. However, this domestic "brain drain" did have a spillover effect in a relatively short time, especially as the infrastructure for communication and transportation developed, and the impact turned out to be less negative than the "brain drain" to foreign countries.

Starting from the early 1980s, light industries largely depending on manual labor became successful in Taiwan, especially those geared toward the export market, such as bicycles, textiles, Christmas tree lights, canned mushrooms, and plastic goods. Further, as the government in Taiwan started to enjoy a budget surplus and determined to invest in science and technology and upgrade industries, the need for high-skill workers increased. More and more Taiwanese expatriates decided to return home to start new careers and fulfill their dreams in their homeland. Many of them were already quite experienced and had acquired special skills and the spirit of entrepreneurship. With the help of forward looking government policies, a good labor market, and the relatively low cost of manufacturing, they were quite convinced that they would be able to compete with the rest of the world. Indeed, without those well-educated and experienced returnee scientists and engineers, numbering in their thousands and working in various associated fields in microelectronics, the high-tech industries, especially in the areas of personal computers, communications, and display equipment, would not have taken off.

Toward the end of the 1980s, in spite of the fact that those who left the country still significantly outnumbered those who came home, the return of a large number of "better developed brains" partially compensated for the ill effects of the "brain drain" of the past. At the beginning of the 1990s, there were about 800 very well educated PhD holders returning home annually, twice as many as those PhD holders who were educated in Taiwan. The change from the "brain drain" to a partial "brain return," which we might call "brain circulation," was a blessing to Taiwan. In fact, both the countries sending and receiving the so-called "high-skill migration" can share the benefits directly, even if the "brain circulation" only amounts to a small fraction of the "brain drain," as long as the returning brains are more skilled and experienced than the departing ones.

In the late 1990s, I was invited to attend the "Knowledge Wave Conference" in New Zealand organized by the Prime Minister, Helen Clark.

Government officials in New Zealand were quite envious of the success of high-tech industries in Taiwan. Knowing that a large number of scientists and engineers returning from the United States had played a crucial role, they asked me who in Taiwan in the 1960s had the wisdom and vision to send most of our brilliant university graduates to pursue graduate studies in the United States. I told them that it was the miserable living conditions, the repressive regime, martial law, and the low academic level rather than the vision of government officials which caused the exodus of talented young people. However, the government in Taiwan did play a role in creating the environment to entice a "brain return." Of course, they were very surprised. New Zealand, a beautiful country with excellent living conditions, did not suffer sufficiently from the "brain drain" to build up an expatriate talent pool in the United States to be able to tap. In order for the developing countries to derive the benefit from the "brain circulation" involving countries with advanced science and technology, it is essential to encourage a large number of talented young students to study abroad. Perhaps it is worth pointing out that 25 years ago I dreamt of helping Taiwan establish some world-class research and academic institutions, such that students could pursue their advanced degrees in Taiwan at the highest level. Working with many accomplished scholars, the dream was realized to a great extent. At the present time, Taiwan has become a democratic society, and the economy as well as academic institutions have vastly improved. With excellent job opportunities available, there is not as much incentive for young people to go abroad. Although we do not have to worry about "brain drain" as much at present, we are also losing the opportunity to derive the benefit from "brain circulation," since the talent pool in the United States is diminishing quickly. For a small place like Taiwan, this turn of events is certainly not what I expected.

It seems to be apparent that the game of "brain gain" and "brain drain" can be played more effectively between a developing country and a developed one. However, during the last few decades, several developed countries have tried to imitate the United States and benefit from high-skill migration by offering attractive conditions, but without resounding success. Aside from Australia and Canada, most of the densely populated developed countries lack the necessary magic to accept foreigners with open arms, making them believe that "all men are created equal" and providing them with the opportunity to become permanent residents or citizens in a relatively short time.

For developing countries, it is not a good idea to build a barrier to stop the "brain drain" or seek compensation from recipient countries for their loss of talent. Instead, what they need to do is to change the situation from a "brain drain" into a "brain circulation." Many newly industrialized countries or regions in Asia have been able to do this successfully. One of the conditions necessary to promote an effective "brain circulation" is to provide good education such that university graduates will be admitted to excellent graduate schools in the advanced countries, and for the home government to have a good policy to attract them back again later. It is of utmost importance for the returning talents to be convinced that they can still compete effectively with the rest of the world after coming back to their homeland. Patriotism alone will not be enough to attract talented people back home.

As we examine the development of human society at the beginning of the 21st century, we discover that two important changes, which will have very significant consequences for the future of mankind, are taking place. Unfortunately, we have not paid enough attention to them, and they might cause great difficulties for human society in the not-too-distant future. Firstly, the Earth, which used to appear "infinite" to human beings, has become "finite." As the population on Earth has increased to six billion and human activities have intensified during the last century, we have moved into an entirely different situation in which harmonious relations between the biosphere and human beings have been broken. Yet we are still following the trajectories for the development of human society in the past, when the Earth was practically "infinite," and we are thus heading in the wrong direction altogether.

Secondly, the globalization process is not yet complete. Some economic activities are globalizing and crossing national boundaries, yet competition based on the nation state is as strong as ever. In the half-globalized world, it is not surprising that we will have to tackle such problems as the widening gap between the rich and the poor, both within and between countries. These problems, as well as those created by high-skill migration, could easily be avoided if the entire world were to be completely globalized, or if the entire world were to become one community.

In spite of the fact that globalization of the world economy is driving us toward a borderless society, the differences between peoples in various regions will not vanish overnight. The establishment of a new, common global culture, together with more effective ways of communicating among all peoples, will certainly take time. Differences of cultural heritage, language, and religion that make this world so rich and colorful will not, and should not, be made to disappear. As the world shrinks in relative terms, and contact between its peoples becomes more frequent, whether or not differences in civilization are likely to cause an inevitable clash, as suggested by the well-known scholar, Samuel Huntington (1996), would seem to be entirely dependent on how well people learn to communicate and to understand, appreciate, and respect cultural heritage. To become good citizens of the global village, we need to learn quickly — and also to teach our young people — to take a global view of different peoples. In this respect, the promotion of extensive "brain circulation" would certainly be the best first step.

If we examine the influence of the United States on the developing countries in the Asia-Pacific region, perhaps one could argue that the most important factor is higher education, especially when expatriates of various countries return home to assume important positions and exert their influence. Unfortunately, most of the universities are more interested in raising funds from their successful alumni and recruiting the best possible students than in helping developing countries to move forward. But the world's most distinguished universities should aim for global influence through the creation of new forms of social thought, the accumulation of new scientific knowledge, and the development of new technologies for mankind, and also by helping developing countries to establish a healthy mechanism for "brain circulation."

In 1994, after spending 32 years in the United States, I returned to Taiwan, thus becoming a part of the "brain circulation." My return to Taiwan did encourage some "big brains," for example, members of the United States National Academy of Sciences and professors holding chairs at first rate universities, to join the trend. The mutual gains derived from sending "young brains" to places where knowledge creation is most efficient and providing the best environment for them to develop will be both richer and fairer than those arising from a competition over talent, as long as sufficient numbers of "big brains" return. Working together, we can make the most of the many opportunities presented in the nascent century of human capital.

This is the first time in human history that all human beings on Earth have been faced with learning to work together and live together as one family in a global village — in other words, to establish "one community for the entire world." The time has come for finally realizing that the planet Earth on which we live is only finite in space, capacity, and natural resources and that, in a sense, we have "over developed" in an unsustainable way. This is a necessary awakening — vital for the survival and sustainable development of mankind. I believe that if we make the correct choice at this crossroads, then the 21st century is likely to be seen as the great turning point, or great transition — the beginning of a new era in the history of mankind.

Reference

Huntington, Samuel (1996). *The Clash of Civilizations and the Remaking of World Order.* New York: Simon & Schuster.

CHAPTER 2

TRANSNATIONAL BUSINESS AND DIPLOMACY IN THE ASIA PACIFIC

Alfonso T. Yuchengco

The Phenomenon of Globalization

Put most simply, "globalization" is shorthand for the way in which trade, investment, and industry are spreading around the world more or less uniformly, overleaping political borders and national cultures. In fact, the process is nothing new. Globalization has been going on, in fits and starts, at least since the Western powers first appeared on the world stage in the 15th century.

Indeed, Japanese intellectuals recall an even earlier episode of globalization, when a pre-industrial trading system, mediated by the Arabs, stretched from West Asia and the Mediterranean across the Indian Ocean through Southeast Asia and dynastic China, clear to the Japanese islands.

The most recent wave of globalization, previous to our time, was stimulated by the Industrial Revolution. It started spreading from Britain in the 1830s and lasted until early in the 20th century. And it was Meiji-era Japan that became its major beneficiary. Although cheap manufactured products from Manchester and Bombay wiped out Japan's textile industry, tea and silk gave it an export niche market. That wave of globalization, stopped by World War I, was replaced by 50 years of autarky, as the great powers sought in national self-sufficiency the strength they needed to fight World War II.

The Globalist Revival in Our Time

In our time, the revival of open trade was stimulated by the founding, in 1948, of a United Nations agency to promote international trade — the General Agreement on Tariffs and Trade. The great trading nations agreed on a system that ensured a reasonable degree of financial and economic stability and discouraged protectionist tendencies. The American dollar became the global currency and the United States the "lender of last resort." As a result, global output between 1953 and 1975 grew on average by a remarkable 6 percent a year overall.

Beneficiaries of our new episode of globalization

The greatest beneficiaries of this new episode of globalization have been Japan, once again, and East Asia's "Four Little Dragons" of Taiwan, South Korea, Hong Kong, and Singapore. Their export-oriented development strategies that tapped into rich western markets set off an "East Asian Economic Miracle" that also stimulated the economies of Malaysia and Thailand and to a lesser extent, those of Indonesia and the Philippines.

Ironically, East Asia was also first to experience the downside of globalization in the regional financial crisis that started in Thailand in July 1997. Since then, globalization's perceived disadvantages have set off an ideological backlash, which has itself become a world-wide counter-movement. On balance, however, globalization can be more beneficial than harmful for poor countries whose leaders ensure that economic growth is shared by the rich and the poor in equal measure.

Transnational Business in a "Flat" World

My task here is to start off our discussions on transnational business and diplomacy in the Asia Pacific. Transnational businesses are both big and small corporations that typically operate openly and freely across national boundaries. Empowered by the new communications and information technologies, these transnational corporations enjoy both global markets and global supply chains. Even services, knowledge work, and high-end manufacturing have now become tradable. Nowadays, capital, skilled workers, and technology move effortlessly across borders, and almost every phase of production is disaggregated and outsourced. An international corps of managers, technologists, and creative people has also formed.

The new computer transnational, Lenovo, is a fairly typical example of this new breed of corporation. Although Lenovo originated in China, it has become a true transnational. Right now it is ranked number three in the global market for personal computers. Lenovo has a Chinese chairman of the board, an American chief executive officer, an American chief operating officer, and a Chinese chief financial officer. Its headquarters are in New York, it has factories in Virginia state and in Beijing, and it is listed in the Hong Kong stock exchange.

This new episode of globalization might give the world economy its biggest stimulus yet

Our episode of globalization is unique in its scope. In fact, *The Economist* calculates that it might give the world economy its biggest stimulus in history (*The Economist*, 2006a). Even the Industrial Revolution fully involved only one-third of the world's population. This current episode of globalization is incorporating once-closed countries into the world economy.

The end of the Cold War has enabled the ex-socialist economies of China, India, Russia, and Eastern Europe to rejoin the world. Meanwhile, the inward-looking countries of Latin America and their Southeast Asian cousin, the Philippines, are beginning to appreciate the benefits of market liberalization. These new entrants have effectively doubled the global work force and they are multiplying the quantity and variety of the global product.

The Balance of Economic Power is Shifting to the "Emerging Economies"

Already the balance of global economic power is shifting to these emerging economies. China and India between them are redrawing the geography of trade and tilting the global economic-power balance in Asia's favor.

China is widely expected to become the largest economy before 2040. By then also, India will have become the third-largest economy, after that of the United States. The European Union will then be no higher than number four. Already Asia has become an alternative engine of the global economy.

In 2006, *The Economist* expected the American economy to come "perilously close" to a recession in 2007, as its housing boom threatened to go bust (*The Economist*, 2006b). But no longer does the world catch a cold whenever America sneezes. *The Economist* said the Asian economies would remain buoyant; and Asia has, since 2001, accounted for over half the world's economic growth. Not only is globalization incorporating more and more countries. It is also becoming a two-way street.

No longer does globalization simply mean Europeans and Americans expanding their markets and production platforms to other parts of the Earth. Now, it also means increasing investments by non-American and non-European companies in the United States and in Europe. The emerging economies are accumulating capital and venturing into corporate acquisitions in the West. And already industrializing Asia is reaching out worldwide for raw materials that the poor "South" used to export to the rich "North." And, even now, this is having political repercussions in East–West relations. For instance, Chinese investment in the oil industry of the Sudan, a state the Americans regard as hospitable to Islamist terrorists, is causing tensions between Beijing and Washington.

Lenovo caused some consternation in Washington when it acquired IBM's personal-computer business. And a Chinese state corporation's bid for the American oil company, UNOCAL, had to be withdrawn because of opposition from Congress. Meanwhile, Mittal Steel's acquisition of the French steel company, Arcelor, evoked racist objections in Western Europe because Mittal Steel, though registered in Luxembourg, happens to be owned by an ethnic Indian entrepreneur.

The Political Implications of Economic Globalization

Will this shift of economic power from West to East produce a shift in political and military power as well? The scale of America's military spending attests to its determination not to be overtaken by a rival power or even by a combination of rival powers. In March 2006, China estimated that its military spending had risen by 12.6 percent over the previous year (Congressional Hearings, 2006), although it is still less than a fifth of what the United States spends. Washington also seems to be trying to contain China economically. And at a time when Beijing is reaching out all over the world for strategic raw-material sources to keep up its economic growth, fiascos like that of the UNOCAL bid will undoubtedly remind Chinese leaders of the boycott the Western powers imposed on Japan's raw-material imports in 1940, which sealed Tokyo's decision to attack Pearl Harbor. However, China itself also seems to be limiting access to its home markets. In September 2006, *Time* reported that "several recent acquisitions of large Chinese firms by foreign companies have been stalled after a storm of public protests over the impact such sales could have on China's economic security" (Elegant, 2006). One such transaction was the $375 million bid by New York's Carlyle Group for China's leading construction-machinery manufacturer.

Globalization's Positive Effects on Relationships Between the Big Powers

Despite these problems, globalization has generally been a positive factor in big-power relations. The regime of open trade and investment has linked great-power economies in complex strands that mitigate the tensions raised by power-politics.

For instance, Japan's ruling politicians may regard China as a strategic rival. But Japanese business leaders regard it as a valued economic partner. It is largely by trading with China and by investing there that Japanese transnationals have revitalized the Japanese economy. Chinese–American commerce itself is expanding exponentially. In President Hu Jintao's own estimate, over 9 percent of all the foreign direct investment (FDI) in his country comes from American corporations. But China's surplus in two-way trade, now in the neighborhood of US$250 billion, has become an irritant. Although America's deficit is partly the result of "off-shoring" by its multinationals, it is building up pressure on China to revalue the yuan and threats of a new round of protectionist legislation from a populist Congress sensitive to the loss of American jobs. Even breaches of intellectual property rights by Chinese corporations prevalent among late industrializers have become emotional issues in China–US relationships.

Leveraging economic power for political goals

Meanwhile, China is leveraging its economic power to gain political advantage. Beijing is expansively deploying the "soft power" being generated by its remarkably open economy. China has not merely helped to revive the Japanese economy. It has also become a growth engine for the ASEAN states. Even Australia's enduring boom is due almost entirely to its export of mineral and gas resources to China.

In the United Nations, China has become visibly more activist. India, too, has become a key diplomatic player, not only in the Asian subcontinent but also in Southeast Asia. In summary, the scale and scope of globalization in our time may be changing international relations at their most basic level. Let me now turn to the problems and prospects of diplomacy in this fast-changing world.

Diplomacy in this Changing World

Political negotiations may dominate the front pages. But issues of fair trade, tariffs, and investments have always been the bread-and-butter of diplomatic activity. Economic relations are still diplomacy's most common topics, and more and more these are multilateral as well as bilateral. Mutual accusations of currencies being deliberately undervalued, of surpluses being dumped in export markets, and of punitive tariffs, are the coin of much of international diplomacy in our time.

In recent years, these traditional issues have been joined by the problems of economic migrants, of "hot money," portfolio capital that can wreak havoc on the puny economies of developing states, and of copyright infringements on a large scale. Another political problem will come from protectionist demands by working people in the rich countries that see their jobs being exported to cheaper production platforms in the poor countries.

The problem of the economies being left behind

The big winners in the global market-opening are the developing countries that, early on, caught the gravy train of export trade. But development is leaving some behind, particularly the African countries south of the Sahara. And these states where globalization is passing by will very likely become a key problem of global diplomacy. Close to a dozen African states have already collapsed in anarchy and genocide. If they are to become viable, these failing states need special WTO export concessions that the rich states are unlikely to give.

Economic migrants flowing to the rich countries

Like unequal trade, economic migration is a worldwide problem. In every region of the globe, both skilled and unskilled workers are flowing from the poorer to the richer economies. In my country alone, the Philippines, one in ten of our 80 million people is abroad, not always legally, and our diplomats posted abroad spend much of their time and effort trying to ease the travails of illegal entrants, abused domestics, and entertainers lured into prostitution or drug-dealing. Our loss of doctors, nurses, engineers, and even middle-level managers is also beginning to worry our policymakers.

Deadlock in the Doha Round of the WTO

Among the outstanding international economic issues, the most polarizing is that of agricultural subsidies and protective tariffs in the rich countries. As we know, a deadlock over this question has caused the collapse of the Doha Round of the World Trade Organization, the successor organization to GATT. The scandal of farm subsidies in the rich countries is most flagrant in the case of the European Union's high-living cows. According to the Australian Trade Minister, Mark Vaile, the typical cow in Europe receives a government subsidy equivalent to US$2.20 a day, which is more than double what 1.2 billion of the world's poorest peoples must live on.

Small States are Forming Regional Communities to Gain Economies of Scale

The failure of multilateral negotiations to open up the global market is driving the smaller states to form regional free-trade areas to protect their home markets and to gain economies of scale. The ASEAN states, for instance, are at last taking seriously their efforts at economic and political consolidation.

Washington may resist what it sees as Beijing's determination to assert itself as the paramount East Asian power. But Southeast Asians are more ready to accept that China will sooner or later become a great power, and that it is unrealistic to think that outsiders can prevent such an outcome.

For the moment, Southeast Asians have set aside their anxieties about how this resurgent China will exercise its regional preeminence. They have embraced China as an engine of growth for the region. In 2007, China's trade with the 10 ASEAN states was scheduled to catch up with ASEAN's US$120 billion trade with the United States.

ASEAN-10 plus China conclude a free-trade pact

The framework for cooperation between the ASEAN-10, the 10 nations of ASEAN, and China is the free-trade arrangement that the two sides started carrying out in 2004, and which is to become fully operational by 2010.

By then, the ASEAN-10 *plus* China will become the largest free-trade area in the world in population terms. In 2005, it represented a market of 1.75 billion people, a combined GDP of over US$2.6 trillion, and an external trade value of US$1.3 trillion.

As the ASEAN-10 *plus* China expands to incorporate Japan and the Republic of Korea, East Asia should be able to sustain economic growth from within itself because of its increasingly wealthy home market and its large savings pool. This arrangement will also leave Washington outside looking in on an East Asian Economic Grouping, at least until the projected APEC free-trade-and-investment area comes on stream in 2020.

The Future of Transnational Business and Diplomacy in the Asia Pacific

Given the global scale of their own economies, both the United States and Japan are reluctant to enter multilateral arrangements that limit their freedom of maneuver. Since multilateral trade negotiations are deadlocked, both Washington and Tokyo are briskly negotiating bilateral pacts with the ASEAN states. In Washington's case, these trade agreements seem designed to further political as well as commercial policy. One of the first East Asian free-trade pacts that Washington concluded in 2001 was with

Hanoi, its Vietnam War adversary. Meanwhile, both Japan and South Korea have been negotiating their own arrangements for liberalizing trade with the ASEAN states. All the ASEAN states (except Thailand) have concluded a trade agreement with Seoul. Manila has signed its own "Economic Partnership Agreement" with Tokyo. ASEAN sees multilateralism as the only check against competing nationalisms and an East Asian economic community as the easiest way of ensuring enduring stability in our region.

Toward an Asia-Pacific Community

Looking forward to the next 10 to 15 or 20 years, East Asia still seems the region with the greatest risk of major armed conflict. Our statesmen need to sustain peace in the Asia Pacific, to manage events so that they do not spiral out of control, and to maintain policies that favor open markets, free trade, and financial stability.

In Western Europe, we have an example of how France and Germany, which had fought four wars over the previous 200 years, put their armed rivalry behind them. Over this past half-century, Western Europe has moved beyond its civil wars to form a single community. In fact, Europe is giving birth to a new world order, as its separate states give up portions of their national sovereignty on behalf of a new communal venture. The new Europe is an "empire" built on consensus and common desire rather than on power and conquest.

We in the Asia Pacific must learn from the European example. For it is not fated that the hegemonic power, the United States, and the rising power, China, should come to blows. The two powers are not just rivals. Both have a stake in each other's prosperity, not only because they are trade and investment partners but also because together they can decide on global war or peace.

China is not just reshaping the global economy. The global economy is also reshaping China. Already China is moving, if by fits and starts, toward an economic structure based on the rule of law, a more efficient allocation of capital, and improved corporate governance. In a word, China's stake is growing in the rules-based global market system that the United States has done the most to promote over this past half-century.

The Pacific peace will be built on the balance of mutual benefit

Community, then, seems the wave of the future. Indeed, the instruments of an East Asian, and of a larger Asia-Pacific, community are already being laid. The Pacific peace will be security cooperation based not on the balance of power but on the balance of mutual benefit. Clearly, it must be built on an understanding among the most affluent and most powerful countries in our part of the world, the United States, Japan, and China. Indeed, a constructive Chinese role in organizing the Pacific peace would demonstrate China's commitment to becoming the "responsible stakeholder" that Washington has challenged Beijing to become.

Japan, too, must take up greater responsibility in the region. In fact, one of the challenges in ensuring the Pacific peace is the relationship between Beijing and Tokyo. In the interest of regional peace, these two powers should stop allowing the historical past to get in the way of the Asia-Pacific future. In the end, of course, relations among the great Asia-Pacific powers will always be based on an interplay of competition and cooperation.

The strategic challenge will be for all our countries and all organizations devoted to regional cooperation to ensure that the spirit of cooperation is always stronger than the competitive impulse. The only real solution, the only lasting solution to our regional rivalries, is to embed all our countries in a network of economic, political, and security relationships in an East Asian and ultimately, in an Asia-Pacific community of consent.

It will be the historic task of East Asia's rising generation of political, economic, and cultural leaders to make these regional institutions work. But it is the burden and the glory of our Asia-Pacific leadership today to complete laying the foundations on which these structures are to be erected, on behalf of our Asia-Pacific posterity.

References

"China's Influence in the Western Hemisphere" (2006). Hearing before the Subcommittee on the Western Hemisphere of the Committee on International Relations, House of Representatives, available at http://www.foreignaffairs. house.gov/archives/109/20404.pdf (accessed April 6, 2006).

Congressional Hearings (2006). "China's Influence in the Western Hemisphere." Hearing before the Subcommittee on the Western Hemisphere of the Committee on International Relations, House of Representatives, April 6, 2006. Available at http://www.foreignaffairs.house.gov/archives/109/20404.pdf/.

Elegant, Simon (2006). "China's Unwelcome Mat." *Time Magazine*, September 18, 2006.

The Economist (2006a). "Surprise! The Power of the Emerging World." *The Economist*, September 16, 2006.

The Economist (2006b). "Asia and the World Economy: The Alternative Engine." *The Economist*, October 19, 2006.

CHAPTER 3

INTERNATIONAL MOBILITY OF THE HIGHLY SKILLED: THE ROLE OF THE GLOBAL KNOWLEDGE NETWORK

Yasuo Uchida

Reflecting the global knowledge-based economy, the mobility of the highly skilled, particularly in the fields of science and technology, has become more international in terms of both supply and demand of the work force. Interestingly, the international movement of the highly skilled has grown not only in numbers but also in complexity over the last few decades. The highly skilled now move either temporarily or permanently using globally extended and multifaceted professional networks. The internationalization of higher education has been a further major factor in the increased complexity of these movements.

The world market is more unified than ever, and firms of various nationalities are increasingly interrelated. Intellectual global networking is becoming stronger and more important in the knowledge-based economy. The "brain circulation" discussed by Professor Lee (see Chapter 1) is one dimension of this process. Innovative high-tech activities are connected with the global science community through the cyber infrastructure. As this trend is evident not only in OECD member countries, but also in East Asian newly industrialized countries (NICs), India and so on, I refrain from using the conventional concept "brain drain" in my discussion.

The Global Knowledge Economy and Professional Networking

These issues can be explained in terms of the four factors discussed by the OECD, innovation, new technology, human capital, and enterprise dynamics (OECD, 2002), which are all closely interrelated. Naturally, in the knowledge-based economy, the capacity to produce and use knowledge has far more importance in determining economic development than ever. Human capital is a significant determinant of growth, since innovation and new technologies are not able to become productive without a well-trained and qualified work force.

Professional networking is increasingly varied, from institutional linkages to informal relations. In whatever form, it promotes business and scientific cooperation, and bolsters innovative environments. Networking promotes increasing communication flows and the diffusion of information or knowledge, leading to widespread economic outcomes. Developments in global networking have created a global science and technology community, within which the highly skilled move to work either temporarily or semi-permanently, whether for professional fulfillment or a better lifestyle.

The Definition of the Highly Skilled

Who are the highly skilled? An adequate definition should be made for further discussion. The highly skilled are roughly those who have successfully completed education at the tertiary level, often in a science or technology field of study, although other fields such as economics or management science may also be included. Some may not be so strictly qualified as above, but are still employed in science and technology occupations where the above qualifications are normally required.

Students studying overseas are a major component of the international migration of the highly skilled. Asian countries are the main countries of origin, accounting for 45 percent of the total number of students moving to OECD countries. As seen in the United States which is the best example, the share of foreign students has been much higher in science than in other fields, and especially so in mathematics, computer science, and engineering. In engineering, the share of foreigners in graduate enrolments rose from around 30 percent in 1987 to over 35 percent in 1997. In mathematics the corresponding figures were around 25 and 35 percent, while for the natural sciences they were around 17 and 23 percent. For the whole field of science and engineering, the proportion of foreigners in graduate enrolments rose from around 20 percent in 1987 to around 24 percent in 1997. In the social sciences, by contrast, the share was smaller and fell slightly from 13.5 percent in 1987 to 12 percent in 1997 (National Science Foundation, 2000).

Brain Circulation in Taiwan

As Professor Lee has shown in Chapter 1, the international mobility of the highly skilled originating in Taiwan has been very dynamic for four decades. The return migration of the highly skilled science and technology workforce is considered a crucial factor in the rapid and solid economic development Taiwan has seen. However, cause-and-effect relations between the highly skilled and economic development are complex. Taiwan experienced an outflow of the highly skilled in the 1960s and 1970s. But it is unclear how much this outflow negatively impacted industrial development in Taiwan in those years in which basic manufacturing was still dominant. It was at a subsequent stage that the more highly educated and trained highly skilled came back to Taiwan.

By the leverage of its fundamental economic success and accumulated capital, Taiwan shifted its policy stance toward developing high technology industries. The establishment of the Hsinchu Science-Based Industrial Park (HSIP) in 1980 symbolizes this initiative. With the government's careful planning and incentives, HSIP provided HS returnees with good professional opportunities and a high-quality living environment. As the figures of the HSIP administration show, the number of firms rose from less than 20 in 1981 to over 200 in 1996 and over 700 by 2000. In the same period, annual sales rose to around NTD300 billion in 1995 to over NTD900 billion in 2000.

This return of this brain-power was certainly promoted by active government intervention, but, very importantly, other enabling factors were already in place: the Taiwan business sector recognized well the strategic importance of moving into high-tech industry and had the financial means to do it. Their understanding and strategy included firm-based international linkages. For example, more than 70 HSIP firms now have offices in Silicon Valley, and their executives and scientists work on both sides of the Pacific.

The late 1980s saw accelerating growth in numbers of highly skilled returnees. A 1990 survey in the Taiwan population census suggested that about 50,000 emigrants returned in the 1985–1990 period. Of these, 43 percent had at least a university education and more than 30 percent were employed as professionals and managers. The 1990s saw a growing number of US-educated returnees to Taiwan. HSIP was the major destination for hundreds of returnees, who joined new or existing firms or launched their own enterprises. The HSIP administration figures show that the number of returnees increased from 27 to 92 in the starting period from 1983 to 1987. These returnees also actively recruited friends staying overseas through their professional networks during the period of inward labor transfer from 1993 onwards, reaching a total of over 4,000 by 2000.

Interestingly, the number of foreign PhDs started growing significantly from 1990, and HSIP has become a far more international science park, strengthening its competence by attracting greater numbers of the highly skilled, both native and non-native. By 2000, the number of native PhDs hired by HSIP stood at around 570, while the number of foreign PhDs was slightly higher at around 640.

The International Mobility of the Highly Skilled in Japan

Japan has the second-largest national science and technology system after the United States, as measured by research and development (R&D) expenditures and number of researchers (Kobayashi and Saito, 2003). Its development was promoted by an indigenous supply of the highly skilled. However, as Japan's population ages, ongoing science and technology development faces a shortage of competent highly skilled workers.

The general immigration law was relaxed in 1989 to facilitate the entry of the highly skilled. Besides immigration measures, mutual accreditation of IT engineers, civil engineers, architects, and so on has been launched with some Asian countries. Scholarship programs for foreign students and post-doctoral programs for foreign scientists have been strengthened. In reality, growth rates of highly skilled entrants have been increasing at a rapid pace (Table 3.1), but the total numbers of highly skilled foreigners residing in

Table 3.1. New non-temporary entrants in Japan.

	1992 Share (%)	1998 Share (%)	1992–1998 Annual growth rate (%)
Professors	0.32	0.54	9.19
Researchers	0.32	0.46	6.13
Instructors	0.96	1.25	4.33
Engineers	1.12	2.15	11.42
Total high-skilled science and technology	2.72	4.4	8.25
Total non-temporary	100	100	−0.09

Source: Japan Immigration Association (1999: Table 4).

Japan are still limited. In 2001, there were only 169,000 resident foreigners with special and/or technical skills.

At the same time, many baby-boomers, who were an important age cohort in the post-war period of high-speed growth of the Japanese economy, are now retiring. But neither inter-organizational knowledge clusters nor professional networks extending beyond corporate boundaries have been well developed in Japan. Japan is also losing its veteran Japanese highly skilled because of inflexible personnel management, enforcing obligatory retirement

In contrast, the Taiwan Ministry of Economic Affairs is gathering information on the skills and experience of retirees from Japanese firms working in Taiwan as technical advisers. In fact, Taiwan executives have hired Japanese engineers, and they offer prospective employees attractive options, including contracts to work in Taiwan for just one week per month. About 200 Japanese retirees have reportedly been hired by Taiwan firms so far on this program. As more imminent retirees seeking to continue utilizing their skills hook up with companies shifting their focus from low costs to higher value, there is a quietly developing concern about a brain drain from Japan.

Conclusion

As in trade and business, the boundaries and points of exchange in the science and technology field have become increasingly global, and a global science and technology community is already in existence. The trend toward a more global system has many positive attributes, and thus national policymakers should not resist this development. Instead, they need to modify their domestic regulatory frameworks, such as immigration policies, licensing, and education, to bolster innovative capacity through improving the utilization of the globalized science and technology workforce.

References

Japan Immigration Association (1999). *Statistics on Immigration Control.* Tokyo: Japan Immigration Association.

Kobayashi, Shinichi and Yasharu Saito (2003). *International Mobility of Highly-Skilled Personnel. Trends in Japan and the World.* Tokyo: National Institute of Science and Technology Policy (in Japanese).

National Science Foundation (2000). *Science and Engineering Indicators.* Arlington Virginia: National Science Foundation. Available at http://www.nsf.gov/statistics/seind00/.

OECD (2002). *International Mobility of the Highly Skilled.* Paris: Organization of Economic Cooperation and Development.

CHAPTER 4

INTERNATIONAL MIGRATION IN ASIA AND THE PACIFIC: KEY FEATURES AND THE ROLE OF THE UNITED NATIONS

Keiko Osaki

As of 2004, there were 58 million international migrants in the Asia-Pacific region, 53 million in Asia and 5 million in the Pacific region (United Nations, 2005). The region has seen a marked increase in the cross-national mobility of people during the past few decades and this trend seems to continue unabated. Widening inter-country disparities in income and opportunities, coupled with demographic imbalances between countries in the region, compel people to move to improve the quality of life for themselves and their families. With more and more countries involved in migration streams, international migration has become a structural reality of many societies in the region. This chapter reviews key features of international migration in Asia and the Pacific region, and discusses how the United Nations (UN) has addressed this issue, which is attracting growing attention.[1]

Contemporary International Migration in the Asia-Pacific Region

The Asia-Pacific region has experienced a phenomenal growth in international migration during the past few decades. While the region continues

---

[1]The views expressed in this paper are those of the author and do not necessarily reflect those of the United Nations.

to see outflows of people for settlement in the traditional countries of immi-gration, namely Australia, Canada, New Zealand, and the United States, the mobility of people seeking temporary employment within the region has become increasingly important.

In Asia, two distinctive labor migration systems have emerged. The rise in oil prices triggered an economic boom in the oil-producing countries of the Middle East in the early 1970s. Shortly after, a large number of migrant workers were attracted to the region to find temporary employment, first in the construction sector and later in service industries. Today, the area still continues to house many migrant workers, with Saudi Arabia being the primary host. The migrant workers were drawn into the area originally from neighboring countries, but later increasingly from South and Southeast Asia.

Since the 1980s, the newly industrialized economies in East and Southeast Asia have also emerged as hubs of temporary migration. These include Brunei Darussalam, Hong Kong, China, Japan, Malaysia, the Republic of Korea, Singapore, Taiwan, and Thailand. As a result, labor migration in Asia has become more intra-regional. The sustained economic growth, coupled with a diminishing supply of domestic workers resulting from low fertility, increasingly made these economies seek manpower from neighboring low-income and labor-surplus countries. During the 1990s, such movements of temporary migrant workers intensified. It also became clear in the 1990s that a large number of skilled professionals were partic-ipating in migration streams, adding complexity to the international labor mobility in the region.

The dynamic growth of labor migration in Asia has been also asso-ciated with the emergence of new countries supplying workers, with some of them actively promoting labor deployment. Hence by the mid-1990s, in addition to India, Pakistan, and the Philippines which have a long history of deploying their workers in large numbers, countries such as Bangladesh, China, Indonesia, and Sri Lanka had joined the group of countries that were key sources of the migrant workforce. The official records available from those countries show that there has been a marked increase in the placement of workers over the past three decades (see Figure 4.1). It should be noted that the actual number of migrant workers leaving those countries is likely to be greater than those officially recorded, because there are unknown flows of people who move without registering with the national authorities.

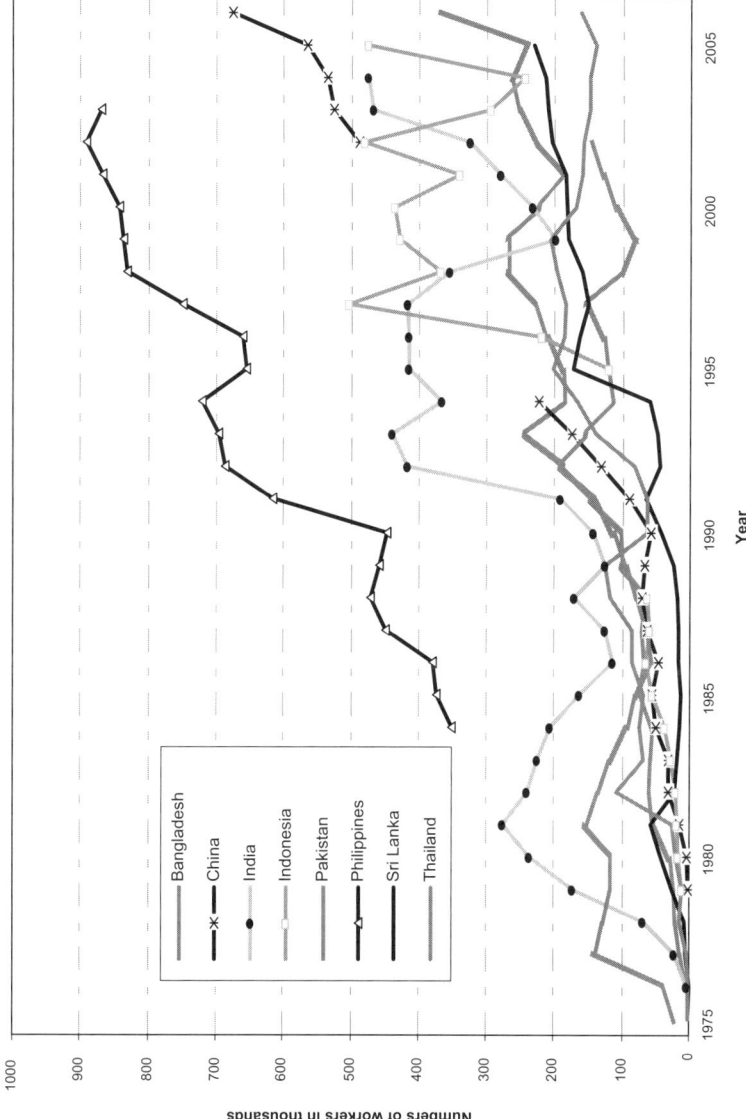

Figure 4.1. Outflow of migrant workers in selected Asian countries, 1975–2006.
Source: Database on international migration maintained at UNESCAP. The number for the Philippines includes rehired workers.

Figure 4.1 indicates that over the past decades, the Philippines continues to top the list of key countries of origin of migrant workers. In 2005 alone, the country deployed over 980,000 persons as migrant workers, or just under 2.7 percent of its national workforce. The destinations of migrant workers differ among source countries. While the Philippines deploys its workforce globally, source countries in South Asia such as India, Pakistan, and Sri Lanka send their workers primarily to the oil-producing countries of the Middle East.

Key Features of International Migration

As mentioned above, a salient feature of international migration in the Asia-Pacific region is a large volume of temporary labor migration. With few exceptions, international migration in the region is primarily intended to fill gaps in the labor market temporarily rather than lead to permanent settlement. The jobs that migrant workers are engaged in within the region tend to concentrate both at the bottom and top of the employment ladder. A large number of migrants are found in agriculture, construction, labor-intensive manufacturing, cleaning and catering services, or jobs which are often referred to as "3D" (dirty, dangerous, and demanding). It has been argued that there is often a mismatch between skills and the jobs that migrants take at their destinations. Thus, workers often leave their jobs at home for higher paying, but less skilled jobs abroad. More recently, Asia has also become a major supplier of skilled workers. The presence of Asian business professionals, managerial workers, and medical professionals, as well as information and communication technology (ICT) personnel working outside their own countries, is growing within and outside the region.

Feminization is also an important feature of international labor migration in the region. There are a significant and increasing number of women who cross borders for employment. In fact, women constitute a large majority of migrant workers leaving key source countries, namely, Indonesia (79 percent), the Philippines (71 percent), and Sri Lanka (66 percent) (see Table 4.1). Migrant women in the region are engaged in a wide range of economic activities, but are found predominantly in domestic work and in the health, manufacturing, and entertainment industries. Demand for female migrant workers has been persistent in relatively affluent economies where

Table 4.1. Percentage of females in the outflows of migrant workers, selected countries, 2000–2003.

| Country | Year | Number of migrant workers deployed, annual average (in 1000s) | | Percent female |
		Total	Female	
Indonesia	2000–2003	387	306	79.2
The Philippines	2000–2002	266	188	70.5
Sri Lanka	2000–2003	195	129	66.1
Republic of Korea	2000–2002	226	80	35.5
Thailand	2000–2003	165	28	16.8

Source: Database on international migration maintained at the Emerging Social Issues Division (ESID), ESCAP. *Note*: The figures for the Philippines refer to newly hired workers for overseas development only.

local women are drawn into the labor force, or where the need for care provision for the elderly is on the rise due to population aging. In theory, women can improve their status and autonomy through migration by playing important roles as family providers and development agents. However, in reality, they are often subject to abuse, exploitation, and isolation in their places of employment.

Undocumented migration has become a cause for serious concern for the countries in the region. Large numbers of undocumented migrants are known to exist, for example, near the borders between Malaysia and Indonesia, and also between Thailand and Myanmar. When Thailand conducted a nation-wide registration campaign in 2004, about 1.3 million undocumented migrants were registered (Huguet and Punpuing, 2005). There are also approximately 200,000 undocumented migrants in Japan and 300,000–500,000 in Malaysia. Human trafficking has been a fast growing transnational problem and a major source of concern for many governments in the region. A strong commitment by governments to combat such irregular migration is seen in initiatives such as the adoption of the South Asian Association for Regional Cooperation (SAARC) Convention on Preventing and Combating Trafficking in Women and Children for Prostitution in 2002, and the signing of the Memorandum of Understanding (MoU) on trafficking in 2005 by the member countries of the Coordinated Mekong Ministerial Initiative against Trafficking (COMMIT).

Remittances made by migrants are the most visible outcomes of international migration, and the increases in the size of remittances flowing into the region have been robust over the years. Figure 4.2 shows the world's top 10 countries receiving migrant remittances in 2007, which includes three Asian countries, namely India, China, and the Philippines. Remittances represent one of the most important sources of external funding in many countries of Asia and the Pacific. They sometimes exceed the flows of official development aid (ODA) or of foreign direct investment (FDI), and hence become a structural element in the national economy. In the Philippines, remittances sent home by migrants have acted as a relatively stable source of foreign exchange earning for many years (Hugo, 2007).

While international migration can have a positive impact on the lives of migrants and their families, it is not free from negative consequences. In particular, the long-term social impact of migration has received marginal attention. Temporary labor migration, in most cases, does not allow migrants to bring their family members to the country of employment. Thus, separation of families due to migration has been a source of great concern,

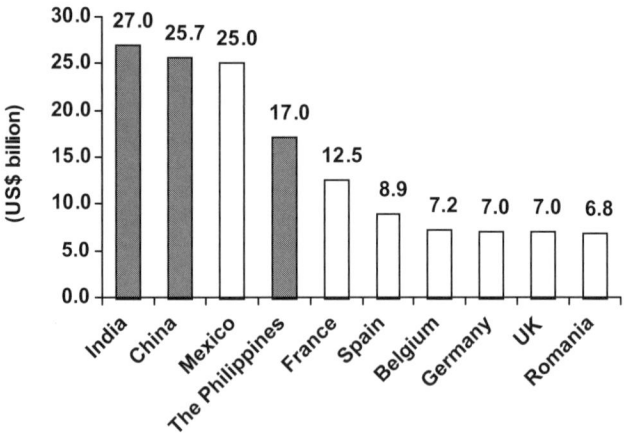

Figure 4.2. Top 10 recipient countries of migrant remittances in 2007 (in US$ billion). *Source*: Ratha *et al.* (2007). *Note*: Remittances include workers' remittances and compensation of employees received.

as it can be detrimental to family cohesion, marital stability, and children left behind. It is estimated that between 3 and 6 million children have been left behind by Filipino parents working overseas; the equivalent figure for Indonesia is one million, while for Thailand it is half a million (Bryant, 2005).

Debates on International Migration and Development at the United Nations

The UN approach to the issue of international migration is often criticized for its ambiguity. This may be partly due to the structure of the organization. While there are several UN bodies responsible for selected dimensions of migration, no single office in the UN system has a mandate to work systematically on the full spectrum of international migration issues (United Nations, 2005). For example, the Office of the United Nations High Commissioner for Human Rights (UNHCHR) is responsible for ensuring the implementation of universally recognized human rights and of key human rights instruments relating to international migration, including the International Convention on the Protection of the Rights of All Migrant Workers and Members of Their Families. The Office of the United Nations High Commissioner for Refugees (UNHCR) has a long history of leading and coordinating international action for the protection of refugees, and seeks solutions for problems of refugees and asylum seekers. The International Labor Organization (ILO) has long promoted the equality of opportunity and treatment of migrant workers in relation to the local people.

As the issue of international migration has moved to the forefront of the policy discourse on managing globalization, there have been increasing demands for the UN to seek the best means to address this complex issue, especially in relation to socioeconomic development. However, the quest by the member states to find the best mechanisms to address the issue within the UN system took nearly 10 years of discussion at the General Assembly (United Nations, 2007). Some states had considered that the issue was politically too sensitive or that the timing was not yet ripe for the international community to tackle. Others were of the view that, despite the importance of the issue, there was not much common ground for discussion between the countries sending and receiving migrants. In particular, the idea of convening an international conference on international migration was not favored by some member states, in view of the financial constraints on the Organization (United Nations, 2003).

The debates at the General Assembly, however, finally resulted in the decision to hold a High-Level Dialogue on International Migration and Development in 2006, following resolution A/RES/59/208. Providing a venue for dialogue between interested parties can help in generating trust and fostering the cooperation necessary for the management of international migration. It was considered that the UN was well placed to promote such a dialogue (United Nations, 2003).

The decision to have this dialogue prompted a number of activities related to international migration at national, regional, and global levels. In the Asia-Pacific region, the United Nations Economic and Social Commission for Asia and the Pacific (UNESCAP) considered the issue of international migration and development at the Committee on Emerging Social Issues in 2005, and held a side event at its 62nd Commission in Jakarta in 2006. Through a number of studies and technical meetings, regional concerns and the challenges of migration were reviewed for presentation during the dialogue.

At the global level, the Global Commission on International Migration (GCIM) composed of 19 expert commissioners and supported by over 30 governments, produced a report containing a series of principles and recommendations to strengthen the national, regional, and global governance of migration. The report was presented to the Secretary-General of the United Nations in 2005. In response to one of the recommendations of the report, the Secretary-General then expanded the Geneva Migration Group, consisting of heads of the major UN bodies involved in international migration and the IOM, and created the Global Migration Group for coordination and cooperation among key UN entities (United Nations, 2007). In January 2006, the Secretary-General also appointed his Special Representative on International Migration and Development to promote participation of member states in the Dialogue at the highest possible level (United Nations, 2007).

The High-Level Dialogue on International Migration and Development that took place in New York on 14–15 September 2006 was the first-ever UN event entirely devoted to the issue of migration and development at the General Assembly. The overall purpose of the Dialogue was to discuss the multidimensional aspects of international migration and development in order to identify appropriate ways and means to maximize its development benefits and minimize its negative impacts. The Dialogue was a great success, and was attended by representatives of 127 countries. The debates and deliberations during the Dialogue were rich and lively, touching upon a wide range of issues, including remittances, labor migration, rights of migrants, migrant integration, irregular migration, and trafficking in persons. The Dialogue at its end adopted the Chairman's summary, which was legally non-binding.

The Dialogue was a breakthrough in migration debates in many ways, as it brought about a paradigm shift in viewing the interlinkages of international migration and development. Migration had long been considered as a means to flee from poverty, or a failure of governments to create decent local jobs. Hence, the migration debate was often preoccupied with its potentially negative dimensions. At the Dialogue, however, participating governments underscored international migration as an integral part of the development process. The phenomenon now affects virtually all countries in the world, developed or developing. The member countries also concluded, perhaps most importantly, that migration could be a positive force for development if it was supported by the right set of policies. The consensus therefore emerged that it was necessary to strengthen international cooperation to promote the positive impact of international migration on development, while respecting human rights and addressing the root causes of migration (United Nations, 2007).

Where does the UN go from here to advance the issue of international migration? There are ongoing debates among member states of the UN on the possible follow-up activities to the Dialogue. While concrete decisions were expected to be made at the General Assembly in 2008, the Belgian Government announced during the Dialogue the establishment of a Global Forum on International Migration and Development, as a state-led venue for discussion of the issue of migration and development. The first Global Forum took place in Belgium in July 2007. Whether the international dialogue on international migration and development will be furthered within or outside the UN system, it seems that the interests of the international community in the subject will only continue to grow in the coming years.

References

Bryant, John (2005). "Children of International Migration in Indonesia, the Philippines and Thailand: A Review of Evidence and Policies." Innocenti Working Paper No. 2005-05, Florence, UNICEF Innocenti Research Centre.

Hugo, Graeme (2007). "International Migration and Development in Asia." Paper presented at the 8th International Conference of the Asia Pacific Migration Research Network, Fuzhou, China, May 25–29, 2007.

Huguet, Jerrold W. and Sureeportn Punpuing (2005). *International Migration in Thailand*. Bangkok: International Organization for Migration.

Ratha, Dilip, Sanket Mohapatra, K.M. Vijayalakshmi and Xhumei Xu (2007). "Remittance Trend 2007." (Migration and Development Brief 3). Washington DC: World Bank Development Prospects Group, Migration and Remittances Team, available at http://siteresources.worldbank.org/EXTDECPROSPECTS/Resources/476882-1157133580628/BriefingNote3.pdf (accessed April 11, 2008).

United Nations (2003). *International Migration and Development: Report of the Secretary-General*. A/58/98. New York: United Nations.

United Nations (2005). *World Economic and Social Survey 2004: International Migration*. New York: United Nations.

United Nations (2007). *Fifth Coordination Meeting on International Migration*. New York: United Nations.

CHAPTER 5

GLOBALIZING HOUSEHOLDING: TOWARD A MULTICULTURAL AGE IN EAST ASIA

Mike Douglass

The Household and Globalization

> Households are seen neither as isolates nor as small units of social organization related to national economies, but instead as basic units of an emerging world-system. (Smith *et al.*, 1984: 8)

More than two decades ago, Smith *et al.* (1984) published an edited volume on the thesis that the household is neither merely a unit of consumption nor an institution that only responds to higher national and international economic forces, but is instead essential to — and the social basis for — capitalist accumulation on a global scale. More specifically, the household is charged with the physical and daily reproduction of labor — more generally, social reproduction — and it carries out its tasks largely outside of the market through pooling of unpaid and paid labor and resources, including income, among its members. The market itself could not readily accomplish these tasks, which involve bearing, raising and educating children, preparing food and running a household, and taking care of members when unemployed, infirm or in need of psychological and moral support.

The household also serves as a base to organize and socialize individuals for the rigors and formalities of employment in the modern enterprise. In this sense, it helps to discipline labor to accept labor processes characterized by expectations of workers being physically and emotionally prepared to adhere to the routines of coming to places of work on time and

doing the often repetitive work assigned to them.[1] Contrary to GNP formulations, which treat the household economy as being unproductive and
solely as a unit of consumption, the Smith, Wallerstein and Evers volume
sees it as being the foundation of national economies and the world economy
as a whole.

Authors contributing to the volume go even further to state that without
the household playing its assigned roles in social reproduction, "any
economy would collapse" (Evers *et al.*, 1984: 26). To them, a fully automated or wholly market driven form of social reproduction is "utopian."
They bolster this view by arguing that non-wage household labor continues
to occupy significant portions of labor time even in societies where wage-
work prevails. From this evidence, they express the view that the institution of the household will necessarily continue to reproduce itself, even as
commodification of social relations advances into all realms of exchange.
People might send all their laundry to the cleaners and order fast food
delivery every night, but they will still engage in labor pooling and income
sharing as household members to reproduce labor power for the system
at large.

More recent studies suggest, however, that the household cannot be so
readily assumed to persist in the contemporary world. A major indicator
of the apparent decline of the social reproductive role of the household,
which was not readily apparent two decades ago, is the world-wide trend
toward below replacement fertility that is seeing absolute population decline
beginning in the more economically advanced societies of the world. High
divorce rates, late marriage with no children, the institutional warehousing
of the elderly, the phenomenal increase in single resident housing units —
more than 50 percent in major cities in the North — are all indicators
of retrenchment of the household and the apparent decline of its role
in sustaining society and economy. In addition, the currently ascendant
neoliberal regime of national and international economic policies is found to
undermine the household, particularly among the poor, by severely reducing
the state-provided social services, economic security and welfare support

---

[1]As noted by Smith (1984), labor does not simply "magically appear at the factory gates"
where it is organized by labor market principals. Its power and availability are instead daily
reproduced in the household.

needed to stay afloat in a world that is witnessing falling real incomes for the lower income classes in, among others, high income economies (Bezanson, 2006).

East Asia is not immune to the stresses on the household that are being documented in the West. Absolute population decline has just begun in Japan, and Korea, Taiwan, Hong Kong, and Singapore — the original "tiger" economies of Asia — are not far behind (Douglass, 2006). These trends are bringing an impending crisis in the respective national economies as the labor force begins to shrink dramatically, dependency ratios rise, and welfare systems become insolvent in their rapidly aging societies.

One emerging way of attempting to shore up the household and its role in social reproduction is to engage in householding through global linkages. Summarized in this paper as "global householding," its major features are the increasing attempts to form and sustain the household through global movements and transactions among household members that have several possible dimensions: marriage; child-bearing and adoption; education of children; hiring foreign domestic helpers and caregivers; and moving not only from low- to high-income economies but, as retirement ages approach, also moving from higher to lower income societies as a way of stretching fixed incomes. None of these elements exist in isolation of the others, but are more accurately part of lifecycles of households through time.

Despite the advent of the age of global householding through these many dimensions, the household remains a phantom in migration studies. Mainstream research continues to view the global movement of people as part of a transnational labor process composed of individual decision makers — frequently viewed as members of ethnic "diasporas" — who migrate around the world for work and income. Though migrants send tremendous amounts of remittances to their households back home, and these households in turn provide many types of support to migrants, the household remains far in the background rather than in the foreground of routine data collection and research on migration. Even new research falling under the rubric of the "transnational family" neglects the role of the household in social reproduction. A large umbrella for disparate studies rather than a consistent framework or paradigm for research, its basic concepts vary substantially among the publications using its title. What constitutes "family" or "transnational," for example, has diverse, frequently ambiguous meanings.[2] More to the point of the discussion here, "family" itself often fades into the background of many transnational family studies, which tend to focus on the agency of individuals who overcome domination by others in the family rather than, e.g., the broader role of the family as an institution in society.[3] The term "transnational" also has various, if not contradictory, meanings in this literature.[4]

Global householding represents a significantly different take on migration and is put forth here to theorize more explicitly about and link the household to larger structural issues such as demographic transitions and shifts in the global economy as well as questions of human agency (Douglass, 2006). Table 5.1 presents key dimensions of global householding, each of which contrasts with other formulations, including transnational family.

First, the household is used as a way to open the treatment to many possible configurations that go beyond kinship or marriage typically used in conjunction with the term "family" (Folbre, 1986; Wallerstein and Smith, 1992). Defined here as a social unit that reproduces itself not only through the physical bearing of children but more broadly through income-pooling and labor-sharing, the household forms what some have called "an economy

---

[2]Many studies do not define family at all, and while some (Sørensen, 2005) try to show that "family" has a wider meaning than "kin" or "marriage," transnational family studies do not in the main explore alternatives to heterosexual marriage or the kin-based family.

[3]Such transnational family studies are often aimed at showing how contestations and role reversals within families are brought about by, e.g., the feminization of international migration and women's increasing role as family breadwinners that is shifting power and roles among its members (Constable, 2005; Piper and Roces, 2003; Parreñas, 2005).

[4]UNFPA (2006: 33) defines "transnational families" as "those whose members belong to two households, two cultures and two economies simultaneously" (Jolly et al. 2003; Parreñas, 2001). Others use it for a family that has moved as a whole from its home country to a new country (Bryceson and Vuorela, 2003). Some (Silvey, 2006) simply mean that that at least one family member is working abroad but do not imply that identities or long-term residence has shifted to more than one country. Still others use the term to describe a "mixed marriage" with one spouse coming from a foreign country (Bacas, 2006). The point to be made here is not that these definitions are not valid, but rather that a study claiming to have "the" definition does not match that of others claiming the definitive definition as well (UNFPA, 2006; Sørenson, 2005; Jolly et al. 2003; Smith and Guarnizo, 1998; Pries, 1999; Levitt, 2001; Guarnizo, 2003; Levitt et al. 2003; Morawska, 2003; Yeoh and Willis, 2004; Constable, 2005).

Table 5.1.   Key dimensions of a global householding research framework.

Dimension	Global householding
Basic unit	Household as an income pooling/(paid and unpaid) labor division and sharing social institution; not only kinship or marriage-based
Relations in the household	Cooperative as well as contested; "economy of affection" as well as "mini-political economy"
Household–society relationship	Social reproduction — reliance on the household in the physical and daily reproduction of society.
Key elements/lifecycles of householding	Marriage/forming household partnerships; child-bearing/adoption; children rearing, including education; daily household maintenance; care of others in the household, including the elderly
Migration motive and driver	Sustaining households with individual betterment; non-economic as well as economic motives
Time dimension	Household through lifecycles and generations
Spatial scale(s)	Multiple local–global scales within and beyond the nation-state; not simply "transborder" or "transnational"

of affection" (Friedmann, 1992) with motives that are not subordinated to the market but in many ways seeks to counter its negative impacts on individuals in the family.

Households need not be based either on biological relationships or on a common residence. They can take many forms, including those with fictive kin, same-sex and unmarried couples, and friends who develop long-term co-residential arrangements (Jellinek, 1991).[5] For example, domestic workers now being recruited by the hundreds of thousands from lower-income countries in Asia are, by the definition used here, intricately involved

---

[5]In the United States, what are now termed "non-family households" — residential units with only one person or those headed by an unmarried person, now comprise approximately one-third of all households (U.S. Census Bureau, 2000).

in householding in higher income societies of Taiwan, Singapore, Hong Kong, and to a lesser extent Korea and Japan. In this context, sources of — and decisions about — generating income and resources pooled by the household are seen in relationship to each other, which also figures into explicit divisions of household labor that can see, for example, one or more members migrating abroad to educate a child while another remains in the home country to earn income to support them (Lee and Koo, 2006).

Second, an open view is taken of the household with regard to the expected interpersonal relationships within it. This is not intended to dismiss research showing the many ways in which patriarchy and traditional family structures make the household an arena of struggles for equality and decision making power — a "mini-political economy" in Friedmann's (1992) terms.[6] Rather, it is also to accept that households are also arenas of genuine caring and of selfless actions for the good of others and the household as a whole. It also allows for implicitly and explicitly negotiated realignments of decision making authority that do not necessarily result in reinforcing the subordination of some of its members to others. As problematic as it might be, forming and sustaining households is a prevailing social desire that has felicitous as well as undesired outcomes for its members.

Third, in addition to focusing on individuals within the household, a key concern here about global householding is its role in social reproduction and, further, the world economy (Smith *et al.*, 1984, 1992). In East Asia this relationship is now becoming a central policy question: how can a society continue to enjoy prosperity in the face of rapid population decline due to the diminishing capacities of its households in social reproduction? Policies to increase fertility rates and to recruit not only foreign workers — including domestic helpers — but also foreign spouses are rising in prominence along with those concerned with gender equality and protection of rapidly growing numbers of foreign workers. Each of these policy issues confronts questions about the globalization of householding.

Fourth, in its role in social reproduction, householding is seen as a longitudinal process involving tasks related to lifecycles, including

---

[6]Intra-family contestations over roles and power constitute one of the major themes of transnational family research, adding the important understanding that the family is not a black box but instead has power relations and differential distribution of its resources among its members (UNFPA, 2006; Bacas, 2006; Bryceson and Vuorela, 2002; Appadurai, 1996; Wilson and Donnan, 1998).

marriage/forming household partnerships; child-bearing/adoption; children rearing, including education; daily household maintenance; and care of others in the household, including the elderly. A very large share of research on transnational families focuses only on marriage or the situation of adult women such as domestic helpers. While important, using "family" only to this extent neglects such phenomena as worldwide increases in international adoption, the tremendous growth in recruiting of children and young adults from abroad for education, and a more recent phenomenon in Asia of retirement from higher to lower income societies. Each of these elements presents its own issues and bottlenecks as householding globalizes. To understand how householding provides the "glue" of a very large share of global migration, they all need to be taken into account.

Fifth, following from the above interest in household–society relationships, the understanding of global householding needs to go beyond the reductionist view of migration as simply a labor process for economic gain. While the household is an arena of income production and pooling, a full global householding perspective takes a more multifaceted view of the motives for migration. Marriage and having children, while having economic dimensions, cannot be reduced to economic motives alone or even in the main, nor can the adoption of children from abroad or sending of children to foreign countries for education be seen solely as a selfish economic investment by parents for future returns. While ambiguities certainly exist in, for example, the "mail order bride" phenomenon now appearing in East Asia concerning whether a foreign-born person is married to add to household labor or for the sake of having a family and children, the one-sided view of marriage migration as simply an aberrant labor process cannot possibly capture either all its motives or all the outcomes. Genuine desires to form households, have progeny, and care for others without a dominant concern for economic gain must also be considered.

Sixth, as a corollary to the understanding of householding as life-cycle process reproducing the household as a social institution, research on global householding is necessarily a longitudinal process that extends through generations. Studying this process through time allows for the assessment of the changing circumstances and capacities for household formation and reproduction. As such, it can also better understand and theorize about the impacts on households of macro-elements of globalization, such as the current massive global shift of labor-intensive manufacturing to China or the rise of an urban middle class in Asia that is presenting a high demand for foreign domestic workers, on households and householding. This affords opportunities for linking, e.g., behavioral decisions within households to broader changes in structural features of the world system. It can help address questions of why the household is "going global." Why is it now rising out of certain societies and not others? What are the patterns and why do variations exist even among countries at the same levels of per capita income? These questions tend to be overlooked in other formulations of migration research.

Seventh, by using "global" instead of invoking "transnational," global householding as a concept avoids the trap of reifying the nation-state as the only meaningful level to analyze householding and policies that affect its fortunes. Although the nation-state remains a powerful entity in regulating migration, it is not the only level of governance of migration. For example, local governments are increasingly taking a larger role in promulgating *de facto* immigration policies, as was evidenced during the struggle in Japan over the national requirement to fingerprint foreign residents, which several local governments refused to carry out, leading to it being rescinded. Local governments in Japan have also been taking the lead changing policies to allow foreign residents to hold public service jobs.

In addition, as with the world economy as a whole, the use of nation-state and national borders to demarcate internal phenomena from international phenomena is increasingly anachronistic. Throughout Asia, rural–urban migration within nation-states is linked with globalization. Yet when a person migrates from the village to work for a global corporation in the big city within a country, this continues to be viewed as an internal or domestic act. The same person moving to a foreign country to work for the same corporation is said to be a transnational migrant. In fact, both are part of global circuits of capital linking rural households to major cities in their own countries and to global flows of labor, finance, resources and commodities beyond national borders. In this regard, the use of "national" also disguises the fact that more than two-thirds of all world trade are now within corporations rather than among nations (UNCTAD, 2006). Goods are not traded among countries but are instead circulated through global corporate circuits of finance, inputs for production, and commodities. Localities are directly linked to these systems as labor, too, increasingly circulates from rural to urban to global and back again as part of global circuits.

Further, while the idea that going across borders signals a shift to "diaspora" or other notions of identities being displaced, there is a recognition that the national border is only one type of border involved. Koreans living in autonomous regions in China and the Commonwealth of Independent States, small-scale societies in Indonesia, the Philippines, and most other nations of Asia face similar identity questions when moving within the nation in which they were born and hold citizenship. The nation-state in Asia has been a work in progress since the era of high imperialism in the 19th century, well before the advent of the modern transnational corporation. The advent of contemporary globalization with the emergence of giant corporations deploying the global factory system away from the North to the South from the 1960s has further challenged the nation-state building process by circumventing national border controls through its control over flows of all forms of capital.

Householding is now beginning to have multilevel global–local rather than simple internal versus transnational linkages. For example, migrants from the rural Philippines working in Taipei use their incomes to buy houses in Manila to move their families from rural regions to the big city (Huang and Douglass, 2004). Porio (2007), in a revealing study of global householding in the Philippines, shows how extended families combine remittances and unpaid labor to move members from the countryside to Metro Manila and abroad in constantly shifting patterns of rural–urban migration, migration abroad and return migration to various parts of the Philippines. This does not mean that the national border is not a formidable point of regulating migration flows, but rather that to call rural–urban migration "internal" and movements abroad "transnational" misses the point that the distinction between national and international is now blurred in all of these household relationships.

Global Householding in East Asia

The perception of migration as a means to improve the family's situation runs strong in migrants' motivations ... With repeat migrations, which allows migrants and their families to recover the costs of migration, migrants are able to put their earnings into other investments: land, better/durable housing structures, the education of children/family members, or capital to set start a business. (Asis, 2003: 6, 10)

The fastest economically developing area of the world over the past several decades, East Asia now displays the entire panoply of global house-holding. The higher income economies are now evocative of the experiences in Europe in their accelerated demographic transitions that are mirrored in increasing difficulties in household formation. Falling fertility rates, the advent of aging societies and the changing gender roles in the household with the rise of career women, have brought new issues and stresses to these countries and territories, including Japan and the four Asian tigers of Taiwan, Korea, Hong Kong, and Singapore, in keeping both households and societies thriving. Plummeting birth rates and a shrinking labor force have already created crises in filling jobs, covering welfare costs of non-working populations, and caring for children and the elderly.

In response, the formation and sustenance of households is increasingly relying on the global movement of, and transactions among, household members beyond national territorial boundaries. Currently, an estimated 175 million people live outside of their country of birth. While still a small share of the world's population, it has been steadily increasing, and by the year 2050 estimations show that it will reach at least 230 million. This does not include spouses or children of migrants born in the current country of residence; nor does it include non-resident migrants who make up an increasing share of global migration. To account for non-migrating household members, these numbers need to be increased by multiples of four or five to fully capture the extent to which migration is imbedded in global householding. Thus, the 175 million becomes 700 million if only a multiple of four is used. Asia already accounted for one-quarter of global migrants, or about 45 million, in 2000. Using a conservative multiplier of four non-migrants to every migrant in a household, this number swells to 180 million.

All of these globalizing householding relations confront and challenge received notions of identity with a single nation-state, as well as the rights to public goods and services in places of residence that attend accepted notions of citizenship. They also bring into stark contrast the intention of most migrant receiving societies to simply extract labor power from migrants while migrants themselves have hopes of a fuller life and spend enormous amounts of energy building and nurturing households to care for the whole lives of their members (Douglass, 1999; Douglass and Roberts, 2003). Global householding is nonetheless a risky endeavor that is fraught with capricious and, from a household perspective, harsh immigration policies, human trafficking, and exploitation. At the same time, however, it also has positive outcomes that allow for optimism and hope as well.

In addition to technological revolutions, the sources of the contemporary shift toward global householding are many. Among the most crucial are the demographic transitions toward below replacement fertility in migrant receiving countries, implicit choices made by women and men to develop careers instead of marrying or having children during child-bearing ages, and the high costs of living in home countries after retirement.[7] Most of these factors, particularly below replacement fertility, are only just now beginning to be experienced in the world. As such they are as yet difficult to either comprehend or anticipate in terms of the impacts they will have in just a decade or two decades from now.

In the case of below replacement fertility, for example, very high burdens will be placed on households by rapidly increasing ratios of non-working to working populations and the inability of governments to continue to expand social security and welfare funds at a rate commensurate with the pace of the aging of their societies. Such trends amount to deep social, economic, and ultimately political crises that require far sighted policies to anticipate and prepare societies to meet them. By the beginning of this century more than half of the population in the world was already experiencing below replacement fertility (Harbison and Robinson, 2003). Pacific Asia already has a number of societies that are at or soon will be below replacement fertility, including Japan, Korea, Hong Kong, Singapore, and Taiwan.

Largely unanticipated only two decades ago, immigration has now become a major dimension of local life within Pacific Asia.[8] In 1993 approx-imately 3 million people were documented as having moved across national

---

[7]The slow-down in population growth has reached middle-income countries as well, resulting in the weakening of traditional family structures (Harbison and Robinson, 2003).
[8]Until the late 1980s, migration to Japan from other Pacific Asia countries almost wholly consisted of women in the sex industry (Douglass and Roberts, 2003). Since that time, new layers of workers in construction, low-wage assembly, and services have been added.

boundaries to other destinations in the Pacific Asia for work, study, marriage, family reunion, retirement, or as political or environmental refugees.[9] In 2003 the estimated number had increased to 10 million. Due to immigration laws declaring much of this migration to be illegal, both the 1993 and 2003 figures are thought to significantly underestimate actual numbers. Again, if multiplying by four, even the conservative number of 10 million jumps to 40 million.

As elsewhere, the sources of the rising levels of migration and global householding in Pacific Asia are multiple, but in the center of almost all of them is the formation and sustenance of households in the home region or country and migrant destinations.[10] Nurturing households over global space is promoted by income differences among Pacific Asian countries that are wide and continue to widen. Recruiters and middlemen have formed networks to greatly facilitate the flow of people, money, goods and services related around the world. In key migrant sending countries, governments and families alike have become dependent upon migrant remittances to sustain their economies. Support groups are also appearing in migrant host societies to assist in overcoming legal and other barriers to entry and long-term stay.

As noted above, in addition to these factors, the demographic surprise of the 21st century in Pacific Asia is the incipient process of long-term population decline in several higher income economies that is already leading to chronic labor shortages and depopulation of non-metropolitan regions. These societies are all rapidly aging as well, which is having multiple impacts, including the growing need for assisted living and long-term care of the elderly, heightening stress on public welfare and pension systems, and new forms of poverty related to living on fixed or declining income streams. In contrast, population growth remains high in key migrant sending countries, such as the Philippines, which are providing growing quantities of global migrant labor.

All of these factors reflect expanding processes of global householding. In many cases this process represents a disjuncture in local demographic, social, and economic factors traditionally working to provide for household

---

[9]About half of Asia's international migrant labor comes from Indonesia, the Philippines, and other Southeast Asian countries. When they go abroad, half remain in Southeast and East Asian countries such as Malaysia, South Korea, and Taiwan.

[10]With more than 300,000 emigrants leaving per year, China had become the largest source of international migrants by the beginning of this century (United Nations, 2002).

formation within existing societies. These disjunctures include numerical gender imbalances, changing gender differences in preferences for marriage, and near or below replacement fertility within societies. They also follow from differences among countries in income-earning opportunities that are manifested in householding through migrant support and remittances to one or more households in the home country and possibly abroad as well. In terms of international adoption, concerns for intergenerational continuity figure into this process as well. Finally, they are created by insufficient welfare and social safety nets for societies with increasing shares of aging, non-working populations who are beginning to look abroad for living more cheaply in their senior years.

As noted, most research on migration continues to assess all of the above data and trends as evidence of globalizing labor processes. Such a view is flawed in several ways. First, it implicitly assumes that the motivation for migration is solely economic and for income. In so doing, it misses not only the extent of migration that is forced due to natural disasters, war and other calamities, but also migration that is directly driven by other motives that are imbedded in global householding. In this same sense, migration for income is not an end itself but is rather a means for reciprocal support among household members. From this perspective, migration as labor process also fails to uncover the social bases — householding — that promote and sustain the movement of people over the globe. All of these points can be exemplified by a step-by-step consideration of the lifecycles of householding, the principal elements of which include:

- Marriage/partnering
- Bearing children
- Raising and educating children (and adults)
- Maintaining the household on a daily basis
- Dividing labor and pooling income from livelihood activities
- Caring for elder and other non-working household members.

Marriage

The marriage market in Asia is becoming rapidly globalized, and just in time for tens of thousands of single-but-looking South Korean men, most of them in the countryside where marriageable women are in scant supply. With little hope of finding wives of their own nationality and producing

children to take over the farm, the men are pooling their family's resources
to raise money to find a spouse abroad. (Demick, 2006: 1)

Marriages with spouses from foreign countries are increasing in several
Pacific Asia societies. One of the factors behind this trend is the continuing
urban transition, which in higher income societies has already depleted rural
populations and left especially men, many of whom are obligated to carry
on with family farms, unable to find brides due to an observed preference
by women for urban work, householding, and lifestyles.

In Japan and Korea, local governments have joined with farmers to
sponsor searches for potential spouses from other Asian countries. For
example, Haenam, a district in the southwest of Korea, plans to provide
unmarried men with 5 million won ($5,500) for expenses spent on bringing
in foreign spouses. As a result of such efforts, the greatest local shares of
marriages with a foreign partner in total marriages tend to be in rural prefectures between local farmers and women from countries such as China,
the Philippines, Thailand, and Vietnam. In Japan, the number of marriages
between Japanese men and foreign women reached about 30,000 per year
by 2000. Most of these marriages are with "mail order" brides. While only
about 1.4 percent of the population in Japan is from abroad, in 2002 these
marriages accounted for about 5 percent of the national total.

The Taiwan and Korean cases are even more striking. Currently, one-
third of all marriages in Taiwan is between Taiwan and non-Taiwan residents. In addition to mainland China, Vietnam has become a principal
source of spouses for Taiwan men. For the three years from 2004 to 2006
approximately 80,000 women moved from Vietnam to Taiwan for marriage
(Cheng, 2007). One thousand Vietnamese women and Taiwanese men marry
every month. Approximately 148,000 brides moved from mainland China
for marriage in Taiwan between 1993 and 2002.[11]

In Korea 14 percent of all new marriages in 2005 were between a Korean
and foreign spouse. More prominently, nearly 40 percent of all rural marriages were with a foreign spouse (*The Chosun Ilbo*, 2006; *Asia Pacific Post*,

---

[11] One-third of international marriages registered in Ho Chi Minh City are between Vietnamese women and Taiwanese men. Interestingly, the government of Taiwan has made it
more difficult and costly to marry a person from mainland China than from other countries.
Longer waiting periods and income tests are imposed on women from mainland China, but
not on women from Vietnam or elsewhere (Tsai, 2003).

2006). As summarized by a newspaper reporter in Korea, "As the number of international marriages increases in the rural areas, rural villages are experiencing their own kind of 'globalization'" (*JoongAng Daily*, 2006).

Although the highest shares of marriages with foreign spouses are in rural regions, the greatest numbers are in the metropolitan regions. Over time, as the experience of Taiwan shows, the rural initiatives also spread to the cities. As divorce rates continue to rise and marriage rates among men and women within the same country fall, global householding initiated by marriage with a foreign spouse can only be expected to increase as well. To the extent that this is already a billion dollar industry and is gaining more acceptance in the countries in which the couples choose to reside, it will become a common occurrence, especially in the higher income societies.

Bearing and adopting children

Four out of every 10 men in rural areas [of Korea] marry non-Korean Asian women. Experts say this will result in around 2 million mixed-race births by 2020. (*Asia Pacific Post*, 2006)

"There are only old people around here," said Le Pho, a 22-year-old Vietnamese woman who married a South Korean a year ago and is now pregnant. Her child will be the first born in the village, Seogok-ri, in more than 20 years. (Demick, 2006: 2)

In 2004 one out of every 7.5 newborn babies was delivered by an immigrant mother. In the same year some 41,000 children of these mothers were in primary school in Taiwan, accounting for 2.17 percent of all primary school students, a 55 percent increase from the previous year. Children from cross-border marriages in high school reached 5,500 in 2004, a growth of 61 percent over the previous year. These numbers combine to show how cross-border marriages are already contributing significantly to the reproduction of the household and social reproduction as well in Taiwan. (Huang, 2006: 455)

One of the principal motives for marriage with a foreign spouse is to have children and to carry on the family line. In 2005 South Korea and Taiwan tied for the lowest birth rates in the world at 1.1 per woman (Demick, 2006). For men, particularly those in heavily depopulating rural regions of high-income countries, namely, Korea, Taiwan, and Japan, marrying a foreign woman is their only chance of having progeny. While not sufficient to reverse trends toward below replacement fertility in these countries, data on rates of birth clearly show that these marriages result in more children than do local marriages.

When having their own children becomes impossible, couples can turn to international adoption. Sending Asian babies to the West for adoption has long been practiced, and continues to occur today. The preference for male children found in many Asian countries produces not only results in highly imbalanced sex ratios favoring males but, paradoxically, also a very large number of female children made available for adoption abroad. China, which now has 120 boys for every 100 girls under age four, is experiencing significant levels of abandonment or the putting up for adoption of female children and is now a principal source of (female) babies for adoption in the West. Korea and Vietnam are also sources of children for adoption. From 1951 to 2001 children from abroad adopted in the United States totalled 265,677. Of that number 156,491 came from Asia. The annual number more than doubled between 1991 and 2000.

Adoption of children from abroad is as yet uncommon in most Pacific Asia countries. However, unreported adoptions are said to be occurring in many countries, and recently the Government of Korea moved to ban surrogate motherhood after a Korean couple engaged an American woman to bear their child (Lee, 2005).[12] In the case of Singapore, adoption is becoming a more open option, but some of it still remains underground. In 2005, applications for adoption processed by the Singapore Government totalled 556; foreign children accounted for 56 percent of this number. Smuggling of babies from Indonesia — some are stolen from parents — is reported to be a significant part of adoption in Singapore (Arshad, 2006).

Late marriage and other factors such as rising divorce rates are leading to physical and social inhibitions against bearing children. Yet the desire to have children remains strong. As of 2004 some 640,000 couples in Korea were unable to conceive and spent about 8.6 billion won a year on fertility treatment. Just as the marriage of rural men to foreign women seemed

---

[12]Up to the late 1980s as many as 9,000 Korean children were being sent abroad for adoption every year (Freundlich and Lieberthal, 2000).

improbable just a few years ago but is now becoming routine, so might the adoption of foreign children into families in Pacific Asia.

Child rearing and education

> ... [Korean] Fathers were not passive or reluctant participants ... to the contrary, they were often the initiators of this family splitting [sending wife with children abroad for education] for the sake of children and, despite the great difficulties they have to endure, they seem to have no regret about their decisions. Furthermore, despite long periods of physical separation, our *kirogi* fathers seem to be able to maintain stable and normal relationships with their wives and children ... In general, *kirogi* families reveal strong family solidarity, but this solidarity is based on a more flexible and pragmatic form of family relations than the traditional patriarchal model. (Lee and Koo, 2006: 551–552)

One of the most striking trends in householding in Pacific Asia is sending children abroad for education. Households in almost all countries in the region do this in large numbers. In Korea and Taiwan it has taken the form of husbands remaining at home while wives and children move abroad for many years for the sake of the children's education and, in the case of Korea, to avoid military service as young adults (Huang, 2006; Lee and Koo, 2006; Bang and Ko, 2006).

China reportedly has the largest number of people who have studied abroad. In 2002 the Ministry of Education reported that 460,000 Chinese have studied in 103 countries and regions, with the United States attracting 150,000, the largest portion (*People's Daily*, 2002). For young people under age 22, from 1999 to 2002, their numbers increased at an annual rate of 40 percent.

In parallel with these trends, such countries as the United States and Australia have been positioning themselves as a center for schooling and higher education for people from Asia. In the United States which had 572,000 foreign students in its educational system in 2003, such prestigious universities as MIT have 70 percent of their graduate students from abroad. Three-quarters of all long-term visitors from Asia in Australia are in educational programs.

Daily household maintenance and reproduction

> In the eyes of the state, the FDW [foreign domestic worker] is not so much
> a worker within a key industry in the national economy but an appendage
> of the Singaporean household, brought in by private contract, and made
> necessary only because the "family" (and within it, women in particular)
> are no longer able to absorb what was traditionally unpaid work. (Huang,
> Yeoh and Asia, 2003: 93)

> In contrast to the waning number of migrant workers in the construction
> and manufacturing sectors due to the decline in those sectors of Taiwan's
> economy, the volume of [foreign] domestic workers keeps a steady growth
> rate. By the end of 2005, the total number of the domestic workers already
> exceeded 143,000. This number accounted for 43 percent of the total
> migrant workers in Taiwan. (Huang, 2006)

The advent of the age of global migration has also brought a new age of
global householding to many Pacific Asia countries in the form of households in higher-income countries hiring domestic helpers and caretakers for
children and the elderly from lower income countries in the region. For the
first time in history, middle class families, not just elites, can avail themselves of having full time domestic workers due to the ease and much lower
cost of recruiting them from such countries as the Philippines, Thailand,
Indonesia, China and, more recently, Vietnam (Wee and Sim, 2003). In
2003 three quarters of a million legal foreign workers, almost all women,
were working in these occupations in just Hong Kong (240,000), Taiwan
(120,000), Singapore (150,000), and Malaysia (240,000). In Singapore one
in seven households now has a domestic worker from abroad, and two-thirds
of households say that they cannot take care of domestic chores, including
taking care of children and the elderly, without a (foreign) domestic helper
(Lam *et al.*, 2006).

Domestic workers typically find themselves involved in two or more
households in their home countries and in the countries in which they
work. Filipina domestic workers in Taiwan, for example, are simultaneously
breadwinners for their households in the Philippines and surrogate mothers
for children of Taiwanese families (Lan, 2003). Similarly, Indonesian maids
in Singapore are found to be remitting about two-thirds of their wages of

about $150 a month to their households in Indonesia (*Migration News*, 2004).

In addition to caring for children and daily household cleaning and food preparation, foreign workers are increasingly involved in caring for the elderly. In Taiwan, such workers have become the backbone of sustaining a system of filial piety that makes putting elders in a long-term care facility unthinkable for many families despite the fact that all adults in the family are engaged in their own jobs outside of the house. On call 24 hours a day, seven days a week, these foreign care givers provide the semblance of a caring Taiwanese family that cannot, in fact, take care of elders having advanced health problems. Japan, facing a similar situation, is also now opening up for foreign nurses working in elderly care.

Whether these workers are considered to be members of the families that employ them is perhaps debatable (Lam *et al.*, 2006). Nonetheless, they are clearly indispensable to the reproduction of hundreds of thousands of households in many countries in the Pacific Asia region. With very large shares of urban middle class families having both husbands and wives working and aging populations growing more numerous, this element of global householding is likely to continue to expand.

Labor migrant and household remittances

An estimated 2.2 million contract workers and immigrants, largely women, remitted some US$3.3 billion from Japan, Hong Kong, Singapore and Malaysia "on monthly averages ranging from US$300 to US$500," said the ADB study, *Southeast Asian Workers' Remittances*. (Opiniano, 2006: 1)

Having been successful as a nurse in Germany, Luz [from the Philippines] financed the migration of Rosa and Ben. She partially assisted Vic, when he left for Papua New Guinea, and to Vic's daughters, when they moved to the U.S. in 2001. Luz also supported Sarah when she first arrived in London, and is now partially supporting a brother in the Philippines who is a widower with six children. (Porio, 2007: 16)

Human Rights Watch criticized Singapore for collecting S$530 (US$314) million a year in levies from the employers of 150,000 foreign maids, but does not protect the maids under its regular labor laws. Employers pay

S$200 to S$295 a month for the privilege of importing a foreign maid. There are about 600,000 foreign workers in Singapore. (*Migration News*, 2006: 9)

The number of people moving for work abroad is escalating. Filipinos deployed abroad increased from under 40,000 per year in 1975 to nearly one million per year in 2004. One-third of those in 2004 went to other countries in East and Southeast Asia. Approximately 20 percent of the entire Philippine labor force is now working abroad. For Vietnam, about 31,400 workers were sent abroad in 1999, a 50 percent increase over 1998, and in 2001 about 50,000 workers were sent overseas for work. In 2000 Indonesia, also a major source of global labor, had more than 1.5 million workers in Malaysia alone, and another 90,000 in Taiwan, 70,000 in Singapore, 40,000 in Hong Kong, 12,000 in Korea, and 3,000 in Japan (MIS, 2002). In all cases, the numbers began to increase even more rapidly and have extended to more countries in recent years.

Worldwide remittances from these global workers are now more than double the amount of global aid by governments and international institutions combined and are now equal to annual amounts of foreign direct investment in developing countries (Figure 5.1). In 2003 Pacific Asia accounted for 14 percent of these remittances. Worker remittances to the

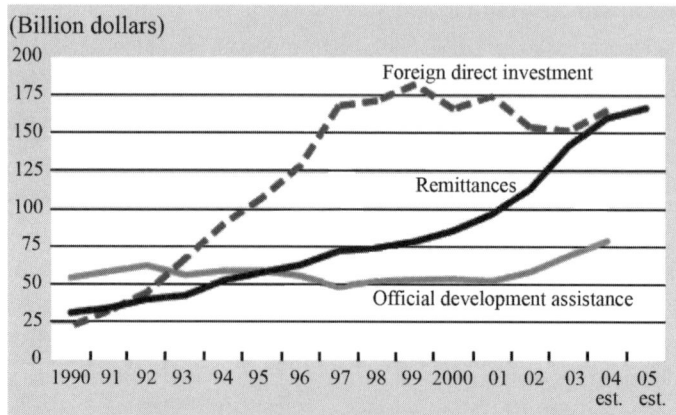

Figure 5.1.   Migrant remittances compared to other international financial flows.
Source: IMF, "Sending Money Home: Trends in Migrant Remittances." *Finance and Development* 42(4) (2006): Figure 1. *Note*: Migrants' remittances include workers' remittances, compensation of employees and migrants' capital transfers.

Philippines alone totaled almost US$8 billion in 2003, which accounted for 10 percent of the country's GDP (*Migration News*, 2004). Remittances to Indonesia from its 1.2 million legal workers abroad were almost US$3 billion in 2003. The Vietnamese government earned US$1.25 billion in remittances from overseas workers, making labor one of the country's key exports (Nguoi, 2003).

When considering in-kind support from families at home, remittances are not just one-way from migrants to households in their country of origin. In a great number of instances, these households take care of the children of the migrants and serve as a sanctuary in between migration episodes. They also give meaning to the sacrifices that especially low-wage migrant workers endure in harsh, highly exploitative employment overseas. Household support is very frequently cited as the main reason for migrating and is the principal source of emotional well-being for people working abroad.

Retirees and the elderly: foreign care givers and retiree emigration from East Asia

"Maid agencies" in Singapore estimate that 30% of the 150,000 foreign domestic workers are hired specifically to care for the elderly. (*The Straits Times*, 11 January 2006)

I do not want to burden my children ... I have three sons and have established good relationships with my daughters-in-law and I want to maintain this pleasant relationship until I die ... I want to maintain my pride as a respected father-in-law. That is why I decided to come to Chiang Mai. I can afford to hire a live-in maid or nurse to look after me here. I would much prefer to be looked after by someone else than my own family members. This arrangement gives me better peace of mind towards ageing. (Interview with Japanese retiree living in Thailand, quoted in Toyota, 2006: 524.)

[Another respondent says] ... Although I have a house and land it is not easy to find a wife for someone like me who graduated with only high school education in Japan, as you know. But I really have to find a wife now. That is why I came to Chiang Mai. I need to find someone who can look after my mother. She used to be quite healthy but now she is getting old and weak, and it got worse since last year. I am rather anxious

regarding how to look after my mother. After the marriage, I can either
take her back to Japan or we can all move to Thailand. I am flexible.
(Toyota, 2006: 526)

One of the most significant trends in the opening of East Asian countries
to foreign workers is to bring these workers, almost always women, to care
for the elderly. Taiwan established this practice several years ago, and now
a very large share of its more than 140,000 domestic helpers are hired to
take care of elderly people (Huang, 2006). Japan is also now taking in a
modest number of nurses, primarily for elderly care.

For seniors facing fixed incomes and diminishing reliance on children to
care for them, an alternative is appearing: move from their costly countries
in East Asia to less expensive ones in Southeast Asia where governments and
private developers are building retirement villas complete with health care
facilities and personnel to attract retirees from richer nations, particularly
Japan (Douglass, 2006). By 2002 one-quarter of the population in Japan
was already over age 65. By 2050 this share is projected to reach 42 percent;
in the same year more than one-third of the population will be over the age
of 80 years. This is taking place in the context of a labor force that began to
decline in numbers in the 1990s and a social security system that is already
paying out more than it takes in. Other countries will encounter similar
issues. In 2050 Korea will have 33 percent of its population over age 65
(United Nations, 2003). Taiwan's population has a similar trajectory.

In view of the rapid increase in retired people on fixed incomes in
higher income economies, governments are already putting forth policies
and developers are already building and advertising retirement communities for expatriates. In Thailand the Government's Board of Investment
has announced that "Thailand wants to attract international retirees and
nursing home patients" and that it will provide tax and other incentives
to developers of retirement communities and resorts (*Leisure Club*, 2004).
Medical and other services specifically targeted for the elderly are part of the
inducements being offered by private sector developers. In 2001 a developer
announced plans to build a retirement village for Japanese at the cost of
B40 billion (US$1 billion) in Northern Thailand (*Bangkok Post*, 2001).
Phuket, Bangkok, Chiang Mai, and Chiang Rai are all advertising schemes
to develop foreign resident communities in Thailand. Saigon South, a huge
suburb of Saigon planned for 1 million people that is being built by Taiwan

developers, also invites retired households to move into its houses and condominiums.

Retirement emigration from Japan is already significant. Toyota (2006) reports that four types of such movers have appeared from the 1990s: seasonal movers who spend winter in Southeast Asia (notably Thailand) and the other half of the year in Japan; totally relocated households that include two generations of retirees, the recently retired and long-retired parents, who move, in part, to avail themselves of domestic helpers who are not allowed to enter Japan; economically displaced seniors who lost jobs during Japan's "lost decade" and more from economic stagnation move to escape household pressures in Japan; and, fourth, single male retirees in search of partners.

All together, the emerging retirement migration shows itself to be diverse and growing in numbers. As Toyota concludes (2006: 530):

> The global householding strategies among the retirees are far more complex than household formation beyond national borders. With the increase in the number of Japanese retirees moving to Southeast Asia, their socioeconomic backgrounds and life strategies also become more diverse. While some move away from Japan in order to maintain their households, others do so in order to avoid contacting their households. Some relocate households to the new country, while others form unstable sexual liaison[s] without clear prospects. For the economically and socially 'displaced' men, their migration appears to be [a] dismantling of or a failure of establishing conventional household[s] in Japan, their escaping from household[s] in a way helps [sustain] the predominant household patterns in Japan. In this sense, global householding can be understood as the process where the complex dynamics of household making and remaking, compelled by various demographic and social factors, are played out at a global scale.

Retirement migration is appearing in other parts of East Asia as well. Old soldiers of the KMT who came to Taiwan in the late 1940s are returning to China; others are also moving from Taiwan to China to not only take advantage of lower costs, but to also participate in China's booming economy (Huang, 2006). If Europe and North America are examples, as the successful retirement experiences become better known, greater numbers are likely to appear in the coming years, especially since several Southeast

Asian countries are focusing on this type of migration as part of their economies.

Conclusions

> Migration policies in the region [East and Southeast Asia] — keeping migration temporary based on the control and surveillance of migrant workers — has gone unchanged in the last 30 years … [and] has resulted in the following outcomes: keeping migration temporary, limiting migrants' participation in the receiving countries in the economy in a specific sector and employer, and preventing settlement by not allowing family reunification. These conditions have real consequences for migrants: they cannot count on job tenure, they are not free to choose better wages and working conditions, and they are not allowed to have a family life. (Asis, 2003: 5)

What is surprising in discourses on global migration is the neglect of the household as a vital institution not only in social reproduction but also as a locus of decision making and motives about migration. It remains a phantom that is only vaguely or incidentally revealed as a background for assessing migrants as labor or spouses. Yet global householding, not labor migration *per se*, represents the singularly most important transformative process in East Asia. Migrants recruited only for their labor typically have visas limited to short-term stays, and they are never afforded the chance to become either permanent residents or citizens. Families cannot accompany them, and they are also often forbidden to marry or have children in the host country.

Global householding through, e.g., marriage, has a quite different outcome that includes permanent stays and possibilities of citizenship, and therefore rights to all privileges accorded to other citizens. In bearing children, global households also contribute to inter-generational multicultural linkages within and among societies in the region and beyond. The globalization of householding is much more likely than people recruited as labor alone to produce layers of sedimentation in the host country that, in the longer term, will transform ethnically homogeneous societies in Asia into genuinely multicultural ones. Few other challenges to the identities and cultures of East Asia are as profound as the localized outcomes of global householding.

Once it is seen as a key social institution in local and global socioeconomic systems, and once available data and cases are brought together to reveal its importance in the contemporary globalization process, the question that arises is whether or not it can be a phoenix that renews energies of householding that seem to be declining within higher-income economies. The answer to this question is as yet unclear for at least three reasons: (1) policy regimes are not, in general, hospitable to global householding, (2) social acceptance is also needed for it to flourish, and (3) the trends are not yet documented sufficiently to be able to make clear trajectories.

Concerning the first point, as noted in the quote above from Asis (2003), policy regimes throughout Asia tend to be inimical to the needs of global householding. Marriage across national boundaries is fraught with difficulties, including, on one end of the spectrum, trafficking and fraudulent representation. On the other end, immigration policies often disallow citizenship rights until many years after marriage and residence, with many countries disallowing non-citizen spouses the right to work outside of the household.

On the second point, social attitudes and discriminatory practices against various elements of global householding are pronounced in many countries. Discrimination in access to private housing, community services, and public spaces are common and usually without legal recourse. Negative attitudes about the traits of people from other Asian countries, such as sensationalized criminal behavior, are allied with this discrimination. Societies in receiving countries are known to channel migrants into certain neighborhoods, which are tantamount to ghettos. Governments also participate in private sector and community regulation through law making and police powers. In addition, popular and academic writing on the various dimensions of global householding often takes a pejorative view of its nature and impacts. Among the more commonly expressed views are that it is exploitative, morally improper, undermines local culture, and it also tends to steal jobs from locals (Douglass, 2006).[13] The many experiences that counter or caution these views remain in the shadow of the more negative treatments.

---

[13]As exemplified by such statements by a foreign bride support group that "Multinational marriage matching is mainly operated by marriage brokers and the process is quite the same with a business transaction" and thus "the value of marriage is distorted" (Liao, 2003: 1).

Third, with tracking of global householding in its many dimensions still not routine, trends are as yet difficult to assess. In some areas, such as marriage, available statistics do show stunning growth patterns. Nonetheless, even this data is not easy to retrieve, and other aspects of global householding such as adoptions, schooling abroad, remittances, and retirement migration are typically found at the case study rather than national data level. Placing householding in the center of migration analysis is needed for an assessment of its future prospects.

When householding goes global, a myriad of agents, governments, and local social practices present formidable challenges to its success even while they also facilitate it as, e.g., brokers or local governments assisting farmers in finding foreign wives. Yet those engaged in global migration and householding are beginning to find allies, support groups, and even government support. While much attention has been given to the nation-state represented by the central government, what is apparent from numerous studies is the heightening role of the local state — prefectural, district and municipal governments — in global householding. Local governments, for example, have been a vanguard in recruiting foreign brides for men in rural areas. They have also developed programs to assist in education and welfare of foreign members of households (Tegtmeyer-Pak, 2003). Faced with having to deal with global householding issues on a daily basis, local governments have also begun to depart from national policies with regard to services provided to and rights of migrants. In Japan, for example, Kanagawa Prefecture has raised the banner stating, "foreign residents are citizens, too" (Tegtmeyer-Pak, 2003). Others have opened lower level civil service employment to long-term foreign residents as well. Where local governments have significant autonomy from the center, the differences between the national and local state seem to be widening across a number of areas of work and residential issues faced by foreign workers. Yet the local state remains relatively unexplored as an agent in the governance of migration, and the changing role of the local state deserves much more attention in assessing the future of global householding.

Despite the manifold barriers confronting global householding, available indicators suggest that it will continue to expand in East Asia, especially in terms of marriage and childbearing, education of children, and recruitment of domestic workers. Other forms, such as international adoption, might well increase over the longer term, as will retirement migration. Though it cannot be predicted that they will somehow substantially compensate for the difficulties appearing in householding within East Asian countries, global householding is now a permanent and expanding feature of their societies, the future of which will, in part, depend on its successes.

References

Appadurai, Arjun (1996). *Modernity at Large: Cultural Dimensions of Global-ization*. Minneapolis: University of Minnesota Press.

Arshad, Arlina (2006). "The Baby Trade." *The Straits Times*, January 22, 2006.

Asia Pacific Post (2006). "Koreans Marry International Soulmates." August 10, 2006. http://www.asianpacific post.com/ portal2/ff8080810d224e23010d23.

Asis, Maruja (2003). "When Men and Women Migrate: Comparing Gendered Migration in Asia." United Nations Division for the Advancement of Women (DAW) Consultative Meeting on "Migration and Mobility and How This Movement Affects Women." Malmö, Sweden, December 2–4, 2003.

Bacas, J.L. (2006). "Cross-border Marriages and the Formation of Transna-tional Families: A Case Study of Greek-German couples in Athens." *Transnational Communities Programme Working Paper Series, WPTC-02-10*. www.transcomm.ox.ac.uk/working%20papers/WPTC-02-10%20Bacas (accessed October 2, 2006).

Bangkok Post (2001). "Massive Population Shift towards Developing World." July 1, 2001.

Bezanson, Kate (2006). *Gender, the State, and Social Reproduction: Household Insecurity in Neo-Liberal Times*. Toronto: University of Toronto Press.

Bryceson, Deborah and Ulla Vuorela (eds.) (2002). *The Transnational Family*. New York: Berg.

Bryceson, Deborah and Ulla Vuorela (2003). "Transnational Family Strategies and Education in the Contemporary Chinese Diaspora." *Global Networks* 5(4): 359–377.

Cheng, Zoe (2007). "The Biggest Leap." *Taiwan Review*, January 31, 2007. http://taiwanreview.nat.gov.tw/ fp.asp?xItem=23746&CtNode=119.

Constable, Nicole (ed.) (2005). *Cross-Border Marriages: Gender and Mobility in Transnational Asia*. Philadelphia: University of Pennsylvania Press.

Demick, Barbara (2006). "S. Koreans Search Far and Wide for a Wife Facing a Shortage of Prospective Rural Brides, Many Men Are Forced to Look Abroad." *Los Angeles Times*, September 24, 2006, http://www.sfgate.com/cgi-bin/article.cgi?file=/c/ a/2006/09/24/MNGHULA2T61.DTL.

Douglass, Mike (1999). "Unbundling National Identity: Global Migration and the Advent of Multicultural Societies in East Asia." *Asian Perspectives* 23(3): 79–128.

Douglass, Mike (2006). "Global Householding in Pacific Asia." *International Development Planning Review* 28(4): 421–445.

Douglass, Mike and Glenda Roberts (eds.) (2003). *Japan and Global Migration: Foreign Workers and the Advent of a Multicultural Society.* Honolulu: University of Hawaii Press.

Evers, Hans-Dieter, Wolfgang Clauss, and Diana Wong (1984). "Subsistence Reproduction: A Framework for Analysis." In *Households and the World-Economy*, edited by Joan Smith, Immanual Wallerstein and Hans-Dieter Evers, 23–36. Thousand Oaks, California: Sage.

Folbre, Nancy (1986). "Hearts and Spades: Paradigms of Household Economics." *World Development* 14(2): 245–255.

Freundlich, Madelyn and Joy Kim Lieberthal (2000). *The Gathering of the First Generation of Adult Korean Adoptees: Adoptee's Perceptions of International Adoption.* Washington, DC: Even B. Donaldson Adoption Institute.

Friedmann, John (1992). *Empowerment: The Politics of Alternative Development.* Oxford: Basil Blackwell.

Guarnizo, Luis E. (2003). "The Economics of Transnational Living." *International Migration Review* 37: 666–699.

Harbison, Sarah F. and W.C. Robinson (2003). "Globalization, Family Structure, and Declining Fertility in the Developing World." *Review of Radical Political Economics* 35(1): 44–55.

Huang, Li-ling (2006). "A World without Strangers? Taiwan's New Households in the Nexus of China and Southeast Asia Relations." *International Development Planning Review* 28(4): 447–473.

Huang, Li-ling and Mike Douglass (2004). "Sunday in Hyperspace: Taipei's Little Philippines." International Dialogic Conference on "Globalization and Civic Space," Globalization Research Center, Honolulu, August 15–17, 2004.

Huang, Shirlena, Brenda Yeoh and Maruja Asis (2003). "Filipino Domestic Workers in Singapore: Impacts on Family Well-being and Gender Relations." UNESCAP Ad Hoc Expert Group Meeting on Migration and Development, Bangkok, August 27–29, 2003.

IMF (2006). "Sending Money Home: Trends in Migrant Remittances." *Finance and Development* 42(4). Washington, DC: International Monetary Fund.

Jellinek, Lea (1991). *The Wheel of Fortune: The History of a Poor Community in Jakarta.* New York: Allen & Unwin.

Jolly, Susie, Emma Bell and Lata Narayanaswamy (2003). *Gender and Migration in Asia: Overview and Annotated Bibliography.* (BRIDGE Bibliography No. 13). Brighton: Institute of Development Studies.

JoongAng Daily (2006). "More Bi-racial Kids Being Born in Korea." April 7, 2006.

Lam, Theodora, Brenda S.A. Yeoh and Shirlena Huang (2006). "'Global House-holding' in a City-State: Emerging Trends in Singapore." *International Development Planning Review* 28(4): 475–497.

Lee, Yean-Ju and Hagen Koo (2006). "'Wild Geese Fathers' and a Globalized Family Strategy for Education in Korea." *International Development Planning Review* 28(4): 533–553.

Leisure Club (2005). "Retirement Resort." http://www.retirement-resort.com/concept.htm.

Levitt, Peggy, Josh Dewind and Steven Vertrovec (2003). "International Perspectives on Transnational Migration: An Introduction." *International Migration Review* 37: 565–575.

Liao, Cecilia (2003). "An Observation of the Multinational Marriages in Taiwan." Garden of Hope Foundation, E-News, 014, July 27, 2003.

MIS (Migration Information Source) (2002). "Indonesia's Labor Looks Abroad." http://www.migrationinformation.org/Feature/display.cfm?ID=53.

Migration News (2004). "Asia." *Migration News* 11(2), 2004.

Migration News (2006). "Asia." *Migration News* 13(1), 2006.

Morawska, Ewa (2003). "Disciplinary Agenda and Analytic Strategies of Research on Immigrant Transnationalism: Challenges of Inter-Disciplinary Knowledge." *International Migration Research* 37: 611–640.

Nguoi, Lao Dong (2003). "Guest Workers Send $1.5b Back Home." *The Labourer*, December 22.

Opiniano, Jeremiah M. (2006). "More Remittances from Women Emphasize Feminization of Migration? ADB Study." Tinig.com. http://www.tinig.com/2005/more-remittances-from-women-emphasize-feminization-of-migration-%E2%80%93-adb-study.

Parreñas, Rhacel S. (2001). *Servants of Globalization: Women, Migration and Domestic Work.* Stanford: Stanford University Press.

Parreñas, Rhacel S. (2005). *Children of Global Migration: Transnational Families and Gendered Woes.* Stanford: Stanford University Press.

People's Daily (2003). "Chinese Studying Abroad Top the World." June 18, 2002. http://english.peopledaily.com.cn (accessed 19 June 2003).

Piper, Nicola and Mina Roces (eds.) (2003). *Wife or Worker? Asian Women and Migration.* Lanham, Maryland: Rowman & Littlefield.

Porio, Emma (2007). "Global Householding and Filipino Migration: A Preliminary Review." *Journal of Philippine Studies* 55(2): 211–242.

Pries, Ludger (1999). *Migration and Transnational Social Spaces.* Aldershot: Avebury.

Silvey, Rachel (2006). "Consuming the Transnational Family: Indonesian Migrant Domestic Workers to Saudi Arabia." *Global Networks* 6(1): 23–40.

Smith, Joan (1984). "Nonwage Labor and Subsistence." In *Households and the World-Economy*, edited by Joan Smith, Immanuel Wallerstein and Hans-Dieter Evers, 64–89. Thousand Oaks, California: Sage.

Smith, Joan and Immanuel Wallerstein (1992). *Creating and Transforming Households: The Constraints of the World Economy.* Cambridge: Cambridge University Press.

Smith, Joan, Immanual Wallerstein and Hans-Dieter Evers (eds.) (1984). *Households and the World-Economy.* Thousand Oaks California: Sage.

Smith, Michael P. and Luis E. Guarnizo (eds.) (1998). *Transnationalism from Below.* New Brunswick: Transaction.

Sørensen, N. (2005). "Transnational Family Life across the Atlantic: The Experience of Colombian and Dominican Migrants in Europe." Paper presented at the International Conference on "Migration and Domestic Work in a Global Perspective." Wassenar, the Netherlands, May 26–29, 2005.

Tegtmeyer-Pak, Katherine (2003). "Foreigners Are Local Citizens, Too." In *Japan and Global Migration: Foreign Workers and the Advent of a Multicultural Society,* edited by Mike Douglass and Glenda Roberts, 242–269. Honolulu: University of Hawaii Press.

The Chosun Ilbo (2006). "More Koreans Marry Foreigners or Tie the Knot Again." http://english.chosun.com/cgi-bin/printNews?id=200603300034, October 22, 2006.

The Straits Times (2006). "Tailor-Maid for the Elderly," *The Straits Times*, 11 January, 2006.

Toyota, Miki (2006). "Aging and Transnational Householding: Japanese Retirees in Southeast Asia." *International Development Planning Review* 28(4): 515–531.

Tsai Ting-I (2003). "Foreign Spouses Need to Wait for Residency: MOI." *Taipei Times*, March 26.

U.S. Census Bureau (2000). *Census 2000 Demographic Profile, DP-1: Profile of General Demographic Characteristics*. Washington, DC: U.S. Census Bureau.

UNCTAD (2006). *Trade and Environment Review, 2006*. Geneva: United Nations Conference on Trade and Development.

UNFPA (United Nations Population Fund) (2006). *State of World Population 2006*. New York: UN Population Division.

United Nations (2002). *International Migration 2002*. New York: UN Population Division, Department of Economic and Social Affairs.

United Nations (2003). *World Population Prospects: The 2002 Revision*. New York: UN Population Division, Department of Economic and Social Affairs.

Wallerstein, Immanuel and Joan Smith (1992). "Households as an Institution of the World-economy." In *Creating and Transforming Households: The Constraints of the World Economy*, edited by Joan Smith and Immanuel Wallerstein, 3–23. Cambridge: Cambridge University Press.

Wee, Vivien and Amy Sim (2003). "Transnational Labor Networks in Female Labor Migration: Mediating between Southeast Asian Women Workers and International Labor Markets." SEARC Working Papers Series, No. 49, Hong Kong, City University of Hong Kong.

Wilson, Timms M. and Hastings Donnan (1998). *Border Identity: Nation and State at International Frontiers*. Cambridge: Cambridge University Press.

Yeoh, Brenda S.A. and Katie Willis (eds.) (2004). *State/Nation/Transnation*. London: Routledge.

CHAPTER 6

MIGRATION POLICY: MAJOR ISSUES FOR JAPAN AND OTHER OECD COUNTRIES

Susumu Yamagami

Introduction

It has been often suggested that the movement of people has become increasingly globalized in parallel with that of goods and money. Beginning the paper with such a statement may invite the counterargument that the international movement of people is not a new phenomenon but has a long history. Certainly people have moved beyond boundaries from ancient times. More recently, the discovery of new continents brought about a new wave of movements of people, and the 19th and early 20th centuries witnessed large flows of people between the European colonial powers and their colonies, as well as the movements from East Asia to Australia and North America. However, coupled with revolutionary advances in transportation and communication technologies, the current flows of international migration have been transforming the global demographic landscape quantitatively and qualitatively.

Moreover, the countries that used to be countries of emigration such as the European countries and Japan are now net recipients of immigrants, while most OECD countries are now facing almost identical issues such as aging societies, decreasing birth rates, relatively high unemployment rates, and an increase in both legal and illegal immigrants. Because they face similar problems, and because of consultations and policy coordination in OECD, G8 and other forums, the OECD countries have adopted increasingly similar policies. Through consideration of the current status of international migration, this chapter intends to review the major issues that Japan and other OECD countries have been facing, and the migration and immigration policies they have adopted.

The Current Status of International Migration

According to the estimates of the UN Population Bureau, out of a world population of six billion, 175 million or 2.9 percent were migrants. The figure here does not include irregular migrants for which there are no reliable figures in many countries. According to the same source, the number of international migrants in 1965, 1975 and 1985 were 75 million, 84 million and 150 million, respectively (IOM, 2003: 4–5). Glancing at these figures, it appears that the increase in international migration between 1965 and 1975 was relatively modest, while in the following decade it became much more rapid.

The International Organization for Migration (IOM) summarizes the recent trends in international migration as follows.

(1) Contrary to the general impression that international migration is a movement of people from the developing countries to the developed countries, the proportion of migrants in the countries of the "North" was 36.5 percent in 1965 and 40 percent in 2000. This means that the majority of migrants are received by the developing countries.

(2) Female migrants now account for 48 percent of the total and many of them are moving independently from their family or male partners, a phenomenon known as the feminization of migration. These female migrants are frequently forced to leave because of poverty or scarcity of jobs, and are more exposed to trafficking or sexual exploitation than other migrants.

(3) The movement of highly educated or qualified professionals is also increasing. The World Bank estimates that 70,000 African professionals and university graduates are heading for Europe and North America every year. At the same time, many scientists in Europe are moving toward North America (IOM, 2003: 6).

However, at the same time, as the IOM also writes, most of the world's population are not involved in international migration but remain where they are born. They may lack the resources or networks that make migration possible, while individual reasons for not wishing to leave home, family and friends are also a major factor (IMO, 2003: 6). Contrary to the generally accepted assumption, it is not necessarily the case that most migrants are poverty-stricken people in a one-way movement from the South to the North in search of a better life.

Immigrants in OECD Countries

The OECD publishes an annual report on the status of migrants in OECD countries, entitled *Continuous Reporting System on Migration: Annual Report* and usually referred to as the "SOPEMI Report." This report was originally intended to compile data on migrant workers in Western Europe and North America. However, since a dramatic increase of refugees and asylum seekers came to be noted in the 1980s, a considerable portion of the report came to be devoted to the trends among these groups. When the inflow of foreign laborers into Japan became visible in the early 1990s, Japan joined this system, and recently the Republic of Korea has also joined the group. The SOPEMI Report of 2004 (OECD, 2004) analyzes the status of migrants in 2002, and some basic figures from the report are as follows.

- In the United States, more than one million migrants were given permanent residence, while 1.3 million migrants (excluding students) were given temporary residence.
- 2.5 million migrants were reported for the (then) 15 countries of the European Union. Of these, 660,000 were reported in Germany, 418,000 in the United Kingdom, and 388,000 in Italy.
- Some 344,000 migrants were reported for Japan (OECD, 2004: 23).

The report also analyses permanent and longer-term migration in some countries, divided into those who have moved for employment, for family reunification, or as refugees. In 2002, according to the report, 69 percent of permanent immigration in the United States was for family reunification, while the figures for France, Canada and Switzerland were 75 percent, 64 percent and 52 percent, respectively (OECD, 2004: 30–31). Given this trend, some countries including Ireland, Italy, France, and Denmark, are moving to restrict the number of admissible family members. In Denmark, new requirements were introduced for a husband and a wife to be reunited: both have to be 24 years or older, and evidence of "attachment to Denmark" rather than other countries — in terms of length of stay, the presence of other relatives in the country, education, and knowledge of the Danish language — has to be produced. As a result of the introduction of these measures, the number of entrants for family reunification in 2002 fell by 25 percent from the previous year, to 8,151 for 2002 compared with 10,950 for 2001. In the United Kingdom and Australia on the other hand, a majority of immigrants are looking for employment, while in the Nordic countries there is a much higher percentage of refugees among immigrants, more than 40 percent in Sweden, and more than 20 percent in Denmark and Norway (OECD, 2004: 30–31).

In many OECD countries, the number of temporary migrants for employment in 2002 increased from the previous year; for example there was an increase of 10.2 percent for the United Kingdom, compared with 14.4 percent for France, 5.5 percent for Germany, 1.8 percent for Japan, and 7.6 percent for South Korea. In the United States, on the other hand, the figures fell due to the tighter controls introduced after 9/11 (OECD, 2004: 30–31). Nonetheless, the United States still received 118,000 highly skilled workers as temporary migrants in 2002 (OECD, 2004: 32).

Turning to the illegal and irregular migrants, it is not easy to estimate figures for them in many countries. In the United States, estimates range as high as 12 million (IOM, 2003: 58). In Western Europe, reliable estimates may be even more difficult than in the United States. The IOM estimates that every year 500,000 illegal migrants arrive in the EU, and as an indicator of the scale of the problem in Europe, it cites the fact that one million illegal migrants had sought amnesty or regularization/legalization of their stay in the previous five years (IOM, 2003: 60). In Japan, the figures for overstayers (those who have entered legally but who have not departed or obtained permission for an extended stay) can be calculated quite accurately from the records of the Ministry of Justice. The number of overstayers as of 2004 was estimated at around 207,000 (Japan Immigration Association, 2005: 7, 38). In addition there are estimated to be some tens of thousands of clandestine entrants, those who did not follow the legal procedures for entry into Japan.

The IOM estimates that these illegal migrants make up between a third and a half of new migrants to the developed countries, while many asylum seekers who are not recognized as refugees nor have been given asylum on humanitarian grounds are also staying illegally in the countries where they asked for asylum (IOM, 2003: 58–59).

Factors Affecting the Migration Policies of OECD Countries

The background to — and reasons for — the recent increase in international migration have been analyzed and discussed by many observers. They have focused on the movement of people from the developing countries to developed countries, pointing out pull factors in the developed countries, such as standard of living, job opportunities, and protection of human rights; and push factors in the developing countries, such as poverty, joblessness, natural disasters, population pressure, oppressive regimes, civil wars, and political turmoil. As early as 1981, Sadruddin Aga Khan, the former UN High Commissioner for Refugees, reported on the causes of mass movement of refugees, referring to push factors such as high birth rates, shortage of food, inflation and unemployment; and to pull factors in some countries in the North such as abundant economic opportunities, a reputation for protecting human rights, liberal immigration laws and regulations, and targets for accepting refugees (Saddrudin Aga Khan, 1981). More recent studies have also shown the importance of the rapid dissemination of information through IT, as well as information provided by earlier migrants and assistance offered through social networks. It is also frequently pointed out that there exist various criminal organizations that assist illegal migrants as a business. The IOM reports on this aspect of migration as follows:

> Migrant smuggling is now a ten billion US$ a year growth industry, serving approximately half of the irregular migrants worldwide. The United Kingdom estimates that over 75 percent of its illegal entrants used the services of smugglers. Well-tuned to market economics and with operational flexibility insufficiently constrained by legal mechanisms, these smuggling groups offer a range of services to the various consumers. An organized trip from Morocco to Spain is possible for as little as US$500, while more elaborate passages and border crossing from Asia to the United States may cost above US$50,000. (IOM, 2003: 60)

The current domestic situation in developed countries may be roughly summarized as follows.

(1) The average unemployment rate in OECD countries is around seven percent, which nurtures a sense that foreign laborers are taking jobs from local citizens. In the case of Japan, the unemployment rate is relatively low compared with other OECD countries.

(2) On the other hand, most OECD countries are facing aging societies and low fertility rates, leading to an awareness of the necessity of foreign laborers.

(3) The remarkable international development of science and technology means that highly educated or talented workers are very much in demand.

(4) After 9/11, the importance of security considerations has been increasingly recognized. After 9/11, the United States introduced finger printing at ports of entry for foreigners, while the United Kingdom has also introduced a system to compare iris images if necessary at major ports of entry. Japan has also amended the immigration law so as to make it possible to fingerprint foreign travelers at ports of entry. There is also recognition of the need to incorporate biometric data into passports.

(5) Illegal and irregular migration, including bogus claims for asylum, has been seen as one of the gravest policy issues facing OECD countries.

Immigration Control Policies Undertaken by OECD Countries

As seen so far, the situation and issues surrounding migration are now very similar across the developed countries. The issue of illegal or irregular migration is seen as a major and urgent concern in all OECD countries, and the responses are also similar. In the last two decades, these have included: the introduction of so-called "employer sanctions" in order to penalize employers of unauthorized foreign migrant, more severe penalties for crimes relating to human smuggling and trafficking, measures to cope with falsified asylum claims, granting amnesty to certain unauthorized foreigners so as to decrease the number of illegal migrants, and promoting international cooperation both regionally and globally. It also should be added that measures have been generally strengthened to counter terrorism since September 11, 2001.

Employer sanctions

Employer sanctions were introduced as a major counter-measure against the increase of illegal migration in the United States and Europe since the latter half of the 1970s, with the incorporation into immigration control legislation of penal sanctions against hiring unauthorized foreigners.

In the United States in the late 1970s, amidst the increasing concern about illegal immigrants, the Department of Labor tried to enforce strict implementation of labor standards relating to minimum wages, overtime, and the employment of minors, and in industries such as agriculture, textiles, construction, laundries, and restaurants. The adoption of this Special Targeted Enforcement Program (STEP), together with the strengthening of border controls by the immigration authority, was expected to deter the inflow of illegal migrants. However, STEP did not bring about the expected results, and in the 1980s, newer and more innovative mechanisms came to be explored. In the amendment of the Immigration Act (Immigration Control and Reform Act) in 1986, new provisions targeting potential employers of foreigners were introduced. In employing any person, an employer had to confirm whether such a person was eligible to work legally, and violations of this rule were to be punished. The duties of an employer under the new regulation became widely known. However, the extent to which employers of foreigners did obey the new rules has been a matter of discussion. The inflow of illegal immigrants seeking employment continued, while forgeries of documents, including passports, green cards, and visas dramatically increased. Thus, in the new Immigration Act of 1990, stricter penalties were stipulated for forging documents.

Western European countries used to accept foreign guest workers on a large scale until 1973. However, hit by the first oil shock, they moved to halt acceptance of new foreign workers. Reflecting this policy shift, the main emphasis in legal migration in Western Europe shifted from labor migration to family unification. Meanwhile, many countries also started to see dramatic increases in numbers of illegal migrants seeking work and asylum seekers claiming persecution in their home countries. Within this context, many countries began to impose penalties on employers for hiring foreigners without confirming that they had valid work permits.

In Japan as well, amidst a dramatic increase in the numbers of overstayers and foreigners working illegally in the late 1980s, a new provision was introduced into the immigration control law so as to punish the employers and brokers responsible for foreigners working illegally.

As for the effectiveness of the employer sanctions thus introduced, Castles and Miller summarize it as follows:

> Laws punishing employers for unauthorized hiring of aliens constituted the centerpiece of many immigration policy reforms in the 1970s in the United States and Western Europe. Such 'employer sanctions' are often coupled with 'legalisation programmes', which give work and residence permits to former undocumented workers who fulfill certain conditions. These carrot-and-stick measures, it is argued, remove the motivation for undocumented work, since employers run serious risks of punishment and workers are better off with legal status, and no longer undercut local wage levels. However, in practice, these programmes may come up against powerful interests; employers may have the political clout to prevent effective enforcement, while migrant workers may reject legalization for fear that it will make it harder for them to find jobs ... A number of analysts have been dismissive of the efforts by European governments to enforce employer sanctions. They thereby ignore the development of a credible state capacity to deter and punish illegal employment of aliens since 1970 in several Western and Northern European states. The overall record of employer sanctions enforcement, however, appears very uneven. It is sometimes suggested that enforcement of employer sanctions in the USA had failed by 1999 because the US government announced it was suspending enforcement ... Already by 1994, the Commission for Immigration Reform concluded that the employer sanction system adopted in 1986 had failed, because many unauthorized foreign workers presented false documents to employers. (Castles and Miller, 2003: 95–98)

It is also virtually impossible in Japan to verify to what extent the introduction of penalties did deter potential employers from hiring foreigners either entering or staying illegally.

Human smuggling and trafficking

In the preceding section, I touched upon the IOM estimate that illegal migration-related businesses amounted to a US$10 billion industry. While activities related to illegal migration are expanding, the major concern of the international community in the last decade has been the criminal organizations engaging in human trafficking. These organizations have increased in viciousness, sophistication and ability to network. Recently, the term "human trafficking" has increasingly replaced "human smuggling." When I attended the Working Group on Organized Crime or the Pacific Rim Immigration Information Group in the late 1990s, "human smuggling" and "human trafficking" were used almost interchangeably, with some difference in nuance. However, according to UN High Commissioner for Human Rights, Ann Gallagher:

> smuggled migrants are moved illegally for profit; they are partners, however unequal, in a commercial transaction... By contrast, the movement of trafficked persons is based on deception and coercion and is for the purpose of exploitation. The profit in trafficking comes not from the movement but from the sale of a trafficked person's sexual services or labour in the country of destination. (Castles and Miller, 2003: 115)

The IMO Report mentioned above also stated that:

> Trafficking is different from smuggling, although abuse and violence can occur in both circumstances. Trafficking, however, amplifies many of the problems linked with irregular migration overall ... Trafficking affects mainly, but not exclusively, women and children. They are most frequently trafficked for sexual abuse or/and labour exploitation, though they sometimes end up falling into begging, delinquency, adoptions, false marriages or trade of human organs. (IOM, 2003: 61)

The same report also estimated the number of victims of trafficking as 700,000 annually, based on the estimates of the United States State Department (IOM, 2003: 61), of whom 120,000 were trafficked into the EU through the Balkan countries. Human trafficking for sexual exploitation has spread worldwide and in Japan it is frequently claimed that foreign and domestic criminal organizations are bringing in many women for the sex industry, recruiting them under the guise of entertainers and hostesses. As the seriousness of the issue has come to be recognized, many governments, international organizations and NGOs are showing increasing concern and launching joint initiatives to tackle this problem. In particular, the IOM has been tackling the issue of trafficking as one of its highest priorities since the late 1990s. Many of the governments concerned have agreed to coordinate their efforts, to promote exchanges of information on the criminal organizations and brokers that are reaping huge benefits from human smuggling and trafficking, and to crack down on them and impose maximum penalties. Within this context, the Japanese Immigration Law was recently further amended so that the brokers and others engaging in illegal entry *en masse* could be heavily penalized, with up to 10 years imprisonment and/or a fine of 10 million yen. The maximum penalties under the Immigration Control and Refugee Recognition Act in Japan until 1990 used to be three years imprisonment and/or a fine of 300,000 yen. However, it came to be seen within Japan that these penalties would not deter illegal entry and other immigration related crimes. In the international community meanwhile, it was frequently suggested that the penalties were so light that Japan might turn into an avenue for human trafficking to other countries. With such shifts in both the domestic and international contexts, the penalties for crimes related to immigration control were made much more severe.

An international agreement, symbolizing the advance in common understanding and effective progress internationally, was enforced at the end of 2003, namely the "Protocol to Prevent, Suppress and Punish Trafficking in Persons, especially Women and Children." Under this agreement, all the parties concerned agree to give adequate consideration to the victims of trafficking, share information, and take appropriate measures for preventing their passports from being forged. Thus, the international community is now requesting the states concerned to cooperate and take action in domains traditionally left to each nation's sovereign discretion.

Increasing numbers of asylum seekers

More than two decades have passed since the increasing numbers of asylum seekers in the developed countries came to be a major policy concern for immigration control. Glancing at the inflow of asylum seekers into Germany, the number increased from 20,000 in 1983 to around 100,000 in 1986 (OECD, 1988: 19–20), reaching a peak of 440,000 in 1992 (OECD, 2001: 280). This figure has been gradually declining since, through successive amendments of domestic legislation restricting the conditions for asylum application. It fell to 130,000 in 1995, 80,000 in 2000, and 50,000 in 2003 (OECD, 2004: 315). Nonetheless, the figure of 50,000 is still considered rather high. The corresponding figures for France, the United Kingdom and the United States stood at 30,000, 30,000, and 100,000 respectively in 1993, and at 50,000, 60,000 and 60,000 in 2003 (OECD, 2001: 280; 2004: 315).

As mentioned above, the number of asylum seekers in Europe increased dramatically in the 1980s, though the origins of the increase lay in the 1970s. After the first oil shock, the Western European countries began to halt or drastically reduce the new recruitment of foreign guest workers, and from then on the asylum seekers began increasing. It was noted that the abuse of asylum procedures for the determination of refugee status was also increasing, to allow migrants to stay longer in the countries concerned. Moreover, some people destroyed their passports intentionally in order to make it difficult to establish their identities and deport them. At successive meetings of the Executive Committees of the UNHCR during the 1970s and 1980s, many representatives from Western European countries were discussing the problem of these "manifestly unfounded or abusive claims" (Yamagami, 1990: 7–8; Schonwalder, 1999). Asylum seekers continued to increase, reaching a peak in 1992. In that year, the 15 countries of the European Community received 670,000 applications, of which 440,000 were filed in Germany. In order to cope with such an increase, Germany stipulated in its Alien Act that persons coming for economic reasons or fleeing from poverty in general or from warfare should not be recognized as refugees and would be denied asylum (OECD, 1988: 19–20). However, even this legislation did not change the trend in asylum seekers. Faced with such a situation, Western European countries came to recognize that the issue was common to all the countries in the European Community, and that they would need a common immigration and asylum policy. EC countries coordinated their asylum procedures in 1988 and decided that an application submitted in one country would be judged by that country for all EC members; other member countries would no longer receive applications from anyone whose claims had been turned down by another country. In July 1992, the EC

Immigration Ad Hoc Council, whose members were politicians and Home Ministry officials discussed policies to deter the flow of asylum seekers from the developing countries. They reconfirmed the established principle that "asylum seekers must remain in the first safe country they arrive at."

The Maastricht Treaty establishing the EU empowered Justice and Interior Ministers to establish a common asylum policy for the entire EU. In December 1992, the Justice and Interior Ministers Meeting held in London adopted the three conclusions. According to an article in the UNHCR magazine, *Refugees*:

> The first embodied a safe third country concept allowing states to refuse individuals access to their asylum procedures if the applicant could have sought protection in another "safe" country. In the second, concerning manifestly unfounded asylum applications, member states were given wide scope for rejecting asylum requests on formal grounds and for limiting appeal possibilities. The third conclusion on "safe" countries of origin allowed for an accelerated procedure in the case of claimants coming from countries in which there is generally no serious risk of persecution. (Telöken, 1993: 11)

The basic thinking behind these conclusions may be summarized as follows:

(a) On applications submitted by persons coming from a "safe" country in which there is generally no risk of persecution, a decision not to recognize them as refugees should be taken expeditiously.
(b) For those who passed to their destination through a "safe country," a request for asylum should have been filed in that country, and therefore the destination country should not have to receive such a request.
(c) Anyone to whom either (a) or (b) applies should be returned to the other "safe" country from which they came.

In Germany, an amendment of the law on asylum procedures was actually made in accordance with these principles (Schonwalder, 1999: 86). Access to the asylum procedures would be denied to a person who entered Germany through any of the EU member countries or other "safe" countries, and an application from a person whose country of origin was on the list of countries in which there was no risk of persecution would in general be considered as groundless. In this revision of the asylum regulations, all the countries adjacent to Germany were now "safe" countries, and therefore anyone who entered Germany by land would not be recognized as a refugee. In addition, an extensive list of "safe" countries of origin was prepared, while the visa requirements in "risky" countries were toughened. Given these measures, and even though the number of applications decreased dramatically, it is remarkable that tens of thousands of applications for asylum are still filed every year.

In the United Kingdom also, the concept of a "safe" country was incorporated into its legal system. The 1996 British Asylum and Immigration Act made it explicit that a person coming from countries in which there was generally no serious risk of persecution should be subject to an accelerated procedure. However, despite this, applications for asylum have been increasing, which continues to be a major political issue.

Together with these kinds of amendments of domestic procedures, the EU countries began to conclude re-admission agreements with surrounding non-EU countries in the early 1990s so as to facilitate deporting those denied asylum. In September 1992 Germany concluded an agreement with Romania to send back most of the 40,000 Romanians who had moved there, and began to make agreements with neighboring countries to send back those who had passed through their territories on their way to Germany. According to the UNHCR magazine cited above, in Brussels in 1994, a meeting of Justice and Interior Ministers agreed on a model re-admission agreement which could be concluded between EU and non-EU countries, with the purpose of making it possible to send asylum seekers back to countries they had passed through en route to the EU. As a result, Europe came to be covered by a dense web of such re-admission agreements (UNHCR, 1993: 11).

Compared with the situation of asylum seekers in Europe, the question has frequently been raised of why the number of applications for refugee status in Japan has remained so low. According to the SOPEMI Report (OECD, 2004: 216), 2782 applications had been filed since 1982. Of these applicants, 305 were recognized as refugees, and another 259 were specifically authorized to stay in Japan for humanitarian reasons. The number of applications has been increasing since 1996, but the figure is still small in comparison with the EU and North America. In 2002, there were 250 applicants of which 10 were recognized as refugees and 40 were authorized to stay for humanitarian reasons (OECD, 2004: 216). Although Japan has accepted resettlement of more than 10,000 Indochinese Refugees and Displaced Persons, both the number of applicants for refugee status and those recognized as such are very small in number. Based on these figures, strong criticisms have been made of the Japanese government and the Ministry of Justice. Some critics argue that the requirements for being given refugee status are too strict in Japan and that therefore only a few are actually filing applications. Some other foreign critics suspect a maneuver by the Japanese government to discourage applications. Against this background, I have explained elsewhere the process for the determination of refugee status in Japan, including the reasons why the applications are so few in number (Yamagami, 1995). What I wrote there may be summarized as follows:

(1) After the problem of refugees following the Second World War, Japan did not face any significant refugee problems until that of IndoChinese refugees in the 1970s. In those days, the borders of socialist countries neighboring Japan were so tightly controlled that few people from the Soviet Union, China or North Korea could cross them to come and seek asylum in Japan.

(2) In Europe, in the process of coping with the refugee problems after the Second World War, procedures for asylum were established and asylum seekers from the east were offered asylum rather generously. Because of this, many who would not normally have been given residence were tempted to apply for asylum as a means to stay in the West.

(3) In Japan, many illegal foreign workers arrived with tourist visas and later engaged in remunerative activities. As long as they could expect to work without being arrested, they did not have much incentive to apply for refugee status.

(4) In reality there are many people who need protection in the international community other than victims of political persecution as stipulated in the refugee convention. These people may not necessarily be given refugee status, but be could offered consideration on humanitarian grounds in permitting their residence.

In retrospect, half of the Vietnamese boatpeople who were rescued on the high seas and brought directly to Japan expressed a desire to resettle in other countries such as the United States and France. Refugees therefore often prefer Europe and North America as their final destinations rather than Japan.

Strengthening Immigration Control and Amnesty for Illegal Migrants

As already seen above, each OECD country has been strengthening immigration controls in order to cope with the increase in illegal migrants and unauthorized foreign workers. The measures include the introduction of employer sanctions, more severe penalties against human smuggling and trafficking, facilitation of the removal of illegal migrants, strengthening visa requirements, and obligating the airlines to confirm travel documents.

In parallel with these measures, many countries have adopted regularization or legalization policies for certain illegal or irregular migrants. The 1986 Immigration reform and Control Act of the United States legalized the residence of residents who had been staying illegally since 1982, who had worked in the agricultural sector for more than 90 days, or who came from Haiti or Cuba. Under this program, around 2.7 million residents had their status legalized (Castles and Miller, 2003: 99). These regularization and legalization programs for illegal migrants were undertaken by the United States, France, Spain, Italy and other countries since the 1990s. Some of them were reported in the SOPEMI Report for 2001, which reads as follows:

> In Spain, a regularisation operation has been incorporated into the transitional provisions of the new Rights and Freedoms of Foreigners Act of January 2000. It applies to all foreigners permanently on Spanish soil on 1 June 1999 and who either held a work permit and/or a residence permit between 1 February 1997 and 1 February 2000, or requested such a permit before 31 March 2000, or lodged an asylum application before 1 February 2000 as well as to family members of nationals of third countries, nationals of Member States of the European Union or of Spanish nationals. Almost 245,000 applications for regularization had been lodged; of these, almost

one third had been filed by Moroccan nationals wishing to obtain residence and employment permits, mainly for agriculture, domestic services and construction ... Following the regularization operation that took in Greece during 1998, almost 371,000 undocumented people received a white card entitling them to enter the labour market and enjoy equal employment rights ... The regularization operation in Italy that began in 1998 was continued into 2000. A Decree of October 1998 established a quarter of 38,000 workers who could be regularized in 1998, of whom 3000 were Albanian, 1500 Moroccan, and 1500 Tunisian. Of the 250,000 applications lodged in 1998, some 39 percent of them were still being examined at mid-January 2000. In June 2000, the government announced that 40,000 residence permits would be issued to undocumented migrants during that year, and 53,000 files would have been examined by the end of July.

In Belgium, the regularization programme implemented in January 2000 looked at 35,000 cases (concerning approximately 52,000 people of whom 17 percent came from the Democratic Republic of Congo and more than 12 percent from Morocco). Regularisation gives entitlement to unlimited stay and access to the labour market. The regularization procedure would end by October 2001.

In March 2000, Switzerland carried out a programme to regularise certain categories of foreigners who had entered the country before 31 December 1992 and were now in serious personal need. This operation, known as Humanitarian Action 2000, concerned almost 13,000, most of whom were Sri Lankan nationals.

In December 2000, the United States Congress adopted the Legal Immigration and Family Equity ACT (LIFEA). In particular, it enables almost 400,000 undocumented migrants to apply for regularization as long as they can prove that they entered the United States before 1 January 1982. (OECD, 2001: 103)

The background to this legalization and regularization undertaken in many countries was that, before strengthening immigration control for the future, it was thought important and wise to secure the understanding of those sectors of the economy which needed migrant labor, by regularizing the status of migrants already working there. It was thought to be inappropriate both from social and humanitarian considerations to keep illegal migrants uncertain about their future for a lengthy period. If the labor services of the illegal migrants were needed, it would be desirable to regularize their stay and apply labor laws and social security legislation to them. According to Castles and Miller:

> Illegally resident aliens responded slowly and cautiously to legalization. Governments were disappointed and eased rules and regulations to encourage more applications. Perhaps most importantly, legalization enabled governments to learn more about illegal migration flows and processes. They were generally more complex than had been thought and principally involved aliens from countries which also sent large number of legally admitted aliens. (Castles and Miller, 2003: 99)

On the other hand, governments both in Germany and Japan have been very reluctant to adopt such a legalization program or amnesty, because they believe that such a policy would invite new waves of illegal migrants hoping for future legalization of their stay. Despite a general orientation toward legalization, in Japan, around 10,000 illegal entrants and over-stayers are given special residence permission annually by the Minister of Justice through his discretion on a case-by-case basis. In the discretion exercised by the Minister of Justice, such factors as length of stay in Japan, family situation, and ties with Japanese society are taken into account.

Measures to facilitate the entry of foreign workers

As seen so far, OECD countries have been toughening immigration controls in order to cope with the increase in illegal migrants. However, at the same time, faced with increasingly aging populations and declining fertility rates, and with the need for highly skilled workers in the IT and other industries, many OECD countries are easing their rules and requirements in certain sectors to facilitate recruitment. According to the 2004 SOPEMI Report, many countries were trying to attract temporary and seasonal workers in order to overcome the labor shortages afflicting certain sectors of industry. Migration for temporary employment had continued in countries such as Australia, Germany, Japan, Korea, and New Zealand, while numbers of visas for seasonal workers had increased sharply in the United Kingdom,

Norway, and Germany. Canada was promoting the admission of skilled workers (based on language skills and diplomas, professional experience and adaptability), investors, entrepreneurs, and researchers. In France, two new agreements on exchange programs for young professionals had been signed with Bulgaria and Romania, bringing the total number of agreements to 13, enabling young professionals aged between 18 and 35 to work abroad (OECD, 2004: 103).

As seen above, Western European countries are now making cautious moves to foreign workers in order to offset the labor shortage in certain sectors which have arisen since the curtailment of the guest worker recruitment schemes in 1973. At the same time, in elections in many countries, a considerable number of votes are being cast for rightist parties that advocate xenophobic policies. Most governments are conscious that however severe the labor shortage might be, expanding the admission of non-skilled laborers amidst high unemployment is a very sensitive issue that requires a careful approach. In Germany, there used to exist strong advocates for a resumption of foreign worker recruitment in certain sectors, especially restaurants and agriculture, ever since the cessation of recruitment in 1973. However, the subsequent resumption of temporary worker admission was explained within the context of efforts to support new democratic governments in Central and Eastern Europe and to secure their cooperation in efforts by Germany and the rest of the EU to curb illegal migration and human trafficking (Castles and Miller, 2003: 101).

Looking at the situation in Japan briefly, in 2004 the Ministry of Justice issued certificates of eligibility with the residence status of either "Engineer" or "Specialist in Humanities/International Services" to 13,214 foreigners, including 2615 Americans, 1999 Chinese, and 1462 Koreans, with the understanding that they would engage in professional jobs or jobs requiring experience. This figure showed an increase of 13.7 percent from the previous year. Similarly 5264 foreigners applied successfully for a change of status from "College Student" to employment in 2004, including 3445 Chinese, 811 Koreans, and 179 Taiwanese, a 39.3 percent increase from 2003. As seen in these figures, the number of foreigners authorized to work in Japan has been expanding (see also the chapter by Liu Farrer in this volume).

Measures for security since September 2001

The terrorist attacks of September 11, 2001 reminded people of the necessity to deal with the security threat posed by terrorists within the globalized flow of people and information. In addition to a geographical and quantitative expansion of human mobility, technological progress in the forgery of travel documents has made many governments explore new ways of identifying individuals, toughen entry inspection and the examination of visas, and further promote international cooperation to counter terrorism.

Thus, the security measures in the United States came to be strengthened. Non-immigrant aliens are subject to fingerprinting at the port of entry, while applicants for non-immigrant visas have been required to undergo individual interviews since August 2003. Before August 2003, applicants for immigrant visas were usually requested to appear before visa officers (OECD, 2004). Due to such measures and a cautious approach in adjudicating visa applications by visa officers, it now takes longer to issue a visa. As a result, a switch of destination for study and research away from the United States to other countries has been noted.

The United States has requested other countries to adopt strict counter-terrorist measures. In particular, the United States requested some 30 countries previously exempt from tourist visas (including Japan) to incorporate biometric data into their passports to prevent forgery and/or falsified usage. The United States made it explicit that it would halt visa waivers for countries that refused. Within this context, Japan amended the Passport Act in June 2005 and incorporated a digitalized image of the face that cannot be forged into a passport, in addition to the photo currently included. By this measure, even if the photo were to be forged (which was almost impossible even before), identification through the digitalized image of the face could still be carried out. On the occasion of this amendment, the act of lending one's passport to another person became an offence, regardless of whether such a passport is actually used, with a penalty of imprisonment of up to five years and/or a fine of up to 3 million yen.

In Europe also, concerns about security were increasingly recognized, in particular since the terrorist attacks in Madrid. In Germany, a new immigration law in 2004 eased the conditions for the deportation of persons suspected of terrorism. In the United Kingdom, it was announced that iris-scanning devices would be installed at major airports for the purpose of the identification of passengers. In the Netherlands, the police were authorized to check the identity of any person over the age of 14 in public places (OECD, 2004: 91).

Summary

In the preceding section, I reviewed the policies undertaken by OECD countries in order to deter the flow of illegal migrants and establish an equitable system of control. As seen there, many OECD countries have been facing similar problems and as a result have adopted more or less similar policies. However, those policies do not necessarily achieve the expected results. No country has succeeded in deterring the inflow of illegal migrants effectively, while numbers of asylum seekers in Europe have not decreased as was expected.

As is well known today, policies to halt recruitment of foreign guest workers and encourage the repatriation of foreign workers by providing considerable financial incentives have not worked as intended either. Instead, many foreign family members joined the workers in Europe through family reunification, and as a result, the foreign population (and consequently the number of foreign workers) has dramatically increased. As observed above, there seem to exist certain limitations on the extent to which tougher and more restrictive policies are effective in controlling migration. The scholars following this issue seem largely to share the view that illegal migration is likely to grow in future, however high the barriers to entry are set, and that there is a need to address the root causes of migration by improving conditions in the countries of departure (Castles and Miller, 2003: 119). Castles and Miller write that this entails "not just development aid, but also foreign and trade policy initiatives, designed to bring about sustainable development, and to improve political stability and human rights. This has long been understood in the USA" (Castles and Miller, 2003: 119). Such considerations were said to have prompted the establishment of NAFTA which would increase FDI and job opportunities in Mexico and subsequently reduce illegal migration. However, there is no evidence that NAFTA has reduced economic or demographic pressures in Mexico or illegal migrants (Castles and Miller, 2003: 119). At a symposium organized by the Harvard

Project for Asia and International Relations, in 2005, Evelyn Hu-Dehart of Brown University mentioned that the public was originally told that once NAFTA was established, illegal migration from Mexico would be reduced. However, I suggested to her that if NAFTA did not exist, the migration pressures from Mexico might be much greater than they are now. In this connection, the IOM has cited the views of Wayne Cornelius and others that, without trade liberalization through NAFTA the overall migration to the United States would be far greater in scale than it now is (OECD, 2004).

In Western Europe, the correlation between the progress of regional integration and the flow of illegal migrants has been an issue of great concern. The formation of a single European market in 1993, suggesting a strong image of "Fortress Europe," led to strong concerns that the flow of goods and people from other regions, particularly Eastern Europe, North Africa and Asia, to Western Europe would be hampered significantly. Meanwhile, the Western European countries themselves were concerned that illegal migration might further increase because the people who could not enter legally would choose to move anyway. Against this background, the EU agreed to establish a customs union with Turkey and to remove trade barriers with Morocco, Algeria, and Tunisia in 1996 (Castles and Miller, 2003: 119). However, there was no clear evidence that these measures reduced the pressures of migration to EU member states. Instead, at the EU Summit held in Seville, Spain in 2002, leaders discussed ways to halt the flow of illegal migrants as one of their primary concerns, and agreed to tackle the issue as a basic element of EU foreign policy. They requested countries of transit and origin to strengthen their border controls to prevent illegal departure, and pressed them to accept the returnees from Europe (*Asahi Shimbun*, *Yomiuri Shimbun*, *Japan Times*, June 22, 2002).

Glancing at the trend among overstayers in Japan, their total number reached a peak of some 300,000 in 1993. It then began to show a gradual decline to some 200,000 as of January 2005 (Japan Immigration Association, 2005). This gradual decline may be the result of various factors combined, such as the efforts of the Ministry of Justice, the National Police Agency and others in apprehending illegal migrants and persuading employers not to hire them. Other factors are the increasing perception that illegal foreign migrants are responsible for crime, the relatively low demand for employment in construction-related industries because of the sluggish economy in the 1990s, the increasing employment of the descendants of Japanese migrants to Latin America (Japanese Brazilians and others) in industries such as automobile production, and the replacement of illegal workers by trainees and technical interns in a wide range of industries, including agriculture and small- and medium-sized enterprises. Nonetheless, considering that 30,000 to 40,000 illegal migrants are deported annually, the fact that the figures for dealing with overstayers remains at 10,000 per year means that considerable number of new overstayers are still arriving, and the problem of overstayers remains a major issue to be tackled.

On the other hand there exist certain sectors of the economy in which it is claimed there is already a labor shortage, thanks to the aging population and the collapse of fertility in Japan. Some researchers and organizations have suggested that it is inevitable that Japan will have to bring in several hundred thousand foreign laborers in order to maintain its economic vitality. The Immigration Bureau of the Ministry of Justice also suggests expanding the scope of admissible foreign laborers in order to cope with the decrease of population (Japan Immigration Association, 2005). However, as witnessed in the negotiations for the Economic Partnership Agreement (virtually an FTA) with the Philippines and Thailand, the Japanese government is rather reluctant to accept a large number of nurses and other caregivers, despite strong pressure from the health sector and other governments.

Enlargement of the admissible categories of foreign laborers has been continuously raised and discussed as an urgent policy issue since the late 1980s in Japan. However, no consensus has emerged on whether to accept large numbers of foreigners other than those who are now admitted as specialists, experts or skilled workers. In the 1960s when Japan experienced high rates of economic growth, there was a strong argument that Japan should bring in foreign guest workers as most Western European countries were then doing. However, the failure to do so resulted in a rise in individual workers' wages and helped promote labor-saving methods and automation, which brought about a great increase in economic competitiveness for Japan. Thus, it seems difficult to change a policy that has worked well so far. Moreover, looking at the subsequent developments in Western Europe such as increasing tension between different ethnic groups and a rise of ultra rightist groups, it may not be easy for the Japanese government to shift the policy so dramatically. Nonetheless, considering the demographic forecasts for the Japanese population and relations with East Asian countries in FTA negotiations, it appears most appropriate at this stage to move toward establishing a more liberal regime for human movement beyond national boundaries, and to contribute to regional integration through greater exchanges of people within the region.

References

Castles, Stephen and Mark J. Miller (2003). *The Age of Migration; International Population Movements in the Modern World.* (3rd edition). Basingstoke: Palgrave Macmillan.

IOM (2003). *World Migration 2003: Managing Migration.* Geneva: International Organization for Migration.

Japan Immigration Association (2005). *Kokusai-Jinryû [Immigration Journal]* 216 (May 2005).

OECD (1996). *Continuous Reporting System on Migration: Annual Report.* Paris: Organization for Economic Cooperation and Development.

OECD (1998). *Continuous Reporting System on Migration: Annual Report.* Paris: Organization for Economic Cooperation and Development.

OECD (2001). *Continuous Reporting System on Migration: Annual Report.* Paris: Organization for Economic Cooperation and Development.

OECD (2004). *Continuous Reporting System on Migration: Annual Report.* Paris: Organization for Economic Cooperation and Development.

Saddrudin Aga Khan (1981). *"Questions of the Violation of Human Rights and Fundamental Freedoms in Any Part of the World, with Particular Reference to Colonial and Other Dependent Countries and Territories, Study of Human Rights and Massive Exoduses."* New York: United Nations Commission on Human Rights (U.N. Document E/CN.4/1503).

Schonwalder, Karen (1999). "'Persons persecuted on political grounds shall enjoy the right of asylum — but not in our country': Asylum policy and debates about refugees in the Federal Republic of Germany." In *Refugees, Citizenship and Social Policy in Europe*, edited by Alice Bloch and Carla Levy, 76–90. Basingstoke: MacMillan.

Telöken, S (1993). "It's a Long Way to Harmonization." *Refugees* 2(113): 10–11.

Yamagami, Susumu (1990). *Nanmin mondai no genjô kadai* [The current status of the refugee problem]. Tokyo: Nihon Kajoshuppan.

Yamagami, Susumu (1995). "Determination of refugee status in Japan." *International Journal of Refugee Law* 7(1): 60–71.

CHAPTER 7

THE OCCUPATIONAL AND GEOGRAPHICAL
LOCATIONS OF TRANSNATIONAL IMMIGRANT
MINORITIES IN JAPAN

Tony Fielding

Introduction: Japan as an Unlikely Country of Immigration

In 1990, or thereabouts, the steeply rising curve of *immigration to* Japan cut
the slowly rising curve of *emigration from* Japan. Japan henceforth became a
country of net immigration (Ishikawa, 2003) (Figure 7.1). At this very same
time, however, Japan's economy went from a period of high growth and low
unemployment to a period of low or minus growth and high unemployment.
According to economic theory this cannot be correct: net immigration occurs
in countries which have job conditions and prospects that are good relative to
alternative destinations (i.e., Japan *prior* to 1990), and a country which is in
recession when others are booming (i.e., Japan *after* 1990) must be expected
to experience net emigration. This chapter attempts to address this paradox
by explaining the presence of these immigrant communities in Japan and
by an analysis of their occupational class and geographical locations.

The Historical Background to Contemporary Japanese Migration

Japan's population largely consists of the descendants of immigrants from
the Asiatic continent (for example, the three waves referred to as the *kikajin*
immigrations arriving from Korea between the fourth and seventh centuries). During and after the "golden age" of the Heian period (ninth to

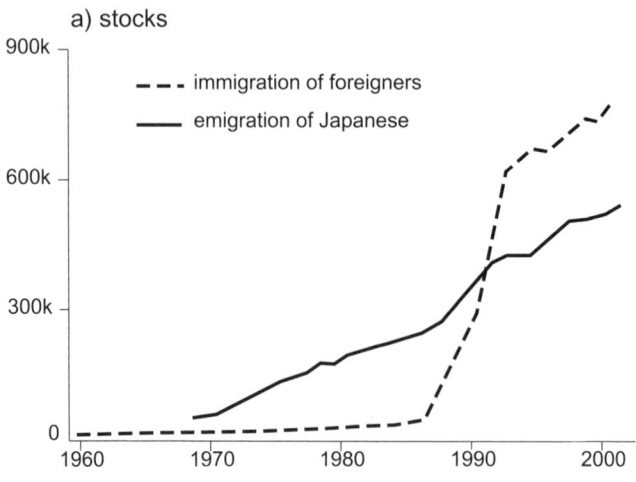

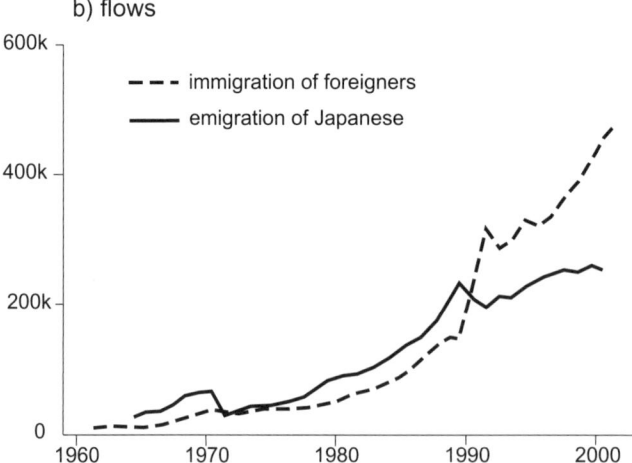

Figure 7.1. Japanese trends in immigration and emigration.
Source: Ishikawa (2003).

twelfth centuries), and saved by the *kamikaze* (wind of the gods) from invasion by the Mongols (late thirteenth century), Japan remained free from foreign invasion but frequently damaged by internal conflict, until effective unification was achieved around 1600. But during the Tokugawa period of semi-feudalism which followed, there occurred perhaps the most striking feature of Japan's migration history, the period of "national seclusion" (*sakoku*). For over 200 years (1639–1854), Japan was virtually a fortress, with no immigration or emigration. During this time it experienced very little contact at all with the outside world, except for that which resulted from Dutch and Chinese trade links through the port of Nagasaki. Many Japanese authors have seen this "national seclusion" as one element in the creation of a Japanese national character which is both uniquely distinct and uniquely uniform. The literature that they have produced is called *nihonjinron* (literally "theories of the Japanese"), which is sharply criticized in some quarters for its links with Japanese nationalism, and with what some claim to be a general hostility towards foreigners (xenophobia).[1]

Japanese Emigration

Overshadowed by the Chinese "diaspora," and now a country of net immigration, it is not widely recognized by students of migration that Japan was, for a long time after the ending of its seclusion in 1868, a country of emigration. The first destinations (1868–1924) were Hawaii and the US mainland; then came Brazil and Peru (after 1908); and, with the expansion of Imperial Japan in the period after the annexation of Korea in 1910, migration to the Asian mainland (it is estimated that there were about 6 million returnees to Japan after defeat in World War II in 1945). Very different in nature is the contemporary exodus of Japanese people, many of them "salarymen," associated with the operations of Japanese industrial and financial institutions in other advanced capitalist countries, and now also in the Asian and Latin American "third worlds" (Goodman *et al.*, 2003). A major contemporary problem associated with this emigration is the ambivalent social standing of returnee women, and the (supposed) special educational problems of returnee children. This problem of return, when combined with unwelcome family pressures and poor job promotion prospects in Japan, often results in young, ambitious Japanese women deciding to settle (often after a period in higher education) in western countries.

---

[1] For a useful collection on the position of ethnic minorities in Japan, see Weiner 1997.

"Oldcomer" Immigrants in Japan

It is standard practice now to distinguish between two very different groups of immigrants in Japan — those who have lived there for several generations (the "oldcomers"), mostly Koreans, but also many Chinese, and those who have arrived in Japan since the late 1980s and early 1990s (the "newcomers"). The oldcomer Koreans number about 600,000 people (there are, of course, also newcomer Koreans in Japan). These oldcomers are mostly second, third and fourth-generation Koreans, the descendants of the 30 percent or so of the 2.3 million Koreans in Japan in 1945 who chose to stay. Although to a very large extent culturally Japanese in language, thought and customs, these people are not Japanese citizens: only a small minority have become naturalized, and therefore they cannot vote in national elections, take public office, or become employees in many public sector organizations. They are "denizens," or permanent residents, rather than citizens. They constitute a large, rather shabbily treated minority, suffering the hatred of a handful of right-wing extremists, but also experiencing a degree of social exclusion (although lessening over time) from the mass of the Japanese population.

When their parents and grandparents came to Japan in the 1920s, 1930s and 1940s, Korea was part of Greater Japan. But during their lives in Japan, the Korean minority have seen their "homeland" first achieve independence, then suffer a very damaging war, then become divided. The division of Korea into two ideologically opposed countries has affected the Korean community in Japan. Most of the Koreans came from what is now the highly developed, capitalist South Korea, but others had family connections with North Korea, and many (including a significant proportion of those originating from the south) sympathized with the *juche* philosophy of the late North Korean leader, Kim Il Sung. This fact, when combined with the effects of social exclusion in the realm of work — which pushes some members of the Korean community towards the seedier end of the non-public sector services, for example gambling (*pachinko*) parlors — and when combined with residential segregation — which results in many Koreans living in the more run-down areas of the cities — provides some Japanese with the reasons they need to justify their feelings of superiority over, and distrust of, the Korean minority (Ryang, 2000).

"Newcomer" Immigrants in Japan

Newcomer migrations have become just as much of an issue for popular and political debate in Japan as the much larger South Asian, African, and Caribbean migrations to western Europe. It is not surprising perhaps, given the Japanese government's determination to exclude unskilled foreign workers, that some of this newcomer migration is illegal.

Who are these newcomers, whose numbers now significantly exceed those of the oldcomers? For the most part, and irrespective of their educational qualifications or jobs they did before they left their countries of origin, they work in Japan in unskilled and semi-skilled jobs, especially in the construction, manufacturing (e.g., car components) and service industries (e.g., as "entertainers"). They are classic "gap-fillers" — they do the kinds of jobs that the Japanese themselves do not want to do. Employers, finding it impossible to recruit reliable Japanese labor for the "3K" jobs (involving work that is strenuous, dirty and dangerous — *kitsui, kitanai, kiken*) turn to foreign workers, who are only too willing to do these jobs at rates of pay that are far more (five, or even ten times greater) than the wages that they can earn in their home countries. In the early period of the build up of immigration from the late 1970s until the mid-1980s, the majority of the newcomers were young Asian women recruited by agents to work in the Japanese sex industry, as bar hostesses, strippers and prostitutes. But by the late 1980s, the immigration stream had become male dominated with Asian men working in the construction industry during the boom years of the "bubble economy," but also in factories and workshops, often as students or "trainees". By the early 1990s these men had been joined by the *nikkeijin* — men and women of Japanese descent, migrating from South America to work (for better pay and in better conditions than Asian newcomers) in the larger factories, mostly in the car components and electrical engineering industries (Tsuda, 2003). Also, some women come to Japan as "mail order brides" to marry Japanese men. Throughout the post-war period, of course, a minority of those migrating to Japan have been professional, technical and managerial staff associated with international business and higher education.[2]

---

[2]For useful references on recent immigration, see Douglass and Roberts, 2000; Hirabayashi *et al.*, 2002; Komai, 2001 and Sellek, 2001.

The "New Immigration Model" Applied to Japan

The model

The introductory section above has provided the context for what follows. The key theoretical question about contemporary immigration to Japan is: "how can a country that has been experiencing low growth or recession throughout the 'lost decade' of the 1990s (with rising levels of unemployment and many business failures) nevertheless witness high levels of immigration and a rising population of (semi-) permanent foreign residents?". The solution to this paradox is to be found in the "new immigration model" (King, Fielding and Black, 1997). The new immigration model is designed to apply to countries which have experienced net emigration in the past, but which have recently turned into countries of net immigration. It was developed to explain the paradox that several countries of southern Europe (for example, Spain) were seeing their immigration numbers rising at the same time that they were experiencing high and/or rising levels of unemployment. How could it be the case that one group of employers were failing to provide enough jobs for members of the host population, while others were actively recruiting immigrant workers? (see Figure 7.2).

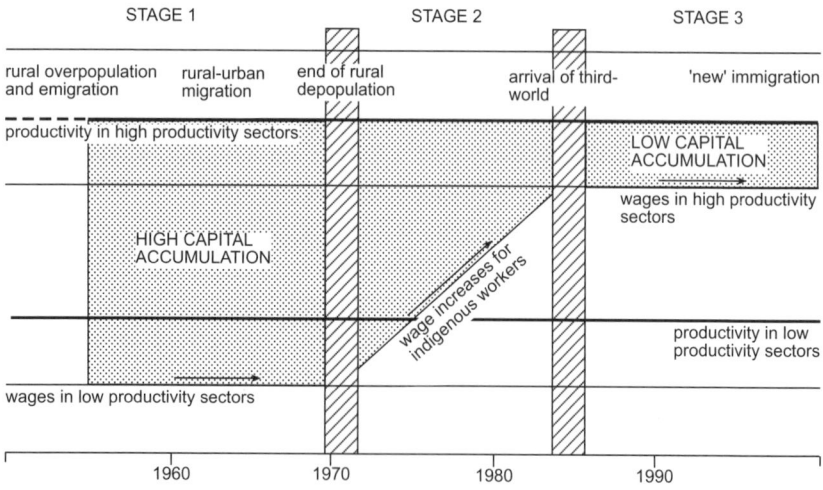

Figure 7.2.   A schematic representation of the "New Immigration Model."

The distinguishing feature of the conceptual model set out in Figure 7.2 is that it links profitability, labor market conditions and both internal and international migration flows, within a two-sector (high productivity–low productivity) national economy. The model has three stages:

Stage 1. Due to a surplus rural population (which was still encouraging emigration) and high levels of rural-to-urban migration (viz. "economic development with unlimited supplies of labour," Lewis, 1954), wage levels were kept to a low level — low enough to allow profitable employment in the low productivity sector as well as high profits and very rapid capital accumulation in the high productivity sector. By the early 1970s, reduced regional income inequality and an effective end to rural labor surpluses alter the conditions for capital accumulation and we enter Stage 2 of the model.

Stage 2. Now the shortage of indigenous labor resulting from past heavy investments (due to high profitability in the high productivity sector) is forcing wages up to levels close to those in the dominant high-income countries (the United States, Germany etc.). This has the immediate effect of making the low productivity sector unprofitable, and it has the longer-term effect of reducing the profitability of the high productivity sector. The result is that, by the mid-1980s, we reach Stage 3 of the model.

Stage 3. Employers in the low productivity sector seek out new sources of low-wage labor (that is, immigrant workers), while at the same time the employers in the high productivity sector disinvest and lay workers off because the margins between labor costs and market price are too tight for profitability. The outcome is inevitable — the number of unemployed among the indigenous workforce goes up at the same time that the number of immigrant workers goes up. So the paradox is resolved!

The application of the model to Japan

Does this conceptual model apply to Japan? Yes, in my opinion, it does. We saw mass migration from rural areas to the major cities in the 1960s as highly profitable companies invested heavily in new factories and offices.

In the early 1970s, there was a precipitous decline in rural-urban migration, and a long period of labor shortages set in. This caused wages to rise to levels which were uncompetitive internationally, which in turn led to the "hollowing out" of the Japanese economy as firms increasingly invested abroad rather than at home. At the same time, the employers in low productivity sectors turned to the use of immigrant workers. The result has been a long period of low growth/recession from 1990, an unemployment level at the historically high level of 5.5 percent, and about 2 million foreigners living permanently or semi-permanently in Japan, many of them arriving in the last few years of the 1990s when the economic prospects were at their worst.

Limitations of the model

The "new immigration model" is not designed to explain everything that calls for explanation about Japanese international migration. I am fully aware of the fact, for example, that 1990 coincided with a change in Japanese immigration law which facilitated the arrival of *nikkeijin* migrants from South America. Nor does it even encompass all of the economic factors in Japanese immigration (several of which were discussed in Fielding and Mizuno, 1996). Rather it is a means to meet a more limited objective — to explain how a country in recession could, against expectations, experience high levels of net immigration.

Implications of the Model for the Occupational Class Locations and Spatial Segregations of Immigrant Minorities in Japan in 2000

This model has both strengths and weaknesses for explaining the social class and geographical locations of immigrant migrant communities. From the 2000 Census we can identify eight immigrant groups by country of origin: (i) Koreans (mostly "oldcomers," but with some "newcomers"); (ii) Chinese (mostly newcomers); (iii) people from the Philippines (mostly women — see Figure 7.3); (iv) Thais (a similar pattern to the Philippines); (v) other South and South-East Asians (mostly men from Muslim countries such as Indonesia, Malaysia, Bangladesh, Pakistan and Iran);

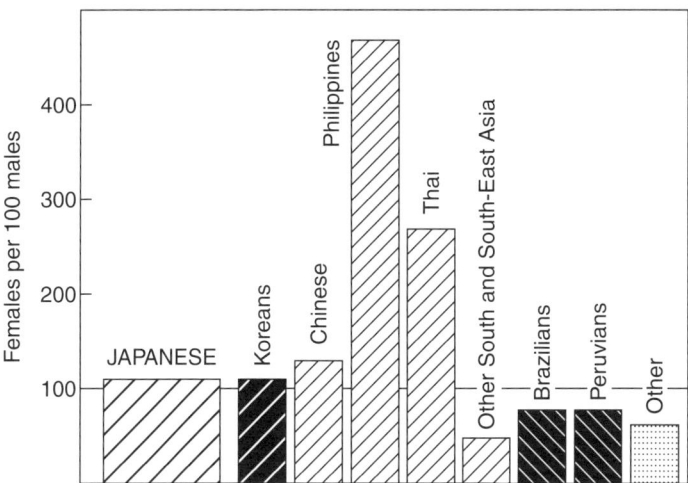

Figure 7.3. Japan: Sex ratios (females per 100 males) for foreigners in 2000. *Source*: 2000 population census.

(vi) Brazilians (mostly people of Japanese descent); (vii) Peruvians (also mostly of Japanese descent); and (viii) Others (mostly people from western countries such as the United States, Canada, Australia, New Zealand, and the countries of the European Union (EU)). The presence in Japan of six of these eight groups is relatively well explained by the "new immigration model" outlined above. The two exceptions are the Koreans and the "Others."

Koreans

(i) *Social class location.* Most Koreans in Japan are second, third and fourth-generation permanent residents. Although they arrived to work as manual laborers in the coalmines, and in construction and manufacturing, their occupational class structure now resembles in many respects that of the host population (Figure 7.4a). This convergence towards the host society's class structure has been observed in other immigrant countries such as the United States (Clark, 2003) and the United Kingdom (Fielding, 1998). There are, however, some interesting differences. Notice that Koreans are under-represented in the professions, and in clerical white-collar jobs. This reflects the difficulty that Koreans have had historically in obtaining formal qualifications through

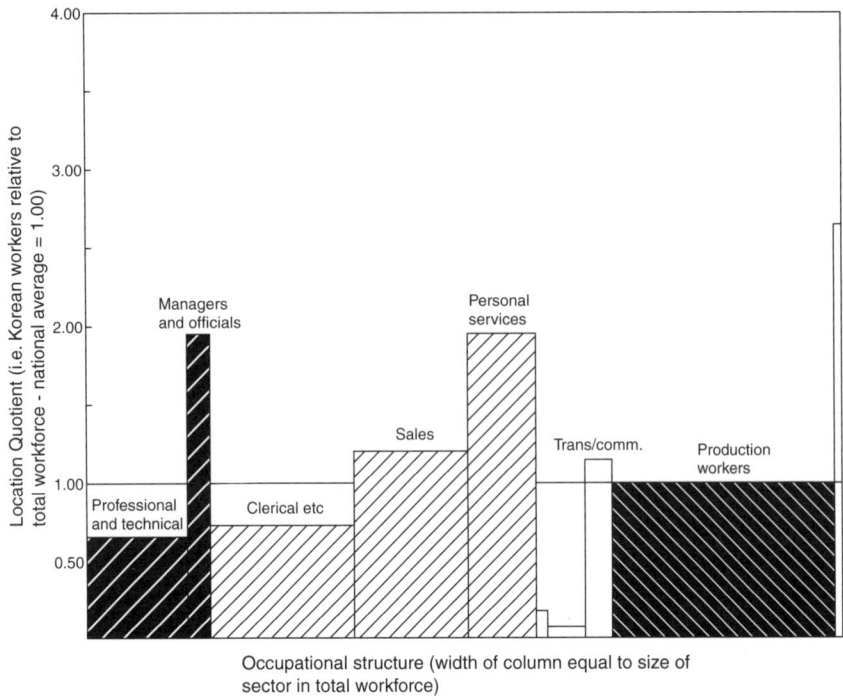

Figure 7.4a. Japan: Occupational structure of Koreans in 2000 (relative to total workforce).
Source: 2000 census.

the Japanese university system, and their partial exclusion from the big-corporation, highly regulated section of the service sector. Their non-citizen status explains their almost total lack of presence in the security (army and police) services, and their urban concentration is reflected in their lack of involvement in agriculture, forestry, and fishing. What is, perhaps, surprising is the fact that their presence as blue-collar production workers is only the same as for the total population. In part, this undoubtedly reflects the deindustrialization of Japan's largest cities and the move of manufacturing investment to small town and rural areas. The Korean population is especially concentrated in the less-regulated end of the service sector, notably personal services (e.g., gambling), and in the category "managers and officials." It turns out that for the Korean population this latter category consists very largely of the owner-managers of small and medium-sized businesses. It seems

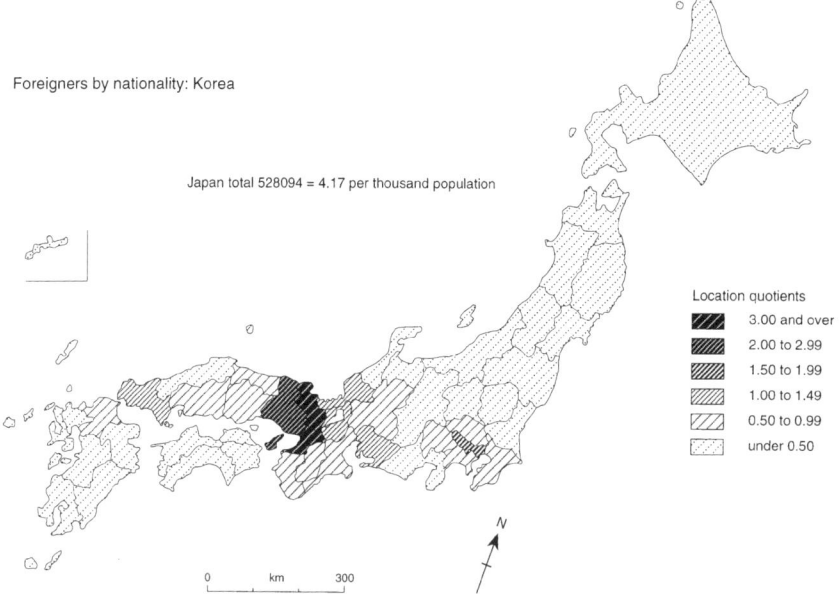

Figure 7.4b.   Japan's Korean population in 2000.
Source: 2000 census.

that, as in other countries where the paths to upward social mobility through the professions and the large business sector are blocked, it has been through the petty bourgeoisie that the social promotion of Koreans into the middle classes has been achieved.

(ii) *Spatial segregation.* Given the relative similarity of the class structure of the Korean population to that of the host society, one might have expected a geographical distribution of Koreans that matched that of the indigenous Japanese. This is clearly not the case: ethnic Koreans are very heavily concentrated in the Kansai region of Japan, especially in the Osaka, Kyoto and Kobe areas (and to a much lesser, though increasing, extent in Tokyo) (Figure 7.4b). This results from the original settlement process when Koreans, many of them from Cheju Island, came to the main industrial region of Japan in the early twentieth century, which was, of course, the Kansai region. Their strong presence in Yamaguchi Prefecture in western Japan also reflects this early settlement process. It is interesting, however, to note that the high level of regional concentration is not matched by an exceptionally high level of segregation at the

Table 7.1.   Indices of dissimilarity for foreigners in Aichi Prefecture 1995.

	Japan	Korea	Brazil	China	Philippines	Peru	USA
Japan	—	23.8	37.4	32.0	23.8	43.6	35.4
Korea	23.9	—	50.0	27.2	25.8	53.7	36.5
Brazil	36.3	48.3	—	54.9	45.1	24.7	57.7
China	35.0	29.3	54.4	—	26.2	58.4	26.6
Philippines	18.3	23.8	42.5	28.9	—	52.6	37.5
Peru	39.7	49.2	23.0	55.5	44.0	—	58.1
USA	36.6	36.5	57.3	26.2	35.5	56.7	—

Above the diagonal = Population census.
Below the diagonal = Alien registration statistics.
Source: Iida, 2001.

local level. In the Table of Indices of Dissimilarity for Aichi (Nagoya) Prefecture constructed by Iida (Iida, 2001), the degree of segregation between the Korean population and the ethnic Japanese is the lowest or second lowest of all the groups studied (values around 23.8 percent) (see Table 7.1).

Chinese

(i) *Social class location.* For the minority "oldcomer" Chinese, much of what has been said about the Korean population applies also to them. But most of the Chinese living in Japan today are "newcomers." They work in factories and workshops and in the less-regulated parts of the service sector (e.g., catering) (Figure 7.5a). Ethnic Chinese have been the main targets for the "trainee" and "foreign student" programs, both of which have been seen by many commentators as "side-door" means for circumventing the official policy which prohibits the immigration of manual workers. It is not surprising, therefore, that the Chinese are very strongly represented in the manual production worker occupational class, as well as in the less-regulated personal services sector. What is, therefore, a surprise is the importance of professional and technical occupations. Clearly, the United States is not the only destination for highly skilled Chinese emigrants, as Liu–Farrer's paper in this volume also shows.

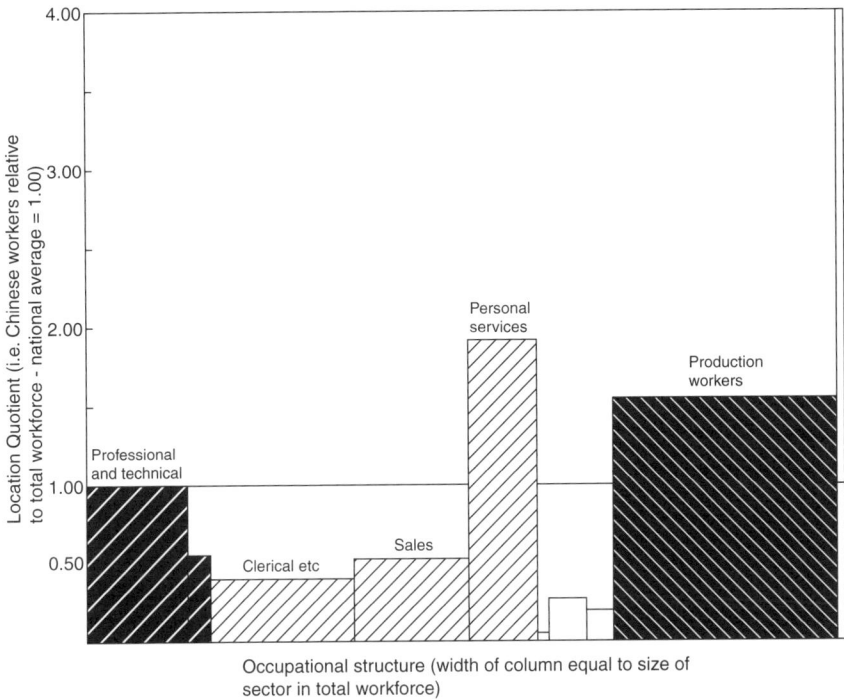

Figure 7.5a. Japan: Occupational structure of Chinese in 2000 (relative to total workforce). *Source*: 2000 census.

(ii) *Spatial segregation.* There is a strong unipolar concentration of Chinese nationals in Tokyo Prefecture, but also some representation of Chinese in much of central, mostly urban, Japan. At the more local scale, Chinese people are fairly similarly located to other Asian new-comer populations (and to Americans), but not to *nikkeijin* or to the host population (Figure 7.5b).

Filipinos

(i) *Social class location.* The lack of convergence to the occupational class structure of wider society is striking — people from the Philippines, over 80 percent of whom are women, are highly concentrated in just two categories, production workers and "personal services" (Figure 7.6a). This last category includes the many Filipinas who work in the Japanese

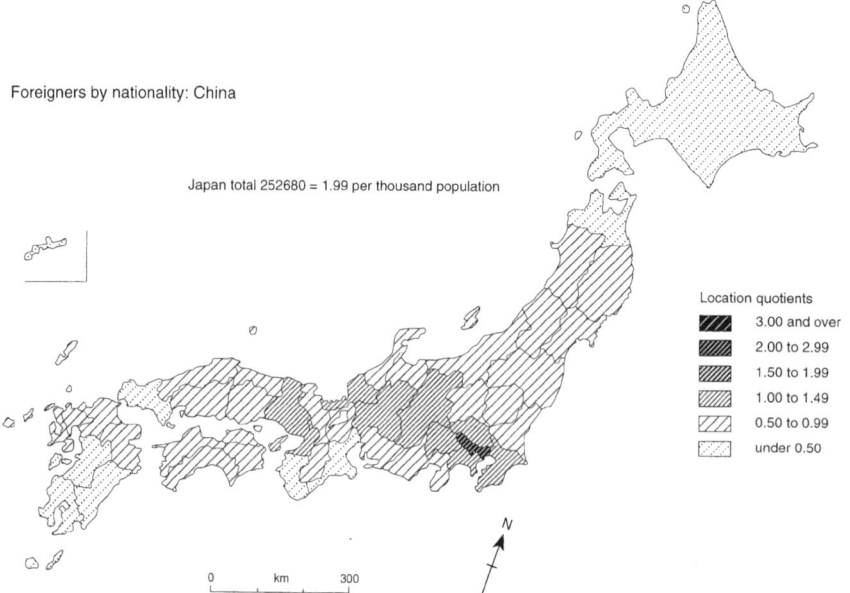

Foreigners by nationality: China

Japan total 252680 = 1.99 per thousand population

Location quotients
3.00 and over
2.00 to 2.99
1.50 to 1.99
1.00 to 1.49
0.50 to 0.99
under 0.50

0   km   300

N

Figure 7.5b.   Japan's Chinese population in 2000.
Source: 2000 census.

sex industry (unlike other countries their representation in domestic labor and the caring services is still fairly low). Among the other occupational categories, only "professional and technical" workers gets anywhere close to reaching the norm for Japan as a whole.

(ii) *Spatial segregation.* At the broad regional scale, it is clear that Philippine nationals are highly concentrated in the capital city region (Kanto) including Tokyo itself, and in the prefectures between the capital region and Kansai (Figure 7.6b). These areas might be thought of as the Tokyo metropolitan area's "leisure resort periphery," that is, the places where golf clubs and mountain resorts (e.g., for skiing and hot springs) are found within easy driving distance from the capital. At the more local level, given both its recent arrival and its occupational concentration, the Philippine population is remarkably co-located with the ethnic Japanese population. One reason for this might be the high degree of marriage and co-habitation between Philippine women and Japanese men (some of these marriages being officially sponsored by local authorities in rural areas).

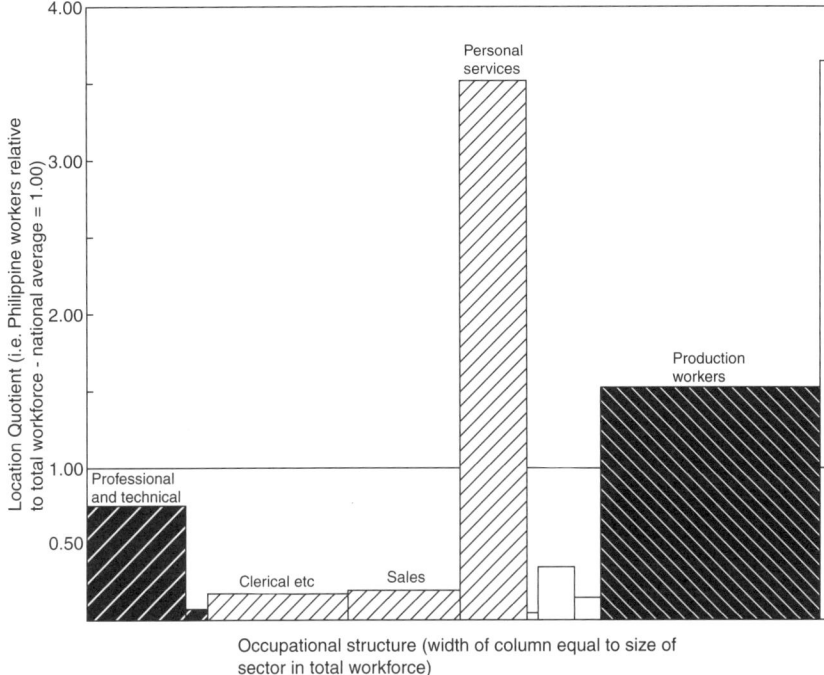

Figure 7.6a. Japan: Occupational structure of Filipinos in 2000 (relative to total workforce).
Source: 2000 census.

Thais

(i) *Social class location.* With about 70 percent of the Thais in Japan being women, some of whom work in the sex industry, it is to be expected that there would be similarities with the occupational class profile of those from the Philippines. However, the differences are also interesting. Thai nationals are much more strongly represented in the manual production worker category, and some also work in "agriculture, forestry, and fishing." Above all, there are very few Thais in professional, technical and managerial occupations (Figure 7.7a).

(ii) *Spatial segregation.* The regional concentration of Thais is quite remarkable: yes, the value for Tokyo itself is high, but the highest values are for the prefectures around greater Tokyo (Chiba, Ibaraki and Tochigi in the east, and Nagano and Yamanashi in the west) where

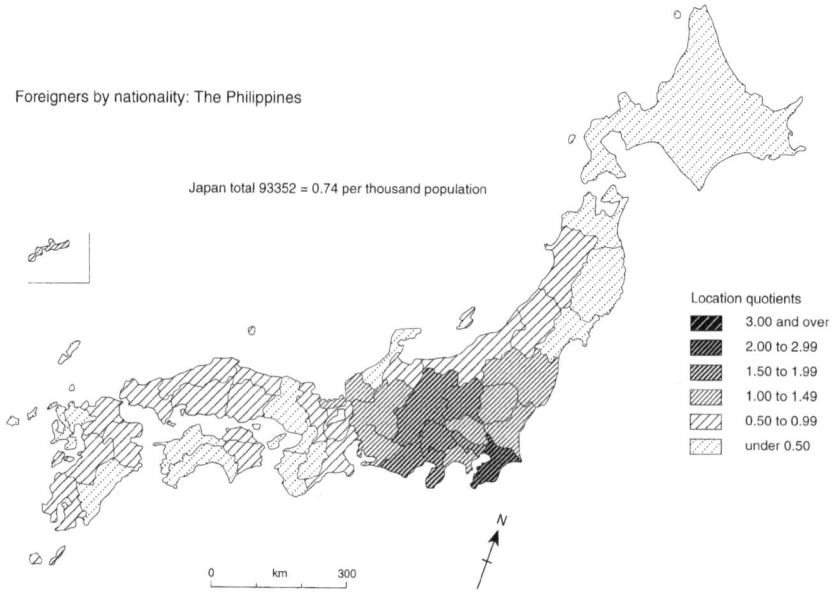

Foreigners by nationality: The Philippines

Japan total 93352 = 0.74 per thousand population

Location quotients

▨	3.00 and over
▨	2.00 to 2.99
▨	1.50 to 1.99
▨	1.00 to 1.49
▨	0.50 to 0.99
▨	under 0.50

0   km   300

N

Figure 7.6b. Japan's Filipino population in 2000.
Source: 2000 census.

concentrations of greater than three times the national average are to be
found. This represents an even stronger version of the "resort periphery"
tendency than was seen for people from the Philippines (Figure 7.7b).

Other South and South-East Asia

(i) *Social class location.* These people, mostly immigrants and predominantly men, are located in classic "gap-filler" occupations, notably as
manual production workers. The "new immigration model" has clearly
been relevant for all of the groups discussed so far (apart from the
Koreans), but here we see it operating in its pure form. In Tokyo itself,
and in industrial areas close by (e.g., Gunma Prefecture to the northwest
of Tokyo), labor shortages in manufacturing industry have been, and
remain, severe, and male workers from South and South-East Asia have
been recruited to fill the gap (Figure 7.8a).

(ii) *Spatial segregation.* There is a regional concentration of immigrants in
the wider Tokyo region, and along the Tokaido urban-industrial belt to
the Nagoya and Kansai industrial regions (Figure 7.8b).

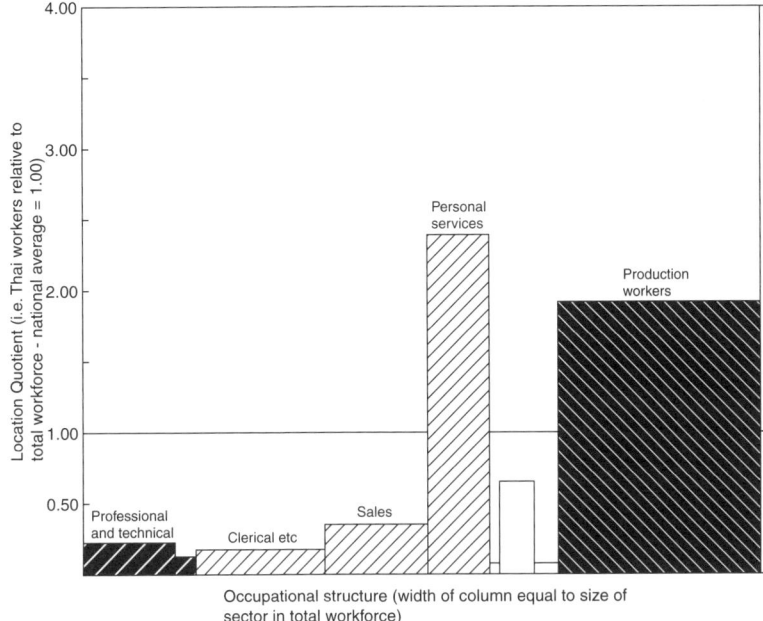

Figure 7.7a.   Japan: Occupational structure of Thais in 2000 (relative to total workforce). *Source*: 2000 census.

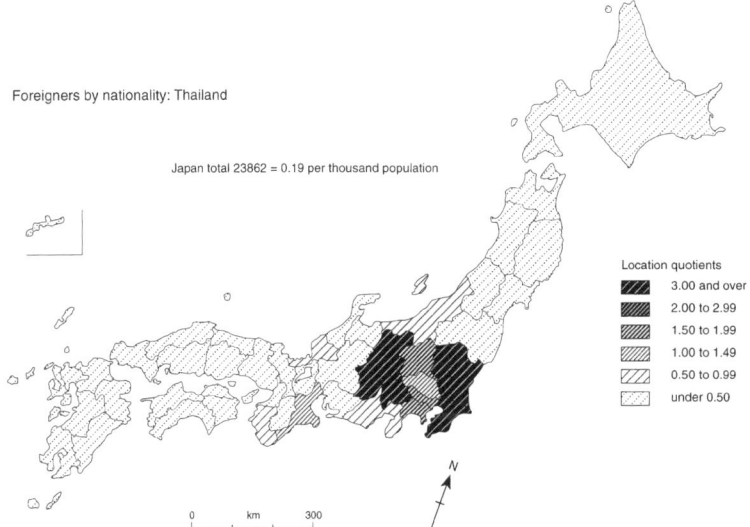

Figure 7.7b.   Japan's Thai population in 2000. *Source*: 2000 census.

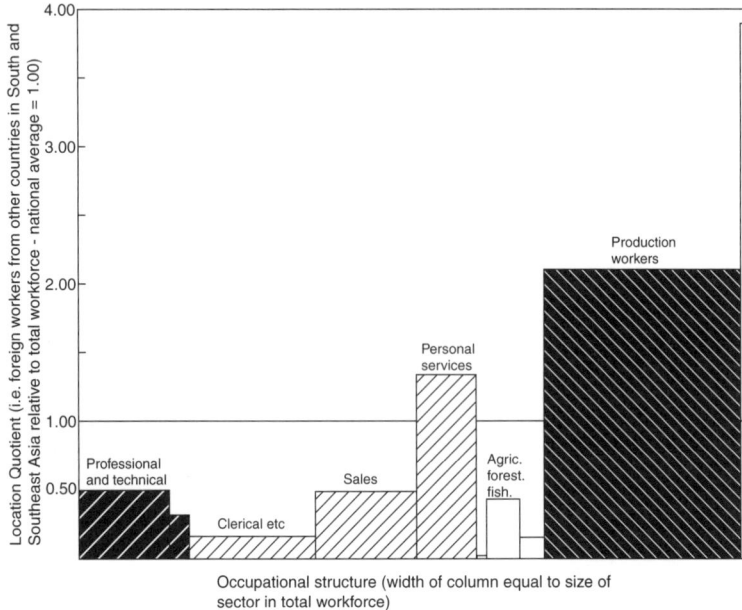

Figure 7.8a.   Japan: South and South-east Asia in 2000 (relative to total workforce).
Source: 2000 census.

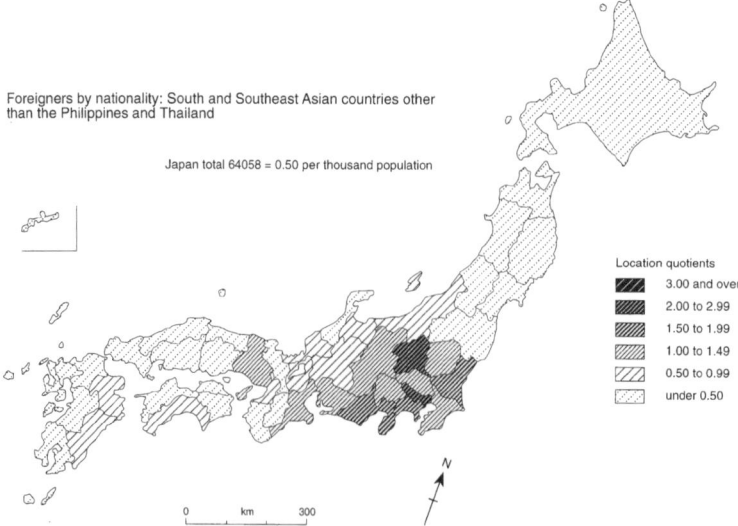

Figure 7.8b.   Japan's other South and South-east Asian population in 2000.
Source: 2000 census.

Brazilians

(i) *Social class location.* To a quite extraordinary extent, we see here a "one-class" immigrant minority. Men and women of Japanese descent recently "returning" from Brazil, whatever their social class location in their country of origin, overwhelmingly work as manual laborers in the manufacturing industry in Japan (Figure 7.9a).

(ii) *Spatial segregation.* The distinctiveness of the regional spatial distribution of Brazilians is no less extraordinary than that of their class location. Brazilian *Nikkeijin* are very heavily concentrated, not in Tokyo itself or its suburbs, not in Kansai, but overwhelmingly in the towns and cities around and to the west of Tokyo where some large, but mostly medium-sized firms, supplying the key components for Japan's highly successful export industries (notably cars and consumer electronics), are to be found (Figure 7.9b). At the local level, as one would anticipate

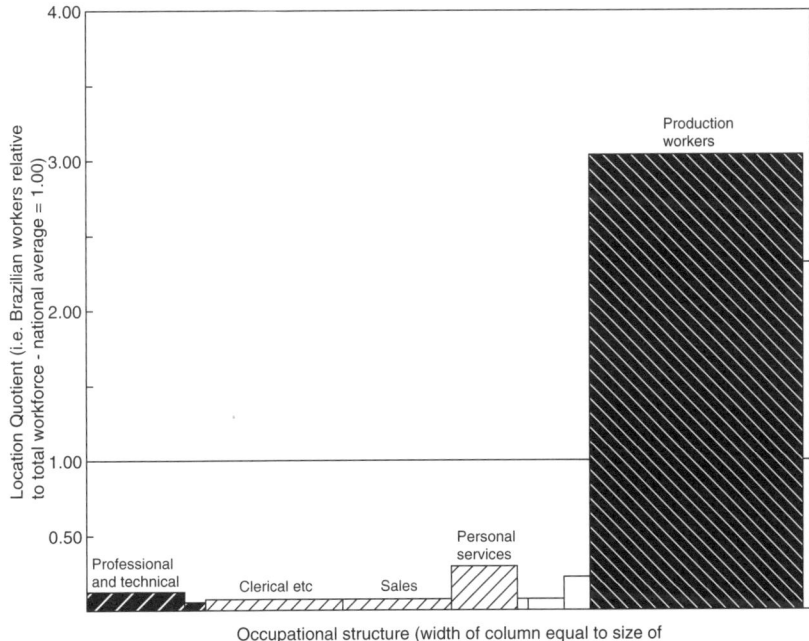

Figure 7.9a.   Japan: Occupational structure of Brazilians in 2000 (relative to total workforce).
Source: 2000 census.

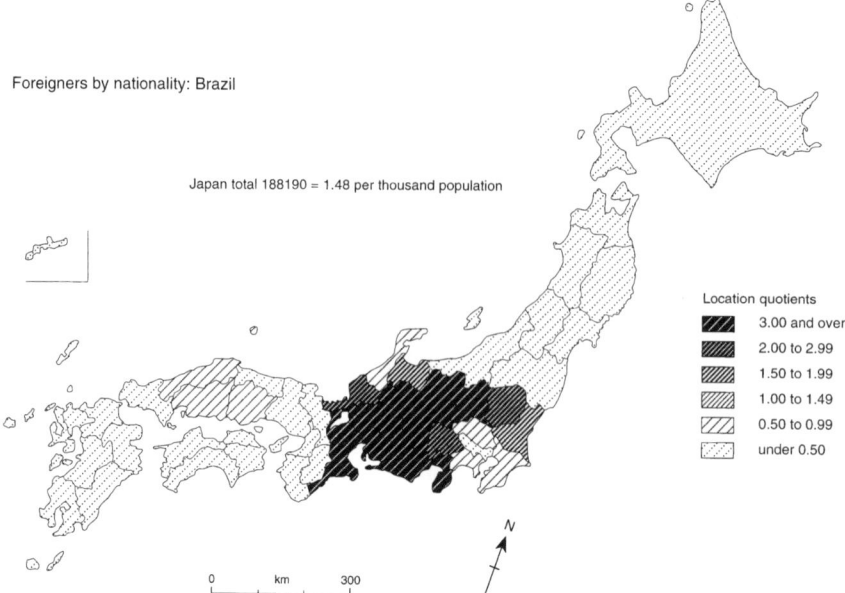

Figure 7.9b.   Japan's Brazilian population in 2000.
Source: 2000 census.

for a recently arrived immigrant group (and in contrast to what might be expected given the fact that these are people of Japanese descent), Brazilians are not located in places occupied by Japanese nationals or by other immigrant groups (with the notable, and to be expected, exception of Peruvians).

Peruvians

(i) *Social class location.* Despite the different history of the Japanese community in Peru, the class profile of Peruvian *nikkeijin* in Japan is, for all intents and purposes, identical to that for Brazilians. This is another one-class community of manual laborers (Figure 7.10a).

(ii) *Spatial segregation.* Once again, both Tokyo and Osaka have values lower than 50 percent of the national average while the prefectures around and to the west of Tokyo reach values which on five occasions exceed three times the national average. At the local level, there is nothing to distinguish the segregation levels of Peruvians and Brazilians. Both are only co-located with each other, and both have the

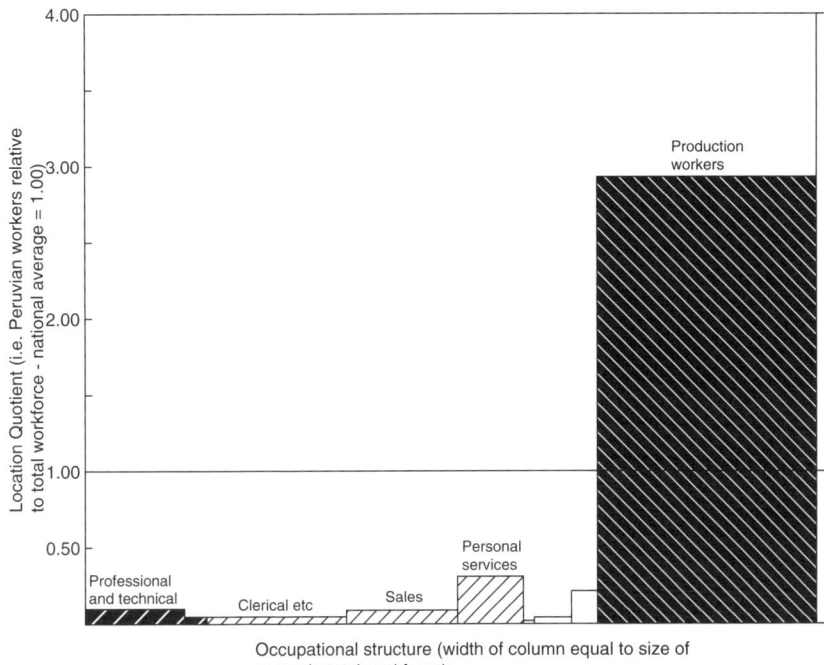

Figure 7.10a. Japan: Occupational structure of Peruvians in 2000 (relative to total workforce).
Source: 2000 census.

highest segregation levels for their links with the Japanese. The highest segregation levels of all are between the Brazilians and Peruvians on the one hand, and the Americans on the other.

Other foreigners

(i) *Social class location.* We now witness the other face of globalization. The vast majority of the foreigners in Japan are there because there are, by Japanese standards, poorly paid, low-status jobs to be done. And with greater interaction through cheap and rapid transport there are workers from distant places available and prepared, by their poverty and powerlessness, to do them, but a small though growing minority of immigrants are in Japan to do very well-paid, high-status jobs, jobs for which special skills and experience are required. This is dramatically demonstrated by the class profile for "other foreigners" (mostly

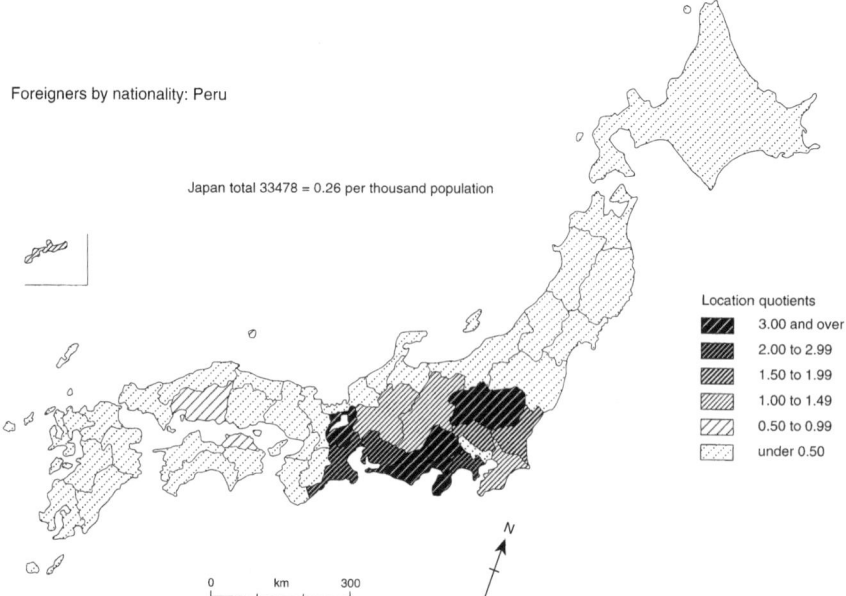

Figure 7.10b. Japan's Peruvian population in 2000.
Source: 2000 census.

westerners in business and higher education). Here professional and technical workers totally dominate the picture, with managers and officials being the only other category to exceed the national average (Figure 7.11a).

(ii) *Spatial segregation.* Westerners are overwhelmingly concentrated in Tokyo itself, with minor sub-concentrations in prefectures containing the port cities of Yokohama and Kobe, and in Okinawa (due to the presence of the United States military) (Figure 7.11b). At the local level, it is only with the Chinese that westerners are, to some degree co-located (mostly, one suspects, because of the importance of the main city centers for both groups).

To summarize

The findings of this analysis of the 2000 Census results for immigrant minority groups in Japan can be summarized as follows: there are five

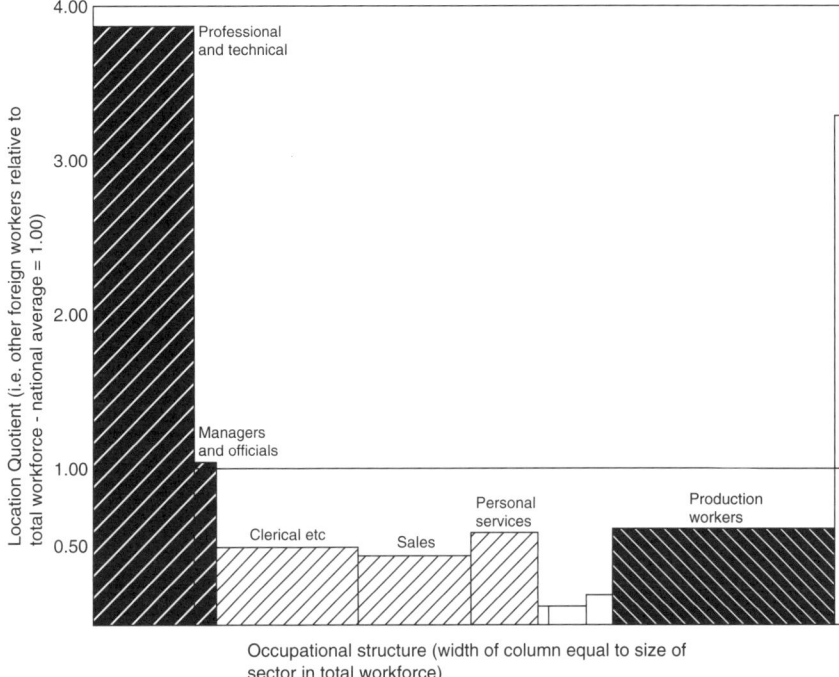

Occupational structure (width of column equal to size of sector in total workforce)

Figure 7.11a. Japan: Occupational structure of other foreigners (mainly westerners) in 2000 (relative to total workforce).
Source: 2000 census.

patterns of class location/spatial segregation combinations, which are:

(i) the Korean case, characterized by a class location profile that is similar to that of the host population, but with a very distinctive regional distribution centered in Kansai;

(ii) the Chinese case, characterized by working class dominance but with some professional middle-class elements, and a spatial distribution highly centered on Tokyo;

(iii) the Philippine and Thai cases, both of which are dominated by female members of the service-sector working class, with a spatial distribution which is Tokyo-centered, but extends to the wider periphery of the Tokyo region;

(iv) the Brazilian and Peruvian *nikkeijin* cases, joined by a less-distinctive South and South-East Asian group, which are male-dominated manual

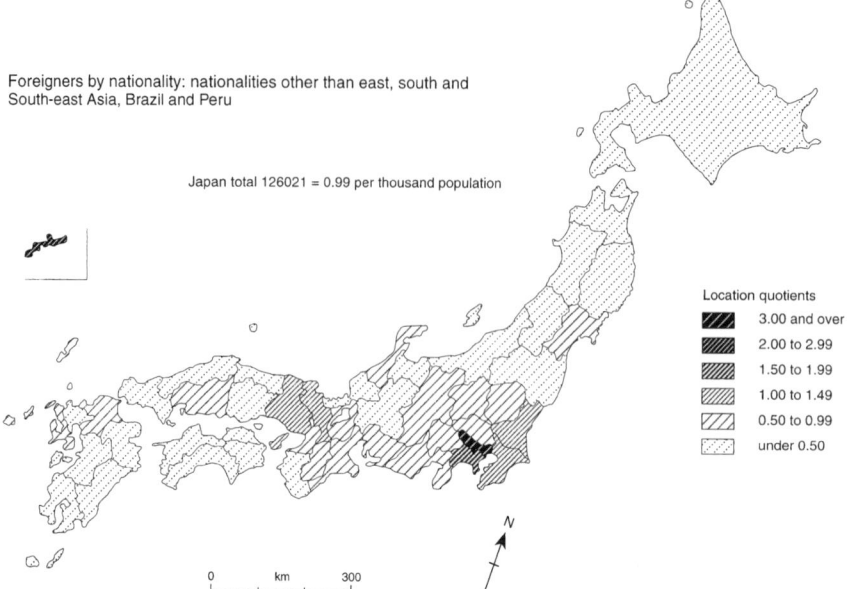

Foreigners by nationality: nationalities other than east, south and
South-east Asia, Brazil and Peru

Japan total 126021 = 0.99 per thousand population

Location quotients
3.00 and over
2.00 to 2.99
1.50 to 1.99
1.00 to 1.49
0.50 to 0.99
under 0.50

0   km   300

Figure 7.11b. Japan's other foreign population (mostly westerners) in 2000.
Source: 2000 census.

working class, with a spatial distribution reflecting labor-shortage
areas, mostly around and to the west of Tokyo and

(v) the westerner case, characterized by a professional, technical and
managerial workforce, spatially centered on Tokyo itself.

The "new immigration model" is relevant to all of these cases except (i) and
(v). Please notice also that, to an unusual degree, Japan has very different
spatial distributions for its main immigrant groups.

Themes which Relate to, and Develop out of, this Research

Testing the "new immigration model"

The general and highly schematic nature of the "new immigration model"
means that it does not produce simple quantitative predictions which are
testable. However, it is in harmony with the underlying logic of the model
that international migration in the 1980s and 1990s has, to a significant

degree, substituted for internal migration in the 1950s and 1960s. If, and it is a big "if," the spatial patterns of labor demand remained constant over time, then the spatial distribution of gross in-migration rates for internal migration in the early post-war years should match the distribution of gross immigration rates for international migration in the recent period.

This relationship is explored in Figure 7.12. It shows that there is indeed a statistically significant positive relationship between the two rates ($r = +0.53$), and that the residuals from the regression line ($y = 1.74 + 1.09x$, where y is immigration 1995–2000, and x is inter-prefectural in-migration 1959–1960) are interpretable in terms of the changes in regional growth performance (growth of Tokyo, but relative decline of Kansai), and the particular labor needs of the areas in which manufacturing industry expanded in the 1960s and 1970s (e.g., Gunma and Shizuoka Prefectures).

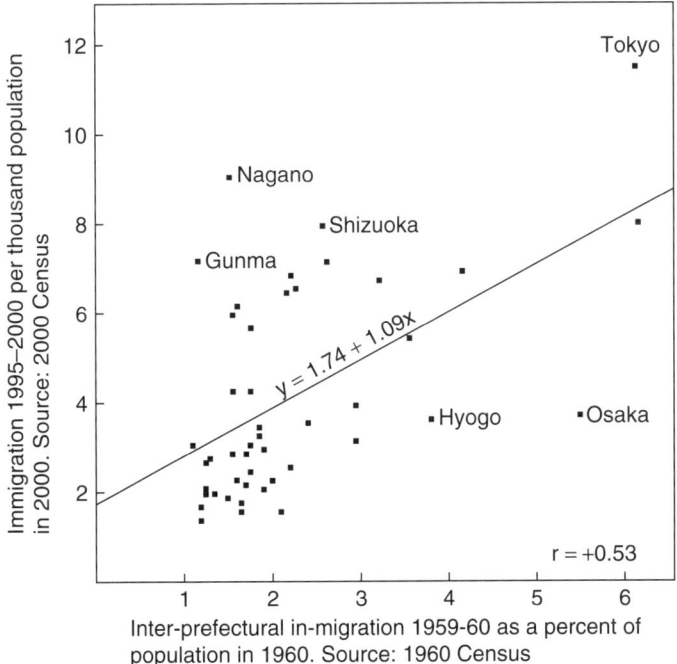

Figure 7.12. Japan: The relationship between international migration in the late 1990s and internal migration in the late 1950s: Date for Prefectures.
Source: 1960 census.

Japanese immigration policy

Finally, previous sections have referred indirectly to the widely held perception that Japan is, uniquely, a classless (i.e., "everyone is middle-class"), racially and culturally homogeneous society. This view has a major impact on Japanese immigration policy which, in my opinion, strongly represents a Walzer-type communitarian position modified by considerations of pragmatism and profit. This is shown in Figure 7.13, in which Japanese and EU immigration policy positions are compared. One of the unintended side-effects of the belief expressed by the Japanese government, that Japan is a country which has no ethnic or other socially excluded minorities, is to bring together immigrant and indigenous minorities in a celebration of their differences from mainstream Japanese, for instance in local festivals.

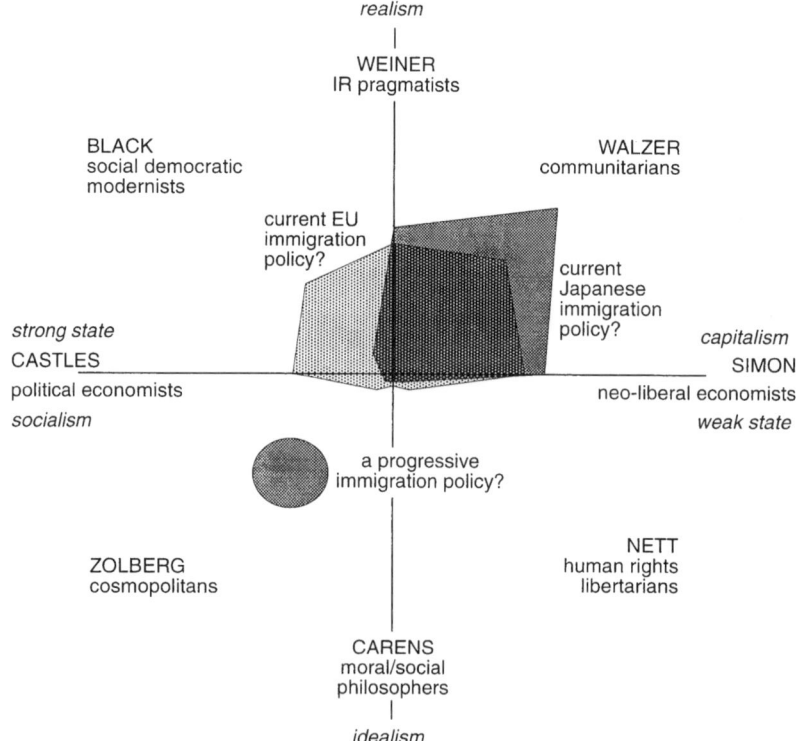

Figure 7.13. Diagram to show the position of Japanese and EU immigration policies in relation to political and philosophical perspectives on immigration issues.

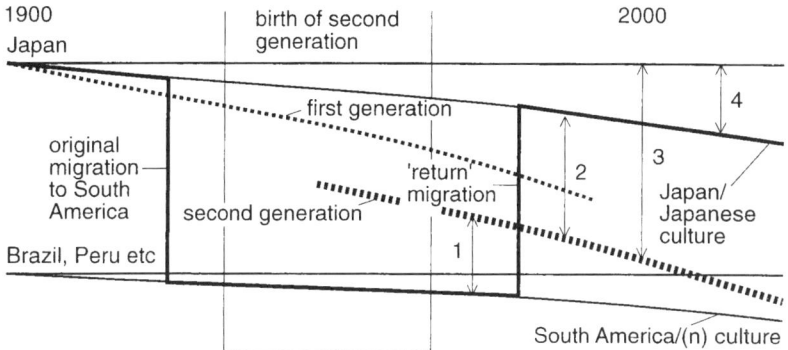

Figure 7.14. Diagram to show identity shifts for second-generation "Returnee" Japanese migrants (Nikkeijin) from South America to Japan. 1 = distance of Japanese South-Americans from contemporary Brazil, Peru etc. (i.e., feeling "Japanese" in South America). 2 = distance of "returnees" from contemporary Japan (feeling "South American" in Japan). 3 = distance of "returnees" from nostalgic (e.g., parental) image of Japan. 4 = distance of contemporary Japan from traditional Japan. Drawn by Tony Fielding in November 2005 but based on research by Anastasia Christou (both at Sussex Centre for Migration Research).

Furthermore, the racialized blood-line notion of Japanese national identity produces the bizarre result that while Koreans in Japan are regarded as "foreigners" (when actually they are, in almost every respect, Japanese), *nikkeijin* are regarded as Japanese (when actually they are, in almost every respect, including language, religion, and lifestyle, Latin American foreigners). This "un-Japanese" character of *nikkeijin* "returnees" is shown in Figure 7.14.

Conclusions

This chapter first provided a historical and conceptual background for an analysis of stratification within transnational migrant communities in Japan. It then explored the connections between occupational class structure and spatial segregation for each of the eight main immigrant groups. Finally, it measured links between internal and international migration, and proposed a characterization of Japanese immigration policy in the context of political and philosophical positions on immigration issues.

References

Black, R. (1996). "Immigration and Social Justice: Towards a Progressive European Immigration Policy?" *Transactions of the Institute of British Geographers* 21(1): 64–75.

Carens, J. (1996). "Realistic and Idealistic Approaches to the Ethics of Migration." *International Migration Review* 30(1): 156–170.

Castles, S. and G. Kosack (1975). *Immigrant Workers and Class Structure in Western Europe.* Oxford: Oxford University Press.

Clark, William A.V. (2003). *Immigrants and the American Dream: Remaking the Middle Class.* New York: Guilford Press.

Douglass, Mike and Glenda Susan Roberts (eds.) (2000). *Japan and Global Migration.* London: Routledge.

Fielding, Anthony J. and Masaaki Mizuno (1996). "Japanese Migration and the Economic Development of the East Asian Region." Research Papers in Geography 23, University of Sussex.

Fielding, Anthony J. (1998). "Immigrant Workers and Class Structure in England and Wales: A Longitudinal Study of the Social Mobility of Britain's 'Black' and 'Asian' Populations." In *Idô to Teijû [Migration and Settlement]*, edited by M. Sato and Anthony J. Fielding, 269–293. Tokyo: Dobunkan (in Japanese).

Goodman, Roger, Ceri Peach, Ayumi Takenaka and Paul White (eds.) (2003). *Global Japan.* London: Routledge Curzon.

Hirabayashi, Lane Ryo, Akemi Kikumura-Yano and James A. Hirabayashi (eds.) (2002). *New Worlds, New Lives: Globalization and People of Japanese Descent in the Americas and from Latin America in Japan.* Stanford: Stanford University Press.

Iida, Nakamura (2001). "Residential and Social Incorporation of Foreign Residents in Japan in the 1990s." DPhil thesis, Oxford University.

Ishikawa, Yasufo (2003). "Nihon no kokusai jinkô idô no tenkanten" (The turning point of Japan's international migration). *Ôyô Chiikigaku Kenkyû [Applied Regional Research]* 8(2): 1–13.

Japan: Statistics Bureau (2004). *2000 Population Census of Japan: Volume 8, Results of Special Tabulation on Foreigners.* Tokyo: Ministry of Public Management, Home Affairs, Posts and Telecommunications.

King, Russell Anthony Fielding and Richard Black (1997). "The International Migration Turnround in Southern Europe." In *Southern Europe and the New*

Immigrations, edited by Russell King and Richard Black, 1–25. Brighton: Sussex Academic Press.

Komai, Hiroshi (2001). *Foreign Migrants in Contemporary Japan*. Melbourne: Trans Pacific Press.

Lewis, Arthur W. (1954). "Economic Development with Unlimited Supplies of Labour." *The Manchester School of Economic and Social Studies* 22(2): 139–191.

Nett, R. (1971). "The Civil Right We Are Not Ready For: The Right to Free Movement of People on the Face of the Earth." *Ethics* 81(3): 212–227.

Ryang, Sonia (ed.) (2000). *Koreans in Japan*. London: Routledge.

Sellek, Yoko (2001). *Migrant Labour in Japan*. Basingstoke: Palgrave.

Simon, J. (1990). *The Economic Consequences of Immigration*. London: Blackwell.

Tsuda, Takeyuki (2003). *Strangers in the Ethnic Homeland: Japanese Brazilian Return Migration in Transnational Perspective*. New York: Columbia University Press.

Walzer, M. (1983). *Spheres of Justice*. New York: Basic Books.

Weiner, Michael (1995). *The Global Migration Crisis*. New York: Harper.

Weiner, Michael (ed.) (1997). *Japan's Minorities*. London: Routledge.

Zolberg, A.R. (1992). "Labor Migration and International Economic Regimes." In *International Migration Systems*, edited by M.M. Kritz, L.L. Limm, and H. Zlotnik, pp. 315–334. Oxford: Oxford University Press.

CHAPTER 8

BETWEEN PRIVILEGE AND PREJUDICE: CHINESE IMMIGRANTS IN CORPORATE JAPAN'S TRANSNATIONAL ECONOMY

Gracia Liu-Farrer

In early 21st century Japan, hundreds of thousands of Chinese people are working in the Japanese business sector as full time or part-time corporate employees. Among them, a large number are specifically engaged in the transnational economy between Japan and China. China's increasing importance as a mass market for Japanese products and an offshore production site for Japanese manufacturers has provided an expanding occupational niche for bilingual and bi-cultural Chinese immigrants in Japan. Similarly, the employment of Chinese has brought opportunities for Japanese companies to enter the Chinese market and take advantage of Chinese labor resources.

In 2005, 35,741 Chinese people working legally in Japan held two types of visas, namely "Specialist in Humanities/International Services" and "Engineer." The "Specialist in Humanities/International Services" visas are mostly granted to those who are employed by Japanese companies to work with China in transnational businesses, typically in positions such as translators and overseas sales representatives. Engineer visas are usually granted to professionals in information technology and other technical fields. With the rapid expansion in offshore production, becoming transnational "bridge engineers" or "bridge software engineers" is a step up on the career mobility ladder. However, work visa holders are only a small percentage of Chinese immigrants actually working in Japan. In 2005, the economically active included also a majority of the 106,269 permanent residents, 54,569 Chinese spouses of Japanese nationals, over 30,000 long-term residents, and over 100,000 Chinese people who had acquired Japanese citizenship since the 1970s. Although no official figures have ever been collected about the exact employment status of these immigrants and the nature of their jobs, my interviews and survey suggest that many permanent residents and naturalized citizens are veteran workers in the transnational economy between Japan and China. They are valued, aside from specific professional capacities, for their bilingual and bi-cultural skills.

The employment of Chinese people for transnational businesses in corporate Japan suggests that an occupational niche has emerged for skilled immigrants, characterized by their role in the transnational economy. This occupational niche indicates a convergence of three previously often dissociated identities: those of immigrants, corporate employees, and actors in the transnational economy. It is evident that the transnational economy has provided Chinese people in Japan with a niche in the primary labor market through which they have gained economic mobility and an entry point into a previously ethnically exclusive society, as well as a vantage point enabling them to avoid being marginal. In this paper, I will elaborate the mechanisms involved in the making of such an occupational niche. I will also argue that the Chinese employees' new-found niche by no means emancipates them from the structural and institutional constraints immigrants are often subject to in Japan. Their Chinese immigrant status frequently hinders them from advancing up the mobility ladder in Japanese firms, as well as denying them the prestige appropriate to their economic positions. The uncertain outcomes of the interaction of privilege and prejudice are particularly clear among Chinese women employees. Some Chinese women are subject to double prejudice due to the gender inequality in Japanese corporate culture and their status as immigrants. Others, however, have managed to enter career tracks that are denied to their Japanese women colleagues, through being foreigners and capable bicultural professionals.

Immigrants and Professionals

Patterns of international migration and modes of immigrant economic incorporation have changed dramatically in recent decades with economic globalization. In many industrial countries, more and more immigrants have entered as students, technical workers, and professionals. Social scientists have consequently accorded increasing attention to these new types of immigrants. The categories of immigrant professionals under frequent scrutiny include Indian and ethnic Chinese IT professionals. For example, based on her research in Silicon Valley in California, Saxenia (2002) highlighted the foreign IT professionals' importance in the region's economic development as well as in the transnational technical exchanges between the United States and Asian countries. In the Eastern Hemisphere, Xiang (2003) studied how Indian IT workers strategize their career mobility transnationally and evaluate their success according to their own map of the world system.

However, although stressing immigrant employees' hyper-mobility and economic roles in the global economy, social scientists have yet to examine their actual corporate experiences. Although entering the primary labor market in the host country, the corporate world, is a classical symbol of successful economic incorporation and upward mobility, immigrant employees, particularly those from less developed regions and non-white racial groups, often clash with the existing racial and gender stratification in the host corporate structure. Many questions could be asked about their lives as both immigrants and professionals. For example, how do immigrants overcome legal and cultural constraints to find jobs in the corporate world beyond their professional networks? What are their mobility patterns and the conditions affecting their career trajectories upon employment? How do they interpret their corporate experience and what are their strategies to better their social and economic standing?

Transnationalism: Blurring the Boundaries Between the High and the Low

The presence of transnational Chinese employees also poses a theoretical challenge to the existing literature on transnationalism. In recent years, social scientists have observed that many patterns of immigrant adaptation are not exclusively local processes within the host society's national boundaries. Immigrants at every stage of the migration process maintain various ties with their home countries, such as transnational religious practices (see Hagan and Ebaugh, 2003; Levitt, 1998), entrepreneurial activities (Portes, Guarnizo and Haller, 2002; Landolt *et al.*, 1999; Itzigsohn *et al.*, 1999), and transnational political activism (Bacsh, Schiller and Blanc, 1992). These kinds of immigrant transnational practices represent immigrants' grass roots efforts to circumvent their marginal social positions in the host country (Portes, 2003). Guarnizo and Smith (1998) categorized these transnational practices as "transnationalism from below." In current migration literature, the transnationality of immigrants' economic adaptation is primarily artic-ulated through informal and disparate entrepreneurial efforts. There is very little literature on immigrants' institutionalized transnational activities such as within a host country's corporate structure. However, Light *et al.* (2002), relying on census data, discovered that the increase of immigrants from certain countries actually increased the volume of American exports to these countries. They speculate that this is because of their ability to speak the foreign language, which otherwise hinders most Americans from entering these markets. This observation raises the question of the exact roles of immigrants in the processes of the export business.

"Transnational corporate employee," on the other hand, has become a title for the actors in multinational corporations who move around the world through intra-firm channels. The term frequently invokes the image of the managerial and professional elites carrying IBM computer cases and flying business class between nodes in the web of a global conglomerate. In the literature on international migration, they are not usually included in the cat-egory of immigrants, firstly because of the impermanence of their settlement in any non-native country, and secondly because "immigrants" implies the unflattering image of being low-wage labor. In most cases, the transnational employees under investigation are from an advanced industrial country, and are assigned to positions as managers or specialists in a subsidiary in a developing country or another strategic location in the firm's global web. Studies of them often focus on the channels of their international flows and trajectories of their mobility (Findlay, 1998; Beaverstock, 2005). Prejudice and discrimination are rarely issues confronting these corporate elites.

The Chinese who are employed in corporate Japan are both economic immigrants in terms of the means and motivations of migration, and trans-national corporate employees in terms of their titles and functions. They often find themselves to be racial and cultural "Others," like immigrants elsewhere, even though they occupy a strategic economic position that makes them indispensable in economic development. Therefore, they blur the boundaries between the high and the low, the privileged and the victims of discrimination. The complexity of their social and economic statuses inevitably affects their career mobility outcomes.

Data and Methodology

I spent most of the three years from January 2002 to December 2004 conducting field research in Tokyo. I gathered both qualitative and quantitative data. The qualitative data includes ethnographic research, first at Chinese social dance venues in Tokyo in 2002 and then at two Chinese immigrant churches in Tokyo from 2003 to 2004. I conducted open interviews with 123 individuals recruited from my ethnographic field sites and through personal networks. The quantitative data used in this paper includes a sample survey of 218 Chinese immigrants which I designed and administered between May and December 2003, and statistical reports published by the Japan Ministry of Justice and the Japan Immigration Association on foreign residents. Among these 218 respondents, 12 directly wrote down "Overseas Representative" as their job titles and 7 reported themselves to be software engineers (SEs). However, these numbers are only suggestive because it was a self-administered survey and 62 respondents did not answer this specific question.

When planning this chapter, I used the selective coding methods of grounded theory (Strauss and Corbin, 1990). I came up with the main categories in this analysis by coding 28 interviews, mainly but not exclusively with immigrant employees in corporate Japan. Seventeen of these 28 interviewees reported themselves to be overseas representatives of companies in Japan, and 11 of them were in the software industry. Although most of the 11 technical employees were not yet "bridge engineers" or "bridge SEs," they nonetheless expressed their opinions about such a position.

The Making of a Labor Market Niche in the Transnational Economy

Corporate employees in Japan's transnational economy have become an important group among the Chinese people in Japan primarily because of the increasingly close economic relationship between Japan and China in the last two decades. The Chinese market was not open to the outside world until the 1980s. Two decades on, China has become the most important production site and one of the most important consumer markets for the Japanese business world. In 2002, Japan poured some US$4.2 billion directly into factories and other operations in China (Belson, 2004), and became the number one foreign investor in China excluding Hong Kong (Chinese Statistical Year Book, 2004). Japan was also the number one importer of Chinese workers (ibid.). Not only do big conglomerates such as NEC and Mazda carry out most of their production in China (and want to sell a large portion of their products there), but numerous medium and small Japanese firms are also active, and to some degree desperate, players in the transnational economy between Japan and China. Chinese and Japanese governments, despite political disputes over territory and history, actively promote such economic exchanges. Starting in September 2003, the Chinese government has granted visa exemption to Japanese citizens scheduled to visit China for less than 15 days. Japan is the first foreign country to enjoy such a visa exemption. In this economic context, Japanese firms actively recruit people who are bilingual and have cultural familiarity with both countries.

However, the making of the transnational niche labor market is not solely a result of Japanese firms' corporate strategies. Its existence is first of all premised upon the existence of large groups of skilled immigrants. The first group is of Chinese students. Since the mid-1980s when Japan opened its door to international students, hundreds of thousands of Chinese students have arrived in Japan on either language or university student visas. One important trend in contemporary international education is the overlapping of student mobility and labor migration (Liu Farrer, 2007b). First, students from all over the world are statistically concentrated in a few affluent developed counties. Five countries, the United States, Japan, United Kingdom, Australia and Germany, absorbed over three quarters of the 343,126 Chinese students abroad in 2004. Second, the students from poorer developing countries in Asia, the Caribbean, Latin America and Africa tend to stay in the host country upon graduation. Statistics show that 79 percent of Indians and 88 percent of Chinese who received doc-toral degrees in science and engineering from United States universities in 1990–1991 were working in the United States in 1995 (Cervantes and

Guellec, 2002). The top two source countries of international students in the United States are China and India. In 2001, 96 percent of Chinese and 86 percent of Indian students who had been awarded doctorates in the United States in 1996 were still residents there (Finn 2001).

In the case of Japan, according to the statistics published by Japan Student Services Organization (JASSO), among the known 24,961 foreign students who graduated from Japanese tertiary schools in 2004, only 13.3 percent went back to their own countries for either employment or further education and 1.0 percent went to a third country to work or study.[1] Over two-thirds or 68.6 percent were either employed or continuing their education in Japan. The remaining 17 percent were listed in the "other" category, which could mean self-employment, marriage and other arrangements, including loss of legal status. Third, in the past two decades, in an increasingly knowledge- and technology-based economy, international student migration is seen as bringing to the host countries valuable human resources. For example, the Australian immigration law explicitly links international student mobility with skilled migration, and encourages students to stay in Australia by giving them qualification points for permanent residency (Ziguras and Law, 2006). In Japan, new policies were passed to allow foreign students a six-month grace period upon the expiration of student visas to look for employment in Japan. Agencies such as the Foreign Students' Career Support Center (a subsidiary of the Ministry of Health, Labor and Welfare), the Japan Student Services Organization (JASSO), and individual schools have made great efforts helping foreign students obtain job information and honing job searching skills. These mobility trends, statistics, and policy measures point to one reality — international education has become a *de facto* means of labor migration.

Aside from the educationally channeled labor migrants from China, Japan has also been aggressively recruiting engineers from other Asian countries since the 1990s. Every year, thousands of Chinese technical professionals arrive in Japan through intra-firm transfer and direct issuance of work visas to engineers. These skilled Chinese immigrants increasingly

---

[1] In 2004, a total number of 28,903 foreign students were expected to graduate. However, JASSO had only 24,961 cases in its data. A further 3942 were labeled "unclear."

see their career opportunities lying in transnational economies and regard themselves as the bridging agents between the Japanese and Chinese economies. Therefore, once employed, they actively help expand the cross-border economy in different ways and consequently carve out a niche for themselves. First, their presence in the company makes it possible for the employer to start business activities in China. Many Japanese firms, especially small and medium firms who have never had foreign employees, hire Chinese students to seek business opportunities in China. Secondly, Chinese employees sometimes take the initiative to expand the company business into China. One informant, Chao Shen, a law school graduate from a Japanese university, reported that he was not hired to do business with China initially. When Chao started his career at a Japanese technology marketing firm, he was an intellectual property legal advisor. For the first few years, Chao traveled mostly to Europe and North America. He later reminded his boss about the potential market for patented technologies in China. Very soon, as the only Chinese person in the company of 50 employees, Chao found himself immersed in the transnational economy between Japan and mainland China, and the company had to hire more Chinese workers to lighten his workload.

In short, the occupational niche in the labor market Chinese immigrants have accessed in Japan is not just a vacancy emerging in the existing cross-border business between Japan and China, but also a result of the increasing international skilled migration, partly as a result of international education and the conscious efforts of these skilled Chinese immigrants to expand the transnational economy. It is an occupational niche that is still enlarging and developing.

Becoming Transnational Employees

Transnational employees, as I have explained previously, have mostly come from two groups of Chinese in Japan: the student migrants, which has in fact been one of the largest groups of migrants from China to Japan; and the employees that Japanese firms recruit directly from China, as in the case of the majority of software engineers. In this section, I will introduce the different ways in which these two groups enter corporate Japan, and the different occupational niches they occupy.

From school to work

Many long-term migrants from China to Japan arrive originally as students, in a situation where two-thirds of foreign students on Japanese campuses are Chinese. In recent decades, the most popular ways for Chinese to enter Japan have been first as technical trainees and next as students. From 1984 to 2004, over a quarter of a million Chinese citizens arrived in Japan with either university or pre-university language student visas.[2] In any given year since 1990, current students have been 20–30 percent of the total registered Chinese population in Japan. After completing their targeted education, some Chinese students continue their education or find employment in a third country; some go back to China; and a large number of them start working in companies in Japan. According to Ministry of Justice statistics on visa changes, in the past several years over half, and sometimes two-thirds, of employment visas have been granted to Chinese students. In my own survey of 218 people from May to December 2003, 32 respondents held employment visas in Japan.[3] Among them, 19 entered Japan as students. In addition, among 34 survey respondents who obtained permanent residency or naturalization in Japan, 16 were former students.

Most Chinese students working for Japanese companies occupy positions in transnational trading and marketing because of Chinese student preferences for gaining entry into the Japanese corporate sector and the cultural competence they have accumulated during their school years, as well as from the demand by corporate Japan for bilingual and bi-cultural human resources. Chinese immigrants who arrived in Japan on student visas have at least high school education in China. Many had work experience before coming to Japan. Very few have financial support from family or scholarships to cover both tuition and living expenses. Since Japanese law grants part-time work permits to foreign students, most Chinese students work on odd jobs through language school and university programs. Their part-time jobs put them side by side with Japanese employees and expose them to

---

[2]From 1984 to 2004, 81,403 Chinese entered Japan as university degree students and 135,050 as pre-university students — mostly students in Japanese language programs. The figures are compiled from Japan's Ministry of Justice's annual reports on population entry and exit statistics.

[3]In the survey, I over-sampled undocumented immigrants — a category that is not included in the Japanese Immigration Office's data.

different aspects of Japanese social life. As a result of both studying and working in Japan, most Chinese students quickly acquire language proficiency and gain an understanding of Japanese work ethics. Moreover, Chinese students, facing the choices of schools and majors after the language school, tend to make decisions based on two criteria: whether they have a good chance of getting in and whether it has employment potential. As a result, a high percentage of Chinese students in Japan are enrolled in undergraduate programs in social science and humanities majors, particularly economics or business.[4] Except for some academic high achievers, Chinese students often enroll in less competitive private universities.

The majority of Chinese students have chosen to stay on in Japan after graduation. The 2004 Statistics provided by JASSO indicate that only 8.2 percent of foreign college graduates returned to their home countries for employment (JASSO, 2004). The majority were either employed in Japan or chose to continue their education in Japan. These Chinese students, upon employment, were usually granted a "Specialist in Humanities/International Services" visa. In fact, in 2004, two-thirds of Chinese students who obtained employment visas were in this category. These people's employment often has to do with their bilingual skills and their Chinese cultural backgrounds. Their jobs are inevitably related to business dealings with China or other Chinese speaking regions. In my survey of 35 former students currently working in Japan, 10 of the 26 who responded to the question gave their occupational titles as "overseas representatives" or "representatives."

Transnational engineers and bridge software engineers

In early 1992, a Japanese software resource company set up an incubator unit in Fudan University, Shanghai, and selected 50 Fudan science graduates, promising to send them to work in Japan. For a year, these young men and women were assigned to graduate student dormitories, and given a monthly allowance of about US$30. They spent five days a week studying software programming, Japanese language, and Japanese management principles. There were classes taught on Japanese social etiquette, including how to dress for work and how long the skirts worn by women employees

---

[4]Based on statistics published by Ministry of Education, Culture, Sports, Science and Technology. These are available online at http://www.mext.go.jp, accessed on October 31, 2006.

should be. After the training, the students were assigned to posts in different corporations in Japan. Such programs went on for several years. In the mid-1990s the unit became an independent software house in Shanghai, dispatching programmers to Japan as well as developing software in Shanghai. Wang Jie was in the first cohort of this program. He was assigned to a subsidiary of Mitsubishi Corp with a five-year contract. He lived in the software company's employee dormitory, an hour's train ride away from the office, and was paid a fraction of what a Japanese employee of his position was paid. His salary, according to his own understanding, only became comparable to the amount earned by his Japanese colleagues in the final year. After fulfilling the five-year contract, he became free and found a job in an IT department in a multinational firm in Tokyo.

Wang Jie was among the early technical recruits by Japanese corporations, and he arrived in Japan with a trainee visa. From the mid-1990s, with the increasing demand, the Japanese government encouraged the import of technical workers. Chinese immigrants arrived in Japan with intra-firm transfer visas or engineer visas. Many software companies appeared in China. Some had branches in both China and Japan, and served as overseas employment agencies, charging fees from both the Chinese programmers and the companies that hired them. Since the late 1990s, big Japanese firms such as Toyota and NTT have been recruiting graduates with science majors directly from the campuses of prestigious Chinese universities. Some new recruits work in Chinese branches of these multinational corporations and are then transferred to work on projects in Japan. Others are immediately flown to Japan to receive on-the-job technical and language training. Sixteen of my survey respondents and seven of the eleven IT people I interviewed arrived in Japan with engineer or intra-firm transfer visas. In Japan, the majority of foreign technical employees are from China.

In the field of technology, two types of transnational employees have emerged. One includes the bridge software engineers or, in some non-IT industries, bridge engineers. The IT workers that I have interviewed defined a bridge software engineer as a person who could design a program with Japanese clients and lead the Chinese programming team to complete the project. They pointed out that skills in software development and management and language and communication competence were crucial in fulfilling the role of a bridge software engineer. As a result, becoming a bridge software engineer is considered a milestone in the career path of a technical worker, a role that is increasingly in demand, and a type of vacancy many IT people aspire to fill.

Another type of transnational technical worker is emerging in the field of technology, often affiliated with firms that have either partners or branches in Japan. When there are demands for programmers in Japan, they go to Japan. Their stay in Japan depends on the length of a particular project and whether new projects are waiting to be staffed. Lin Feng, a young man I met in Tokyo, stayed in Tokyo for a stretch of two years working on two different projects. When his employer in Japan had no more projects lined up for him, he was recalled by his Chinese employer, a subsidiary of a state-owned corporate giant, to recuperate and participate in internal software development in China. During the three years I was in touch with him, he spent a total of eight months in China.

Career Mobility in the Occupational Niche

The occupational niche in the transnational economy where Chinese immigrants are situated is stratified, but the logic of mobility for Chinese transnational employees is different from that of Japanese employees in the same corporate structure. In Japan, until very recently, employee mobility was vertical, especially among men working in larger firms. Their structural locations mirrored their educational credentials and seniority. They also stayed put in the same company. In the mid-1990s, scholarly research about Japanese employee career mobility still reported an over 80 percent retention rate. Thus Japanese corporate employees, once hired, tended to remain with the same firm till retirement (Ishida *et al.*, 1997). The Chinese employees in corporate Japan, however, tend to move horizontally, and compared to their Japanese colleagues, are almost hyper-mobile. Such career mobility patterns on the one hand reflect a corporate Japan that wants to take advantage of these human resources in the transnational economy, but is not yet able to eliminate prejudice toward immigrants from China and to change the rigid corporate structure. On the other hand, they represent the immigrants' own calculation of the opportunities and stakes and their life aspirations. In this section, I focus on the analysis of overseas representatives and software engineers. These two groups' mobility patterns have a lot in common, but because of different employment channels and work styles they also have different career trajectories.

Horizontal mobility

Each of the occupational categories of "Overseas Representative" and "Bridge SE" contains a hierarchy within itself, with differentiation between support staff such as sales assistants, translators, and sales staff in the marketing business on the one hand, and programmers, SEs, and project managers in the IT industry on the other. However, Chinese people rarely advance internally along the corporate ladder, but rather migrate out to other business institutions. Two reasons can be seen for this phenomenon. First, Chinese employees tend to work for small- and medium-sized firms. As the Ministry of Justice's data shows, almost half of the foreign students who graduated from Japanese universities with doctoral, master's and bachelor's degrees since the late 1990s were employed in enterprises of fewer than 50 people. Their entry salaries were also decreasing over the years (Ministry of Justice, 2006). While in 1997 only a third of them were offered a monthly salary of less than 250,000 yen, in 2005 half of the students who were granted employment visas made less than 250,000 a month. Although there is no breakdown of the data according to nationality, it would be no surprise if over half of these Chinese employees were working for small firms and earning less than 250,000 a month, given that Chinese immigrants make up over 60 percent of those who succeeded in changing their status from students to employees. Upon graduation, in order to be able to stay in Japan, Chinese immigrants are not always in a position to choose employers or bargain for benefits. Since the majority of them are not from prestigious universities, they have limited access to big firms. The Ministry of Justice has a set of criteria for employment visas and one of them is earning a total annual income of more than 3 million yen. Several interviewees communicated that their employers would not have hired them if they had had to pay this much. Employers often manipulated the figures. Occasionally there would be two contracts with the Chinese employee, one for visa application purposes, and the other for real.

There are two consequences resulting from being employed in small- and medium-size firms. One is a short food chain. If a company consists of only a few dozen people, there is hardly room for promotion. The other problem with a small or medium-size firm is its lack of job security. With the economic downturn, many smaller firms have found it harder and harder to survive. They now turn toward the Chinese labor market for hope. They hire Chinese students in Japan in order to launch a business with China. However, with their own destiny still pending, they can hardly afford job security for their Chinese employees. As a consequence, Chinese employees of small Japanese firms tend to move out and look for jobs elsewhere when they can no long contain their frustration over lack of promotion and salary increments, or when they feel the company is in a precarious situation.

The second reason for Chinese employees' horizontal mobility is the blocked vertical career ladder. Many interviewees reported that despite their hard work, they had little chance for promotion because they were foreigners. By being foreigners, Chinese employees are considered temporary workers. Many are in fact contract employees, with no chance to experience the typical on-the-job training Japanese firms have been famous for. They are hired for their immediate utility. In the case of Qin Ailing, who worked for a multinational electronic appliances company's marketing department and enjoyed the same benefits as her Japanese peers, she was classified as a Type-B employee. She was neither a Type-A permanent employee as were most of her Japanese coworkers, nor a contract employee, but a non-Japanese employee whose tenure was indefinite and who was not required to sign up for a retirement pension. She could only become a Type-A employee if she became a Japanese citizen — a possibility she had been considering for several years. And despite her frequent trips between Japan and China and the excessive workload she shouldered, she was pessimistic about promotion in the immediate future.

As a consequence of negligible job security and promotion prospects in a small firm and the assumption of impermanence in bigger firms, Chinese immigrants rarely feel the need to commit to one employer, but keep their eyes open for better opportunities. The flourishing transnational economy creates enough vacancies for them to move to advance their careers. However, true hyper-mobility happens only to some, typically in the IT industry.

IT people move, and move around the globe. Three important conditions that have enabled IT people in Japan to move between employers to better their employment situations are, first, the sheer demand for their skills; second, the dense and vast professional networks; and third, the competitiveness of the market, and therefore the need to keep learning and updating one's knowledge. Chinese IT people in Japan are usually affiliated with the numerous IT resource firms — "soft-houses" in their own words (Wang, 2005). They staff projects in other companies and organizations. With the mushrooming of soft-houses, skilled individuals are in great demand. Other than looking for clients, soft-house owners are also in a constant search for programmers, both in Japan and in China. Each project usually recruits IT people from different soft-houses, and, individuals compare each other's houses and spread information about new job opportunities through on-the-job networks. Clients who establish their own projects sometimes also attract these individuals to become their permanent employees. Chinese immigrants rarely turn down such opportunities because these clients are often bigger companies who offer better benefits, more prestige, and higher job security. The other reason for IT people to move is the fear of becoming technologically obsolete. Therefore, after software engineers realize that their jobs have been reduced to system maintenance, they start to become anxious and aspire to change jobs. However, despite all these reasons for mobility, according to Wang's study of 60 Chinese IT professionals in Japan (Wang, 2005), only half of them changed jobs two or three times, although the lifetime employment history of close to two-thirds of all his research subjects was shorter than 10 years.

Vertical mobility

With the expansion of their company businesses in China, some Chinese employees in corporate Japan do get promoted. People in sales assistant roles can become sales representatives and enjoy international travel. However, according to my interviews, true promotion into leadership positions has happened mostly to men, especially men with permanent residency or naturalized citizens. Among the few people I interviewed who actually had a title other than the generic "overseas representative," one worked for a company of two dozen people that exclusively did business with China. He had obtained permanent residency and worked for the company for 16 years. The company basically relied on him for all business deals. He was given the title of division leader (*buchô*). Another man who worked for the overseas marketing department at a large steel company was given the position of group leader (*kachô*). He earned the title by actively acquiring clients in China independently. If he left, the company would lose most of their Chinese clients. Therefore, it seemed that those truly indispensable Chinese employees, usually men, with outstanding records may have a chance for promotion, especially if they show true commitment by becoming Japanese citizens. Shen Chao, the person who expanded his firm's business into China, was asked by his boss to naturalize in order to be entitled to a leadership role. "I showed them the kind of commitment they needed only by naturalization."

Among the technical people, corporate titles are less important than a person's actual tasks and whether they have a leadership role in a project. IT people accumulate licenses and work experience. Some also try to master the language. The important career milestone for Chinese IT people in Japan is to become a bridge software engineer. It is a leadership role that is both challenging and in great demand in the transnational IT business. It is a niche which is so far filled mostly by Chinese IT professionals who have work experience with Japanese clients and are familiar with Chinese culture and work style.

Going home

Going home is the pinnacle of a Chinese employee's transnational corporate career. For most Chinese, "home" means a big Chinese city, not necessarily the town they have left behind. Li Wei, who worked for the steel company mentioned above, was talking to his boss about sending him back to China to be in charge of one of their Chinese branches. Although growing up in northern China, he bought a condo in Shanghai and was hoping to move back in two or three years. He was being interviewed by other Japanese firms having branches in Shanghai or its surrounding area because his boss told him that the company headquarters needed him more than the branch did. He was willing to reduce his salary if he could be sent back to China. Japanese company logic is that, because it is cheaper to live in China, Chinese employees should expect less than they are paid in Japan. This logic does not apply to Japanese expatriates sent to China who usually go with better packages than they would have in Japan because they expect to keep the same lifestyle. Given that most Japanese goods have to be imported, they are paid higher salaries, not to mention that the company has to compensate them for the inconvenience of living in a foreign country. In fact, such a difference in logic has consequently created a niche for Chinese employees who have both work experience with Japanese firms and cultural familiarity with both countries. They are pseudo-expatriates, holding a status somewhere between Japanese expatriates and local employees.

Such is the dream position for most corporate male employees I have interviewed because they do not see themselves staying in Japan for the rest of their lives despite their permanent residency, Japanese spouses, and Japanese citizenship. One reason they gave for desiring to go home was to escape the stressful work environment and feeling of constraints (*ya yi*) in Japan, both because stress and constraints characterized Japanese social life according to their own experience and because they were immigrants in a country they perceived as "exclusive" and "narrow-minded." The other reason, of course, was that the amount of money and prestige they could have as pseudo-expatriates would allow them a cushy life in China and a social status they would never be able to enjoy in Japan. More practical reasons often involved children. Many of my interviewees had sent or wanted to send their children back to China for education.

Becoming transnational entrepreneurs

Transnational entrepreneurship is another desired option of career mobility. Many Chinese employees choose to become entrepreneurs when they have sufficient business networks or when some opportunities suddenly emerge. For Chinese IT professionals in Japan, transnational entrepreneurship is almost a natural career choice. Software development is a profession for the young, according to many software engineers, when one still has the brain power. Being a boss, on the other hand, is all about business experience and networks — something one accumulates with age. Some Chinese IT professionals have worked in the Japanese IT industry long enough to understand the ways it operates and have obtained enough access to clients. On the other hand, being closely connected to the IT industry in China through professional and social networks (such as classmate networks), they can cut the cost significantly by either expanding offshore production or recruiting programmers from China.

One important characteristic of the entrepreneurship taken up by former overseas representatives and other Chinese employees in sales and marketing is the close relationship between their corporate business and their own independent business (Liu Farrer, 2007a). A Chinese entrepreneur often starts his or her own company by working in the same type of business as their former employer, either as a competitor or as a supplier or client of their former boss. These Chinese entrepreneurs learn specific trade knowledge and skills through working for Japanese companies. For example, An (An, 1998) who imported construction material from China to Japan worked in a Japanese trading company in the same business for three years, first learning to prepare import and export documents and then moving on to sales and marketing. He realized that he alone could do the work shared among the 120 people in that company. He left the company and set up his own business. Fifteen entrepreneurs in my data continued the same business after they left their previous employers. Several others found their niche markets when they were working for a Japanese institution. In fact, corporate experience not only trained the immigrant entrepreneurs in their trade but also provided partners or a first group of employees in some cases. Several entrepreneurs took their former coworkers — their subordinates or supervisors — together with them when they left their former employers.

The mobility of corporate Chinese women

Chinese women in corporate Japan present a mixed picture regarding their career prospects. On the one hand, many Chinese women take up the so-called *sôgôshoku* — a career track that has mobility potential instead of *ippanshoku* — the dead-end career track in which many Japanese women are found (Brinton, 1992). Chinese women are frequently sales representatives traveling internationally. Some of my interviewees therefore believed being Chinese could actually give them leverage to overcome the gender barrier in the corporate structure. Anqi, a sales representative at a Japanese manufacturing company, took business trips by herself to Taipei and Shanghai almost every month. She said she was the only woman in her company who did not have to wear a cream-colored uniform, and she was the only woman employee in the marketing department.

On the other hand, some Chinese women are pessimistic about their career future in corporate Japan because of the double disadvantages of being both Chinese and women. Chen Lan, a woman who graduated from a private university, found employment with a medium-sized trading company in 1999. As Lan reported, "Although I am in charge of an important part of the company business, I can never become an office manager, let alone a branch manager. The Japanese men would be horrified with a Chinese woman sitting on top of them." Another informant Yao Lin left the trading firm where she had worked for 5 years when she turned 30. She said, "Japanese men are so very narrow-minded. Guess what the men in my company had said to me for years? '*Toshi mo soro soro, kekkon mo soro soro deshô*' (You are about the age. Get married soon). I couldn't stand it and had to quit."

Because of these two perceived disadvantages of being both a woman and a foreigner in corporate Japan, some career-minded women such as Yao Lin have chosen to become self-employed. In 2002 when I interviewed her she was 32, still single and the owner of a small trading firm. In 2005, Chen Lan also quit the trading firm and started her own business in the same trade, partnering with her former boss, the office manager. Other women kept changing firms. For example, Ailing, before joining one of the biggest electronic appliance companies, had worked for both a real estate giant and a policy institute. Both of her previous employers had prestige in Japan. However, she considered the corporate culture in both companies oppressively male-dominated. She chose her latest employer because it was in high-tech business and therefore hopefully more progressive.

As a step in the mobility process, "going home" for Chinese men means being sent back to a big Chinese city as a pseudo-expatriate. However, for women, it often means quitting the job and taking up a domestic role. Lin Yueling was once a magazine editor in China. She obtained a master's degree in a Japanese university and started working for a Japanese firm as a sales representative. Although a natural career choice for a Chinese person with her background, Yueling did not like sales and found her work environment stressful. Feeling miserable, she accepted the first marriage proposal that came her way. She did not love the man she married, but marrying him meant she could leave her corporate job and still live in Japan. As much as she dreaded working in a Japanese company, she also dreaded the idea of going back to China carrying the same suitcase but with added age. She did not know what she could have found in China. When I met her, she was several years into marriage, and a part-time Chinese teacher.

Conclusion

This chapter has discussed the occupational niches for Chinese employees in corporate Japan's transnational economy. The existence of such a group and the fact that their population has been rapidly expanding has theoretical significance for both international migration studies and social mobility research. They represent a new pattern of transnational economic adaptation, indicating that a labor market niche is emerging for bilingual or multilingual immigrants, particularly international students in the global economy. Their mobility outcomes suggest that economic globalization has created a multiscalar transnational labor market. Within it, there are not only the globe-trotting corporate elites moving within the multinational corporate structure; but also individuals from different backgrounds occupying a hierarchy of positions.

Specifically, the case of Chinese employees in corporate Japan shows that many of these transnational employees are, on the one hand, presented with unprecedented opportunities brought about by increasing demand for their cultural and linguistic competences in the expansion of the transnational economy. On the other hand, they carry the baggage and stigma of immigrants in a previously ethnically homogeneous corporate structure. They have to confront many social and organizational constraints and advance their careers through frequent compromises and alternatives. Their lack of bargaining power in employment — lower wages, entering predominantly small firms, difficulty in vertical mobility, and being sent abroad as pseudo-expatriates — all indicate that they are still branded with the mark of immigrants from a developing country. The occupational opportunities available to Chinese women and the career mobility withheld from them further signal the tension of a labor market position marked by uncertain careers sandwiched between occupational privilege and social and institutional prejudice.

References

An, Jianxing (1998). "Ye cao de zhong zi [The Seeds of Grass]." In *Fu ji dong ying xie chun qiu* [*Writing History in Japan*], edited by Duan Yaozhong, pp. 1–8. Shanghai: Shanghai Education Press.

Beaverstock, Jonathan V. (2005). "Transnational Elites in the City: British Highly-Skilled Inter-Company Transferees in New York City's Financial District." *Journal of Ethnic and Migration Studies* 31(2): 245–268.

Belson, Ken (2004). "Japanese Capital and Jobs Flowing to China." *New York Times*, February 17, 2004.

Brinton, Mary C. (1992). *Women and the Economic Miracle: Gender and Work in Postwar Japan*. Berkeley, California: University of California Press.

Cervantes, Miguel de and Dominique Guellec (2002). "International Mobility of Highly Skilled Workers: From Statistical Analysis to Policy Formation." Paper presented at the *International Mobility of the Highly Skilled*, OECD, Paris.

Findlay, Allan M. and F.L.N. Li (1998). "A Migration Channels Approach to the Study of Professionals Moving to and From Hong Kong." *International Migration Review* 32(3): 682–703.

Finn, Michael G. (2001). "Stay Rates of Foreign Doctorate Recipients from U.S. Universities, 2001." Oak Ridge Institute for Science and Education, www.orau.gov/orise/pubs/stayrate03.pdf (accessed January 29, 2007).

Guarnizo, Luis E. and Michael P. Smith (1998). "The Locations of Transnationalism." In *Transnationalism from Below*, edited by Michael Peter Smith and Luis E. Guarnizo, pp. 3–34. New Brunswick, New Jersey: Transaction Publishers.

Hagan, Jacqueline and Helen Rose Ebaugh (2003). "Calling Upon the Sacred: Migrants' Use of Religion in the Migration Process." *International Migration Review* 37(4): 1145–1162.

Ishida, Hiroshi, Seymour Spilerman and Kuo-Hsieu Su (1997). "Educational Credentials in Promotion Chances in Japanese and American Organizations." *American Sociological Review* 62: 866–882.

Itzigsohn, Jose, Carlos Dore Cabral, Estner Hernandez Medina and Obed Vazquez (1999). "Mapping Dominican Transnationalism: Narrow and Broad Transnational Practices." *Ethnic and Racial Studies* 22: 316–339.

JASSO (2004). Gaikokujin Ryûgakusei Shinrô Nado Jôkyô (Heisei 16 nendoban). Tokyo: Japan Student Services Organization, available online at www.jasso. go.jp/statistics/intl_student/data05_d.html.

Landolt, Patricia, Lilian Autler and Sonia Baires (1999). "From 'Hermano Lejano' to 'Hermano Mayor': The Dialectics of Salvadoran Transnationalism." *Ethnic and Racial Studies* 22: 290–315.

Levitt, Peggy (1998). "Local-level Global Religion: The Case of U.S.-Dominican Migration." *Journal for the Scientific Study of Religion* 37(1): 74–89.

Light, Ivan, Min Zhou and Rebecca Kim (2002). "Transnationalism and American Exports in an English-Speaking World." *International Migration Review* 36: 702–725.

Liu Farrer, Gracia (2007a). "Producing Global Economies from Below: Chinese Immigrant Entrepreneurship in Japan." In *Deciphering the Global: Its Spaces, Scalings, and Subjects*, edited by Saskia Sassen, pp. 257–281. London: Routledge.

Liu Farrer, Gracia (2007b). "Educationally Channeled International Labor Migration: Post-1978 Student Mobility From China to Japan." PhD diss., University of Chicago.

Portes, Alejandro (2003). "Conclusion: Theoretical Convergencies and Empirical Evidence in the Study of Immigrant Transnationalism." *International Migration Review* 37: 874–892.

Portes, Alejandro, Louise E. Guarnizo and William J. Haller (2002). "Transnational Entrepreneurs: An Alternative Form of Immigrant Adaptation." *American Sociological Review* 67: 278–298.

Saxenia, Annalee (2002). "Brain Circulation: How High-Skill Immigration Makes Everyone Better Off." *The Brookings Review* 20(1): 8–31.

Wang, Jin (2005). "Nihon no gaikokujin kôdô jinzai dônyû seisaku to zainichi Chugokujin — Chugokujin IT gijyutsusha ni taisuru jitai chôsa o chûshin ni" [Japan's Policies towards Importing Highly Skilled Foreign Manpower and the Chinese in Japan — Research about Chinese IT Engineers]. In *Chûgokukei ijyûsha kara mita Nihonshakai no shomondai* [*Japanese Social Problems in the Eyes of Chinese Migrants*], edited by Tajima Junko, pp. 87–107. Tokyo: Research Foundation for Safe Society.

Xiang, Biao (2003). "Indian Information Technology Professionals' World System: the Nation and the Transnation in Individuals' Migration Strategies." In *State/Nation/Transation: Perspectives on Transnationalism in the Asia-Pacific*, edited by Brenda S.A. Yeoh and Katie Willis, pp. 161–178. London: Routledge.

Ziguras, Christopher and Siew-Fang Law (2006). "Recruiting International Students as Skilled Migrants: The Global 'Skills Race' as Viewed from Australia and Malaysia." *Globalisation, Societies and Education* 4(1): 59–76.

CHAPTER 9

MULTICULTURAL COEXISTENCE POLICIES:
RESPONSES OF LOCAL GOVERNMENTS IN THE
TOKYO METROPOLITAN AREA TO THE PRESSURES
OF INTERNATIONAL IMMIGRATION

Stephen Robert Nagy

Introduction

Globalization has had broad and diverse effects on all nations. Significant effects include increased interdependence between nations in the realms of economics, politics, and security. As a consequence of economic interdependence, nations around the world including Japan have been compelled either to have an official immigration policy or to accept migrant laborers, since nations receive "substantial benefit from immigration in terms of economic growth, demographic revitalization, and maintenance of international status and influence" (Huntington, 2004, 180). These essential migrant workers usually find work in industries that are having difficulty in finding native laborers and Japan is no exception to this trend.[1]

The scale of international migration is difficult to measure. However, according to the 2003 report of the International Organization for Migration (IOM), as of 2000, 175 million people were separated from their mother countries. That number increased to 192 million in 2006 and by 2050, it is

---

[1]In 1999, the United Nations (UN) and the Japanese Government estimated a shortfall of approximately 600,000 workers a year beginning in the early 21st century. Considering the declining birthrate in Japan, the only viable means of counteracting this trend is to receive foreign laborers, which has very significant implications for Japanese society as a whole. http://www.un.org/esa/population/publications/ migration/japan.pdf (accessed February 16th, 2005).

estimated that this figure will rise to 230 million, with Japan again being no exception to this global trend.[2]

What is driving this migration? In the case of Japan, the economic gap between the country and its neighbors has been a significant force behind the legal and illegal flows of migrant workers to Japan in an era of globalization. This flow accelerated after the 1985 Plaza Accord which inflated the value of the yen, resulting in an increased economic gap between Japan and her neighbors. Also, instability in the Middle East contributed to making Japan a more attractive destination for migrant laborers, as did a revision of Japanese immigration policy to allow individuals of Japanese ancestry (up to the third generation) to return to Japan for work. Furthermore, the dynamics of "push-pull relationships" (Tullao and Cortez, 2003) have further contributed to the increase in Japan's foreign migrant population, as well as the increasing ease of communication and transportation. In concrete terms, the population of foreign residents has seen a steady increase in overall numbers in Japan, from 1,121,672 registered foreigners in 2002 to 1,997,459 in 2006.[3]

As of 2005, Japan's population began to decline owing to low birth rates, a reality that will affect the country's future economic vitality (*The Economist* 2005: 29–30). Like other nations, Japan is using foreign workers to compensate for this trend and as a result it has revised its immigration policy to compensate for its labor shortage.[4] According to the Statistics Bureau of Japan, the number of foreigners living, working and studying in Japan reached 2,084,919 in 2006 representing 1.63% of the total population.[5] This figure does not include the number of known illegal foreign residents which according to the Ministry of Justice had climbed to 207,299 in 2006.[6] Moreover, the number of foreign residents could be much higher

---

[2]International Organization for Migration: http://www.iom.int/jahsa/page3.html (accessed October 12th, 2006).

[3]The Ministry of Justice. "Immigration Control 2007." http://www.moj.go.jp (accessed March 30th, 2008).

[4]See the Japanese Ministry of Justice Homepage for a complete explanation of the Immigration and Refugee Recognition Act. http://www.moj.go.jp/ENGLISH/IB/STANDARD/standard01.html (accessed November 15th, 2005).

[5]Ministry of Justice http://www.moj.go.jp/PRESS/070921-1/070921-1.pdf (accessed April 30th, 2008).

[6]Ministry of Justice Homepage: http://www.moj.go.jp/English/issues/issues05.html (accessed September 16th, 2006).

if we consider those children who come from international marriages called *daburu*[7] in Japan (Suzuki, 2004: 23–25).

In the Tokyo Metropolitan Area (TMA), the foreign population had climbed to approximately 360,000 in 2005, almost 3 percent of the total metropolitan population (Sômushô, 2006). More strikingly, in some wards of the TMA, foreigners represent nearly 10 percent of the total municipal population and the proportion is expected to rise in the coming years (Shinjuku Bunka/Kokusai Kôryû Zaidan, 2004).

This increased presence of foreigners residing in Japan, in particular in the TMA, is threatening the supposed culturally homogenous social fabric of Japan. This threat is often articulated as the *gaikokujin mondai* or "problem of foreigners." Education, living conditions, discrimination and racism, housing, finding work, receiving and paying for social welfare programs, and parent-child linguistic and cultural gaps are but a few of the dilemmas that have been associated with the *gaikokujin mondai* since as early as 1984 (Kanagawa Kennai Zaijû Gaikokujin Jittai Chôsa Iinkai, 1985). This is especially true because the TMA has a larger proportion of *newcomers* than other parts of Japan (Suzuki, 2004).

European scholars have voiced their concern over this phenomenon arguing that increased numbers of foreigners can affect "societal security" (Waiver *et al.*, 1993: 23), or more specifically, "the ability of a society to persist in its essential character under changing conditions and possible or actual threat," and "the sustainability, within acceptable conditions for evolution, of traditional patterns of language, culture association, and religious and national identity and custom" (Ibid.). The continued debate over the Muslim scarf and its acceptability in France, and the recent protests over caricatures of the prophet Mohammed published in Denmark are two examples of challenges to European societal security, including national identity and custom, and in particular the traditions of freedom of speech and religion.

Similarly, Huntington stresses that the benefits of immigrants and migrants in the United States can be "negated by costs of high spending on government services, fewer jobs, lower wages, and reduced benefits

---

[7]*Daburu* is the Japanese pronunciation of "Double." It refers to children who have one Japanese parent and one non-Japanese parent. Children who have two parents from different countries but whose parents are not of Japanese nationality are called "international children" or just "foreign children." See: Tabunka Kyôsei Ki-wa-do Jiten Henshû Iinkai (2004: 71).

for native workers, social polarization, cultural conflict, decline in trust in the community, and erosion of traditional concepts of national identity" (Huntington, 2004: 180). He asserts that unbalanced and uncontrolled immigration or migration can weaken the foundations of the United States, especially those religious and socio-economic pillars that have contributed to the development of the United States.

Japanese scholars have also expressed their concern over Japanese societal security, although they usually emphasize issues related to employment and the erosion of national identity. The Japanese "societal security" focus has evolved to center on multicultural coexistence, a response to the cultural misunderstandings and social welfare issues arising from the *gaigokokujin mondai* (So, 2000: 19–38). Unfortunately, the *gaikokujin mondai* has also come to include the misperception of a growing crime rate by foreigners (Herbert, 1996).

The societal security focus in Japan has contributed to (and is perhaps also derived from) a greater role for local governments in dealing with the *gaikokujin mondai*. By expanding the kinds of activities that fall under the rubric of internationalization to include multicultural coexistence, local governments are in the process of creating an infrastructure to integrate foreigners into Japanese communities. This infrastructure includes programs providing assistance relating to communication, lifestyle, and creating and building facilities to promote multicultural coexistence in cities.

This chapter will examine the multicultural coexistence policies, which are collectively called *tabunka kyôsei seisaku*, carried out by three local governments in the TMA, Shinjuku Ward, Adachi Ward, and Tachikawa City, in response to the pressures of migration, in order to develop a better understanding of the kinds of policies and measures that are being instituted to manage increased numbers of foreign residents living, working, and settling in Japan.

Multicultural Coexistence in Three Areas of Tokyo

Multicultural coexistence policy has in one form or another been a part of Japan since the 1960s. Despite this historical background, official plans and policies have only just been introduced in local government. At the national level, things are moving at a slower pace, with the Ministry of

Internal Affairs and Communications releasing an official policy report on the promotion of multicultural coexistence in March 2006. Shinjuku, Adachi, and Tachikawa are examples of local governments that have promulgated *tabunka kyôsei* plans as of 2006. Each has a particular focus and orientation that meets each municipality's needs and direction.

Multicultural coexistence in Shinjuku Ward

Shinjuku Ward has a population of which 9.72 percent are foreign, and this proportion is expected to increase to 30 percent in the coming years (Shinjuku Bunka/Kokusai Kôryû Zaidan, 2004). According to the 2004 statistics, Shinjuku's total population was around 300,000, with nearly 30,000 registered as foreigners.[8] Moreover, compared with 1995, Shinjuku Ward's registered foreign population had increased by 50.3 percent, from 18,815 in 1995 to 28,272 in 2005.[9] In contrast with other wards in the TMA, Shinjuku has by far the largest and most diverse population of foreigners, surpassing its nearest rival, Adachi Ward, by almost 7,000 foreign residents.[10]

Based on a report on policies toward foreigners (Shinjuku Ward, 2006), Shinjuku identified several areas where multicultural coexistence initiatives could be applied, including problem areas where people were dissatisfied.

The specific measures taken to achieve these objectives include: (1) assistance for Japanese language education, (2) the publication and collection of living and lifestyle information, and (3) the promotion of networks in Shinjuku Ward.

As part and parcel of realizing these specific measures, Shinjuku Ward established the Shinjuku Multicultural Coexistence Plaza, a center for information exchange, advisory services, Japanese and foreign language instruction, and cultural exchange events. Through the quasi-governmental

---

[8]For a complete breakdown of the statistics on the registered foreigner population of Shinjuku which, as of January 2004, was 29,143, see http://www.city.shinjuku.tokyo.jp/division/26010chishin/toukei/toukeihyo/2004/04hyo04.xls (accessed October 13th, 2005).

[9]This material was obtained at the February 2006 International Exchange Forum Conference in Tokyo, Japan in which a representative from Shinjuku Ward gave a lecture on the multicultural coexistence policies in Shinjuku Ward.

[10]http://www.toukei.metro.tokyo.jp/tnenkan/2003/tn03qytia0140.xls (accessed October 4th, 2005).

Table 9.1.   Multicultural coexistence-related projects and budget in Shinjuku Ward.

Event/Project	Budget	Description
International Understanding Project	646,000 yen	Promote international understanding through lectures, seminars, and school seminars
Multicultural Disaster Training	932,000 yen	Disaster training for foreign residents
Multicultural Coexistence Project	2,781,000 yen	Disaster training for foreigners, post-multilingual information on homepage, seminars
Japanese Language Classes	4,380,000 yen	Management of volunteer Japanese language classes for foreign residents
Foreign Advisory Service	8,195,000 yen	Multilingual advisory services for foreigners
Multilingual Publications	14,187,000 yen	Multilingual publications providing lifestyle, administrative and culture information to residents of Shinjuku Ward

Source: Tokyo Kokusai Kôryû Dantai Renraku Kaigi (2005).

Shinjuku Foundation for Culture and International Exchange (Shinjuku Bunka/Kokusai Kôryû Zaidan), Shinjuku Ward has budgeted for international understanding projects, international exchange programs, and multicultural coexistence projects as well as others, of which Table 9.1 presents an abbreviated list.

The activities and projects that Shinjuku Ward is pursuing in its overall multicultural coexistence objectives demonstrate the Ward's commitment to ensuring that foreign residents do not become a burden to the municipal government and the Japanese residents of Shinjuku. Japanese language classes and cultural classes provide participating residents with the rudimentary skills they need to maneuver through the complexities of life in Japan as foreign residents. Multilingual advisory services and publications also complement these projects by ensuring that all resident foreigners are aware of their rights and responsibilities as residents of Shinjuku.

The rationale behind these kinds of information, publications, and advisory services is that if foreigners are kept abreast of their rights and responsibilities, and if they have language and cultural skills, they will not cause intercultural friction or be a burden on the Shinjuku local government and community. This strategy includes participation in social welfare, pensions, and national healthcare schemes, and the provision of education and child subsidies providing language and culture training as well as multilingual services is meant to decrease the chances that foreign workers will be exploited, and to increase their ability and desire to seek medical, legal, and other kinds of services when the need arises.

Shinjuku recognizes that the proportion of foreign residents living there will increase in the coming years, and that without the necessary infrastructure these new residents will find integration into Shinjuku challenging, either in the short or long term. Multicultural coexistence activities such as those mentioned above temper the severity of this challenge, attenuating the cultural friction that may occur and limiting the potentially negative impact that poorly integrated foreign residents may have.

In responses to questionnaires and interviews, I found that Shinjuku remained opposed to the idea of voting rights for all residents and voting rights for long-term residents. More significantly though, the Managing Director of International Exchange at Shinjuku's Shinjuku Foundation for Culture and International Exchange suggested in an interview that:

> Multicultural coexistence and internationalization policy are not about creating a municipality that foreigners want to come to, rather they are about maintaining the integrity of the Japanese community, ensuring that the foreigners that do settle temporarily or for the long term do not disrupt the traditional patterns of Japanese life. Multicultural coexistence programs provide foreign residents with knowledge about Japanese customs and manners so they can avoid causing problems with Japanese residents. Moreover, the Multicultural Coexistence and Internationalization Policy is not about voting rights for foreigners. (Interview conducted in September 21st, 2006)

These views on multicultural coexistence are not entirely inconsistent with Shinjuku's approach to planning and implementing multicultural coexistence policy and activities. As highlighted in Table 9.1, Shinjuku financially prioritizes programs that inform foreign residents of their rights and, more importantly, their obligations. This is exemplified in the monthly multi-lingual publication called *Shinjuku News* that informs foreign residents of when and how to pay taxes, where to get vaccinations, how to enroll in national health insurance and social insurance programs, the correct way to dispose of rubbish, and the cultural expectations of the Shinjuku community.

The investment in Japanese language programs for foreigners also illus-trates Shinjuku's limited but inclusive multicultural coexistence policy and activities. Like other wards in the TMA, Shinjuku Ward organizes, liaises with, and provides support for foreigners in the form of facilities and net-working. In terms of budgetary prioritization, Japanese language classes for foreigners are deemed important enough to devote nearly 4.5 million yen to them, with the rationale that, with familiarity and Japanese skills, foreigners will cause less disruption, as they will be more independent.

It should be mentioned that the Japanese language classes offered by Shinjuku and most of the other municipalities in the TMA are not the equiv-alent of English as a Second Language (ESL) or in Japan's case, Japanese as a Second Language (JSL). Rather, they are introductory and interme-diate Japanese conversation courses that aim to facilitate the lives of for-eigners living in Japan. This quasi-commitment to language training raises the question of the degree to which foreign residents can fully access the Shinjuku community with only rudimentary Japanese language skills.

Despite this shortcoming, Shinjuku's multicultural coexistence strategies and initiatives include multilingual publications to ensure that important information is conveyed to all residents. The most recent focus has been on "multicultural disaster training."[11] This program was conceived following the Hanshin Earthquake in 1995, which highlighted the fact that the most vulnerable residents in disaster situations are the old, the sick, the disabled, and the foreign residents, who are often handicapped by limited linguistic skills, cultural savvy, and integration into the community.[12]

---

[11]"Multicultural disaster training is in fact the direct translation of an expression frequently used to describe multilingual disaster training. (Interview conducted on September 21st, 2006.) See *Shinjuku News* No. 6, September 25, 2006 on page 7 for further information on what is offered in a "Multicultural Coexistence Disaster Prevention Drill."

[12]The Director of International Affairs from the Ministry of Internal Affairs and Commu-nication gave a lecture on the Development of Internationalization in February 2006 at the International Exchange Forum Conference in Tokyo, Japan in which he discussed the most

To prevent a similar tragedy from occurring in Shinjuku, the Ward has provided nearly a million yen for multicultural disaster training and nearly 15 million yen for multilingual publications that provide information on what to do in the case of a disaster. Not withstanding the quality and volume of information that has been produced for foreign residents, the Managing Director of International Exchange stated that Shinjuku still faces challenges in getting this information out to foreign residents, getting them to participate in training exercises, and making them aware of community facilities and preparations in case of emergencies.

What is more, the Managing Director told me that this information and participation barrier was compounded by already existing foreign resident communities. For example, Filipinos that settled into Shinjuku accessed other Filipinos through church communities, where they received information on Shinjuku, the TMA and Japan in general. Similarly, those of Korean origin networked with already existing Korean communities, while Chinese networked with existing Chinese communities, to find work, information, and camaraderie. Despite these alternative institutions, the Ward organizes disaster training for foreign residents at least once a year, in Japanese, Chinese, English, and Korean languages.

On the cultural side, Shinjuku is implementing an initiative to create a society in which all cultures are respected and openly practiced through cultural exchange events, international festivals, and foreign language classes. Activities still tend to oppose Japanese culture to foreign cultures, diminishing the sense of togetherness or multicultural coexistence as a community, as illustrated by events such as the Japanese speech contests for foreigners. This juxtaposition of cultures and the treatment of foreigners as what Nobue Suzuki describes as an "undifferentiated mass" (Suzuki, 1995: 158) raise questions as to whether or not multicultural coexistence policies are truly emphasizing pluralism or whether they are implementing a kind of limited pluralism.

Interestingly, Shinjuku organizes its multicultural coexistence policies and practices collectively and comprehensively. Specifically, no less than 21 departments, sections, foundations, or municipal facilities are involved in

---

vulnerable residents in the case of a disaster. For information on the number of foreigners who died during the Hanshin earthquake, see also Gaikokujin Jishin Jôhô Sentaa (1996: 179–180). Tabunka Kyôsei Ki-wa-do Jiten Henshû Iinkai (2004: 128–129).

multicultural coexistence policy and practice.[13] Each administrative bureau proposes its own multicultural coexistence activities. For example, the taxation department publishes material on how to pay residential income tax, the health department provides information on AIDS prevention in multiple languages, and the department of education provides supplementary Japanese language instruction, and has produced a multilingual CD guide on "Japanese school lifestyle." Most innovatively, Shinjuku's attempts to ensure that all foreigners are educated about how to manage and succeed in their lives in Shinjuku have resulted in the production of a multilingual video.[14]

Although each section maximizes opportunities for foreign residents to fully integrate themselves into mainstream Japanese life through inclusionary lifestyle assistance programs, there is the noteworthy absence of the electoral department in this process. This again symbolizes Shinjuku's commitment to only limited inclusion, by not granting or even considering some form of political participation for foreign residents — and more significantly, long-term permanent residents.

Examining Shinjuku's multicultural policies and activities, we see that they do promote a degree of inclusionism and pluralism. Foreign residents are now able to access all administrative services, no longer handicapped by linguistic barriers. Moreover, both their human rights and to a certain degree their civic rights have been protected, with access to all social welfare programs, education, and other local government services. However, even long-term residents have not been given the right to vote, or be represented.

---

[13]This list includes the Culture and International Section and the Culture and International Manager, the Shinjuku Culture and International Exchange Foundation, the Administration Information Section, the Disaster Management Section, the Taxation Section, the National Health Insurance Section, and the Commerce and Tourism Section. See Shinjuku Ward (2006).

[14]This Shinjuku information video was produced in 2002. It features local foreign residents from different nationalities explaining to new foreign residents about how to get a foreign registration card, how to enroll in national health insurance, the proper way to dispose of rubbish, the appropriate way to live in harmony with Japanese neighbors, social rules and expectations, and what to do in a disaster, amongst others. Significantly, the short information video has been produced in English, Chinese and Korean languages to reach the maximum number of newcomers. http://www.city.shinjuku.tokyo.jp/koho/video/No51/index.html (accessed August 6th, 2006).

In terms of pluralism, Shinjuku is making attempts to ensure that all cultures existing in Shinjuku can be expressed openly through cultural exchange programs, the establishment of the Shinjuku Multicultural Center, and by holding foreign language classes. Still, the penchant for separating Japanese culture and Japanese residents from foreign residents sets up a dichotomy, a guest versus host paradigm which places the two groups in opposition to each other. In this sense, Shinjuku's multicultural coexistence policies and practices are embodiments of both limited inclusionism and pluralism.

When asked what areas Shinjuku would like to pursue via internationalization, the Managing Director identified five areas: the promotion of deeper international understanding; the inclusion of more foreign residents in the planning, implementation, and initiation of internationalization programs; the promotion of foreign residents in local civil society; multicultural coexistence; and stronger support from the national government. Current obstacles to more effective internationalization were identified as insufficient funding and financial support; a lack of interest on the part of both foreign and Japanese residents; lack of support from national government; and the current official employment system that transfers personnel every two years' and which presents a huge challenge in terms of creating and maintaining a long-term vision.

A plethora of explanations exist for the lack of participation of foreign and Japanese residents in Shinjuku Ward's internationalization activities. First, as previously mentioned, foreigners who settle in Shinjuku gravitate to ethnic centers, where they can get information in their own languages, find employment, and communicate in their mother tongues. As a result, these foreigners unintentionally isolate themselves from Shinjuku society at large.

Another important factor in the lack of involvement in Shinjuku could be the issues of visa status and the fear of forced repatriation. These are apparent in services, information, and programs aimed at those worried about their visa status.[15]

---

[15]For example, within the TMA, a legal advisory service called the Tokyo Relay has been organized, a rotating free legal advisory service offered to all foreign residents (both legal and illegal), involving collaboration between local governments such as Adachi, Shinjuku, and Tachikawa throughout the TMA and the Japan Lawyers Association, as well as local language volunteers. Included in the advisory service is free legal advice in several areas,

Lastly, apathy and resignation are often cited as reasons for not becoming more involved in the local community. In interviews conducted in 2003 in Shinjuku as part of Shinjuku's efforts to find a direction for their multicultural coexistence policies, many foreign residents voiced their opinion that they wanted to participate in Shinjuku society but felt that it was difficult owing to cultural differences between themselves and the Japanese. They also lacked opportunities to participate and felt that participation was not as co-residents of Shinjuku, but as guests and hosts.[16]

Although these policies and practices are limited, they do agree in part with Shinjuku Ward's Internationalization Policy:

> In a basic attempt to create culture and internationalize the local community, the foundation was laid for the purpose of cultivating and refining local culture along with creating a local community in which Japanese and foreign residents can live together by developing a deeper, mutual understanding of each others' culture and customs. (Lifestyle and Culture Bureau of the Tokyo Metropolitan Government, 2000: 12)

The difference between the ideals of Shinjuku's internationalization policy and multicultural coexistence policy and practice is that, while the former emphasizes inclusion of all residents in the Shinjuku community, respecting and understanding each others' cultures, the latter realizes these objectives only to a limited degree.

Multicultural coexistence in Adachi Ward

Adachi Ward highlights the relevance of its multicultural coexistence policy from two perspectives. First and foremost, Adachi has demonstrated quantifiably that a multicultural coexistence policy has become a necessity, given that its population of registered foreign residents had increased

---

including immigration, labor-related matters, and divorce. Volunteer interpreters interview participating foreigners, identify the area of law in which they need counsel, and then act as interpreters for the foreign residents during their discussions with the attending lawyers. The most important and most challenging aspect of the Tokyo Relay is ensuring that participants understand and have faith in the organizers, and that no matter what their visa status may be, they are guaranteed anonymity.

[16]For the complete transcripts of interviews conducted in Shinjuku Ward see, Shinjuku Bunka/Kokusai Kôryû Zaidan (2003). Similar views are echoed by foreigners living in other wards such as Bunkyo Ward. See Bunkyo Ku Gaikokuseki Kumin no Sumiyasusa Chôsa Iinkai (2004: 125–142).

to 21,405 as of 1st January, 2006 (Adachi Ku Kuminbu, 2006). This was nearly a three-fold increase in the number of resident foreigners since 1980.

Significantly, in 1980, 95.6 percent of the foreign population were ethnic Koreans (Ibid.). However, beginning in the 1980s, "newcomers," primarily from China and the Philippines, began to settle in Adachi because of the relatively inexpensive cost of living. Currently, the demographic distribution has altered dramatically since the 1980s, with ethnic Koreans ("oldcomers") representing only 41.7 percent of the foreign resident population (Ibid.). The next two largest groups of foreigners are the Chinese with 28.5 percent, and the Filipinos with 17.0 percent. Other significant numbers include Thais (1.8 percent), Brazilians (1.5 percent), Pakistanis (0.9 percent), Americans (0.8 percent), and Vietnamese (0.8 percent). By 2025, Adachi Ward's foreign population is predicted to rise to 40,000, or 6.7 percent of the total municipal population (Ibid.). Perhaps even more surprisingly, by 2050 the foreign population is predicted to rise to 70,000, or approximately 14.7 percent of the total population (Ibid.). This figure is even higher than some countries with a history of immigration (see Table 9.2). With this expected rise in the

Table 9.2. Percentage of immigrants in Britain, France, Germany, the United States, Australia, and Japan compared with Tokyo, Adachi Ward, Shinjuku Ward, and Tachikawa City.

Country, Region or Ward	Foreign population (estimated)
Britain	4.6% (1999)*
France	5.5% (1999)*
Germany	9.7% (2002)*
United States	12.1% (2005)*
Australia	21.8% (2001)*
Japan	1.6% (2004)□
Tokyo Metropolitan	2.8% (2004)□
Shinjuku Ward	9.72% (2004) ▲
Adachi Ward	6.7% (2005)○
Tachikawa City	1.83% (2005)●

Sources: *ILO website, Center for Immigration Studies website, US Census Bureau; □ Sômushô (2006); ▲ Shinjuku Bunka/Kokusai Kôryû Zaidan (2003); ○ Adachi Ku Kuminbu (2006); ● Tachikawa Shi Sangyô Bunkabu Shimin Katsudôka (2005).

foreign population and in particular the prediction that the newcomers will be predominantly of Asian origin, Adachi Ward is predicting that problems associated with national health care, education, and housing will occur, as seen in the past.

Indeed, Adachi has been transformed since the 1980s from a predominately Japanese Ward to one that hosts a large and diverse population of foreign residents. This increased number of foreigners has impacted Adachi citizens. According to the 34th Annual Household Census[17] of August 2005, which included a survey on multicultural coexistence, 14.1 percent of Japanese residents "hope for the number of foreigners to increase in the future," 61.4 percent "don't care either way" and 22.3 percent "hope that the number of foreigners does not change" (Adachi Ku Kuminbu, 2006).

Those who were positive about the number of foreigners increasing in Adachi cited increased chances for cultural exchange, including language exchanges, as the rationale for their answer. Those who replied negatively cited worries about increased crime, differences related to cultural and lifestyle, differences with regard to thinking, and finally increased social costs (Ibid.).

In this survey, enquiries were made related to the manner in which the municipal government should carry out its internationalization program. Adachi citizens were asked about the following initiatives (see Table 9.3) (Ibid.). The responses are indicative of Japanese residents' awareness of foreign residents living in Adachi Ward. Moreover, these responses highlight what Japanese residents feel should be prioritized vis-à-vis the integration of foreigners into Adachi Ward, with language training, Japanese culture and rule awareness, and advisory services being at the top of the agenda.

The citizens' responses to this 2005 survey have been incorporated to some extent into multicultural coexistence policy and practice. As shown in the responses to the questionnaire and interviews conducted with the Coordinating Manager of Adachi's Multicultural Coexistence Management Section, the Ward has prioritized promotion of world peace, mutual

---

[17]The formal Japanese name is: *Dai 34 Adachi Kusei ni kan suru Yoron Chôsa (Tabunka Kyôsei ni Kan suru Bubun)*.

Table 9.3. Adachi residents' responses to the future direction of international-ization in Adachi Ward and priority areas for municipal government.

Questions related to the future direction of internationalization in Adachi Ward and what area the municipal government should prioritize its resources.	Those who responded positively to the following questions
1 Increase foreigner advisory services at the city hall reception windows	96%
2 Strengthen the Japanese language programs for those foreigners who cannot speak Japanese	70.5%
3 Hold seminars/courses on lifestyle rules in Japan	64.1%
4 Increase the amount of information available in foreign languages at municipal facilities	64.0%
5 Expand the cultural exchange activities at Adachi's International Festival	39.9%
6 Expand assistance to foreigners starting companies or interested in working	37.3%
7 Enrich education related to foreign cultures and languages at local schools and in the local municipality	37.0%
8 Promote citizen-based international exchange, cultivate an international exchange group	32.8%
9 Increase chances for foreign residents to share their views and participate politically	23.6%
10 Establish a regulation which systemizes the promotion of Internationalization	14.1%

Source: Adachi Ku Kuminbu. Kokuminka (2006).

understanding, the "internationalization" of the local community, facili-tating the lives of foreigners, promoting more interaction between foreigners and Japanese, and creating a multicultural coexistent society.

Moreover, when asked about the direction of evolution of Adachi Ward's internationalization program, the Coordinating Manager agreed that the overall direction of policy has changed from an emphasis on cultural pro-grams to one of supporting local foreign residents. However, despite this transition, Adachi's internationalization program still emphasizes interna-tional understanding and cultural programs, and according to the Managing

Director, would like to introduce these kinds of programs at the elementary school level.[18]

The structure of Adachi Ward's overall multicultural coexistence plan is based on the fundamental principle, "richness in difference." The aim of "creating multicultural coexistence in Adachi Ward with the cooperation of people with different mother tongues, culture, and customs," is supported by four additional categories of measures: "communication assistance," "lifestyle assistance," "creation of a multicultural coexistent municipality," and setting up measures for "multicultural coexistence."

Under the umbrella of "communication assistance," Adachi Ward has introduced three concrete measures, including providing information on lifestyles, instructions for information bulletins, and suggestions for the enrichment of Japanese language volunteer classrooms. This information is distributed to all municipal facilities including police stations. The enrichment of Japanese volunteer classes takes the form of creating a network between Japanese language volunteer groups, establishing Japanese language classrooms targeted at children, and including cultural elements into Japanese language classrooms.

These initiatives strive to include all foreign residents in the "information loop" that exists within Adachi Ward by providing multilingual information at a host of locations. Importantly, they tap into localities and facilities that foreign residents make use of in their daily lives. Unfortunately though, according to the Coordinating Manager of the Multicultural Coexistence Unit, this distribution system is somewhat incomplete because at present there are no connections with local grassroots organizations that attract foreign residents, such as churches where ethnic Filipinos often gather. In fact, when queried about the current obstacles to more effective internationalization, the manager strongly agreed that despite the need, lack of interest from Japanese and foreign residents has made it difficult to ensure that information is conveyed to all residents.

This problem is magnified by the absence of "orientation" programs to make foreign residents aware of the resources available to them in Adachi,

---

[18] Currently, Adachi Ward dispatches foreign residents to schools to teach staff and students about foreign cultures about 15 times a year, to foster international understanding. It uses a register consisting of a list of names of foreign residents, their country of birth, and their availability for these visits.

including where to find information in their own language.[19] Furthermore, Foreign Registration Sections, the first stop for foreigners settling in wards, are almost always in a separate location from the International Exchange Sections and Multicultural Sections, often resulting in these sources of lifestyle information being by-passed altogether. Separate locations and staff who are often less than adept at communicating with foreigners in foreign languages compound the problems of transferring information to the "newcomers."

In relation to lifestyle assistance, there are five specific measures, including educational assistance, childrearing assistance, the promotion of crisis and disaster management, the establishment of a management and labor office, and setting up a system to recruit and make use of volunteers. Although a number of communication assistance initiatives provide informational support for foreign residents, these lifestyle assistance initiatives are more structural in that they concentrate on educational access and success, skills, knowledge, and awareness of facilities in the case of a natural disaster, the provision of venues, opportunities, and assistance for foreign residents to receive business "start-up" assistance, liaising with Adachi Ward economic groups, information exchange, networking opportunities with Adachi businesses, and assistance in economic activities (Adachi Ku Kuminbu, 2006: 21–22).

All these initiatives embody inclusionism to some degree. The promotion and support for business activities by foreign residents, collaboration and exchanges with local Japanese business leaders, and — perhaps most importantly — the recognition and implementation of these basic measures demonstrate Adachi's vision of a ward in which all residents are contributors with the potential to cooperate and succeed together.

Similarly, initiatives to establish nursery school facilities for foreign residents' children, enhanced training for nursery school staff, educational advisory services, disaster training, aid for foreigners interested in starting their own companies, and the creation of a group of volunteers that could be dispatched to help foreign residents when they encounter educational,

---

[19]In this case, Shinjuku's Information Video may be an excellent model for producing a multilingual vehicle that conveys necessary information about the Ward. Adachi Ward could produce something similar to Shinjuku, but include a Tagolog version owing to the number of Filipinos residing in Adachi.

administrative, or living difficulties emphasize Adachi's structural approach to multicultural coexistence. Structures are being established for foreign residents not only to integrate into Adachi linguistically, but more significantly to weave themselves into the Adachi tapestry through structural changes in the Adachi local government that allow foreign residents easier access to services provided by the local government.

The third basic measure in Adachi's multicultural coexistence is the creation of a multicultural coexistent municipality. This measure includes the creation of networks, the expansion of opportunities to participate in ward administration and planning, the creation of multicultural coexistence awareness, invitations to schools, and exchange activity assistance.

Adachi means to achieve these objectives by expanding exchanges with the Association for Overseas Technical Training,[20] networking with overseas youth groups, increasing the number of exchanges, application and publication of human resource information including information on local services and jobs, increasing opportunities for foreign residents to participate in local administration such as through the yet-to-be established Multicultural Promotion Assembly, and expanding opportunities for foreign residents to visit schools.

To achieve these objectives, Adachi, like Shinjuku Ward, has requested aid from a diverse group of administrative units, including the Citizens' Section, the Board of Education, the Youth Center, and the Cultural Promotion Section. Each has a particular role in helping realize Adachi's multicultural coexistence policy, in this case the objective of creating a multicultural coexistent municipality.

For instance, the Board of Education is coordinating the clarification of "multicultural coexistence awareness," while the Citizens Section is involved in planning and implementing events that represent this vision of multicultural coexistence. The Promotion of Sports Section and the Cultural Promotion Section complement this collaboration by targeting the youth and organizing events for young people.

Adachi's measures to create a multicultural coexistent community include an important initiative to establish a Foreign Resident Advisory Board to enable foreign residents to have a voice in ward administration

---

[20]The Association for Overseas Technical Training: http://www.aots.org (accessed October 8th, 2006).

(Adachi Ku Kuminbu 2006: 19, 27–28). The establishment of this advisory board and efforts to include foreign residents in ward administration demonstrate Adachi's commitment to political inclusionism.

In addition to the advisory board, Adachi Ward is also currently investigating how to involve permanent residents in local referenda.[21] Further, the ward is also conducting research on adopting new legislation that would give permanent residents voting privileges in local elections, demonstrating its commitment to at least some level of inclusion for foreign residents in terms of civic rights.[22]

Finally, whereas the first three measures put forth by Adachi to achieve its vision of multicultural coexistence revolve around participatory assistance, structural reform, and legal reform, the establishment of a multicultural coexistence promotion system institutionalizes this vision. This includes the creation of formal municipal ordinances for the promotion of multicultural coexistence, and strengthening networking with other municipalities, the Tokyo Metropolitan Government, and other associations by making more widely available information on the current multicultural coexistence policy.

The establishment of a formal multicultural coexistence promotion system emphasizes strengthening networks with other organizations that provide aid to foreign residents, collaboration in research and publishing, and evaluation of programs. Although it does not specifically mention them, it also implies strengthening networks with local institutions and private groups in which foreign residents routinely participate, including churches and ethnic associations. According to the Coordinating Manager of the Adachi Multicultural Coexistence Section, this has proved difficult in the

---

[21] At present, many wards are faced with two important issues: first, the building of a nuclear power plant and second, town amalgamation. Adachi Ward is presently conducting research on revising its basic voting ordinances so that permanently settled residents can participate in referenda concerning the above matters as well as other issues as they arise. See Adachi Ku Kuminbu (2006: 27).

[22] In February 1995, the Japanese Supreme Court ruled that the Japanese Constitution did not prohibit long-term permanent residents from voting in local elections. However, the decision was overturned in October 2003. Then in 2004, the House of Representatives scrapped the bill "Bill regarding Local Government Assembly Representative Voting Rights for Permanent Long-Term Residents." Despite this rejection at the level of the House of Representatives, wards like Adachi are still looking into the possibility of overturning this decision and realize some level of suffrage for long-term residents. See Adachi Ku Kuminbu (2006: 27).

past because foreign resident associations generally kept to themselves. Moreover, the manager also emphasized that historically, the oldcomer *Zainichi* Koreans resident in Japan generally faced little difficulty with language or culture. Rather, the challenges they faced lay in the realization of basic human and civic rights and once those were met they no longer needed to be as vocal.

Adachi's comprehensive strategy is very much related to the prediction mentioned above that the foreign population of Adachi will rise to 14.6 percent of the total ward population by 2050 (Adachi Ku Kuminbu, 2006: 32). Moreover according to the 34th Annual Household Census, not only are the numbers of foreigners going to increase, but so are the problems associated with absorbing a large number of non-Japanese speaking foreigners, such as education, employment, and accessing and paying for the social welfare system, as many other previous studies have shown.[23]

After considering these facts, Adachi Ward has put forth a multicultural coexistence plan that hopes to solve some if not all of the problems first identified in the Kanagawa 1984 survey on "The Living Conditions of Chinese and Korean Residents" (Kanagawa Kennai Zaijû Gaikokujin Jittai Chôsa Iinkai, 1985).[24] It has also been carefully planned to consider the future impact of Free Trade Agreements which are currently under negotiation with 15 neighboring Asian countries, along with their potential to increase the movement of people into Adachi Ward and the rest of Japan. The plan has also taken into account the growing economic ties in the East Asian area and the global center of economic power shifting to East Asia, resulting in an expectation that the number of foreign residents will continue to increase into the future in Adachi, as in the rest of Japan (Adachi Ku Kuminbu, 2006).

In short, Adachi's multicultural coexistence policies and practice take the form of participatory assistance in the form of language and cultural assistance; structural modification to promote participation in Adachi

---

[23]For information on problems identified in the Tokyo Metropolitan Area see: Tokyo To Seikatsu Bunkakyoku, Kokusaibu Kokusaika Suishinka (1997).

[24]The 1984 survey vividly illustrated that the local foreign residents, in particular those of Korean and Chinese descent faced problems with discrimination, poor living environments, educational gaps, obstacles to receiving social welfare benefits, lack of pensions and a host of other problems. See Kanagawa Kennai Zaiju Gaikokujin Jittai Chôsa Iinkai (1985).

social welfare programs; legal reform; establishment of an advisory board to explore a degree of civic inclusionism; and lastly, local government legal reform to institutionalize multicultural coexistence policy and practice.

In contrast to Shinjuku Ward, Adachi's multicultural coexistence policies are more inclusive. Specifically, Adachi has made — or is in the process of making — structural reform in its administrative services to allow for real participation rather than just language supplementation as seen in the Shinjuku case. The establishment of links between foreign residents and Japanese at the business, cultural, and legislative levels is allowing foreign residents to participate at all levels of Adachi society. Even though, as in Shinjuku, long-term foreign residents in Adachi Ward still do not have complete civic rights since they still are not legally eligible to vote, foreign residents enjoy a level of inclusionism that is yet to be realized in Shinjuku Ward. Another noteworthy difference between Shinjuku and Adachi is the employment of a full-time foreign resident to act as liaison, interpreter, or translator for foreign residents, complementing the multicultural coexistence awareness measures.

As in other wards in the TMA, Adachi sponsors culture exchange events, international cultural days, and opportunities for Japanese residents to learn about fellow residents and their native cultures, to promote pluralism in the Adachi community. Multicultural coexistence awareness programs such as "guest teacher programs"[25] introduce non-Japanese cultures to students in Adachi schools and research is currently being carried out on a multinational curriculum for Adachi nursery schools.[26] Cultural and international events promote pride and awareness of the diversity that exists in Adachi.

---

[25] Guest teacher programs are one vehicle used in international cultural exchange and multicultural coexistence. In these programs, a foreign resident would visit a school and give a lecture on their native land. As a participant several times over in these interesting but structurally problematic programs, I noted that "guest teachers" are usually requested to present a stereotypical account of culture and customs. In short, Japanese and foreign cultures are set juxtaposed to each other instead of establishing a relationship based on similarities.

[26] Higher levels of education and their curricula are dictated by the Ministry of Education, Culture, Sport, Science and Technology (MEXT), accounting for the focus on nursery schools only. However still, the Coordinating Manager did voice his interest in expanding multicultural coexistence awareness activities into elementary schools through the vehicle of the guest teacher (Adachi Ku Kuminbu, 2006: 21).

In addition to initiatives to build multicultural coexistence awareness and foster pluralism in nursery schools, the Board of Education in Adachi City is conducting research into the manner in which it can incorporate multicultural coexistence into lifelong learning as part of its Adachi Ward Education Plan. Whether or not the Board can implement multicultural coexistence awareness into the classroom remains to be seen, but it will have to find a way to incorporate it into the mandatory curriculum stipulated by MEXT. In short, if Adachi's Board of Education would like to add multicultural coexistence awareness to the mainstream education system, it will have to find a compromise with MEXT.

Despite these interesting and innovative programs, the tendency remains to contrast foreign culture and foreign residents with Japanese culture and Japanese residents, as illustrated in the "guest teacher" program, the Children's Assembly that allows Japanese and foreign children of Adachi to exchange opinions, and the proposed Foreigners Assembly Advisory Board.

Multicultural coexistence in Tachikawa City

Tachikawa City is the last example of multicultural coexistence policy and practice in this chapter. Tachikawa is small compared to Adachi or Shinjuku. In line with the national trends cited previously, Tachikawa City's foreign population has increased 1.43 times since 1995 totaling 3,304 (Tachikawa-Shi Sangyô Bunkabu Shimin Katsudôka, 2005). Ethnic Chinese and Koreans still make up the majority of the registered foreign population but according to the "Tachikawa City Multicultural Coexistence Plan of 2005," the ethnic Chinese population has increased 2.37 times and the Philippine population 1.2 times since 1995 (Ibid.).

As part of Tachikawa's efforts to realize its multicultural coexistence policy, the municipality has promulgated a four-point plan which includes: (1) the promotion of multicultural coexistence awareness; (2) the creation of a municipality in which foreign residents can live with ease; (3) the creation of an attractive local society through various exchanges and networks; and (4) encouragement of the participation of foreign residents in the local community (Ibid.).

Tachikawa's pillars of multicultural coexistence include a host of concrete measures to ensure its realization. For instance, to promote multicultural coexistence awareness, Tachikawa aims to encourage respect for human rights, create opportunities for teaching about multicultural coexistence, and increase opportunities for international understanding.

According to the guidelines set out to achieve these objectives, Tachikawa aims to treat its foreign residents not as guests, but as individuals who are involved in and contribute to the development of Tachikawa as a whole. Moreover, through the distribution of pamphlets and other materials, Tachikawa is striving to promote human rights awareness among all residents. Initiatives to improve multicultural coexistence also include holding symposia featuring themes such as multiculturalism and human rights.

This basic objective of Tachikawa's multicultural coexistence plan and activities is demonstrative of the city's desire to protect the human rights of residents and foster awareness of multicultural coexistence. While it does not address the connection directly, the emphasis on human rights may be related to implementing international conventions to which Japan became a signatory at the municipality level.[27]

Despite this initiative to protect the human rights of foreign residents, it is noteworthy that there is an absence of specific measures put forth by Tachikawa City to grant civic rights, in particular voting rights, to long-term or permanent residents. The absence of any concrete measure to fully include foreign residents may be indicative of Tachikawa's reticence to become fully inclusive, that is to include foreign residents in the direct decision-making processes of the city. Despite this, Tachikawa's Multicultural Coexistence Plan does include an initiative to take note of the opinions of foreign residents vis-à-vis local government affairs, and Tachikawa has formed a Multicultural Coexistence Promotion Committee

---

[27] See for instance ILO convention No. 97, which stipulates that migrant workers should receive equal treatment to nationals in terms of working conditions, including access to public services, wages, and the right to join unions; No. 143 which calls for granting labor rights to all migrant workers including irregular workers; No 118 adopted in 1962 which calls for equal treatment for nationals and foreigners, and No 157 adopted in 1982 which states that migration should not lead to loss of benefits such as pensions. (http://www.ilo.org/ilolex/english/convdisp1.htm, accessed July 24th, 2006).

which includes foreign residents, demonstrating its commitment to at least limited inclusionism.[28]

As part of its initiatives to create opportunities for training in multicultural coexistence awareness and international understanding, the Tachikawa Multicultural Coexistence Plan has delegated awareness training programs to the Tachikawa Board of Education. These initiatives are aimed at providing Tachikawa students with opportunities to experience foreign cultures, and develop international awareness.

However, questions still remain. How will these programs work out? Will there be cooperation with MEXT in terms of curriculum development? And at what level in the Japanese education system will these programs be instituted?

Emulating Adachi Ward, a guest teacher program could be instituted, but here again the municipality is faced with the dilemma of the manner in which to introduce foreign cultures, languages, and international viewpoints. This becomes especially problematic when MEXT stipulates the core requirements with regard to educational content. Furthermore, questions remain as to whether or not multicultural coexistence programs are going to be regular, long-term programs that students engage in through the school year, or whether they will be sporadic one-off affairs that emphasize cultural differences as opposed to similarities. Programs that become regular components of the curriculum, emphasizing the role of foreign residents in the Tachikawa community and cultural similarities, will foster both inclusionism and pluralism. Programs that contrast Japanese and foreign culture, as seen in previous guest teacher programs, will most likely have the opposite effect. Unfortunately at the moment, programs in Tachikawa and other local governments in the TMA are more representative of the latter.

What is required for programs which emphasize the role of foreign residents in the Tachikawa community to be realized is structural change, as seen in Adachi Ward. Structural change in educational curriculum and programs administered by the Tachikawa local government would strengthen

---

[28]Through living in Tachikawa City for eight years and meeting the current coordinating manager of the Tachikawa Internationalization Unit, I was directly recruited to participate in the Multicultural Coexistence Promotion Committee. The coordinating manager told me that realization of the plan required foreign resident participation, Japanese language skills (although not a necessity), and a monthly commitment to attend meetings which would result in proposals to promote multicultural coexistence.

the inclusive and pluralistic nature of Tachikawa's multicultural coexistence program. This could take the form of hiring foreign residents as teachers and public servants, to demonstrate that all residents are contributors to Tachikawa society.[29]

Tachikawa's second basic objective, the creation of a municipality in which foreign residents can live at ease, includes proposals to create a more pleasant living environment and to internationalize the city's administration. As with Shinjuku, Adachi, and other wards in the TMA, specific measures include the creation of multilingual administrative guidebooks and opening a specific reception window at the Tachikawa Multicultural Center for foreign residents to help find solutions to their problems.

The basic premise behind this initiative is that foreign residents are obliged to pay taxes like their Japanese counterparts. As a result, administrative services should secure the rights of foreign residents by striving to represent and fulfill their needs. This includes providing multilingual material on the local government's services such as health care, social insurance, pensions, and disaster information, to facilitate living in Tachikawa. These administrative services should also include Japanese language assistance to aid foreign residents in adapting to local municipal life. In short, the internationalization of administrative services should aim at ensuring that the diversity of residents in Tachikawa can receive services and information in the language of their choosing.

Multilingual materials and reception windows are examples of structural changes in the Tachikawa administrative organization that aim to encourage inclusionism through removing the linguistic and cultural barriers that previously challenged foreign residents. However, full inclusionism as an end goal may be paradoxically unattainable, not only for Tachikawa but also the three other municipalities examined in this chapter, given that multilingual guides and services as exemplified in Tachikawa's second multicultural coexistence measure would remove the need to integrate into Tachikawa society linguistically and culturally. The same policies that

---

[29]At the local government level, inclusionary policy has taken many forms and is neither comprehensive nor unified across Japan. For example, as previously mentioned the municipalities of Kawasaki, Kyoto, and Osaka have granted foreigner residents the right to work in managerial positions in local governments. Kawasaki City has created a foreigner resident advisory council with elected representatives and opportunities to voice concerns and proposals to the local chamber of councilors. See Jichitai Fo-ramu (2005).

foster inclusionism and pluralism may also unintentionally prevent their full achievement.

Tachikawa's third basic objective of the creation of an attractive local society through various exchanges and networks includes four specific measures: creating opportunities for international exchange, welcoming foreigners through tourism, strengthening sister city exchanges, and continuing to promote international cooperation. Taken together, the focus of these individual measures is connecting Tachikawa City and its residents to the international community through tourism, a sister city relationship, international cooperation, and by creating opportunities for international exchange. The rationale behind creating these connections is that through more contact with people, information and culture from abroad, Tachikawa City and its residents will be better able to cope with the challenges of an increasingly globalized world. In other words, repeating the comments of the Coordinating Manager of Tachikawa's International unit, more contact and exchanges with cultures and people from abroad will be one step in the move from an "information oriented society" to an "internationally oriented society."

To achieve these measures, the Tachikawa City Multicultural Coexistence Plan includes increasing opportunities for exchange between Japanese and foreigners who live, work, or study in Tachikawa and the creation of networks with nearby associations whose mission is to promote international exchanges with foreign and Japanese residents. The former is meant to widen the number and variety of opportunities for exchange, while the latter is meant to provide Tachikawa with more tools to expand the scale and effectiveness of its multicultural coexistence activities.

The specific activities that fall under the category of creating opportunities for international exchange include a Japanese speech contest for foreigners, an introduction to Japanese culture such as the tea ceremony and flower arrangement, an international festival, and sister city exchanges.

As with other cities, the activities that Tachikawa City is proposing are problematic for three reasons. First, the events separate foreign and Japanese residents as well as foreign and Japanese cultures. For example, there is no speech contest for Tachikawa residents, but only a Japanese speech contest for foreigners which creates an opposition between guests and hosts, or between Japanese and non-Japanese.

Second, opportunities for exchange are centered on traditional Japanese culture such as the tea ceremony or flower arrangement. Again, Japanese culture is being opposed to foreign culture in a teacher-student relationship rather than a relationship based on equality or co-residence. Equally interesting, the culture being introduced is not widely practiced by the majority of Japanese. This is important, in that foreign residents are being introduced to culture that has little relevance in modern Japanese society, and thus has little relevance for those trying to understand or cope with modern Japan.

Third, it should also be noted that exchange opportunities are specifically designed for foreign residents as opposed to all residents, again creating a divide between Japanese and foreign residents.

The fourth basic objective of Tachikawa's Multicultural Coexistence Plan is encouraging the participation of foreign residents in the local community. Specifically, Tachikawa aims to create venues where foreign residents' opinions can be voiced, an atmosphere which encourages participation, volunteer activity opportunities, and a local community that foreign residents can participate in. Through harnessing the talents, abilities, and networks of resident foreigners, Tachikawa hopes to deepen multicultural coexistence awareness in Tachikawa. This includes enlisting foreign residents, as guest teachers for seminars on international understanding, as language teachers, and as community leaders. It also involves including foreign residents in Parent-Teacher Associations (PTA) and children's activities.

To encourage the participation of foreigners in Tachikawa society, it is recognized that foreigners need the means to facilitate that participation. Subsequently, the Tachikawa Multicultural Coexistence Plan has proposed measures to help the formation of ethnic associations, to foster leaders among the foreign residents, and to survey foreign residents' opinions through questionnaires related to lifestyle.

Although these initiatives are admirable, they are problematic from several standpoints. First, according to the Coordinating Manager of the Internationalization Unit of Tachikawa, the lack of interest of Japanese and foreign residents in internationalization and multicultural coexistence initiatives in Tachikawa remains a hurdle. They lack awareness of the programs and the need for them, and their lack of interest and pessimism is reinforced by media reporting of domestic and international events.[30]

Second, considering the diversity and number of foreign residents in Tachikawa and other municipalities in the TMA, the challenge remains of organizing ethnic associations that represent the interests of the foreign residents. In the case of a Foreign Assembly Advisory Board of the type created in Kawasaki city and proposed for Adachi Ward, questions remain as to how this organization will represent the voices of all the foreign residents. The creation of ethnic associations, although useful for networking, also strengthens the ethnic identity of each group and weakens their collective identity as Tachikawa city residents. Third, the historical experience of many ethnic groups in Japan and their mistreatment may provide an obstacle to forming an organization which identifies them as outsiders.[31]

Drawbacks aside, the Tachikawa policy and its associated activities to foster multicultural coexistence, especially through the participation of foreign residents, encourage both pluralism and inclusionism. The support and assistance for the creation of ethnic associations creates diversity in the municipality and avenues for voicing concerns to the local administration. By virtue of creating ethnic associations, the policy encourages diversity and subsequently pluralism in the Tachikawa area. Surveying foreign residents' views also is inclusive in practice, attempting to include the opinions of all residents in policy development.

---

[30]The media in Japan often report that crimes committed by foreigners have increased significantly in the past 20 years. However the same media fail to report that crime rates by Japanese are still more than double those committed by foreigners. Moreover, the arrests of foreigners are on the whole associated with visa-related issues rather than violent crime. These misleading media stories create negative images related to foreigners and subsequently pessimism vis-à-vis-vis policies that are related to foreigners. International issues such as belligerent statements by North Korea, anti-Japanese riots in China, and South Korea have similar effects. For more information on crime statistics, the National Police Agency publishes an annual report breaking down crime rates demographically. The statistics divide incidents dealt with by police into "crimes" and "offenses." The former include violent incidents while the latter includes visa infractions, speeding, and prostitution. From these statistics we can see that rates of crimes committed by foreigners are on the whole are lower than those committed by Japanese, except for foreigners originating from South America, generally *Nikkeijin* living and working in Japan legally. http://www.npa.go.jp/kokusai2/15b/siryo.pdf (accessed August 2nd, 2006).

[31]Many long-term residents take a Japanese name to avoid being identified as non-Japanese.

Among the three municipalities described here, Tachikawa's multicultural coexistence policies and activities are probably the least influenced by a fast growing foreign resident population. Compared to Shinjuku and Adachi Wards, numbers of foreign residents are low. According to the 2004 Survey on Foreign Residents, foreign residents still face discrimination when it comes to renting apartments. They also have problems finding work, while they see administrative obligations as difficult to understand. They also have difficulties in enrolling their children in nursery schools, and find it difficult to make Japanese friends, as well as a host of other problems.

Like other municipalities in the TMA, Tachikawa's multicultural coexistence policy focuses on inclusion and pluralism. Its multicultural coexistence policy aims to decrease discrimination and promote the respect for human rights. In contrast to its municipal cousins, Tachikawa's multicultural coexistence strategy does not overtly emphasize dissipating intercultural frictions or ensuring that foreign residents do not become a social burden to Tachikawa. Rather, its multicultural coexistence policy focuses on foreign and Japanese residents working together to create a pluralistic community, as embodied by the policy of not treating foreign residents as guests but as potential pillars of the local community.

Conclusion

The municipalities of Adachi, Shinjuku, and Tachikawa have different foreigner demographics and subsequently different focuses of their multicultural coexistence policies and measures. However, despite the differences, several similarities do exist. First, all three municipalities have outlined in their multicultural coexistence plans that language difficulties and a lack of cultural savvy (knowledge) impede foreigners' abilities to meet their obligations as residents, and also to realize their rights to social welfare programs. In response to this problem, these municipalities have produced multilingual lifestyle guides with information ranging from school enrollment, emergency evacuation, and filing tax forms, to detailed instructions on what to do in the case of a health problem. To supplement information provided through booklets, pamphlets, bulletin boards, and monthly publications, all three municipalities have established multilingual advisory services for newcomers and older residents. Newcomer-oriented multicultural coexistence policies are apparent in many kinds of services, information, and programs that contribute to overcoming language and cultural obstacles.

Adachi Ward has Chinese, Korean, and English speakers on hand to help mediate and find solutions to the various problems that foreign residents encounter. In the case of Shinjuku Ward, a Multicultural Coexistence Center has been established where advisory services are provided in Chinese, Korean, and English languages, in addition to several other languages (Tokyo Kokusai Dantai Renraku Kaigi, 2005: 6–9). Above and beyond advisory services, the Multicultural Coexistence Center also serves as a library, lecture room, and skill training area, and it also acts as the headquarters of Shinjuku Ward's multicultural coexistence policy. Tachikawa is attempting to overcome the language hurdle through volunteer language interpreters and translators. Unfortunately though, unlike Adachi and Shinjuku Wards whose interpreters and translators are either full or part-time employees of the local ward, Tachikawa's language interpretation is based on translation volunteers. Because of their status as volunteers, they may have limited professional experience and familiarity with daily administrative challenges, compared with staff who are either full-time or part-time employees.

The three municipal cases studies examined here demonstrate that multicultural coexistence policy reflects local needs. Importantly, the analysis above demonstrates that policies reflect the influence that globalization can have at the local level through global migration and economic interdependence. Specifically, the multicultural coexistence policies that local governments plan and initiate are a direct result of growing numbers of foreigners living in Japan and their settlement patterns in each municipality.

Multicultural coexistence policies initiated at the local government level are also a result of international and global pressures. Obligations to fulfill international conventions and bilateral treaties have compelled local governments to provide for the needs of foreign residents as ordinary residents (Suzuki, 2004). They include securing access to social welfare programs, protection against discrimination, and employment protection. Economically, deepening economic interdependence has created a need for foreign laborers in Japan in order for Japanese manufactures to remain competitive.[32] These trends are exacerbated by Japan's graying population and low birth rate, with no end in sight.

Domestically, because of the "Local Government Law" (Komai, 2001: 119) and the "Foreigner Registration Act" (Ministry of Justice, 2006),[33] local governments have been compelled to develop innovative policies to ensure that the rights of foreign residents are protected and that all foreign residents have access to social welfare (Komai, 2001: 119). Further, multicultural coexistence policies which emphasize inclusionism and pluralism are a reaction to the demands of resident foreigners for equality. *Tabunka Kyôsei* policies are also directly related to rapidly growing numbers of foreigners living in Japan who are settling permanently.[34]

The global movement of people will continue to affect Japan into the future. In particular, the combination of closer economic ties between Japan and her neighbors, recommendations to increase the total population of foreign residents to three percent of the total Japanese population,[35] continued low birth rates, and more and more foreign residents choosing to become general permanent residents will compel local governments and the national government to adopt multicultural coexistence policies that meet the challenge of the global movement of people. The direction of these policies will not only determine whether Japan will maintain its economic vitality, but also the future nature of Japanese society.

References

Adachi Ku Kuminbu (2006). *Tabunka Kyôsei Suishin Kikaku: Ikiiki Wakuwaku "Tabunka Kyôsei Toshi Adachi."* Tokyo: Adachi Ku Kuminbu, Kokuminka.

---

[32]According to the *Shûkan Diamondo*, over 760,000 foreign workers are powering companies like Toyota, Suzuki, Sanyô, Honda and Yamaha. See: *Shûkan Diamondo* June 5th, 2005.

[33]Ministry of Justice: http://www.moj.go.jp/ENGLISH/IB/ib-01.html (accessed July 23, 2006).

[34]According to the Ministry of Justice, in 2005 the number of General Residents (*ippan eijûsha*) increased from 145,336 in 2000 to 349,804 in 2005. Ministry of Justice homepage: http://www.moj.go.jp/press/060530-1/069530-1.html (accessed October 15th, 2006).

[35]"Report on the Future Acceptance of Foreigners/ Kongo no Gaikokujin no Ukeire ni Tsuite." http://www.moj.go.jp/NYUKAN/nyukan51.html (accessed June 30th, 2006).

Bunkyo Ku Gaikokuseki Kumin no Sumiyasusa Chôsa Iinkai (2005). *Bunkyo Ku Gaikokuseki Kumin no Sumiyasusa Chôsa Hokusho.* Tokyo: Bunkyo Ku, 2004.

The Economist (2005). "Greying Japan: the Downturn." 7–13 January, 2005, pp. 29–30.

Gaikokujin Jishin Jôhô Sentaa (1996). *Hanshin Daijisai to Gaikokujin: "Tabunka Kyôsei Shakai" no Gentai to Kanôsei.* Tokyo: Akashishoten/Gaikokujin Jishin Jôhô Sentaa.

Herbert, Wolfgang (1996). *Foreign Workers and Law Enforcement in Japan.* London: Kegan Paul International.

Huntington, Samuel (2004). *Who We Are? The Challenges to American Identity.* New York: Simon and Schuster.

Jichitai Fo-ramu (2005). "Jichitai ni okeru Chiiki ga Ichidai to Natte Kokusaika he no Torigumi: Gaikokujin no Sumiyasui Machi Nihonjin mo Yasui-Tabunka Kyôsei Shakai o Mezasu. Kawasaki Shi Jisaku." Jichitai Kokusaika Kyôkai 191(9).

Kanagawa Kennai Zaijû Gaikokujin Jittai Chôsa Iinkai (1985). *Kanagawa Kennai Zaijû Gaikokujin Jittai Chôsa Hôkokusho: Kankokujin, Chôsenjin, Chûgokujin ni tsuite.* Kanagawa: Kanagawa Kennai Zaijû Gaikokujin Jittai Chôsa Iinkai.

Lifestyle and Cultural Bureau of the Tokyo Metropolitan Government (2000). *The 2000 Report on the "Current Situation of International Policies of Wards, Cities, Towns and Villages in the Tokyo Metropolitan.* Tokyo: Shinei Print.

Shinjuku Bunka/Kokusai Kôryû Zaidan (2003). *Shinjuku-Ku ni Okeru Gaikokujin Jumin to no Kyôsei ni kansuru Chôsa Hokusho (Heisei 16 Nen 3 Gatsu).* Tokyo: Shinjuku Bunka/Kokusai Kôryû Zaidan.

Shinjuku Bunka/Kokusai Kôryû Zaidan (2004). *Tabunka Kôysei no Machi zukuru (Gaikokujin Jissaku) no Suishin ni Tsuite.* Tokyo.

Shinjuku Ward (2006). *Shinjuku Ku ni Okeru Tabunka Kyôsei Oyobi Gaikokujin Kanren Jigyô Heisei 18 Nendo.* Tokyo: Shinjuku Ward Office.

Shûkan Diamondo, June 5th, 2005.

So, Yon Dal (2000). *Tabunka Kyôsei Shakai he no Tenbô, Kyôsei Shakai e no Chihô Sanseiken: Teiju Gaikokujin no Shiminteki Kenri no?* Toko to Kongo no Tenbô, pp. 19–38.

Sômushô (2006). *Tabunka Kyôsei no Suishin ni Kansuru Kenkyukai: Chiki ni okeru Tabunka Kyôsei no Suishin ni Mukete.* Tokyo: Sômushô.

Suzuki, Eriko (2004). "Gaikokujin Shujuu Chiiki ni miru Tabunka Kyoushakai no Kadai: "Kyousei" wa Nani Ka?" *Tabunkaka suru Nihon wo Kangaeru: Kokkyo wo Koeta Hito no Idô ga Shinten suru Naka de.* (FIF Special Report No. 8.) Tokyo: Fujita Mirai Keiei Kenkyujo.

Suzuki, Nobue (1995). *Nihongo wa Kokusaigo ni Nariuruka.* Tokyo: Kodansha.

Tabunka Kyôsei Ki-wa-do Jiten Henshû Iinkai (2004). *Tabunka Kyôsei Ki-wa-do Jiten.* Tokyo: Akashi Shoten.

Tachikawa Shi Sangyô Bunkabu Shimin Katsudôka (2005). *Tachikawa Shi Tabunka Kôysei Suishin Puran.* Tokyo: Tachikawa City Office.

Tokyo Kokusai Kôryû Dantai Renraku Kaigi (2005). *Tokyo Kokusai Kôryû Daitai Renraku Gikai Dairetori-Heisei 17 Nendopan.* Tokyo: Tokyo Kokusai Kôryû Dantai Renraku Kaigi.

Tokyo To Seikatsu Bunkakyoku (1997). *Tokyo To Zaijû Gaikokujin Seikatsu Jittai Chôsa Hokusho.* Tokyo: Tokyo To Seikatsu Bunkakyoku, Kokusaibu Kokusaika Suishinka.

Tullao, Tereso S., Jr. and Michael Angelo A. Cortez (2003). *Movement of Natural Persons Between the Philippines and Japan: Issues and Prospects.* Manila: Japan-Philippines Economic Partnership Research Project.

Waiver, Ole, Barry Buzan, Morten Kelstrup and Pierre Lemaitre (1993). *Identity, Migration and the New Security Agenda in Europe.* London: Pinter.

CHAPTER 10

MIGRATION UNDER THE JAPAN–PHILIPPINES FREE TRADE AGREEMENT

Michael Angelo A. Cortez

Introduction

With the movement of capital, goods, and services, comes the movement of people as a driving force of globalization. It can be argued that if the movement of capital, goods, and services can be allowed, why not the movement of people to address the asymmetries in demographics and manpower in trading countries? This chapter explores the impact of the recently forged free trade agreement between the Philippines and Japan on the movement of people. In an earlier study prepared for the Japan–Philippines Economic Partnership Agreement (JPEPA), Tullao and Cortez (2003) suggested that the flow of temporary workers from the Philippines to Japan should be restructured, from entertainers to what an aging society really needs, health workers and nurses. Exploring this aspect of the Japan–Philippines free trade agreement is relevant in the context of strengthening economic relations between the two countries. Japanese investors are known for their commercial presence, particularly in the electronics and automotive industry, in developing countries like the Philippines. Since the re-establishment of diplomatic ties, Japan has become the top aid donor to the Philippines, contributing US$9.4 billion over the past 23 years or 51 percent of all foreign loans. On the other hand, the Philippines is reputed to be the leading exporter of labor in the world, ranging from the semi-skilled to professional and technical workers.

Considering the asymmetric demographic and development trends between the two countries, this chapter explores the possibility of meeting the needs of both countries to increase productivity, within the context of bilateral trade. Japan's aging population requires the assistance of health service providers while the Philippines attempts to maximize employment opportunities in the domestic economy and abroad. While Japan's health sector has been closed to foreign corporations and their personnel, the aging population and the burden on public health expenditure are making it necessary to open up this sensitive sector as part of the free trade agreement with the Philippines.

Factors Affecting the Movement of People

Temporary labor migration can be explained from three major theoretical perspectives. The first sees it as a macroeconomic response and adjustment mechanism to asymmetries in demography and economic development in the host and sending countries. The second views migration as a rational individual response to wage differential between countries. The third looks at household decisions to maximize family income and minimize the scope of economic risks.

The host country is normally characterized by rapid economic growth accompanied by low population growth. This combination results in high demand for labor due to economic expansion, coupled with a low level of labor force participation due to demographic decline. On the other hand, the sending country is normally marked by lethargic economic performance coupled with rapid population growth. This economic and demographic mix produces a pool of unemployed workers. This asymmetry in demographic and development trends between the two countries is resolved through the migration of workers from the labor surplus to the labor deficit country. If a labor deficit country wishes to maintain a restrictive policy toward the entry of workers, it will have to adapt by increasing the wage rate to increase participation in the labor force. The *pull factor* of higher wages in labor receiving countries and the *push factor* of high levels of unemployment and poverty in source countries are the most obvious and popular reasons for the temporary movement of migrant workers (Wickramasekera, 2002). Ballescas (2003) adds high population growth rate, slow domestic growth, and high levels of unemployment and underemployment as other push factors that make migrant workers seek greener pastures. The pull factor in the case of Japan is the aging population and the subsequent shortage of young workers.

Young Japanese workers have developed negative attitudes toward jobs classified as "3K" or "3D" jobs: *kitanai* (dirty), *kiken* (dangerous), and *kitsui* (difficult). While the Japanese are culturally obligated to taking care of their elderly, changing work and family patterns have led to a shift toward hiring health workers to assume the responsibility. The ability of the Japanese to pay for health services and the comparatively attractive wages that working in Japan can serve as pull factors for Filipino labor migration from the first perspective mentioned above. The second perspective explains migration in terms of the personal decisions of the workers to improve their standard of living, while the third points to the development of a migration culture among families and networks of migrants. Incidentally, Ballescas (2003) has presented a more detailed explanation of temporary labor migration of Filipino workers to Japan. Citing a study by Truong (1996), Ballescas suggests that Filipino female migration to Japan can also be seen as fulfilling the reproductive requirements of the Japanese population. With declining fertility rates, and as more female Japanese workers become career centered and reject domesticity, some Japanese men have looked to Filipino female entertainment workers to address their reproductive and marital needs.

The Historical Flow and Demographic Profile of Filipino Workers to Japan

Based on recent estimates from the Philippine Overseas and Employment Administration (POEA), 667,226 Filipinos are currently deployed in more than 200 countries and trust territories around the globe, including the Middle East, Asia, Europe, the Americas, Africa, and Oceania. Although skilled and professional workers from the Philippines are spread around the world, workers with certain skills tend to cluster in specific countries. For example, Filipino domestic helpers tend to be concentrated in Hong Kong and Saudi Arabia, entertainers in Japan and other Southeast Asian countries, IT professionals and nurses in the United States, and nurses in the United Kingdom.[1]

---

[1] POEA statistics are currently to be found on the Internet at http://www.poea.gov.ph/html/statistics.html.

In 2005, Japan ranked fifth as a destination for overseas Filipino workers, with 42,586 workers deployed. This was even though deployment had decreased by 42 percent from 74,480 workers in 2004, when Japan ranked fourth, as a result of a crackdown on illegal workers and stringent new requirements for professional entertainers. However, Japan is still the second most popular destination for newly hired workers. In 2004, 71,166 workers were hired, though in 2005 the number decreased to 38,756.

The Commission on Overseas Filipinos estimates that there were around 83,303 workers on a permanent basis and 238,522 temporary workers in Japan as of 2004. The number of irregular migrants was estimated at 31,428. In Asia, Japan has the highest number of permanent and temporary Filipino workers. Malaysia and Singapore, however, have more irregular migrants, given that Japan has tightened its immigration measures. According to the United Nations Economic and Social Commission for Asia and the Pacific (ESCAP 2002), migration is structural and demand driven. Women's migration and their concentration in domestic services and the entertainment sector suggest that the labor market is not only segmented but also gendered. Since entertainers, dancers, musicians, and singers are clustered mainly in Japan, based on disaggregated information on outbound professions by the POEA, Table 10.1 summarizes the outflow of overseas foreign workers (OFWs) and is broken down by gender. Performing artists are referred to as "guest entertainers" in Japan and as such are accorded recognition as "professionals." These professional entertainers worked under contract with agents and talent managers in the Philippines and club managers in Japan. The large-scale flow into Japan's entertainment market passed the scrutiny of immigration rules that required them to have artist certification from their home governments or other documentary credentials. From a mere 5,508 Filipino entrants into Japan in 1960, the number increased several fold to 20,477 in 1970 and 129,053 in 1998. In 2002, of the total 667,226 OFWs deployed by the Philippines, some 77,870 went to Japan, though as mentioned above, the number fell after the immigration crackdown in 2004.

Filipino migration to Japan used to be predominantly male in the 1970s, reflecting the general exodus of migrant contract workers for the Middle East and elsewhere. However, at the beginning of the 1980s, migration to Japan became female dominated. In 1970, there were 8,789 female and 11,688 male Filipino migrants. In 1980, the number of female migrants

Table 10.1.   Deployed new hires of Filipino overseas foreign workers by sex and skills, 1992–2000.

Year	Sex	Choreographers dancers	Composers, musicians and singers	Professional nurses	Domestic helpers
1992	Male	1,552	416	536	1,334
	Female	33,979	2,572	4,230	46,243
1993	Male	370	247	599	1,135
	Female	12,342	941	5,231	60,244
1994	Male	846	387	948	1,559
	Female	26,620	1,963	5,357	63,833
1995	Male	657	221	1,133	1,241
	Female	14,498	1,220	6,295	59,698
1996	Male	647	245	640	1,017
	Female	13,445	1,869	4,017	60,184
1997	Male	802	283	669	745
	Female	24,833	4,164	3,552	46,785
1998	Male	720	485	663	1,035
	Female	25,923	7,781	2,892	45,868
1999	Male	606	610	828	777
	Female	28,731	13,602	4,497	52,268
2000	Male	1,063	919	1,273	1,367
	Female	34,475	23,048	6,410	66,890

Source: POEA (2003). www.poea.gov.ph.

jumped to 14,962, overtaking that of Filipino males (12,940). By 1990, the number of Filipino males in Japan had doubled to 24,956 while the number of females had soared 5.5 times to 83,336. The numbers of male migrants continued to rise slowly, to 26,856 in 1993, but with a slight decrease in female migration (79,538 in 1993), even though the latter still predominated (Ballescas, 2003).

Filipino male temporary labor migration has consisted mostly of trainees under Japan's training system. Japanese firms in the automotive and semi-conductor industries in the Philippines send their workers to Japan for training. The changes in female migration have reflected both changing bilateral arrangements between the two countries and market realities. A study of Filipino female labor migration to Japan by Osteria revealed that most of the domestic helpers seeking work in Japan were either hired directly or came as tourists. Relatives working in Japan were also instrumental in facilitating recruitment. Entertainers were on average younger than domestic helpers by nine years. However, domestic helpers were better educated than entertainers, as evidenced by a high percentage of women with college education. While entertainers were mostly single, domestic helpers were usually married, widowed, or separated (Osteria, 1994).

Current Level of Remittances and Volume of Workers

OFW remittances from Japan grew at a steady rate from US$122 million in 1997 to US$300 million in 2005. Table 10.2 summarizes OFW remittances from Japan. The remittances from Japan in 2005 were 25 percent of the total from all over Asia; and 3 percent of the total worldwide, which had by then overtaken the US$10 billion mark.

To understand the need for home-help services, the complex interaction of economic development and demographic factors has to be considered (Figure 10.1). Economic expansion leads to increased demand for workers. For demographic factors, Japan's declining fertility rates and the increase in life expectancy of the population have decreased the labor force participation rate while at the same time increasing the dependency ratio. The high

Table 10.2.   Remittances of overseas Filipino workers from Japan, 1997–2005.

Year	Sea-based	Land-based	Total
1997	8,873	122,502	131,375
1998	7,333	100,474	107,807
1999	43,820	230,111	273,931
2000	46,739	323,358	370,097
2001	18,248	373,623	391,871
2002	25,402	465,623	491,025
2003	41,499	304,558	346,057
2004	48,567	259,561	308,128
2005	55,709	300,950	356,659

Source: Bangko Sentral ng Pilipinas www.bsp.gov.ph.

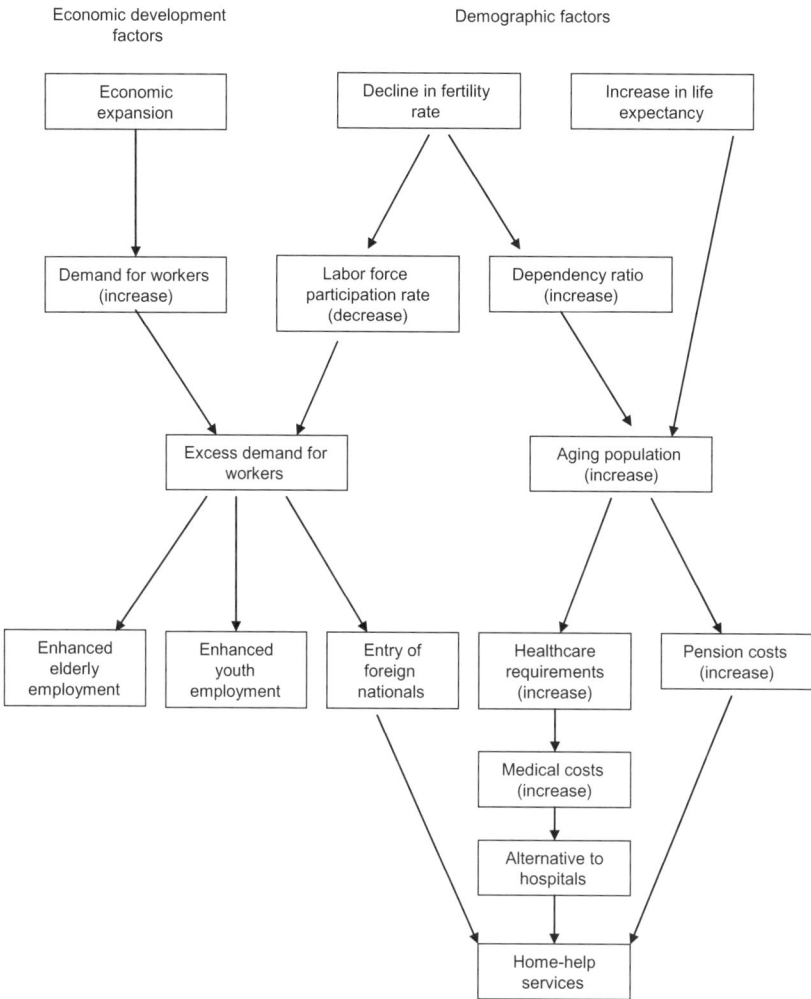

Figure 10.1. Factors explaining migration from the Philippines to Japan. (Tullao and Cortez, 2003.)

dependency ratio requires an increase in the number of the working population to care for the aging, thus creating a demand for workers. This demand may be addressed domestically by retaining the elderly in the labor force, which in Japan's case is costly since age is correlated with salary, or by encouraging youth employment, which is a more realistic scenario. The excess demand may also be met by the employment of foreign workers.

As aging increases, there are corresponding increases in pension costs and healthcare requirements. Resulting medical costs may lead to new methods of caring for the elderly, such as home-help care services. Considering the changing work and family values of Japanese workers, employing foreign nationals as home helpers may be seen as meeting Japanese family obligations. Relations within the family may even be improved through the removal of the care burden from family members (Saito, 2003).

Japan's Aging Population

In 2001, Japan had a population of 127.5 million, a working-age population (15 years old and over) of 108.8 million, and a workforce (those employed plus those classified as unemployed) of 67.5 million. Females made up 41 percent of the workforce. The aging population is apparent in Table 10.3. In 1990, 23.8 percent of Japanese were 55 years or older

Table 10.3.   Japanese population and labor force projections, 1990–2010 (millions).

Age	Population			Labor force		
	1990	2001	2010	1990	2001	2010
0–14	22.5	18.3	17.1	—	—	—
15–29	27.0	25.6	20.4	14.7	15.6	12.3
30–54	44.6	44.5	42.8	36.2	36.4	35.5
55–59	7.7	8.3	8.6	5.6	6.3	6.7
60–64	6.8	7.8	9.9	3.7	4.3	6.3
65–	14.9	22.6	28.7	3.6	4.9	6.6
Total	123.5	127.1	127.5	63.8	67.5	67.4
Share (%)						
55 or over	23.8	30.4	37.0	20.2	23.0	29.1
65 or over	12.1	17.8	22.5	5.6	7.3	9.8

Sources: Ministry of Public Management, Home Affairs, Posts and Telecommunications *Rodoryoku chosa* (labor force survey) and Ministry of Health and Welfare, *Rodoryoku jukyu no tenbo to kadai* (Projections for issues in supply and demand in the labor force) (1999); Sasajima (2003).

while 12.1 percent were 65 years or older. By 2001, the aging population had grown by 30 percent. Those aged 55 years or older made up 30.4 percent of the population, while the proportion of those 65 years or older had risen to 17.8 percent. Aging is a recognized phenomenon in developed countries. However, the trend in Japan differs in its speed. Changes are forecast to take place in Japan in only 21 years, which will take the United States 56 years to attain, compared with 70 years in Germany and 75 years in Britain, By the year 2010, it is projected that 37 percent of Japan's population will be 55 or older, and 22.5 percent will be over 65 (Sasajima, 2003).

Table 10.4 projects that the percentage of the population aged 65 or older could even reach 36 percent by 2050, rising from a projected 28.7 percent in 2010.

Japanese workers work until they are 65 years of age before they are entitled to a retirement pension. The main problem the government faces as a result of the aging of the population is the deteriorating financial health of the public pension system. The government reforms the public pension system every five years, and among the measures it has taken to stem the financial woes are cutting the level of pension payments, increasing the level of contributions, and gradually raising the starting age for the payment of public pensions to 65 between 2001 to 2025 (Sasajima, 2003).

Table 10.4. Estimated Japanese population 65 and over, 1995–2050 (thousands).

Year	Total	Age 65 and over	Total (%)
1995	125,570	18,277	15
2000	126,926	22,041	17
2010	127,473	28,735	23
2020	124,107	34,559	28
2030	117,580	34,770	30
2040	109,338	36,332	33
2050	100,593	35,863	36

Source: National Institute of Population and Social Security Research. Facts and Figures of Japan (2003).

Filipino nurses and caregivers

Nurses

The Philippines has been exporting nurses to the United States, United Kingdom, and the Middle East for many years. Table 10.5 summarizes the deployment of newly hired nurses from 1998 to the first half of 2005. Since the oil boom in the 1970s, Middle-Eastern countries have employed the majority of Filipino nurses abroad. Saudi Arabia led the group of destination countries with a total of 62,025 nurses hired between 1995 and 2005, followed by the United Kingdom with 16,552.

The deployment of Filipino nurses worldwide varies over time, with a rise around the turn of the century, followed by a fall (Table 10.6).

Nurses are lured by the high wages abroad compared to the meager salaries provided by Philippine hospitals. A Filipino nurse would earn roughly US$200 per month in the Philippines as compared to US$4,000 per month in the United States.

Caregivers

With the opportunities in destination countries for health service providers and allied services, a new segment in the Philippine health services sector

Table 10.5. Filipino nurses hired overseas, by country, 1995–2005.

Country	Volume
Saudi Arabia	62,025
United Kingdom	16,552
United States	12,232
United Arab Emirates	4,538
Singapore	4,150
Ireland	3,318
Libya	2,934
Kuwait	2,472
Taiwan	1,205
Qatar	1,049
Total	110,475

Source: POEA (2006).

Table 10.6. Deployment of newly hired
Filipino nurses by year, 1995–2005.

Year	Volume	Change (%)
1995	7,954	—
1996	5,477	−31
1997	5,245	−4
1998	5,399	3
1999	5,972	11
2000	8,341	40
2001	13,822	66
2002	12,335	−11
2003	9,270	−25
2004	8,879	−4
2005	7,748	−13
Total	90,442	

Source: POEA (2006).

has emerged, that of "care-giving." A caregiver can be defined as a person who has responsibility for meeting the physical and psychological needs of an infant or dependent adult. A caregiver provides private household childcare, senior support care or care of the disabled without supervision (TESDA, 2003). This sector, which serves developed countries with aging populations, has attracted increasing numbers of Filipino migrant workers. The POEA classifies care-giving services as skilled, considering the training and certification process a worker has to undergo before deployment overseas. It is forecast that the demand for care-giving will continue to rise in future years. Demand is most likely to grow in countries with aging populations such as Canada (TESDA, 2003). Canada's live-in caregiver program offers temporary employment opportunities for individuals willing to provide care for children, the elderly or people with disabilities in their own homes. Eligibility requirements include the equivalent of high school education, training or experience in a related field, and an ability to work using the English language. Caregivers who complete 24 months of full-time live-in employment during a 36-month period can apply for permanent landed immigrant status for themselves and their dependents (Spigelman, 2000). Table 10.7 shows the aggregate outflows of hired caregivers from 2001 to 2005.

Table 10.7. Annual deployment of newly hired caregivers from the Philippines, 2001–2005.

Year	Number	Change (%)
2001	465	—
2002	5,383	1058
2003	18,878	251
2004	20,394	8
2005	16,146	−21
Total	61,266	

Source: POEA (2006).

As a result of a perceived demand, caregiver training institutions have mushroomed all over the Philippines. In 2004, there were around 758 institutions registered with and regulated by the Technical Education and Skills Development Authority (TESDA). However, TESDA is closely monitoring the registered institutions in order to curb the proliferation of unauthorized training centers. All caregiver programs are being evaluated based on regulations for training caregivers promulgated by the TESDA Board. While nursing schools have introduced care-giving as a vocational alternative, there are institutions that particularly focus on the vocation itself, as well as other technical and vocational institutions that have been spun off to provide training in related services.

TESDA, however, has issued a memorandum that the demand for caregivers is not sufficient to absorb the output of all the training institutions (TESDA, 2004). From 2002 to 2003, around 54,644 students graduated from the care-giving programs of the 758 institutions. However, from the deployment statistics in Table 10.7, it appears that only 36,146 were deployed in 2004 and 2005 combined.

In an attempt to standardize, assess, certify, and monitor the caregiver training program in the country, TESDA has proposed caregiver course modules covering the following items:

- Overview of the live-in care-giver program of Canada
- Introduction to live-in care-giver skills enhancement
- Basic first aid

- Basic life support
- Cardiopulmonary resuscitation (CPR)
- Home and client safety management
- Home management and client care
- Nutrition and food preparation
- Care of children
- Care of the elderly
- Canadian culture, people, and traits
- English as a second language
- Personality development

The above standards are used for registration of programs, assessment, certification, and monitoring of training institutions in the Philippines and may be used as criteria for domestic regulations in other destination countries (TESDA, 2003), such as in the case of Japan.

The Japan–Philippines Free Trade Agreement (FTA)

The Japan–Philippines FTA is the first of its kind for Japan because it includes landmark provisions on the movement of labor. Under the agreement, a limited number of Philippine nurses and caregivers will be allowed to work in Japan on condition that they pass Japanese qualifying examinations. The FTA will also remove tariff duties on more than 90 percent of trade in goods between the two countries. This agreement is intended to strengthen the economic collaboration between the two trading countries by increasing the flow of goods, persons, investments, and services. Under the agreement, Japan agreed to accept 400 nurses and 600 caregivers beginning from the fiscal year April 1, 2007, provided that the countries completed all the procedures including parliamentary ratification of the pact. Japan's vice labor minister thought the numbers "realistic and appropriate," and that they would have no negative effects on the domestic labor market (*Japan Times*, 2006a).

As for domestic regulations, nurses and caregivers would have to pass examinations in Japan to be certified for work. Accordingly, these workers would have to take Japanese language lessons for six months when they arrive in Japan. In addition, specialized training in Japanese hospitals and facilities for the elderly is required. Nurses will be given three years to pass the licensing examination while caregivers will be required to pass the exam within four years. Workers who pass the exam will be allowed to work in Japan indefinitely.

Implications and Policy Options Concerning the Movement of People

Language and cultural training

Since language and culture are major barriers to accessing the Japanese market, TESDA could assess, certify, and monitor the operations of language training centers in the Philippines. All Japan-bound health professionals could be required to take the Japanese Language Proficiency Test and course units in Japanese culture before departure. A set of criteria for training and certification of caregivers catering to the Japanese market could be created, similar to the standards established for the Canadian market. As for language proficiency, the Japanese Language Institute of the Philippines (JPIL) and other Japanese language programs of reputable Philippine universities could be accredited, so that prospective migrant health service workers could learn Japanese and qualify while still in the Philippines. Eliminating the language barrier would allow Filipino health service providers to achieve the remaining requirements more easily. Tertiary health courses could also include units in language and culture to equip the graduates with a working knowledge of their destination country.

Mutual recognition

Expanding training in professional services will require the accreditation of qualifications of service providers in the light of existing differences in training requirements, standards, and licensing mechanisms between countries. In addition, domestic rules governing the practice of a profession entail not only licensing procedures, but also protection against possible risks stemming from the incompetence of service providers. A study by Ramirez (2001) concluded that the quality of Filipino nursing graduates is on par with the other more developed APEC member countries. In order to enhance access by Filipino nurses who are now recognized as service providers in the United States, United Kingdom, and Saudi Arabia, local accreditation bodies like the Professional Regulation Commission (PRC) should now aim at regional accreditation and certification. This will pave the way for local Professional Associations like the Philippine Nurses Association, to enter into mutual recognition agreements within the APEC region. Aiming for international comparability and standards will also serve as a challenge to the Philippine educational system and for nursing education in particular to gain more international respect and recognition (Ramirez, 2001). Another bilateral avenue would be through a Mutual Recognition Agreement (MRA) with Japan on specific key professions and occupations. An MRA is an ideal option because it focuses on particular market access issues including qualifications and technical standard requirements for specific professionals and workers. Bilateral negotiations, as in the case of Japan and the Philippines, are more practicable since countries are able to focus on and resolve key issues related to their two situations. Once bilateral agreements have been achieved, this can lead to other bilateral agreements, which will ultimately extend mutual recognition more widely.

If the MRA is based on recognition of qualifications, the following items should be included:

- Minimum level of education required, including the entry requirements, length of study, and curriculum;
- Minimum level of experience required, including length of conditions or practical training or supervised professional practice prior to licensing;
- A framework of ethical and disciplinary standards; and
- Examinations passed and the extent to which home country qualifications are recognized in the host country.

Aside from enhancing the market access for individual caregivers, the Philippines should explore the liberalization of entry for entry to the Japanese market of Filipino healthcare agencies, and consider how Filipino health professionals, including doctors, nurses, dentists, and physical therapists, can enter the Japanese healthcare sector. The Philippines should work out a mutual recognition agreement with Japan on educational qualifications, professional requirements, and other technical standards so that the qualifications of Filipino health professionals can be recognized in

Japan. Such recognition is a major prerequisite for entry and eventual employment.

Cultural apprehensions

Japanese elderly people have a strong opposition to being taken care of by strangers. They feel that the family should provide the care. The value placed on *inkyo* ("live in hiding") also explains why they want to live quietly, not causing trouble for other people. This tendency among the elderly in Japan was one of the reasons why the detection of sickness was often delayed (Saito, 2003). In the pre-World War II era, the Japanese brought up their children in the expectation of support in their old age. The reason for developing a "Japanese-style welfare society" in the 1970s was to create an inexpensive welfare state where women provided care for their elderly parents at home. Even now, 85 percent of long-term care providers are women (Saito, 2003). Saito mentions another cultural preference of the Japanese elderly, which is to live in hospitals rather than homes for the elderly. They think that old age homes are for poor people. At one time, these homes were places for the elderly who could not be taken care of by their families. As a result, medical expenses for the elderly are increasing year by year in Japan, as the numbers of elderly increase.

Domestic regulations — Numerical quotas

Numerical quotas may no longer hold in the future if market forces mean that the services of foreign workers are no longer needed. This concern, however, can be addressed through special clauses under the agreement like fixing the term of employment. These can be invoked in cases or conditions warranting disengagement from the commitment to employ migrants.

Issues of protection

Discrimination is also a major issue in temporary labor migration. Migrant workers are discriminated against in some host countries as they are seen as taking opportunities from the local labor force. In Japan, workers fear that working conditions of Japanese workers will deteriorate with the entry of a new and cheaper pool of labor. The Japan Nursing Association has cautioned that many hospitals suffer from staff shortages because work rules are inflexible, citing the example of women forced to quit when they have children (*Japan Times*, 2006b). The Nippon Care Service Craft Union is also apprehensive of "importing a makeshift labor force" from overseas instead of utilizing potential workers from Japan. The union argued that unemployed Japanese youth may be willing to work as caregivers but current working conditions are unfavorable and would not allow them to make a living. Importing foreign workers may lower wages in the service sector, and leave them staffed entirely with foreign workers. In relation to this, proper living conditions for foreign workers in terms of salary, education, and medical care have to be ensured to prevent social unrest (ibid.).

Bilateral economic agreements and implementation of guidelines between the Philippines and Japan should include provisions on the protection of overseas Filipino workers in Japan, covering the period from recruitment to their return to the Philippines. Although Japan has strict immigration policies and labor laws that adhere to international standards, the prevalence of abuse, discrimination, nonpayment of wages, violation of contracts and the rising numbers of missing and irregular migrants indicate that the implementation of these laws is very lax. Aside from identifying the flaws in the legal framework of protection, there is a need to regulate migration flows at both ends so that OFWs will not end up as the victims of illegal recruiters, crime syndicates, and unscrupulous employers.

With the exit of highly skilled professionals from the country, the problem of brain drain as a consequence of overseas employment is an issue in the Philippines. However, the brain drain can be transformed into a "brain gain" through technology transfer (see Chapters 1 and 3). Filipino professionals training in Japan should be encouraged to learn to use the latest technology in different fields. The training and experience that they can gain in Japan could be applied in the Philippines upon their return. There should be a mechanism that would ensure the return of Filipinos who have undergone training in Japan to the Philippines, and reduce the temptation to become irregular workers.

Conclusions and Recommendations

Given the aging population in Japan on the one hand, and the ability of the Philippine human resource development institutions to train health workers on the other, it will be of mutual benefit to both countries if the entry of Filipino nurses and caregivers is liberalized to promote increased productivity.

Now that the FTA has been signed,[2] there are issues that need to be addressed for the mutual benefit of the two countries. The first is the language barrier, where Filipino health service providers are compelled to prove their Japanese language proficiency. However, the FTA stipulates that they must qualify while they are in Japan to enable them to stay indefinitely. Government and policymakers should rethink this provision and consider Filipino health workers learning and taking language certification examinations from an accredited Japanese language teaching institution or university in the Philippines.

Second, mutual recognition of qualifications may also facilitate the freer movement of workers. As with arrangements with European countries, Filipino nurses could initially serve as nursing assistants until such time as they prove their competence as required by Japanese quality assurance standards.

Third, cultural apprehension could be addressed by the Japanese government by highlighting the increased productivity of Japanese workers. Similarly, awareness of Japanese culture would help eliminate the cultural barrier between Filipino workers and Japanese patients.

The issue of numerical quotas, however, should be examined to include provisions to allow for changing market forces. The quotas may be limited or extended depending on the success of the movement of health service providers to Japan.

As for the issue of protection, the implementation of FTA guidelines should guarantee international standards and protection against abuse, discrimination, nonpayment of wages, and violation of contracts. The exodus of nurses and care-givers may have detrimental effects on the Philippine healthcare system but, considering that the movement to Japan is only temporary, their exposure to advanced technology and caring procedures may result in a later brain gain. The training and experience they receive in Japan can be applied in the Philippines upon their return. A mechanism for their return should be in place to prevent irregular migration.

Finally, there is a need to strengthen the regulatory measures by both governments to ensure the quality and protection of workers.

---

[2]The FTA has not yet been ratified by the Philippine Senate due to overlapping issues on environment and other political concerns as of December 2007.

References

Ballescas, Rosario (2003). *Filipino Migration to Japan, 1970s to 1990s. Philippines–Japan Relations*. Manila: Ateneo De Manila Press.

ESCAP (2002). "International Migration: An Emerging Opportunity for the Socio-economic Development of the ESCAP Region." Social Policy Paper No. 6. ISBN: 92-1-120103-9 Economic and Social Commission for Asia and the Pacific, United Nations.

Japan Times (2006a). "Japan to Accept 1,000 Filipino Nurses, Caregivers under FTA." *Japan Times*, September 12, 2006.

Japan Times (2006b). "Philippine FTA to Reshape Health Care." *Japan Times*, September 13, 2006.

Osteria, Trinided (1994). *Filipino Female Labor Migration to Japan: Economic Causes and Consequences*. Manilla: De La Salle University Press.

Ramirez, Veronica (2001). "Philippine Maritime and Nursing Education: Bench-marking with APEC Best Practices." Discussion Paper No. 2001-13, University of Asia and the Pacific, APEC Study Center Network.

Saito, Y. (2003). "Elderly Care Policy in Japan during the 20th Century — Historic Review and Prospect for the 21st Century." In *Challenges for Aging Japan — Democracy, Business, Aging*. Tokyo International House of Japan, Ryumonsha, and Shibusawa Eiichi Memorial Foundation; St Louis: Center for International Studies, University of Missouri.

Sasajima, Yoshio (2003). *Labor in Japan*. About Japan Series No. 9. Tokyo: Foreign Press Center.

Technical Education and Skills Development Authority (2003). "Caregivers: Special Breed of Health Workers." http://www.tesda.gov.ph/page.asp?rootID=34&sID=159&pID=52.

Technical Education and Skills Development Authority (2004). "How Saturated is the Caregivers' Market?" http://www.tesda.gov.ph/page.asp?rootID=4&sID=153&pID=34 (February, 2004).

Tullao, Tullao and Michael Cortez (2003). "Movement of Natural Persons between the Philippines and Japan: Issues and Prospects." Discussion Paper Series 04-11, Philippine Institute for Development Studies, 2003, http://publication.pids.gov.ph/details.phtml?pid=2717.

Wickramasekera, Piyasiri (2002). "Asian Labour Migration: Issues and Challenges in an Era of Globalization." International Migration Papers 57. Geneva: International Labor Office.

CHAPTER 11

INTERNATIONAL MIGRATION, BRAIN DRAIN,
AND THE PHILIPPINE ECONOMY'S ROCKY ROAD
TO DEVELOPMENT

Jose V. Camacho Jr.

Introduction

The issues and problems surrounding international migration and the brain drain, especially in developing economies such as the Philippines, will continue to receive more critical attention in the years to come. International migration, which is the flow of people across international borders, and the brain drain, the movement of highly skilled labor from developing to developed economies, will be increasingly difficult to contain against the backdrop of globalization, the revolution in information and communication technology, and the changing demographic patterns in developing and developed countries.

Indeed, the impact and implications of international migration are already immense in both the migrants' countries of origin and destination. For instance, highly skilled people have moved to developed from developing countries that already suffer from shortages of human capital and skilled workers. Moreover, as demonstrated by Ozden and Schiff (2006), "the flow of formal remittances from migrants to their relatives in their country of birth has exhibited a rapid and accelerating rate of growth. The remittance flow has doubled in the last decade, reaching US$216 billion in 2004, with US$150 billion going to developing countries (Ratha, 2005). It surpasses foreign aid and is the largest source of foreign capital for dozens of countries."

The decision to migrate entails a rational comparison by individuals of the economic benefits and costs or the welfare gains and losses, both to themselves and to society in the countries of origin and destination. For countries of origin, these costs include "the loss of skilled migrants' positive impact on society and the resources used to educate them. Migrants are likely to suffer from the separation families, friends, and culture, and from the lack of effective legal protection. Costs for destination countries include the perceived threat to cultural identity and the effect of migrants' competition for the same jobs as natives" (Ozden and Schiff, 2006).

This chapter will examine the patterns, trends, issues and magnitude of Philippine overseas labor migration, and its consequences and impact against the backdrop of a highly globalized world and the Philippine economy. Furthermore, the chapter will describe the quality of human resources that the country has in terms of skills and educational achievement. It will show how the Philippine government has tried to encourage rather than curb the brain drain in view of the country's high levels of unemployment and underemployment. More importantly, the billions of dollars of annual remittances from Filipinos working abroad has become the lifeblood for an economy that is continuously haunted by economic crisis, fiscal deficits, poverty, and a high rate of population growth.

The Philippine Economy and Its Human Resources

One cannot deny that indeed the Philippines is rich in human resources. It has a vast pool of talented and highly educated individuals: engineers, scientists, teachers, doctors, nurses, and other types of moderately and highly skilled labor, such as computer programmers and technicians, and other ICT experts. Every year, the country educates about two-and-a-half million tertiary education students and about one-fifth join the labor force after graduation (Tables 11.1 and 11.2).

The 2005 United Nations Development Program Human Development Report classifies the Philippines as a country with a medium level human development, according to the Human Development Index (Table 11.3). It is a country with comparatively high rates of literacy and basic education participation (Tables 11.4 and 11.5). However, in spite of this rich endowment in human resources, one cannot help but ask why it has lagged behind its

Table 11.1. Higher education enrolment in the Philippines, 2002–2005.

Discipline group	School year		
	2002–2003	2003–2004	2004–2005
Agricultural, forestry, fisheries and veterinary medicine	84,609	78,848	70,824
Architectural and town planning	25,535	22,008	23,225
Business administration and related courses	617,020	557,859	516,928
Education and teacher training	417,619	402,781	366,941
Engineering and technology	354,840	357,514	321,660
Fine and applied arts	10,186	10,828	12,221
General	35,852	41,267	34,234
Home economics	5,788	5,703	5,342
Humanities	29,243	28,534	26,956
Law and jurisprudence	19,428	18,502	19,539
Mass communication and documentation	33,882	27,983	25,299
Mathematics and computer science	271,294	262,970	240,178
Medical and allied	220,195	321,571	445,729
Natural science	28,372	26,221	23,458
Religion and theology	7,642	7,245	7,892
Service trades	15,851	17,347	13,878
Social and behavioral science	73,718	74,731	66,490
Trade, craft and industrial	3,209	1,457	14,946
Other disciplines	172,693	168,009	166,575
Total	2,426,976	2,431,378	2,402,315

Source: Commission on Higher Education (2004).

highly industrialized Asian neighbors in terms of economic growth and development.

The Philippines' economic performance has been likened to a "roller-coaster" ride. As Table 11.6 shows, economic growth in some years since the early 1990s has been negative. The rate of unemployment is endemically high, sometimes reaching double digit levels. The unemployment rate peaked at nearly 11 percent in 2004, the highest recorded since 1991. Although foreign direct investment had increased from US$1.43 billion in 2002 to US$1.49 billion in 2003 (NEDA, 2004), this did not result in lower

Table 11.2. Number of Philippine college graduates by discipline, 2000–2003.

Discipline	School year		
	2000–2001	2001–2002	2002–2003
Agricultural, forestry, fisheries, vet. med.	13,172	13,335	14,765
Architectural and town planning	2,541	3,087	2,746
Business admin. and related	106,559	109,486	110,870
Education and teacher training	71,349	77,555	80,863
Engineering and technology	45,041	48,861	53,487
Fine and applied arts	1,323	1,448	1,522
General	5,238	3,318	3,354
Home economics	957	1,080	1,198
Humanities	4,236	4,871	5,187
Law and jurisprudence	2,214	2,463	2,631
Mass communication and documentation	5,140	5,703	5,140
Mathematics and computer science	33,059	37,354	36,223
Medical and allied	27,296	26,474	33,296
Natural science	4,770	4,950	4,872
Religion and theology	1,052	1,275	1,242
Service trades	2,342	2,641	2,610
Social and behavioral science	13,395	14,090	15,417
Trade, craft and industrial	712	957	395
Other disciplines	23,244	24,891	25,969
Total	363,640	383,839	401,787

Source: Commission on Higher Education (2004).

unemployment. But one has reason to be optimistic with the performance of the service sector, the economy's engine of growth. The expansion of ICT-related businesses continues to be the dominant source of growth and employment in this sector, owing to the brisk investments in call centers, business process outsourcing (BPOs), and software development.

As Table 11.7 indicates, although the Philippine economy experienced a continuous expansion in the 1970s, a pronounced decline occurred in the "lost decade" of the 1980s, when its neighbors achieved an annual economic growth rate of about 6 percent (Balisacan and Hill, 2003). Furthermore, what haunts policymakers is the persistent problem of unemployment, and

Table 11.3. Rank and human development indicators of selected Asian economies, 2005.

Country	Rank	HDI	HDI classification
Japan	11	0.943	High human development
Singapore	25	0.907	High human development
Korea, Rep. of	28	0.901	High human development
Malaysia	61	0.796	Medium human development
Thailand	73	0.778	Medium human development
Philippines	84	0.758	Medium human development
China	85	0.765	Medium human development
Vietnam	108	0.704	Medium human development
Indonesia	110	0.697	Medium human development
India	127	0.602	Medium human development

Source: UNDP (2005) *Human Development Report.*

Table 11.4. Simple literacy rates in the Philippines, 1989–2003.

Year	Combined male and female	Male	Female
1989[a]	89.8	89.8	89.8
1994[a]	93.9	93.7	94.0
2000[b]	92.3	92.1	92.5
2003[c]	93.4	92.6	94.3

Sources: [a]Functional Literacy, Education and Mass Media Survey (FLEMMS); [b]2000 Census of Population and Housing; [c]2003 FLEMMS; National Statistical Coordination Board (NSCB).

the high population growth rate that continues to exacerbate the problem of poverty, particularly in the rural areas. Population growth has increased at a rate of 2.3 percent for the last 10 years, one of the highest among Asian nations (Alonzo *et al.*, 2004). The Asia Development Bank states: "The Philippines provides a concrete example of GDP growth that did not reduce poverty, although the economy recorded growth of more than 4% in 3 of the past 4 years ... growth has not been high enough to keep up with population growth: GNP per capita has lingered at around US$1,000 for the past 20 years" (ADB, 2005).

Table 11.5. School participation rates in the Philippines, 1999–2004.

| Year | Participation rate | |
	Elementary level*	High school level**
1999–2000	96.95	65.43
2000–2001	96.77	66.06
2001–2002	94.31	69.35
2002–2003	94.13	65.06
2003–2004	91.63	66.29

*Based on 7–12 years-old population; **based on 13–16 years-old population.
Source: Department of Education.

Table 11.6. Output growth and unemployment rates in the Philippines, 1991–2005.

| Year | Growth of output, annual change (%) | | | | Unemployment rate (%) |
	GDP	Agriculture	Industry	Service	
1991	−0.6	1.4	−2.7	0.2	9.0
1992	0.3	0.4	−0.5	1.0	8.6
1993	2.1	2.1	1.7	2.5	8.9
1994	4.4	2.6	5.8	4.2	8.4
1995	4.7	0.9	6.7	5.0	8.4
1996	5.9	3.8	6.4	6.4	7.4
1997	5.2	3.1	6.1	5.4	7.9
1998	−0.6	−6.4	−2.1	3.5	9.6
1999	3.4	6.5	0.9	4.0	9.6
2000	4.4	3.4	4.9	4.4	10.1
2001	1.8	3.7	−2.5	4.3	9.8
2002	4.5	4.0	3.9	5.1	10.2
2003	4.5	3.2	3.6	5.8	10.1
2004	6.0	4.9	5.2	7.1	10.9
2005	5.1	2.0	5.3	6.3	10.3

Source: Asian Development Bank (ADB) — Key Indicators 2006 (www.adb.org/statistics).

Table 11.7.   Average growth rate of GDP in selected Southeast Asian countries, 1950–2000 (% per annum).

Country	1950–1960	1960–1970	1970–1980	1980–1990	1990–2000
Indonesia	4.0	3.9	7.6	6.1	4.2
Malaysia	3.6	6.5	7.8	5.3	7.0
Philippines	6.5	5.1	6.3	1.0	3.2
Singapore	NA	8.8	8.5	6.6	7.8
Thailand	5.7	8.4	7.2	7.6	4.2

Note: Each year is a 3-year average of the year indicated, the previous year, and succeeding year.
Source: Balisacan and Hill, 2003.

Table 11.8.   Share of major sectors in Philippines employment, 1970–2000 (%).

Year	Agriculture	Industry	Services
1985	49.7	13.9	36.4
1990	44.8	15.6	39.2
1995	43.5	16.0	40.5
2000	38.6	15.8	46.3

Source: Balisacan and Hill (2003).

The structural change in the Philippine economy deviates from the usual pattern of economic development experienced by East-Asian countries, a structural change which one analyst has described as being "of the wrong kind" (Philippine Human Development Report 2000). Table 11.8 shows that the share of agriculture in employment has continuously decreased, while the share of industry has also steadily declined. This pattern is unlike structural change in other countries of the region. Balisacan and Hill (2003) note: "whereas the more general pattern is for the share of industry to expand, in the Philippine case it too has shrunk, albeit marginally."

The 2005 ADB study of Philippine poverty shows that the incidence of poverty is higher in the agricultural sector (66.2 percent), where most of the employed are laborers (42.5 percent) and farm workers (see Table 11.9). It is also high among the self-employed (43.5 percent), those with family

Table 11.9. Employment of Philippine families by income stratum (%).

	Bottom 40%	Top 60%	Philippines population
Type of economic activity			
Family sustenance activity	76.6	26.9	46.9
Sharecropping	6.7	5.7	6.1
Entrepreneurial activity	74.2	58.9	65.1
Wage and salary employment	53.5	76.5	67.2
By class of workers			
Wage and salary workers	34.4	57.1	48.6
Own-account workers	43.5	32.6	36.7
Unpaid family workers	22.2	10.2	14.7
By major industry group			
Agriculture, fishery, and forestry	66.2	20.9	37.9
Mining and quarrying	0.4	0.3	0.4
Manufacturing	5.1	12.5	9.7
Electricity, gas, and water	—	0.5	0.3
Construction	4.1	6.2	5.4
Wholesale and retail trade	11.5	23.4	18.9
Hotel and restaurant	0.7	3.3	2.3
Transportation, storage, and communication	4.2	9.5	7.5
Financing, insurance, and real estate	0.5	4.5	3.0
Community, social, and personal services	4.6	16.7	12.2
By major occupation group			
Laborers	42.5	22.7	30.1
Farmers	34.1	11.5	20.1
Technicians	0.9	4.0	2.8
Clerks	0.9	6.8	4.6
Service workers	5.1	11.4	9.0
Traders	7.0	11.6	9.9
Plant and machine operators	3.5	10.0	7.6
Special occupations	0.2	0.4	0.3
Professionals	0.4	7.4	4.8
Officials of the Government	5.2	14.1	10.7

Source: 2002 APIS as cited in ADB (2005).

sustenance or entrepreneurial activities, and wage and salary workers (34.4 percent). The study implies: "the basic problem of the poor is not so much lack of employment as the low incomes derived from employment." Although most of the poor have sources of livelihood and employment, these are characterized as low in terms of pay, skills, and productivity (UNDP, 2002; ADB, 2005).

Policies on Overseas Filipino Employment

The migration of Filipinos, particularly to Hawaii and California, started to be noticed during the period of American occupation, from 1898 until World War II. The number of migrant workers considerably increased in the 1960s when the United States started to liberalize its immigration policies (Sicat, 2003: 103). In her analysis of patterns of migration in the Philippines, Low (1970) mentions that "the Philippines is, perhaps, the classic case example cited by Americans during discussions of the brain drain from developing countries ... professional immigration ... has been especially visible because it has concentrated so heavily on one professional area — medicine ... Taking physicians and surgeons alone in the area of high level manpower most relevant to discussion of the brain drain, the scale of Philippine migration was more than six times that of physicians from any other Asian country, including Hong Kong."

Over the years, the deployment of Filipino workers abroad has been a policy choice by the Philippine government and a natural response to high levels of unemployment and underemployment, low levels of economic growth, and a budget deficit. These macroeconomic imbalances are further magnified with the increasing globalization of the international economy (Sicat, 2003: 103). It is in this vein that the Philippine government started to play a facilitating role in generating jobs through helping to organize overseas employment and labor migration.

This active policy of labor export can be traced back to the 1972–1974 oil price boom in the Middle East (O'Neil, 2004). The hike in oil prices made it more profitable for oil refinery industries and construction firms to hire contract workers. With high rates of unemployment and bleak prospects for the economy, President Marcos used the opportunity to deploy skilled Filipino laborers whose remittances formed the lifeblood of their families that were left behind. This deployment of thousands of workers required systematic monitoring and regulation policies, which in turn encouraged more contract workers to be employed overseas (O'Neil, 2004). This led Marcos to create the Philippine Overseas Employment Administration (POEA). The POEA "provides contract labor directly to foreign employers, maritime agencies, and governments. The changes had the effect of bringing the work of Filipinos abroad under the authority of the Philippine government. Whether recruited privately or by the government agency, workers and recruiters enter into a contract that is enforceable under Philippine law" (O'Neil, 2004). In view of criticisms aired by the Catholic Church and non-governmental organizations, POEA was mandated "to be more active in the protection of migrant workers' rights and welfare" and in their safe "return and reintegration."

At present, through its employment facilitation function, POEA conducts comprehensive marketing, research, and development programs in order to generate overseas employment opportunities (POEA, 2004). It provides integrated accreditation and processing services to facilitate the documentation of qualified Filipino workers hired through private employment agencies. In its 2004 Annual Report, POEA reported the following accomplishments through its employment facilitation and promotion, marketing, licensing, and regulation services:

1. Facilitation of the creation of hundreds of thousands of jobs overseas. The number of deployed workers grew by nearly 2 percent from 279,565 in 2003 to 294,914 in 2004.
2. Intensification of promotional strategies, leading to an increase in the demand for a skilled and unskilled workforce in 28 countries.
3. An increase in job orders processed of 212.7 percent.
4. A high level marketing mission that led to signing of memoranda of understanding and placement of workers in South Korea, Taiwan, and Kuwait.

The above accomplishments, according to the former Secretary of Labor and Employment, Patricia Sto. Tomas, was "consistent with the President's priority agenda and with the agency's mandate to manage the overseas employment program." In the same report, she mentioned that "As labor migration remains a dominant fixture in the global economic landscape, we need to constantly review our policies and procedures to make them attuned to the rapid changes in the international environment. Indeed, if we have to keep our position as the world's top supplier of quality labor and ensure our hold on both the traditional and emerging countries of destination for Filipino workers, we need to maintain a strong and healthy partnership with the private sector, as well as with other government agencies involved in the employment of Filipino overseas" (POEA, 2004).

These policy initiatives are consistent with the series of medium term-development plans (MTDP) crafted by the Philippine government, from the Marcos regime in the early 1980s to the current administration. The development plans explicitly state that overseas employment should be a viable option for Filipinos and that it will remain "a legitimate option for the country's workforce. As such, government shall fully respect labor mobility, including the preference of workers for overseas employment. Protection shall be provided to Filipinos who choose to work abroad and programs for an effective reintegration into the domestic economy upon their return shall be put up" (NEDA, 2004; O'Neil, 2004).

In the current development plan (MTDP 2004–2010; NEDA, 2004: 114), it is emphasized that:

> the protection and welfare of overseas Filipino workers (OFWs) is a shared responsibility of the sending as well as the host countries, and this will be a core principle in promoting markets and cultivating bilateral ties with labor receiving countries. For this purpose, government shall pursue forging of bilateral agreements in co-operation with the private sector to secure the employment, security, and protection of OFWs. It shall further sustain the implementation of a comprehensive social service package for OFWs onsite, expand the reintegration program for them including their families and dependents, and intensify country-specific prede-parture orientation seminars. The fight against illegal recruitment shall be sustained through the Presidential Task Force on Illegal Recruitment, and by implementing performance appraisal system of all licensed recruitment agencies. Finally, Tripartite Consultative Councils will be set up to institutionalize OFW and private sector participation in overseas employment.

The Migration of Filipino Workers

One development issue that has constantly confronted the country is that a large number of talented and educated individuals have continued leaving the country to seek "greener pastures" abroad. But more often than not, they have not returned. No doubt, the prospects of high earnings, stable jobs, and decent living conditions in the destination country have made them decide to stay there.

For the period 2000–2004, the number of Filipino workers who went abroad to seek employment averaged about 872,753 per year, increasing at a rate of about 2 percent (Table 11.10). This is attributed mostly to an upward trend in land-based jobs, specifically in 2004 when deployment increased by 8.1 percent, from 651,938 in 2003 to 704,586 in 2004. According to POEA, the total number of deployed workers overseas in 2004 represented about 93.4 percent of the yearly target of 1 million jobs.

There was a marked increase in the deployment of all categories of skilled workers, particularly professional/technical and service workers, from 2003 to 2004. Females made up most of this number, a sizable portion being performing artists, teachers, and health-related workers such as nurses and healthcare assistants (Table 11.11). The top destinations for newly deployed workers were Japan, Saudi Arabia, Taiwan, United Arab Emirates, Kuwait, Hong Kong, South Korea, and other Middle-Eastern countries such as Qatar, Lebanon, and Bahrain (Table 11.12). In terms of these workers' remittances, the Philippines received about US$6.8 billion in 2002, rising to about US$10.6 billion in 2005 (Table 11.13). Policymakers are

Table 11.10. Deployment of overseas Filipino workers, 2000–2004.

Year	Total	Growth rate (%)	Land-based	New hires	Rehires	Sea-based
2000	841,628	0.55	643,304	253,418	389,886	198,324
2001	866,590	3.08	669,639	271,085	390,554	204,951
2002	891,908	2.80	682,315	289,288	393,027	209,593
2003	867,969	−2.68	651,938	279,565	372,373	216,031
2004	933,588	7.60	704,586	284,912	419,674	229,002

Source: Philippine Overseas Employment Administration.

Table 11.11.   Deployment of overseas Filipino workers, by skill category, 2003–2004.

Skill category	2003			2004			Percentage change		
	Female	Male	Total	Female	Male	Total	Female	Male	Total
Professional and technical workers	67,336	11,620	78,956	79,862	13,144	93,006	18.57	13.12	17.80
Administrative and managerial workers	103	284	387	151	339	490	46.60	19.37	26.60
Clerical workers	2,204	1,761	3,965	3,054	2,167	5,221	38.57	23.06	31.70
Sales workers	1,394	1,096	2,490	2,741	1,162	3,903	96.41	6.02	56.6
Service workers	76,296	7,725	84,021	101,595	11,261	112,856	33.10	45.77	34.30
Agricultural workers	29	384	413	20	645	665	−31.03	67.97	61.00
Production workers	18,766	42,586	61,352	20,713	41,978	60,708	10.38	−1.43	2.2
For reclassification	8,975	952	9,927	258	1,368	1,626	−97.13	43.70	−83.60
Total	175,103 76%	66,408 24%	241,511	208,411 75%	72,064 25%	280,475	18.97	8.52	16.1

Source: Philippine Overseas Employment Administration.

Table 11.12. Top ten destinations of new hires, overseas
Filipino workers

Country	2004	2003	% Change
Japan	71,166	58,755	21.1
Saudi Arabia	58,363	51,334	13.7
Taiwan	34,030	35,352	−3.7
UAE	26,653	17,812	49.6
Kuwait	22,640	16,150	40.2
Hong Kong	16,511	14,033	17.7
Qatar	10,919	6,653	64.1
Lebanon	6,155	1,698	262.5
Bahrain	3,683	1,890	94.9
South Korea	3,516	4,080	−13.8

Source: Philippine Overseas Employment Administration.

Table 11.13. Overseas Filipino workers (OFW) remittances,
1999–2006 (US$ in thousands).

For the period	Total	Land-based	Sea-based
1st semester 2006	5,958,866	5,027,704	931,162
2005	10,689,005	9,019,647	1,669,358
2004	8,550,371	7,085,441	1,464,930
2003	7,578,458	6,280,235	1,298,223
2002	6,886,156	5,686,973	1,199,183
2001	6,031,271	4,937,922	1,093,349
2000	6,050,450	5,123,773	926,677
1999	6,794,550	5,948,341	846,209

Source: Central Bank of the Philippines.

hopeful that the level of OFW remittances will continue to rise in the years
to come.

The Migration of Filipino Teachers

The exodus of Filipino teachers to the United States has been a cause of
grave concern for the Philippine educational system, particularly in relation

to its delivery of quality instruction in science and mathematics. As a solid foundation in science and mathematics education is one of the core elements in the country's effort to develop a technologically advanced economy, the migration of science and mathematics teachers to the United States, if it continues unabated, will impede the country's quest to further modernize and industrialize. In this vein, Tabunda's analysis (2005) is instructive as she reveals the following disturbing trends:

1. The demand for science and mathematics teachers in the United States from 1990 to 2004 grew at an average rate of 3.1 percent. For the school year 2003–2004, an additional 1,132 science and mathematics teachers were needed due to increasing enrollment and retirement of teachers. Over a 16-year period, from 1988–2004, the United States accounted for 72.8 percent of the total number of teachers deployed abroad. Other popular destinations for Filipino teachers include Canada (12.4 percent), Australia (9.2 percent), Japan (1.9 percent), and Germany (0.9 percent). Other countries make up the remaining 3.5 percent. Between 2000 and 2004, it is estimated that 818 secondary level teachers were deployed to the United States. These teachers, usually armed with postgraduate degrees and teaching experience, are provided with H1-B visas. This special form of visa is good for six years, allowing them to convert to immigrant status. It is likely that emigration of science and mathematics teachers will increase in the future, as those who are deployed are likely to convert to immigrant status once they become eligible.

2. Even if the Philippines produces a large enough supply of graduates with teacher training, about 84,460 in 2004, only 15 percent of secondary education graduates major in mathematics and another 15 percent specialize in science teaching. The lack of material incentives has generally discouraged the better students from enrolling, thereby resulting in lower graduation rates in science and mathematics education programs. In 2004, only 27.2 percent of the 58,415 applicants passed the licensure examination for teachers to teach in high schools. While the number of applicants for mathematics and science teaching licenses increased during the period 2001–2004, these annual increases can be attributed to the large number of test repeaters. Aggressive recruitment for work

abroad of the country's most qualified, experienced science and mathematics teachers can only result in further deterioration in the quality of science and mathematics instruction in the Philippines, unless even more drastic measures are taken to train the remaining teachers to handle science and mathematics courses.

The above trends have costly implications for the learning outcomes of elementary and high school students as indicated by the dismally low achievement rates in the science, mathematics, and English examinations of the National Achievement Test conducted yearly by the Department of Education (Table 11.14). Over a six-year period, students' performances were way below the 75 percent pass mark. These appalling conditions continue to make worse a situation where fewer and fewer Filipino students gain the necessary skills and competences in elementary and secondary education. Other learning indicators paint a disturbing picture in relation to the Philippines' bid to produce a highly skilled labor force that will make a big difference in a globally competitive knowledge economy. For instance, as Table 11.15 shows, the rates of survival and completion are low, showing a high incidence of drop-outs and inefficiency in the use of school resources.

No wonder that when Filipino students' educational achievement is compared with the performance of other countries in standardized international

Table 11.14. Achievement rates, by subject areas, school year 1999–2005.

	1999–2000	2000–2001	2001–2002	2002–2003	2003–2004	2004–2005
Elementary						
Mathematics	45.69	49.75	—	44.84	59.45	59.10
Science	48.61	49.75	—	43.98	52.59	54.12
English	46.32	47.70	—	41.80	49.92	59.15
High School						
Mathematics	49.99	51.83	—	32.09	46.20	50.70
Science	46.80	45.68	—	34.65	36.80	39.49
English	50.43	51.00	—	41.48	50.08	51.33

Note: Achievement tests were not administered in SY 2001–2002. National Achievement Tests (NAT) were given in Grade IV (for elementary) and 1st year (for secondary) for mathematics, science and English subjects in SY 2002–2003 and SY 2003–2004. In SY 2004–2005, NAT were given to Grade VI (for elementary) and Year IV (for secondary).
Source: Department of Education, National Education and Research Center (NETRC).

Table 11.15. Philippine basic education key indicators,
school year 2002–2003 (%).

Indicators	Male	Female	Overall
Cohort survival rate			
Elementary	66.01	74.06	69.84
Secondary	58.72	73.13	65.83
Drop-out rate			
Elementary	8.44	6.15	7.34
Secondary	16.26	9.96	13.10
Completion rate			
Elementary	62.94	71.18	66.85
Secondary	52.38	67.46	59.79

Source: Department of Education, as cited in NEDA (2004).

tests, the results are discouraging. For instance, the 2000 Philippine Human Development Report illustrates that in the 1999 Trends in International Mathematics and Science Study (TIMSS) Test, the "Philippines ranked 39th — fourth from the bottom and above Kuwait, Colombo, and South Africa. Filipino students in both lower and secondary schools obtained only 31 percent of the correct answers in the math portion. The Philippines math average is only 78 percent of the world average and 42 percent of the scores obtained by Singaporean pupils. In science, the scores of Filipino children in lower and upper secondary schools were below the international median by 77 percent and 80 percent." In the 2003 TIMSS report, the Philippines was placed 41st and 42nd respectively in high school mathematics and science skills among the 45 countries surveyed. The country also failed to move from its 23rd rank among the 25 countries surveyed in elementary school mathematics and science.

The Migration of Filipino Nurses

Nurses, like doctors, are the backbone of any country's healthcare system. In the Philippines, thousands of students are attracted to enroll in nursing degree programs. This is because of the expected high incomes and other benefits that await them when they land a job overseas, particularly in the United States, United Kingdom, or other developed countries such as Canada, Japan, Austria, and Norway. The large numbers of middle-aged professionals who are seeking a more lucrative career change also contribute to the increasing numbers of enrolments in nursing degree programs. These "second degree" shifters include doctors as well as teachers, clerks, government employees, accountants, journalists, and secretaries. More often than not, these "career shifters" are able to take shorter programs since they gain credits for basic science subjects from their earlier education.

As a result of the increase in student enrollment, many private and government-run schools have started to offer degree programs in nursing. This is in spite of the fact that most of these schools are ill-prepared in terms of the competency of teaching staff and adequacy of hospitals and healthcare facilities to offer the degree programs that will guarantee high quality graduates. The efficiency and quality of their output can be best judged in terms of their performance in the nursing licensure examination which is administered yearly by the Philippine Professional Regulation Commission (PRC). In this examination, the schools where examinees graduated can be identified. A quick survey of the June 2006 examination results revealed that there were 360 schools in the country that offered degree program in nursing. It is disappointing to note that more than one-third of these schools had no graduates who passed the national test. The low pass rates from the 1995 to 2006 examinations are also indicative of the poor performance of the graduates from these schools (Table 11.16). To be able to continue operating under Philippine law, it is mandatory that a nursing school must have a pass rate of at least 5 percent. The Commission on Higher Education (CHED) wants to push the rate higher to 30 percent, a level that could close down many of the nursing schools. Yet, in spite of this poor performance, the Philippines sent nearly 85,000 nurses to work abroad as seen from Table 11.17. The top three destination countries include Saudi Arabia, the United States, and the United Kingdom (Table 11.18).

The exodus of qualified nurses abroad to seek greener pastures is indeed alarming and could lead the country to a severe healthcare crisis. This situation greatly undermines the nation's capability to provide adequately for the medical needs of its growing population.

Table 11.16.   Philippine nursing board performance 1994–2006.

Year	Number of examinee	% of examinees that passed
1995	38,389	58.24
1996	25,163	54.22
1997	19,546	50.02
1998	17,101	55.79
1999	13,152	49.86
2000	9,270	49.63
2001	8,269	53.57
2002	9,449	44.75
2003	15,606	48.23
2004	25,294	49.74
2005	50,280	51.60
2006	42,006	42.42

Source: Professional Regulation Commission.

Table 11.17.   Total number of nurses deployed overseas from the Philippines, 1995–2003.

Year	Number of nurses deployed
1995	7,584
1996	4,734
1997	4,242
1998	4,591
1999	5,413
2000	7,683
2001	13,536
2002	11,911
2003	18,450
Total	84,843

Source: POEA, 2004; Institute of Health Policy and Development Studies, 2004 in Galvez-Tan, 2006.

Access to healthcare, particularly in the rural areas, has worsened and become more inequitable. For instance, as reported by Tan and associates (Tan *et al.*, 2005; Tan, 2006), more than 50 percent of the population has no access to health care, especially in regions and provinces where the poverty

Table 11.18. Top 10 countries for deplyment of nurses, 2000–2003.

Destination	2003	2002	2001	2000
Saudi Arabia	5,740	5,704	5,045	3888
United States*	196	320	304	89
United Kingdom*	1,544	3,105	5,383	2615
Libya	52	414	9	17
United Arab Emirates	226	405	243	305
Ireland	207	915	1529	–
Singapore	326	337	413	292
Kuwait	51	108	182	133
Qatar	242	213	143	7
Taiwan	200	131	9	0

Note: *Underreporting has a high probability.
Source: Philippine Overseas Employment Administration (POEA), 2004 as cited in Galvez-Tan, 2006.

Table 11.19. Measurements of access to basic health services, Philippines, 2002–2003.

Percent of children who were delivered by a health professional	59.8% (2003)[a]
Percent of children who were delivered in a health facility	37.9% (2003)[a]
Percent of deaths attended by a health professional	48% (2003)[b]
Percent of children 12–23 months fully immunized	60% (2003)[a]
Contraceptive prevalence rate	48.9 (2003)[a]
Physicians per 100,000 people	124 (2002)[c]
Percent of children who were delivered by a health professional	59.8% (2003)[a]

Source: [a]National Demographic and Health Survey [NDHS], 2003; [b]National Statistics Office, 2004; [c]United Nations Development Program (UNDP), 2003, as cited in Tan *et al.* (2005), Tan (2006).

incidence is high. For instance, some hospitals and clinics in Mindanao "could not operate their new wards due to lack of nurses. The southernmost island of Mindanao has always been deficient in the health human resources, whether in numbers, ratios, or distribution. Mass migration has severely strained this underserved part of the country." As shown in Table 11.19, their analysis also suggests that "5 out of 10 Filipinos die without getting medical attention. Only 60 percent of the population has full access to essential drugs. Ten mothers die every day due to pregnancy and childbirth-related causes. Forty percent of all births are still unattended by healthcare professionals. More than 100 municipalities remain doctorless and nurseless at any time during the past 10 years."

Concluding Remarks

There has been extensive analysis of the impact of migration on the receiving countries' economies, especially on markets for unskilled labor (LaLonde and Topel, 1997). However, the links between migration and development issues in the sending countries have been somewhat neglected, particularly as far as empirical research is concerned (Borjas, 1999). In spite of the advances in social science research and methodology, little attention has been given to empirical work on linkages between migration and development, specifically those that focus on the economies of sending countries in relation to destinations (LaLonde and Topel, 1997; Borjas, 1999). As explained by Ozden and Schiff (2006), this lack can be explained by the

> relatively minor role played by migration in promoting the integration of developing countries into the world economy in the post-World War II era. In contrast to policies regulating trade and capital flows, immigration policies of destination countries continue to be highly protectionist and explain, in part, the absence of large migration flows, especially when compared with the second half of the 19th century. A second reason for this oversight has been the absence of systematic and reliable data on international migration patterns and migrant characteristics at either the aggregate or the household level.

Since the early 1980s, there has been a significant increase in the number of Filipino migrant workers. The forces of globalization and economic liberalization have further intensified their migration. Macroeconomic imbalances also contributed to the large outflow of labor abroad, mainly because of unemployment, economic opportunities, incentives, and rewards system specifically in the sphere of public sector work. Lien and Wang (2005) demonstrate that "skilled migration tends to lower the source country employment level and thus has negative welfare implications for the source country." The large outflow of teachers and nurses as demonstrated in this chapter vividly illustrates an outflow of skilled and educated workers. Sooner or later, this increasing outflow will cause a severe crisis in the education and healthcare systems where the unskilled and semi-skilled workers and professionals are left at home. While this is happening, the government has not made significant progress in creating economic growth and productivity gains, and in generating jobs to hasten and widen labor absorption. Meanwhile, high population growth will continue to exacerbate the problem of unemployment for many young graduates and others who are educated. Even when there are jobs available, the entry of less skilled and less educated workers into a tight labor market can depress wage rates in general, even the wages of those who are highly skilled and better trained, which in turn may induce them to seek more lucrative employment abroad.

However, source countries could potentially reap benefits from the brain drain and skilled labor migration. The empirical studies of Miyagiwa (1991) and Stark *et al.* (1997, 1998) as cited in Lien and Wang (2005) show that the "brain drain may raise the education and income levels of the source country" which as a consequence can lead to a "higher average level of human capital per worker." Positive externalities or "spillover effects" can actually be derived from the brain drain. For instance, as explained by Tabunda (2005), "the recruitment of teachers by the United States could in the short run provide the material incentives that would attract more and better qualified students to take degrees in science and math teaching, just as global demand for nurses has attracted more and better students to the country's nursing programs."

References

Alonzo, R. *et al.* (2004). "Population and Poverty: The Real Score." School of Economics, University of the Philippines, available at http://www.econ.upd. edu.ph/respub/dp/htm/DP2004-15.htm.

Asian Development Bank (ADB) (2006). *Key Indicators 2006*. Manila: Asian Development Bank, available at www.adb.org/statistics.

Asian Development Bank (ADB) (2005). *Poverty in the Philippines: Income, Assets, and Access*. Manila: Asian Development Bank.

Balisacan, A.M. and H. Hill (eds.) (2003). *The Philippine Economy: Development, Policies and Challenges.* New York: Oxford University Press.

Borjas, George (1999). "The Economic Analysis of Immigration." In *Handbook of Labor Economics*, Vol. 3A, edited by Orley Ashenfelter and David Casel. Dordrecht, Netherlands: North Holland.

Central Bank of the Philippines (Bangko Sentral ng Pilipinas). OFW Remittances. Available at www.bsp.gov.ph.

Commission on Higher Education, Philippines (2004). *Academic Year 2003–2004 Higher Education Statistical Bulletin.* Available at www.ched.gov.ph/statistics/index.html.

Department of Education, Philippines. Facts and figures. Available at www.deped.gov.ph.

Human Development Network (2000). *Philippine Human Development Report 2000.* Quezon City: Human Development Network.

Human Development Network (2002). *Philippine Human Development Report 2002.* Quezon City: Human Development Network.

LaLonde, Robert J. and Robert H. Topel (1997). "Economic Impact of International Migration and the Economic Performance of Migrants." In *Handbook of Population and Family Economics*, edited by Mark Rosenzweig and Oded Stark. Amsterdam: North-Holland.

Lien, Donald and Yan Wang (2005). "Brain Drain or Drain Gain? A Revisit." *Journal of Population Economics* 18: 153–163.

Low, Ruth Heather (1970). "Chapter 3 — The Philippines." In *The International Migration of High Level Manpower. Its Impact on Development Process*, edited by Committee on the International Migration of Talent. New York: Praeger.

Miyagiwa K. (1991). "Scale Economies in Education and the Brain Drain Problem." *International Economic Review* 32: 743–759.

National Center for Education Statistics (2004). U.S. Department of Education, Institute of Education Sciences. "Highlights From the Trends in International Mathematics and Science Study (TIMSS 2003)." December 2004. Available at http://nces.ed.gov/.

National Statistical Coordination Board, Philippines. *Simple Literacy of the Population 10 Years Old and Over.* Available at www.nscb.gov.ph/secstat/d_educ.asp.

National Statistical Coordination Board (2004). Philippine Statistical Yearbook. Makati City.

NEDA (2004). "Philippine Medium Term Development Plan (MTPDP) 2004–2010." Pasig City: National Economic and Development Authority.

O'Neil, Kevin (2004). "Labor Export as Government Policy: The Case of the Philippines." Washington D.C.: Migration Policy Institute, available at http://www.migrationinformation.org/USFocus/print.cfm?ID=191.

Ozden, Caglar and Maurice Schiff (eds.) (2006). *International Migration, Remittances and the Brain Drain.* Washington D.C.: World Bank.

POEA (2004). "Annual Report." Manila: Philippine Overseas Employment Administration, available at www.poea.gov.ph.

Professional Regulation Commission, Philippines. Available at www.prc.gov.ph and http://newsinfo.inq7.net/.

Ratha, Dilip (2005). "Workers' Remittances: An Important and Stable Source of External Development Finance." In *Remittances: Development Impact and Future Prospects*, edited by Samuel Munzele Maimbo and Dilip Ratha. Washington D.C.: World Bank.

Sicat, Gerardo P. (2003). *Philippine Economic and Development Issues*, Vol III. Manila: Anvil.

Stark, O., C. Helmenstein and A. Prskawetz (1997). "A Brain Gain with a Brain Drain." *Economics Letters* 55: 227–234.

Stark, O., C. Helmenstein and A. Prskawetz (1998). "Human Capital Depletion, Human Capital Formation, and Migration: A Blessing in a 'Curse'?" *Economics Letters* 60: 363–367.

Tabunda, Ana Maria L. (2005). "Deployment, Emigration and Shortage of Qualified Science and Math Teachers." Available at www.sei.dost.gov.ph/deployment.pps.

Tan, Jaime Galvez, F. Sanches and V. Balanon (2005). "The Brain Drain Phenomenon and Its Implications for Health, in *Filipino Diaspora.*" Paper presented to University of the Philippines Alumni Council Meeting, 24 July 2005.

Tan, Jaime Galvez (2006). "Philippines: The Challenge of Managing Migration." Paper presented to the Academy Health, 2006 Health in Foreign Policy Forum, Washington D.C., www.academyhealth.org/nhpc/foreignpolicy/agenda.htm.

United Nations Development Program (2005). *Human Development Report 2005.* New York: Oxford University Press.

CHAPTER 12

THE GROWING ROLE OF INTERNATIONAL
REMITTANCES IN THE VIETNAMESE ECONOMY:
EVIDENCE FROM THE VIETNAM (HOUSEHOLD)
LIVING STANDARD SURVEYS

Wade Donald Pfau and Thanh Long Giang

Introduction

In detailing the situation of overseas remittances to Vietnam in the 1990s and 2000s, this chapter investigates an important aspect of globalization in the Asia-Pacific region. Indeed, overseas remittances are playing an increasingly important role in the Vietnamese economy. Hernándes-Crossndes-Cross (2005) reports that remittances from overseas totalled US$1.2 billion in 1999. By 2003, they grew to $2.6 billion. In terms of gross domestic product (GDP), this represents a growth from 4.4 percent of GDP in 1999 to 7.4 percent in 2003. Since 2000, overseas remittances have been larger than Overseas Development Assistance and at a level comparable to Foreign Direct Investment. Foreign remittances are undoubtedly having an impact on the Vietnamese economy in numerous ways and deserve to be a focus of research.

In an attempt to fill some of these research needs, this chapter seeks to quantify the impact and the evolution of foreign remittances on the people of Vietnam by using the Vietnam (Household) Living Standards Surveys (VLSS) in 1992/1993, 1997/1998, 2002, and 2004. The objectives of this study include, first, to characterize international remittance receipts and their evolution over time. We will determine where they come from, the percentage of recipient households, and what proportion of household expenditures they represent. We will also analyze the socioeconomic and demographic characteristics of those households receiving remittances from abroad, as well as how the remittance sender is related to the receiver, and how the funds are spent by households. Finally, we will consider the relationship between remittances and inequality in Vietnam. To accomplish these goals, we will initially review the existing studies on foreign remittances. Then, we will present our data and methodology, as well as advantages and limitations of the data. This is followed by our analysis. The last part will present concluding remarks and directions for further studies.

Our findings conclude that overseas remittances to Vietnam come from throughout the world, but are dominated by the United States as a main source. Also, over time, the destinations of foreign remittances are becoming more diverse as they move away from Ho Chi Minh City and other urban areas, to other regions, particularly rural areas. Nonetheless, the percentage of households receiving overseas remittances has held steady at around 5–7 percent of the population. Also, widows, the elderly, female-headed households, and households where the head does not work receive foreign remittances disproportionately. This helps to ensure that foreign remittances actually improve equality in Vietnam with regard to per-capita household expenditures, even though the improvements are quite small. Nonetheless, the improvements to income equality caused by overseas remittances are becoming more substantial over time. We have also determined that overseas remittances are used primarily for consumption, and that they are mainly provided by close family members including children, spouses, and siblings.

Previous Studies of Overseas Remittances

There are a few studies of remittances in Vietnam available to researchers. For instance, Le and Nguyen (1999) used the 1992/1993 VLSS to study domestic and international remittance flows in Vietnam. Their main interest was to determine the impact of remittances on income distribution, finding that while internal remittances tended to reduce inequality, the flow of remittances from overseas tended to go more toward high-income households and thus exacerbate inequality. They also built regression models to delineate who received remittances and how big these remittances would be.

Another study by Cox (2004) uses the 1992/1993 and the 1997/1998 VLSS surveys. Cox considers the issue of private inter-household transfers in Vietnam, which include both remittances and loans. He examines the characteristics associated with transfer receipts, the impact of transfers on inequality, and the flow of transfers between generations. His particular interest is in the elderly and whether private transfers are able to help them sufficiently, in spite of the weak public insurance system. By using longitudinal data from the surveys, he presents evidence that private transfers, primarily remittances, do act as a type of insurance responding to events such as retirement or widowhood. He also compares the role of remittances that flow within regions, between regions, and from overseas sources, and he finds remittances to be a major source of income redistribution, more than twice the size of public transfers.

Another more recent study that includes coverage of remittances is by Babieri (2006). This study uses the 3 percent sample available for public use of the 1999 Census and the VLSS of 1997/1998 to analyze rates of co-residence and flows of remittances between the elderly and their children. This chapter develops a regression model to explain what characteristics determine whether elderly people can expect to receive remittances from their children. Though this chapter is not specifically about international remittances, it seeks to test whether the intensification of migration accompanying economic reform in Vietnam is leading to the breakdown of inter-generational family support in the country. Babieri (2006: 27) concludes that children continue to support their parents and that "geographic distance between adult children and their elderly parents should not be interpreted as a sign of indifference."

More broadly, we can also find a large literature on the theoretical and empirical impacts of remittances. Much of the theoretical literature seeks to explain a two-step process: first people must migrate, and then they must send remittances home. In fact, this literature says little about whether international remittances will lead to greater income equality or to a more unequal distribution of income. Ravallina and Robleza (2003), however, summarize the relationship between migration and equality very well. According to one argument, only the wealthiest people will be able to afford the costs of education, training, and migration for family members necessary to make the receipt of international remittances possible. In this scenario, remittance receipts therefore increase income inequality. The alternative argument is that the wealthiest members of the society tend to be more content, so that it is only those in weaker positions who make the sacrifices needed to send family members overseas. Thus the receipt of remittances tends to promote income equality in the home society.

Beyond the issues of migration, the relationship between remittances and inequality remains unclear. One could expect remittances to flow from the well-off to the less well-off as a type of insurance mechanism that could play an important role in countries with weak social insurance systems. Remittances could also promote economic growth by providing funds for human capital and infrastructure development. These factors would tend to promote equality, or to at least improve the situations of most people in the country. Alternatively, remittances could produce greater inequality by creating a well-off group of recipients who enjoy increased consumption from year to year without feeling a need for work.

Empirical work on the impact of remittance receipts on income distribution has now been completed for a number of countries. For example, Adams (1991) found that while international remittances did reduce poverty in Egypt by a small amount, their overall impact on the income distribution was negative. Adams repeated this analysis for Pakistan in 1992, Guatemala in 2004, and Ghana in 2006, and he generally found that international remittances had a negligible or slightly negative impact on the income distribution (Adams 1992, 2001 and 2006).

Data and Methodology

The VLSSs are organized by household, but they also include some data on each individual in the household, such as age, gender, relationship to household head, marriage status, working status, salary, health, and education. Table 12.1 shows the number of households and individuals interviewed for each survey. At the household level, the surveys provide extensive data on sources of income, business and agricultural enterprises, detailed household expenditures, ownership of consumer durables, poverty incidence, poverty alleviation programs, and housing conditions. The households are representative of the entire Vietnamese population, both urban and rural, and from across the regions.

Remittances are defined in the surveys as the amount of money and monetary value of in-kind benefits received by a household from people not

Table 12.1. Number of households and individuals in the Vietnam (household) living standards surveys.

Year	Number of households	Number of individuals
1992/1993	4,800	24,068
1997/1998	6,002	28,633
2002	29,530	132,384
2004	9,189	39,696

Source: Authors' calculations from VLSS 1992/3 and 1997/8, and VHLSS 2002 and 2004.

living in the household and which do not require repayment. With respect to information about remittances, we can think of the two surveys from the 1990s as being similar to one another, but as different from the two surveys in the 2000s. Generally speaking, the information about remittances in the surveys from the 1990s is much more complete than in the later surveys. For the 1990s, we know specific details about each remittance a family receives. This information includes which family member received it, the relationship of the remittance sender to the receiver, the gender of the sender, and where the sender lives, including which country the remittance came from, if it came from overseas. The 1990s surveys also include details about both remittances received and sent by each household, which allows a researcher to determine whether the household is a net receiver or sender, though this detail is not important for the analysis of overseas remittances, since very little is sent out of Vietnam. For 1997/1998, we even know how the household spent the remittances it received. However, not all of these details are included in the 2002 and 2004 surveys. For the later surveys, we only know the total amount of remittances received by each household, divided into domestic and international remittances. Thus, for the later surveys we cannot discuss the relationship between the sender and receiver, whether the household is a net sender or receiver, and from which country the remittance came.

Other general limitations of the data that bear some relevance to the topic of this chapter include the fact that we generally have only information about relatives who live in the same household (particularly in the later surveys), and therefore it is difficult to identify other relatives who may be living nearby or have migrated to other areas. Thus, we cannot identify which households have family members living overseas and which do not, in order to identify the potential for international remittances. For instance, while we know about receipt of remittances from children, we cannot say what percentage of non-co-resident children provide them. Furthermore, besides wages, most income sources are only identified at the household level, so it is not clear which member is the source of the income. Wealth data are also only available at the household level. This limits the analysis of intra-household sharing.

In this chapter, we will analyze our research objectives by using data tabulations for each survey to observe trends over time. We use the individual and household weights so that the tabulations are representative for the entire Vietnamese population. Thus, we can observe changes in overseas remittance flows during a time period in which the Vietnamese population experienced profound social and economic changes.

Results

In the following Section, different aspects of overseas remittances to Vietnam will be analyzed, in order to gain a better understanding of their impact on Vietnamese households.

Characteristics of remittance flows in Vietnam

The role of remittances in the Vietnamese economy is growing, both in terms of the percentage of households receiving them and in the overall size of the remittances. Though this chapter is primarily concerned with international remittances, we will first provide some evidence of the overall situation of remittances in Vietnam. Remittances can flow either within the same province, between different provinces, or from overseas.

As seen from Table 12.2, data for the origin of remittances are much more extensive for the 1990s surveys than for the 2002 and 2004 surveys. Before going into greater detail about the 1990s, we can see the overall time trend of rapid growth in the proportion of domestic remittances. In 1992/1993, 71.7 percent of the total value of remittance flows came from overseas sources, and this amount gradually fell to 36.8 percent in 2004. With this in mind, we can say much more about the 1990s. In 1992/1993,

Table 12.2. Vietnam's flow of remittances by origin (percent of total value of remittances).

	1992/93 (%)	1997/98 (%)
Source of remittances		
Within same province	18.9	27.8
Between provinces	9.4	17.0
International	71.7	57.3
Source of international remittances		
Laos	0.0	0.0
Cambodia	0.2	0.0
Thailand	0.3	0.4
China	0.2	0.2
Hong Kong	0.0	1.1
Taiwan	n/a	0.8
Australia	7.3	8.6
France	2.8	4.0
Western Europe	9.9	7.7
Former Soviet Union	3.4	3.2
Eastern Europe	9.3	3.9
United States	41.1	57.7
Canada	6.2	6.1
Other	19.2	6.5
North America	47.3	63.8
Europe	22.0	15.6
Australia	7.3	8.6
Asia	4.2	5.6
Other	19.2	6.5
	2002 (%)	2004 (%)
Source of Remittances		
Domestic	61.3	63.2
International	38.7	36.8

Source: Authors' calculations from VLSS 1992/3 and 1997/8, and VHLSS 2002 and 2004.

18.9 percent of the value of remittances moved between households within the same province, 9.4 percent between provinces, and 71.7 percent from overseas. Five years later, in 1997/1998, international remittances represented only 57.3 percent of the total remittance value, while remittances

flowing within a province represented 27.8 percent of remittance value, and
those between provinces represented 17 percent of the total value. The most
popular source for overseas remittances was the United States, which provided 41.1 percent of the overseas total in 1992/1993, and 57.7 percent in
1997/1998. By continents, in both surveys, North America led with the most
remittances, followed by Europe, Australia, and Asia. The "other" category
was also particularly substantial in 1992/1993, representing 19.2 percent
of overseas remittances, but no additional details were provided to indicate
which countries were represented.

As noted, this period was characterized by a growing fraction of the
remittance totals coming from domestic sources. One may wonder whether
this indicates an increase in the absolute value of domestic remittances, or
a decrease in value of overseas remittances. To help answer this, Table 12.3
shows the percentage of households (weighted by household size) receiving
remittances from domestic sources and foreign sources. The percentage
of households receiving international remittances does not increase much
during the period, moving from 5.6 percent of households in 1992/1993
to 7.25 percent of households in 2004. Meanwhile, the percentage of

Table 12.3.   Percentage of households receiving remittances based on origin
of remittances.

	1992/1993 (%)	1997/1998 (%)	2002 (%)	2004 (%)
Receipt of remittances from				
No remittances	79.28	77.32	20.01	12.28
Domestic remittances	16.11	17.83	77.31	86.65
International remittances	5.60	5.60	5.93	7.25
Receipt of remittances from				
No remittances	79.28	77.32	20.01	12.28
Domestic remittances only	15.12	17.06	74.06	80.47
International remittances only	4.62	4.85	2.68	1.67
Both international and domestic	0.99	0.78	3.25	5.58

Note: Columns in the top half of the table do not add to 100 because households
receiving both domestic and international remittances are counted twice.
Source: Authors' calculations from VLSS 1992/3 and 1997/8, and VHLSS 2002 and
2004.

households receiving domestic remittances explodes, particularly between the 1997/1998 and 2002 surveys. In 1992/1993, only 16.11 percent of households received domestic remittances, but this grew to 77.31 percent of households in 2002 and 86.65 percent of households in 2004. Further down Table 12.3, we can see that even for households receiving overseas remittances, it became more common during this period to receive domestic remittances also.

Socioeconomic and demographic characteristics of households with remittances

Table 12.4 describes the socioeconomic characteristics of those receiving international remittances. We examine various characteristics of the household, including its regional location, urban/rural status, marital status, gender, and age of the household head, and whether the household head is employed. For each survey year, there are three columns. First, the percentage of Vietnam's population represented by each category is shown. Then, we see the percentage of overseas remittances received by each category. The third column then shows the ratio of foreign remittances received to the proportion of the population represented by each group. If the ratio is above 1, then the group receives a disproportionate share of remittances from overseas, while those with a ratio less than 1 receive a relatively smaller share. This table demonstrates that recipients of remittances do not represent a random sample of Vietnam's population, and helps to elucidate those who are more likely to receive such remittances.

First, by region, Table 12.4 shows that the South East region of the country consistently receives the most remittances from overseas. Throughout the period, the South East contained about 15 percent of Vietnam's population. Meanwhile, at the low point in 2002, the South East received 29.2 percent of the total international remittances, compared with 49.1 percent in 1997/1998. The South East includes Ho Chi Minh City, which is particularly well known as a home for families who have relatives overseas. After the South East, no region can consistently claim a relatively large proportion of international remittances; though there are regions that consistently receive lower levels of remittances relative to their populations. For the Central Highlands and North East, the ratio of foreign remittances

Table 12.4. Flow of international remittances in Vietnam based on household characteristics.

	1992/1993			1997/1998			2002			2004		
	Percent of population	Percent of foreign remittances received	Ratio of foreign remittances received to population	Percent of population	Percent of foreign remittances received	Ratio of foreign remittances received to population	Percent of population	Percent of foreign remittances received	Ratio of foreign remittances received to population	Percent of population	Percent of foreign remittances received	Ratio of foreign remittances received to population
Region												
Red river delta	20.2	30.9	1.5	19.6	15.8	0.8	21.9	9.5	0.4	22.1	19.5	0.9
North east	14.2	3.0	0.2	15.1	2.8	0.2	11.9	5.7	0.5	11.6	3.9	0.3
North west	2.6	0.2	0.1	2.9	0.0	0.0	2.7	1.0	0.4	3.0	0.7	0.2
North central coast	12.8	1.2	0.1	13.8	6.9	0.5	13.4	9.5	0.7	13.1	10.9	0.8
South central coast	9.5	8.0	0.8	8.5	9.9	1.2	8.5	9.8	1.2	8.7	9.9	1.1
Central highlands	2.3	0.7	0.3	2.8	0.3	0.1	5.8	2.8	0.5	5.0	1.8	0.3
South east	15.9	42.6	2.7	15.9	49.1	3.1	14.6	29.2	2.0	16.2	31.6	2.0
Mekong river delta	22.5	13.3	0.6	21.5	15.3	0.7	21.3	32.5	1.5	20.4	21.8	1.1
Urban/Rural States												
Rural	80.0	20.9	0.3	77.6	25.2	0.3	76.8	49.0	0.6	74.1	49.9	0.7
Urban	20.0	79.1	4.0	22.4	74.8	3.3	23.2	51.0	2.2	25.9	50.1	1.9

(Continued)

Table 12.4. (*Continued*)

Marital status of household head												
Married	85.4	76.7	0.9	86.4	78.7	0.9	85.6	74.5	0.9	84.8	68.2	0.8
Widowed	10.9	15.1	1.4	10.4	11.8	1.1	11.5	17.5	1.5	12.3	23.6	1.9
Otherwise not married	3.7	8.2	2.2	3.2	9.6	3.0	2.9	8.0	2.8	2.9	8.3	2.8
Gender of household head												
Male	77.3	57.5	0.7	78.4	55.0	0.7	79.5	57.0	0.7	78.3	52.1	0.7
Female	22.7	42.5	1.9	21.6	45.0	2.1	20.5	43.0	2.1	21.7	47.9	2.2
Age of household head												
20–29	10.7	2.0	0.2	5.4	2.5	0.5	5.0	4.9	1.0	3.2	3.3	1.0
30–39	29.6	29.4	1.0	28.3	17.1	0.6	26.2	20.5	0.8	23.1	12.5	0.5
40–49	22.5	12.5	0.6	29.4	29.5	1.0	31.5	26.7	0.8	32.4	28.5	0.9
50–59	18.3	27.3	1.5	17.8	19.3	1.1	17.0	15.8	0.9	20.0	22.6	1.1
60–69	13.1	13.5	1.0	13.4	14.7	1.1	11.5	13.7	1.2	11.5	16.4	1.4
70–79	4.9	12.5	2.6	4.9	11.2	2.3	7.0	14.9	2.1	7.4	12.9	1.7
80–89	0.7	2.9	3.9	0.8	5.6	7.4	1.7	3.1	1.8	2.1	3.7	1.7
90 and older	0.1	0.0	0.0	0.1	0.2	4.0	0.2	0.2	0.9	0.3	0.0	0.0
Work status of household head												
Not working	10.7	32.3	3.0	15.2	39.5	2.6	14.0	35.6	2.5	15.3	35.8	2.3
Working	89.3	67.7	0.8	84.8	60.5	0.7	86.0	64.4	0.7	84.7	64.2	0.8

Source: Authors' calculations from VLSS 1992/3 and 1997/8, and VHLSS 2002 and 2004.

to population was at its highest at 0.5 in 2002, and the North West also reached its peak in 2002 with a ratio of 0.4.

Regarding urban/rural status, urban areas consistently claim a larger share of remittances from overseas, though rural areas have been consistently gaining ground over time. In 1992/1993, rural areas contained 80 percent of Vietnam's population, but only received 20.9 percent of the total foreign remittances. By 2004, the rural areas had lost some population so that they represented 74.1 percent of the country's people, while the portion of foreign remittances grew to 49.9 percent. Thus, just as the share of remittances going to the South East region decreased over time, we are able to see evidence of growing geographic diversity in terms of where foreign remittances flow in Vietnam.

The next categories in Table 12.4 are the marital status and gender of the household head. Across the years, households with a married head have tended to receive relatively smaller remittances. Instead, these remittances tend to flow more to widows and those otherwise not married. Similarly, while males tend to head about 78 percent of Vietnamese households (weighted by household size), such households only receive about 55 percent of the foreign remittances over time. By 2004, females headed 21.7 percent of households, and their households accounted for 47.9 percent of foreign remittances. Actually, increasing remittances to female-headed households can be observed over time, as in 1992/1993 females headed 22.7 percent of households and received 42.5 percent of the value of overseas remittances. Contrary to the earlier hypothesis that international remittances would reinforce the wealth of otherwise well-off households, the tendency for overseas remittances to flow to unmarried and female-headed households provides some initial evidence that remittances may be helping to equalize incomes. This is an issue we will turn to again in later sections.

The next grouping in Table 12.4 is by the age of the household head. Here, we can see evidence of overseas remittances being used to support elderly family members, though unlike before, this is a trend that weakens rather than strengthening over time. Nonetheless, these numbers do not provide the full story because we do not know about who else is living with the household head for the purposes of this table. For instance, if a child moves from overseas back to Vietnam to take care of elderly parents directly instead of providing remittances, then the table would show declining remittance flows to the elderly without properly characterizing the shift in type of support. Giang and Pfau (2007) provide some evidence regarding this matter by categorizing elderly households as those who are dependent on younger family members and those who are not. They find that the number of elderly people living as dependents is declining in favor of the elderly living alone. This would imply that a breakdown is occurring as the elderly people also receive less overseas remittances, and so further research is needed in this area using the longitudinal aspects of the dataset.

Finally, Table 12.4 shows that regarding work status, the tendency is for the head of households not to be working when they receive international remittances. In 1992/1993, 10.7 percent of household heads were not working, and these households received 32.3 percent of the overseas remittance flows. By 2004, 15.3 percent of household heads were not working, and they received 35.8 percent of the remittance value. However, this correlation does not reveal the underlying causation. It could be that households who can receive international remittances become lazy and less likely to work, or it could be that such household heads are unable to work and thus their family members are more willing to sacrifice to provide them with remittance income. The aging of the population as well as the flows to widows and others indicates the second scenario is likely, but it could be that both possibilities are playing a role.

Relationship between the senders and receivers of international remittances

Using the 1990s surveys, we can get an idea about the relationship between the senders and receivers of international remittances. As mentioned before, this analysis is not possible with the 2002 and 2004 surveys, because such details are missing from the survey questions. These details are provided in Table 12.5.

In both the 1992/1993 and 1997/1998 surveys, children were the largest source of international remittances, providing 40.2 and 36.7 percent respectively of the total value for those years. Next, the category of siblings and nieces/nephews was also an important source, providing 38.7 percent of the remittances in 1992/1993 and 33.2 percent in 1997/1998. Parents and spouses also provided some remittances, as well as other categories.

Table 12.5.   International remittances, relationship of sender to receiver weighted by remittance amount.

		Age of household head						
	Total (%)	20–29 (%)	30–39 (%)	40–49 (%)	50–59 (%)	60–69 (%)	70–79 (%)	80–89 (%)
Relationship of sender to receiver (1992/1993)								
Grandchild	1.9	0.7	0.7	0.2	3.1	0.1	5.9	4.7
Child/child-in-law	40.2	12.8	6.6	8.9	62.2	63.8	82.2	85.6
Spouse	4.0	*34.2*	7.0	8.2	0.0	0.0	0.0	0.0
Sibling, sibling-in-law, niece or nephew	38.7	32.3	*64.6*	*53.4*	22.9	31.3	6.6	2.5
Parent/parent-in-law	10.0	1.5	19.5	9.4	8.6	0.0	3.3	0.0
Grandparent	0.1	2.2	0.0	0.0	0.0	0.0	0.0	0.0
Other	5.1	16.3	1.7	19.8	3.2	4.8	2.0	7.2
Relationship of Sender to Receiver (1997/1998)								
Grandchild	4.2	0.0	0.0	3.5	4.8	5.1	9.8	4.6
Child/child-in-law	36.7	2.0	0.7	11.8	*48.8*	69.7	78.6	84.7
Spouse	5.6	*53.7*	11.6	6.0	0.0	0.0	0.2	0.0
Sibling, sibling-in-law, niece or nephew	33.2	22.1	*36.8*	*55.1*	34.4	19.4	5.7	1.5
Parent/parent-in-law	5.6	0.0	23.6	2.0	3.8	0.9	4.3	8.8
Grandparent	0.0	0.0	0.0	0.0	0.1	0.0	0.0	0.0
Other	14.7	22.2	27.3	21.7	8.2	4.9	1.5	0.6

Source: Authors' calculations from VLSS 1992/3 and 1997/8.

Table 12.5 also shows the distribution of remittances by relationship status, depending on the age of household head. For households with a head aged 20–29, spouses are the biggest source of international remittances, followed by the sibling category. But for households aged 30 and older, spouses are not a noticeable source. For those households with a head aged 30–49, the sibling category is most important, and for those aged 50 and above, children become the most important source. The "other" category is rather small, consisting of 5.1 percent of the total in 1992/1993 and 14.7 percent in 1997/1998. It is worth noting that in addition to other distant relatives, the "other" category includes all remittances from nonrelatives, demonstrating that most foreign remittances are sent mainly to family members in Vietnam.

Evidence on spending patterns for remittances

How remittances are spent is an important question that can help to characterize the impact of international remittances on the Vietnamese economy. For instance, are they used to purchase food, shelter, or other consumption goods, or for education, or for business investment? It is an important question, though it is only addressed in the 1997/1998 survey.

In this survey, there are 497 reports of international remittance receipt, going to 377 different households. For each of the 497 reports, the interviewee was asked to identify up to three different ways that the remittance was spent. In all 497 cases, a first use was reported, while a second use was reported in 56 cases, and a third use in only 7 cases. For the first use, 86.7 percent (431 cases) identified consumption, 0.4 percent (2 cases) identified education, 3.0 percent (15 cases) identified investment in non-farm production, 1.2 percent (6 cases) identified investment in farm production, 4.6 percent (23 cases) used the funds to build a house, and 4.0 percent (20 cases) identified the use as "other." Regarding the identification of a second use, 40 of the 56 who responded identified a second use beyond consumption. These include 12 cases for education, 11 cases for non-farm investment, 1 case for home building, and 18 cases for "other." This only leaves 14 other cases of second uses, and 9 of these 14 identified consumption as the second use.

While these numbers cannot be used to pinpoint the exact percentage breakdown of spending, because they do not identify the proportions spent on each category, let us ignore second and third uses and assume all of the remittance was spent on the first use. In this case, the remittances for consumption tended to be smaller, because once we weight for the size of the remittance, spending on consumption represented about 73 percent of the value of international remittances. Meanwhile, house construction received 14.4 percent of the remittances, non-farm investment received 6.0 percent of the flows, and education and spending on farm investment were essentially insignificant factors as most of the rest went to the "other" category. Unfortunately, such information is only included in the 1997/1998 survey, but we do find evidence in this case that remittances have a tendency to be consumed, especially if we add home construction to consumption expenditures. Perhaps surprisingly, very little of the expense of education is funded by remittances from overseas.

Impact of international remittances on income inequality in Vietnam

Here we explore the relationship between remittances and income inequality in Vietnam. First, Table 12.6 provides details about the distribution of international remittances to different income groups. For each survey year, we show the share of the total foreign remittances received by a subgroup of the population, the mean amount of foreign remittances and mean amount of per-capita expenditures measured in thousands of Vietnamese Dong (VND), the mean amount of per-capita expenditures minus foreign remittances, and the amount of remittances as a percentage of expenditures. The population subgroups include households not receiving foreign remittances, households receiving foreign remittances, and then these recipients divided into five quintiles, sorted by the total per-capita expenditures of the household.

For recipients of foreign remittances, with an implicit assumption that remittances are consumed and that households would not be able to adjust their expenditures in the counter-factual situation where they do not otherwise receive foreign remittances, we observe that such remittances account for between 40 and 60 percent of household expenditures. The percentage was the highest in 1992/1993, where remittances accounted for 57.1 percent of expenditures. Actually, that year also holds the distinction as being the only year in which the mean amount of foreign remittances (1391.7 thousand Dong) for recipients actually exceeded the mean per-capita expenditures of nonrecipients (1255.3 thousand Dong). Among households receiving foreign remittances, we can also observe that in all years the mean foreign remittance exceeded Vietnam's poverty-line for per-capita expenditures. Finally, with regard to the income distribution divided into five quintiles, we find that the most well off quintile receives a disproportionate share of the foreign remittances, though their share lessens over time from 84.7 percent of the total in 1992/1993 to 69.3 percent of the total in 2004. Also, while the absolute level of remittances tends to increase as one moves up the income distribution, there is not as clear a pattern regarding the percentage of expenditures represented by remittances.

Table 12.6 seems to imply that international remittances lead to greater inequality, especially as recipients on average tend to enjoy about double the per-capita expenditures of nonrecipients. However, Table 12.7, which

Table 12.6. Relationship between remittances and the income distribution.

	Share of total foreign remittances (%)	Mean foreign remittances	Mean per-capita expenditures	Mean per-capita expenditures net foreign remittances	Remittance as % of expenditure
1992/1993 (Poverty line for per-capita real expenditure: 1160)					
Households not receiving foreign remittances	0	0.0	1255.3	1255.3	0.0
Only households receiving foreign remittances	100.0	1391.7	2437.7	1046.0	57.1
Only households receiving foreign remittances					
Expenditure Quintile 1	0.9	199.2	643.4	444.2	31.0
Expenditure Quintile 2	2.5	736.5	819.0	82.5	89.9
Expenditure Quintile 2	3.8	357.1	1072.0	714.9	33.3
Expenditure Quintile 2	8.2	468.2	1524.6	1056.5	30.7
Expenditure Quintile 5	84.7	2354.4	3656.4	1302.0	64.4
1997/1998 (Poverty line for per-capita real expenditure: 1790)					
Households not receiving foreign remittances	0	0.0	2614.1	2614.1	0.0
Only households receiving foreign remittances	100.0	2209.2	5273.3	3064.1	41.9

(Continued)

Table 12.6. (*Continued*)

	Share of total foreign remittances (%)	Mean foreign remittances	Mean per-capita expenditures	Mean per-capita expenditures net foreign remittances	Remittance as % of expenditure
Only households receiving foreign remittances					
Expenditure Quintile 1	0.2	104.3	1160.4	1056.1	9.0
Expenditure Quintile 2	2.8	720.9	1723.5	1002.6	41.8
Expenditure Quintile 2	3.9	831.8	2290.2	1458.4	36.3
Expenditure Quintile 2	11.3	1132.1	3382.3	2250.2	33.5
Expenditure Quintile 5	81.8	3370.6	7635.6	4265.0	44.1
2002 (Poverty line for per-capita real expenditure: 1917)					
Households not receiving foreign remittances	0	0.0	3337.4	3337.4	0.0
Only households receiving foreign remittances	100.0	2895.5	5674.7	2779.2	51.0
Only households receiving foreign remittances					
Expenditure Quintile 1	0.8	290.7	1312.9	1022.2	22.1
Expenditure Quintile 2	2.1	502.1	1889.8	1387.7	26.6
Expenditure Quintile 2	4.8	961.4	2473.6	1512.2	38.9

(*Continued*)

Table 12.6. (*Continued*)

Expenditure Quintile 2	16.1	2227.7	3550.3	1322.7	62.7
Expenditure Quintile 5	76.3	4481.9	8659.2	4177.3	51.8
2004 (Poverty line for per-capita real expenditure: 2077)					
Households not receiving foreign remittances	0	0.0	4189.2	4189.2	0.0
Only households receiving foreign remittances	100.0	3674.1	8013.7	4339.7	45.8
Only households receiving foreign remittances					
Expenditure Quintile 1	0.7	694.2	1645.6	951.5	42.2
Expenditure Quintile 2	5.2	1718.3	2390.9	672.5	71.9
Expenditure Quintile 2	7.8	1692.3	3279.0	1586.7	51.6
Expenditure Quintile 2	17.1	2718.2	4745.5	2027.3	57.3
Expenditure Quintile 5	69.3	5023.1	11709.0	6685.9	42.9

Note: Monetary amounts are measured in thousands of VND per year. Expenditure quintiles are defined in terms of household per-capita expenditures.

Source: Authors' calculations from VLSS 1992/3 and 1997/8, and VHLSS 2002 and 2004.

Table 12.7. Impact of remittances on income inequality in Vietnam: Gini coefficients.

	Excluding remittances	Including domestic remittances only	Including foreign remittances only	Including all remittances
1992/1993 Per-capita income/expenditure				
Income per-capita	n/a	n/a	n/a	n/a
Expenditure per-capita	0.3580	0.3534	0.3344	0.3305
1997/1998 Per-capita income/expenditure				
Income per-capita	n/a	n/a	n/a	n/a
Expenditure per-capita	0.3645	0.3551	0.3583	0.3501
2002 Per-capita income/expenditure				
Income per-capita	0.5036	0.4964	0.5059	0.4988
Expenditure per-capita	0.4113	0.3899	0.3870	0.3703
2004 Per-capita income/expenditure				
Income per-capita	0.5042	0.4943	0.5040	0.4947
Expenditure per-capita	0.4176	0.3868	0.3948	0.3694

Source: Authors' calculations from VLSS 1992/3 and 1997/8, and VHLSS 2002 and 2004.

uses Gini coefficients, suggests otherwise. These figures show the impact of remittances on the income distribution, where the income distribution is defined separately as both per-capita expenditures and per-capita income (household income is only available in the 2002 and 2004 surveys). A Gini coefficient shows the degree of equality with which income or expenditures are divided in a society, with a measure of 0 showing perfect equality and a measure of 1 showing that one household holds all the resources. The conclusion of Table 12.7 is that both domestic and foreign remittances are contributing to greater equality in Vietnam. This is found by first removing all remittances receipts from the income measure of the household, and then calculating the Gini coefficient. Then, domestic remittances are added to the income measure to find a second Gini coefficient. Then, domestic remittances are removed and foreign remittances are added to the income measure to find the Gini coefficient in the third column. The fourth column includes the Gini coefficient with all remittances included.

We observe that the Gini coefficients are smaller after including the remittances, showing greater equality. For instance, in 1992/1993, foreign remittances help to reduce the Gini coefficient from 0.3580 to 0.3344. In 1997/1998, Vietnam is tending toward greater overall inequality, but foreign remittances nonetheless help reduce the Gini coefficient from 0.3645 to 0.3583. In 2002 and 2004, we have Gini coefficients for both income and expenditures. The Gini coefficients for income tend to be larger than for expenditures, because wealthier families tend to save more so that overall expenditures are closer. For income, 2002 shows the only instance of increased inequality, as foreign remittances increase the Gini coefficient from 0.5036 to 0.5049. However, with expenditures, we see the same trend as before. Inequality is increasing in Vietnam, but overseas remittances reduce the Gini coefficient from 0.4113 to 0.3870. Finally, in 2004, overseas remittances again reduce the Gini coefficients; for income the Gini coefficient moves from 0.5042 to 0.5040 (a negligible difference) and for expenditures it moves from 0.4176 to 0.3948. At least in terms of expenditures, we are seeing clear evidence that overseas remittances are improving income equality in Vietnam.

Conclusions

International remittances are clearly playing an important part in the Vietnamese economy. This chapter sought to determine how international remittances are impacting on Vietnamese households. Our findings conclude that overseas remittances come from throughout the world, but the United States dominates as the main source. Also, over time, the destinations of foreign remittances are becoming more diverse as they move away from Ho Chi Minh City and urban areas, in particular, to other regions and to rural areas. Nonetheless, the percentage of households receiving overseas remittances has held steady at around 5–7 percent of the population. Also, widows, the elderly, female headed households, and households where the head does not work receive a disproportionately large share of foreign remittances. This helps to ensure that foreign remittances actually improve equality in Vietnam with regard to per-capita household expenditures, though the improvements are quite small. Nonetheless, the improvements to income equality caused by overseas remittances are becoming more substantial over time. We have also determined that overseas remittances are used primarily for consumption, and are mainly provided by close family members including children, spouses, and siblings.

There is still much more to be said about the role of international remittances, and we hope this chapter will serve as a starting point for further analysis. In particular, it does not account for the macroeconomic impacts of remittances in a general equilibrium framework. If remittances lead to greater investment, then they can be an important source of economic growth. Also, this chapter does not provide much detail about an issue of particular interest to the authors, which is how remittances affect the living standards of Vietnam's elderly. The social insurance infrastructure is still weak, and as economic reform is producing many changes in Vietnamese society, we wish to carry out further research on the overall impact on the elderly.

References

Adams, Richard (1991). *The Effects of International Remittances on Poverty, Inequality, and Development of Rural Egypt*. Research Report No. 86. Washington D.C., International Food Policy Research Institute (IFPRI).

Adams, Richard (1992). "The Effects of Migration and Remittances on Inequality in Rural Pakistan." *Pakistan Development Review* 31(4): 1189–1206.

Adams, Richard (2004). "Remittances and Poverty in Guatemala." World Bank Policy Research Working Paper 3418, Washington D.C.: World Bank.

Adams, Richard (2006). "Remittances and Poverty in Ghana." World Bank Policy Research Working Paper 3838, Washington D.C.: World Bank.

Babieri, Michelangela (2006). "*Doi Moi* and the Elderly: Intergenerational Support under Strain of Reforms." Paper prepared for presentation at the 2006 Population of America Association Meeting, Los Angeles, March 30–April 1, 2006.

Cox, Donald (2004). "Private Inter-household Transfers in Vietnam." In *Economic Growth, Poverty, and Household Welfare in Vietnam*, edited by Paul Glewwe, Nisha Agrawal, and David Dollar, 567–603. Washington D.C.: World Bank.

General Statistics Office of Vietnam (GSO) (2004a). "General Introduction of Vietnam Household Living Standard Survey 2002 (VHLSS2002)." Mimeo.

General Statistics Office of Vietnam (GSO) (2004b). "Main Differences between VLSS 1992/1993, VLSS 1997/1998, and VHLSS 2001/2002." Mimeo.

Giang, Thanh Long and Wade Donald Pfau (2007). "The Elderly Population in Vietnam during Economic Transformation: An Overview." In *Social Issues in Vietnam in Economic Transition and Integration*, edited by Giang Thanh Long and Duong Kim Hong, Vol. 1, 185–210. Hanoi: Vietnam Development Forum.

Hernándes-Cross, Raúl (2005). "The Canada-Vietnam Remittance Corridor: Lessons on Shifting from Informal to Formal Transfer Systems." World Bank Working Paper No. 48. Washington, D.C.: World Bank.

Le Minh, Tam and Duc Vinh Nguyen (1999). "Remittances and the Distribution of Income." In *Health and Wealth in Vietnam: An Analysis of Household Living Standards*, edited by D. Houghton *et al.*, 167–181. Singapore: Institute of Southeast Asian Studies.

Ravallina, N.M. and E. Joelna Robleza (2003). "The Contribution of OFW Remittances on Income Inequality: A Decomposition Analysis." Report for School of Economics, The University of Philippines.

World Bank (2000). "Vietnam Living Standards Survey (VLSS), 1992–1993: Basic Information." (Updated from 1994 version). Washington D.C.: Poverty and Human Resources Division, World Bank.

World Bank (2001). "Vietnam Living Standards Survey (VLSS), 1997–1998: Basic Information." Washington D.C.: Poverty and Human Resources Division, World Bank.

World Bank. "The 2002 and 2004 Vietnam Living Standards Surveys (VHLSS 2002 and 2004)." http://www.worldbank.org.vn/data/VHLSS2002_2004.ppt, (accessed July 6, 2006).

CHAPTER 13

STAYING IN THE GLOBAL ECONOMY:
A PRELIMINARY VIEW OF VIETNAM AFTER THE END
OF THE AGREEMENT ON TEXTILES AND CLOTHING

John Thoburn

Introduction

Textiles and clothing (T&C) have been the archetypal "starter" industries
in industrialization. Following the examples of Britain in the eighteenth
century and Japan in the twentieth, many developing countries have stimulated their economic growth by becoming exporters of T&C. World trade in
T&C was tightly controlled for 30 years from 1974 under a series of international Multi-Fibre Arrangements (MFAs). Access to major markets — prin-
cipally the United States and the European Union (EU) — was restricted by
annual quotas imposed on exporting countries, under which total exports in
a series of tightly defined categories were limited to volumes specified by
country. In 1994 as part of the "Uruguay round" trade negotiations under
GATT,[1] a gradual phase-out of the MFA over a 10-year period was agreed.
This was the Agreement on Textiles and Clothing (ATC), under which all
quotas were to be abolished by the end of December 2004, with textiles and
clothing being "integrated" into the normal WTO rules governing trade.

By restricting the exports of major T&C producers, particularly China,
not only did the MFAs seek to protect domestic producers in Western
markets, but it also served to encourage producers in other developing
countries to enter the global economy as garment exporters. Now that the

---

[1]GATT is the General Agreement on Tariffs and Trade, the forerunner of WTO, the World
Trade Organization.

MFA/ATC is no more, a number of developing countries have become vulnerable to competition from China and other large producers such as India. This chapter looks at the experience of Vietnam[2] as a relatively new entrant to the global market. Vietnam is not as dependent on T&C exports as some other countries, since it has a relatively diversified export portfolio, but T&C is still its largest manufacturing exports. By considering the case of Vietnam, this chapter hopes to provide partial answers to the question of how vulnerable countries can stay in the game, post-MFA, and — indirectly — whether T&C can continue to be drivers of export-oriented industrialization for newcomers to globalization.

The first section looks at the issue of vulnerability and further justifies the choice of Vietnam as a case study. The second section introduces key characteristics of world T&C trade, including the role of global buyers and the pressures facing all producers. The third section discusses the predictions about the impact of the end of the MFA[3] and compares these to the initial outcomes. The fourth section concludes the paper.

Vulnerability and the Choice of Vietnam as a Case Study

Vulnerability: Textiles versus clothing

Although the textiles and clothing sectors are often referred to as if they were a single composite industry, textiles are more capital intensive than clothing, and have become increasingly so (OECD, 2004: 21). Vulnerability to competition usually refers primarily to clothing exporting, although a few developing countries, such as Pakistan, are significant exporters of textiles and face Chinese competition in their export markets. Historically textiles have been more of a driver of industrialization in low income countries than clothing, since garments can be produced in households or by small-scale tailoring using purchased fabrics. Textiles, though more capital intensive than clothing, are typically less capital intensive than the manufacturing

---

[2]For an introduction to Vietnam and its economy, see Thoburn (2007). An overview of globalization issues in Vietnam, as they relate to poverty, can be found in Thoburn (2004). See also Van Arkadie and Mallon (2003) on the Vietnamese economy and reform program.
[3]Strictly speaking, the ATC *replaced* the MFA in 1994. However, virtually everyone has continued to refer to the arrangements as the MFA, and so do we.

average.[4] Often built up under tariff protection as part of import substituting industrialization policies, textiles in developing countries may lack the ability to produce at international standards of quality. And as an import-competing industry, they have been vulnerable to competition in their domestic market as countries reform and liberalize their trade regimes.[5] As a result of this competition, textile production in the world economy has become more concentrated geographically (Brenton and Hoppe, 2006: 151).

Countries that have entered the world market in recent years as garment exporters often have not done so on the basis of clothing using domestic textiles. Indeed, garment exporting to take advantage of unused MFA quotas may not even have been the result of domestic firms expanding into global markets, but of inward direct foreign investment (DFI). In Cambodia, for example, the industry is almost entirely in the hands of foreign firms, although in Bangladesh it is predominantly locally owned (UNCTAD, 2005: 12); but in both cases the export of clothing depends on imported fabrics. A later section will show the key role that global buyers have played in such developments. In this chapter, we focus on vulnerability with regard to garment exporting, taking textile production into account where it affects export competitiveness in clothing. Textiles themselves, however, are important in world trade, accounting for 42 percent of total world T&C exports in 2005 (WTO, 2006). This partly reflects trade in non-clothing items such as industrial and home textiles,[6] but it is also the result of the trade-intensive nature of clothing production. Even China, the world's largest garment and textile exporter,[7] is also the world's second largest textile importing country after the United States (WTO, 2006).

---

[4]This is true of Vietnam, measuring capital intensity in terms of non-wage value-added per worker (Thoburn *et al.*, 2003).

[5]A classic case is South Africa, where a trade liberalization program in the 1990s resulted in much increased import penetration. South African companies adjusted, often developing exports in niche products to make up for their losses of domestic market share, but at the cost of large losses of employment as they restructured to improve labor productivity. See Roberts and Thoburn (2003).

[6]Less than half of world textile production is for use in clothing (OECD, 2004: 36).

[7]This comment refers to exporting *countries*, not counting the EU collectively as a "country." In 2003, China as a textile exporter was second to the EU-15 (UNCTAD, 2005: 4).

The choice of Vietnam

Table 13.1 illustrates a number of countries that are heavily dependent for their export earnings on garment exporting, including Cambodia and Bangladesh, already mentioned. While Vietnam is by no means as heavily dependent on garment exporting as the other countries listed, it is interesting for a number of other reasons too. As Table 13.2 shows, it experienced an exceptionally rapid increase in its T&C exports in the 1990s, as part of its entry into the global economy under its *doi moi* economic reform program, started in the mid-1980s, and following the collapse of its export markets in the former Soviet Union and Eastern Bloc at the start of the 1990s. Whilst its high export growth rate was from a low base, a comparison with South Africa — another new global entrant in the 1990s following years of economic seclusion under *apartheid* — is instructive.[8] While Vietnam's T&C exports were less than South Africa's in 1990, by 2001 they were almost five times greater.

Vietnam's performance as a T&C exporter was also remarkable in that until 2001 it was effectively cut off from the US market. Although the trade embargo imposed by the United States following the ending of the Vietnam–American war had been lifted in 1994, the United States imposed substantially higher — and in T&C effectively prohibitive — tariffs on

Table 13.1. Dependence on clothing exporting (shares of total merchandise exports, 2003).

Cambodia	84%
Bangladesh	76%
Lesotho	65%
Mauritius	53%
Sri Lanka	52%
Laos	42%
Vietnam (share of exports)	18% (incl. textiles)
Vietnam (share of manufacturing employment)	23% (incl. textiles)

Sources: (UNCTAD, 2005: 4), except for Vietnam. For Vietnam sources see Nadvi and Thoburn (2004a and 2004b).

---

[8] South Africa was also used as a comparator country to Vietnam in the research on globalization on which Nadvi and Thoburn (2004a and 2004b) report.

Table 13.2.   Exports of textiles and clothing, 1990–2001: Vietnam and comparisons before the US bilateral trade agreement.

	1990	2001	Average annual growth rate 1990–2001 (%)
Exports (US$ in million)			
China			
Clothing	9,669	36,650	13
Textiles	7,219	16,830	8
Vietnam			
Clothing and textiles	20	2,000	34
(in 1998 C/(T&C) = 88%)			
South Africa			
Clothing	81	222	5
Textiles (narrow definition)	131	232	5
World			
Clothing		195,000	6
Textiles		147,000	3

Vietnam, as Vietnam was then not a member of the WTO. The conclusion of a bilateral trade agreement between the United States and Vietnam in 2001 (the "USBTA") opened the US market to explosive growth in Vietnamese T&C exports. Until 2001, about 80 percent of Vietnam's exports were divided almost equally between the European Union and Japan, a bilateral agreement having been concluded with the EU in 1992, while Japan did not impose MFA quotas or prohibitive tariffs. Following the start of the USBTA, Vietnam's exports of T&C to the United States rose from a negligible amount to almost US$2.9 billion in 2005[9] more than Vietnam's total to all destinations in 2001. Of the Vietnamese T&C exports to the United States in 2005, 95 percent were of clothing, reducing the already low proportion of textiles in the T&C total in the late 1990s (see Table 13.2).

Vietnam, then, appears a rather formidable new entrant to world markets. After an initial grace period, the United States imposed MFA quotas on Vietnam in May 2003 (Nadvi and Thoburn, 2004b: 255). Following the end of the MFA with effect from 1 January 2005, the United States continued to impose MFA quotas on Vietnam as it was not a WTO member, while

---

[9]See http://otexa.ita.doc.gov/msrcty/v5520.htm, accessed February 2007.

virtually all other major exporters, including China (at least initially — see later), had unrestricted access. As of the beginning of 2007, Vietnam has been admitted to WTO membership, but it is too early to say what will be the impact on its T&C exports to the United States.

Vietnam is interesting as a case study also for two further reasons. First, like China, its trade liberalization program has followed an "East Asian" pattern, where exports have been developed rapidly while the domestic market has remained protected (Jenkins and Thoburn, 2003: 1). Now Vietnam's entry into the WTO and its commitments under the USBTA are driving import liberalization.[10] Secondly, and again like China, its T&C sector has a more complex industrial structure than those of other new entrants to the global market like Cambodia or Lesotho. State owned enterprises (SOEs) comprised 25 percent of Vietnam's garment output in 2004, while the domestic private sector comprised 35 percent and the foreign-owned sector 40 percent,[11] although the domestic private sector was under-represented in its share of exports. Vietnam's T&C SOEs have undertaken great restructuring as part of the country's moves into the global economy, as also have China's (Eberhardt and Thoburn, 2007).

The Global Textile and Clothing Trade

Global T&C trade is tightly organized within global value chains (GVCs). This form of institutional structure controls which countries, and which producers within those countries, can enter into global production, and whether their position is sustainable.

Global value chains[12]

To export clothing, producers need to gain access to global value chains (GVCs). Analysis of GVCs looks at the process of selling a product from the

---

[10]Import liberalization has also been driven by Vietnam's commitments under AFTA, the ASEAN Free Trade Area, although there is no space here to discuss them. See Thoburn *et al.* (2003: 10).

[11]The corresponding figures for Vietnam's textile sector were 44 percent for SOEs, 30 percent for the domestic private sector and 27 percent for the foreign sector (VNSY, 2004).

[12]On global value chains, see Nadvi (2004).

supply of raw materials through to the final distribution and marketing of the product (and even recycling). But a GVC is more than a series of input-output relations. Economic actors at certain stages of the chain exercise control over-entry and over-upgrading (of products and processes, and functions) by producers: that is, they exercise *governance* and they can earn "*rents*" (surplus profits). Garments are *buyer-driven* GVCs, where barriers to entry — and rents — are concentrated at the retail end. Production in clothing GVCs is organized by many economic actors without their own factories, though some (sometimes former) manufacturing firms outsource too (e.g. Levi Strauss, Sara Lee). Buyers include department stores (such as J.C. Penney), speciality stores with their own brand (such as The Gap), brands largely without stores (such as Liz Claiborne), supermarkets (such as Tesco), discounters (such as Walmart), and mail order firms. Note though that the US market is more homogenous than the markets in Europe, which exhibit many characteristics of organization and demand that are somewhat country-specific (Palpaceur *et al.*, 2004). In consequence, US orders tend to be much larger and often for lower quality products; this has implications for the kinds of producers who enter the chain.

Another important feature of GVCs in garments is what Gereffi (1999) has called "triangular manufacturing." That is, production is often organized not directly with producers in developing countries, but via garment manufacturing companies based in Hong Kong, Taiwan, or Korea. These manufacturing companies may themselves set up factories in countries from which buyers wish to source, organize fabric supply (sometimes from textile factories of their own), or subcontract from domestic suppliers. This arrangement adds further to barriers to entry for domestic producers in developing countries, in that global buyers often prefer to source from existing vendors (such as Hong Kong manufacturers) setting up in new locations than from domestic producers in those locations.[13]

What then drives global buyers' pattern of world sourcing, and how is this affected by the end of the MFA? There are three key factors: distance and lead times; costs, particularly labor costs (wages relative to productivity); and trade distortions: the MFA in the past, but also tariffs and preferences.

---

[13]This comment is based on interviews by the author with buyers based in Hong Kong in 2001, 2002 and 2006. Hong Kong is a key base from which British and US buyers organized their world sourcing.

For high and fast fashion items, particularly in women's wear, proximity to the final market is required. Items must be available quickly on the shops' shelves if they are to sell before the current fashion changes. This leads to sourcing from adjacent countries such as Turkey in the case of the European Union and Mexico in the case of the United States. There is some conflict between lead times and costs, since, for buyers to access lower labor costs, they generally have to source from further away. So the further away the supplying country, the more likely the buyer is to source either for very standard items, like T-shirts or jeans from countries like Lesotho, or items where there is little fashion change, such as men's suits from South Africa.

The "fundamental" determinants of buyers' patterns of sourcing — lead times and costs — must be considered within a framework of complex trade distortions. The availability of unused MFA quotas in the past has been a major stimulus for buyers to move to new countries of supply and for the foreign investors working for those suppliers to undertake "quota-hopping" DFI. Now, without the MFA, trade preferences and trade barriers fulfill a similar role. Clothing exporters still face highly differentiated trade barriers in different markets, and the average level of tariffs on T&C is high relative to that of manufactured goods as a whole (OECD, 2004: 57). For example, Bangladesh's clothing exports can enter the EU market free of import duty since Bangladesh is a least developed country, whereas Vietnam has to pay around 10–12 percent duty since it is not. Vietnam (as a developing but not least developed country) qualifies for a 20 percent reduction in the duty under the EU's *Generalised System of Preferences* if it meets the EU's stringent rules of origin, but where its clothing is made from imported fabrics it must pay the full duty. In contrast, clothing from South Africa — a richer country than Vietnam — can enter the US market duty free under the US Africa Growth and Opportunity Act (AGOA), although only if they use African (or US) fabrics and yarns.

Buyers are also influenced by whether potential producers of their garments can meet environmental and social compliance standards, such as no excessive overtime, no use of child labor and the avoidance of pollution, although such compliance is a necessary rather than a sufficient condition for sourcing. Some countries have been able to enhance their appeal to buyers by stressing their adherence to social standards: Cambodia is a case in point (ILO, 2005: 36–41). Large buyers, especially those from the United States, regularly audit their suppliers for compliance, although compliance requirements are less strict in cases where traders — usually from East Asia — source from smaller firms (Nadvi and Thoburn, 2004a: 115–8).

Increasing pressures on suppliers

At the time of the abolition of the MFA, a number of long-term challenges were facing clothing exporters. These remain important and include:

• Demands by global buyers for cheaper products, higher quality, and shorter lead times;
• Pressures to meet environmental and labor standards, as noted in the previous subsection;
• Buyers wishing to reduce number of suppliers — both in terms of countries, and of vendors in each country, in order to reduce transactions costs and
• Competition from China, with predictions that China would sweep the board once MFA quotas had gone.

These pressures reflect pressure on buyers as a result of increased competition at the retail end (OECD, 2004: Chapters 1 and 2; UNCTAD, 2005: 7–12). The end of the MFA has offered buyers a chance greatly to reduce their transactions costs by limiting their numbers of suppliers and supplier countries. Producers, such as those interviewed in Hong Kong before the end of the MFA, fear that the world clothing industry would follow the example of the world footwear industry. In footwear, many countries — such as almost all in sub-Saharan Africa — have lost their footwear industries to import competition, particularly from China, and the industry has become geographically quite concentrated (UNCTAD, 2002).

The End of the MFA and its Consequences

The end of the MFA from 1 January 2005 saw a situation where pressures on clothing suppliers had been increasing, and where producers in countries with previously underutilized MFA quotas were vulnerable to buyers switching their purchases elsewhere and to foreign investors moving out.

In clothing production, a factory — whose capital equipment mostly consists of sewing machines — can be moved out in a matter of weeks. Textile production, especially the production of yarns, has heavier and more expensive capital equipment and is therefore less footloose. Now that the MFA is over, trade preferences exert a greater influence on sourcing — for instance pushing buyers toward a country like Bangladesh — than hitherto.

Predictions about the end of the MFA

One of the most influential set of predictions was that made by Nordås (2004) for the WTO, arguing that China was likely greatly to increase its share of the US and EU market (see Table 13.3). China's strengthening position was more pronounced in the United States than the EU, and more pronounced in clothing than in textiles.

Table 13.3.   Estimated percentage market shares in the United States and EU before and after elimination of quotas.

EU clothing	Before	After	US/Canada clothing	Before	After
China	18	29	China	16	50
India	6	9	India	4	15
Turkey	9	6	Mexico	10	3
Other "top 10" exporters	37	32	Other "top 10" exporters	46	22
Rest of world (incl. Vietnam)	30	24	Rest of world (incl. Vietnam)	24	10
EU textiles	Before	After	US/Canada textiles	Before	After
China	10	12	China	11	18
India	9	11	India	5	5
Turkey	13	12	Mexico	13	11
United States and Canada	8	7	EU	16	14
Other "top 10" exporters	24	24	Other "top 10" exporters	35	31
Rest of world (incl. Vietnam)	36	34	Rest of world (incl. Vietnam)	20	21

Source: Adapted from Nordås (2004).

The initial events in 2005[14]

Initially, there was rapid expansion of exports from China to the EU and the United States after MFA quota removal on 1 January 2005. Some buyers rushed in, though others not. In July and August 2005, garments from China were held in EU ports, and from May to August 2005 Chinese clothing exports to the EU and United States more or less stopped. In September 2005, the EU released Chinese products from the warehouses in time for Christmas. New trade restrictions on China were introduced; however, the EU established quotas for imports from China for the period 2006–2007 preset but with some growth. After the EU had decided on quotas, the United States followed, imposing quotas on China for the period 2006–2008. Compared to the EU, the new US quotas had less generous growth provisions and covered a wider range of products than the EU's (e.g., the United States included woven shirts and the EU did not). Quotas on China under these two new systems were set in value terms, not volumes as in the old MFA.

Performances of suppliers

Tables 13.4 and 13.5 show purchases from the United States and the EU, respectively. The US data shown include textiles. These are of minimal importance for Vietnam (or Cambodia, Bangladesh, or Lesotho), but the inclusion of textiles allows us to see how Pakistan and India have been able to increase their exports to the United States substantially. The table makes it clear that there have been losers, most noticeably in Africa, but Mexico has seen its exports fall too.

As Table 13.5 shows, China greatly increased its exports to the EU-15 in the first post-MFA year, as did Vietnam to a certain extent.

Vietnam

Vietnam at the moment seems to be staying in the game, and is seen by buyers as an alternative to China, particularly since China has been restricted in the US market until 2008. Vietnam has skilled workers and low wages, although

---

[14]These comments are based on interviews in Hong Kong in spring 2006.

Table 13.4.   US Imports of T&C ("total MFA categories").

(US$ in billion)	2004	2005	Change for year ending August 2006 (in %)
World	83.3	89.2	2.9
China	14.6	22.4	13.5
Vietnam	2.7	2.8	24.5
Cambodia	1.4	1.7	27.2
Bangladesh	2.1	2.5	21.4
India	3.6	4.6	17.6
Pakistan	2.5	2.9	18.0
Mexico	7.8	7.2	−11.3
Sub-Saharan Africa	1.8	1.5	−19.5
Lesotho	0.46	0.39	−14.4
South Africa	0.16	0.086	−46.2

Source: http://otexa.ita.doc.gov/.

Table 13.5.   Imports of garments into EU-15.

(Million Euros)	2004	2005	% change
China	11,037.9	16,398	48.6
Vietnam	609.6	662.9	8.7
Cambodia	517	474.4	−8.2
India	2,433.8	3,196.8	31.3
Pakistan	905.8	770.2	−15.0
Bangladesh	3,689	3,500.9	−5.1
Lesotho	0.843	0.632	−25.0
South Africa	56.7	39.2	−30.9
Mauritius	512.7	441	−14.0
Turkey	7,519.9	7,868.4	4.6

Source: Eurostat.

the country has issues of corruption, which affect the movement of goods. However, it also has various other problems. First, its textile industry has proved inadequate to meet the needs of garment exporting, and some three-quarters of fabrics used for export garments are imported. Fabrics are often supplied by buyers, and the Vietnamese garment manufacturers are paid a processing fee. Some textile SOEs have integrated forwards into garment production using their own fabrics (Thoburn *et al.*, 2003), but this makes them inflexible, and they often do not know how to source fabrics from elsewhere. As one buyer in Hong Kong explained, buyers want vertical production not vertical integration. That is, they want all stages of production in one country or area, but not necessarily in vertically integrated and inflexible firms.

Second, Vietnam T&C production is largely confined to manufacturing, and does not do product development. Even Hong Kong foreign investors in Vietnam do their product development with buyers in the manufacturer's Hong Kong office and just use Vietnam for manufacturing.

Thus, Vietnam's garment exporting seems to generate less added value to the country than might be first supposed. To increase its gains, Vietnam requires development of its textile industry, particularly through foreign investment to generate international standards of quality. It requires more skill in sourcing textiles, even if these are not produced domestically, to gain the control to move toward "full package" production.

China

Although China is a formidable competitor, in the longer run it faces some problems. Its wage levels are rising, especially in the southern province of Guangdong, one of the hearts of the export garment industry. Wages have been rising too in central coastal China, the greater Shanghai region, a historic center of textile production. Although moves to the interior of China to access lower wages are possible in principle, interior provinces suffer from poor infrastructure and long distances to market, and it is difficult for firms to persuade managers to go. Also, people from the interior are becoming less willing to migrate and live in dormitories, which has been a way in the past that the coastal regions have ensured a labor supply. More fundamentally, there will be a future labor shortage as China's one-child policy affects first population growth and then reduces the size of the working population. Some regions are trying to get out of T&C (like Shanghai), and buyers say that China is keen for "diplomatic reasons" to leave lower value-added products to less developed countries.

Conclusions and Reflections

Barriers to entry into export garment production have become higher in recent years as a result of changes at the retail end of the global value chains for garments. There has been increasing concentration in the US retail sector: new entrants have been challenging existing firms, with a large fall in the share of department stores and a rise of discounters like Walmart. There are now shorter fashion seasons, causing buyers to search for lower prices for given quality and for faster lead times. So, firms need to keep prices low and to upgrade their products, processes, and functions. Buyers require producers to be able to work with them in developing new products, and prefer to source from countries with a strong textile industry in order to shorten lead times. In this sense, the barriers to entry, and to the sustainability of the position of recent entrants, have grown larger, and T&C exporting has become a less easy route to industrialization than in the past.

At the same time, the continued existence of a distortionary[15] pattern of trade preferences increases the trade-intensity of the global T&C industry. For instance, Jordan has become an exporter of clothing to the United States on the basis of a bilateral free trade agreement with the United States, while importing its textiles from China. Vietnam has succeeded in becoming a major exporter of clothing without strong preferences, first to the EU[16] and Japan, and from 2001 to the United States. Nevertheless, it remains vulnerable if the restrictions on Chinese T&C exports to the EU and the United States are lifted after 2007–2008, although it is also likely that buyers will wish to retain some degree of diversification in their sourcing, even though their range of suppliers is currently being reduced. However, Vietnam's lack of a globally competitive textile industry of sufficient capacity to service its export garments remains a significant weakness, and Vietnam has far to go before it becomes a partner in product development.

---

[15]This is not to say that all preferences are undesirable. Clearly the EU's Anything but Arms preferences for least developed countries, under which Bangladesh benefits, or the US AGOA, which gives African countries duty free access, can be justified on the basis of special help for the poorest. Nevertheless, there is a strong suspicion that some preferences are more political than developmental.

[16]Although Vietnam has GSP access to the EU, often its clothing exports do not qualify under EU rules of origin, because the fabrics are imported.

References

Brenton, Paul and Mombert Hoppe (2006). "Life after Quotas: Early Signs of the New Era in Trade in Textiles and Clothing." In *Trade, Doha and Development: A Window into the Issues*, edited by Richard Newfarmer. Washington D.C.: World Bank.

Eberhardt, Markus and John T. Thoburn (2007). "China, the World Trade Organization, and the End of the Agreement on Textiles and Clothing: Impacts on Workers." In *Marginalisation in China: Perspectives on Transition and Globalisation*, edited by H.X.Q. Zhang, Bin Wu and R. Sanders. London: Ashgate.

Gereffi, Gary (1999). "International Trade and Upgrading in the Apparel Commodity Chain." *Journal of International Economics* 48(1): 37–70.

ILO (2005). *Promoting Fair Globalization in Textiles and Clothing in a Post-MFA Environment*. Geneva: International Labour Office.

Jenkins, Rhys O. and John T. Thoburn (2003). *"Can Trade Reform Reduce Global Poverty?"* Brighton: Institute of Development Studies Policy Briefing. www.ids.ac.uk/ids/bookshop/briefs/PB19.pdf (accessed August 19, 2003).

Nadvi, Khalid (2004). "Globalisation and Poverty: How Can Global Value Chain Research Inform the Policy Debate." *Institute of Development Studies Bulletin* 35: 20–28.

Nadvi, Khalid and John T. Thoburn, with Bui Tat Thang, Nguyen Thi Thanh Ha, Nguyen Thi Hoa, Dao Hong Le and Enrique Blanco de Armas (2004a). "Vietnam in the Global Garment and Textile Value Chain: Impacts on Firms and Workers." *Journal of International Development* 16(1): 111–123.

Nadvi, Khalid and John T. Thoburn, with Bui Tat Thang, Nguyen Thi Thanh Ha, Nguyen Thi Hoa and Dao Hong Le (2004b). "Challenges to Vietnamese Firms in the World Garment and Textile Value Chain, and the Implications for Alleviating Poverty." *Journal of the Asia Pacific Economy* 9(2): 249–267.

Nordås, Hildegunn Kyvic (2004). *The Global Textile and Clothing Industry Post the Agreement on Textiles and Clothing*. Geneva: World Trade Organisation, http:www.wto.org.

OECD (2004). *A New World Map in Textiles and Clothing: Adjusting to Change*. Paris: Organisation for Economic Cooperation and Development.

Palpacuer, Florence, Peter Gibbon and Lotte Thomsen (2004). "New Challenges for Developing Country Suppliers: A Comparative European Perspective." *World Development* 33(3): 409–430.

Roberts, Simon and John T. Thoburn (2003). "Adjusting to Trade Liberalisation: The Case of Firms in the South African Textile Sector." *Journal of African Economies* 12(1): 74–103.

Thoburn, John T. (2004). "Globalisation and Poverty in Vietnam: Introduction and Overview." *Journal of the Asia Pacific Economy* 9(2): 127–144.

Thoburn, John T. (2007). "Viet Nam." In *Handbook on the Northeast and Southeast Asian Economies*, edited by Anis Chowdhury and Iyanatul Islam. Cheltenham: Edward Elgar.

Thoburn, John T., Nguyen Thi Thanh Ha and Nguyen Thi Hoa (2003). "Globalisation and the Textile Industry of Vietnam." Globalisation and Poverty Discussion Paper no. 10. http://www.gapresearch.org/production/DP10% 20Vietnam%20textiles.pdf.

UNCTAD (2002). *Trade and Development Report 2002*. New York and Geneva: United Nations Conference on Trade and Development.

UNCTAD (2005). *TNCs and the Removal of Textile and Clothing Quotas*. New York and Geneva: United Nations Conference on Trade and Development.

Van Arkadie, Brian and Raymond Mallon (2003). *Viet Nam: A Transition Tiger?* Canberra: Asia Pacific Press at the Australian National University.

VNSY (2004). *Viet Nam Statistical Yearbook*. Hanoi: General Statistics Office.

WTO. Various Years. *International Trade Statistics*. Geneva: World Trade Organization.

CHAPTER 14

EMERGENCE OF THE GLOBAL DEVELOPMENT
NETWORK IN THE PERSONAL COMPUTER INDUSTRY

Yumiko Nakahara

Introduction

Research and development (R&D) activities used to be the least globalized
of all the functions of multinationals. In the 2000s, globalization means that
R&D activities are increasingly being relocated to developing countries and
their function is expanding to include product development.

From the late 1980s, the personal computer industry began to employ
a form of production totally different from the conventional vertical integration in which a multinational carried out all the steps in the production
process. This form of production can be described as the "global production
network" or GPN. As discussed below, it entails the division of the whole
production process into several steps located in geographically dispersed
places, some outside the company's own boundaries and national borders.
Further new features of the industry have emerged since the early 2000s.
From this time, the product development process also began to be subdivided into several steps located in a wide geographic area, including developing countries.

How can we conceptualize these new phenomena? Using the personal
computer industry as a case study, here I propose a theoretical framework to
describe the globalization of research and development activities, with the
locations expanding to include developing countries, and with the locations
expanding to include product development. First I review other studies of

the globalization and networking of R&D, and then I analyze the process of globalization of research and development after 2000, along with the reasons for it. Finally, I propose a conceptual framework to describe the globalization of development activities in the personal computer industry. The final section provides a summary of findings and conclusions.

Globalization and the Networking of R&D Activities

Studies of the globalization of R&D activities began to appear in the 1960s and 1970s. At that time, the main interest was in the issues of establishing foreign R&D units and coordinating several R&D units within one multinational company (Ronstadt, 1978). However from around 1990, research interests expanded to include collaboration with external R&D institutions such as universities, research institutes, and other organizations (see for example Development Bank of Japan, 1988).

Some studies employed the concept of "network" to describe the globalization of R&D. For example, Westney (1998) classified global R&D activities into six types, and identified the most dispersed and advanced type as "flexible network or heterarchy." Gassman and von Zedtwitz (1999: 235, 243–245) distinguished five typical forms of international R&D organizations, and described the most dispersed of these as "integrated R&D networks," integrated networks of R&D units located internationally and creating synergy. Von Zedtwitz and Gassman (2002) presented a similar idea. On the other hand, Hayashi (2004) described the collaboration between various domestic and foreign R&D units within one multinational and its external linkages with outside R&D organizations, including universities, as the "networking of R&D." Ernst (2005: 173–175) referred to the geographically dispersed multilayered structure of microchip design as a "global design network." The United Nations Conference on Trade and Development (UNCTAD, 2005) employed an idea similar to that of Ernst.

However, these studies of the globalization of R&D based on concepts of networks did not discuss the geographical dispersion of R&D in relation to that of the whole production process. In the personal computer industry, as I will explain later, the geographical dispersion of the whole production process preceded that of R&D activities. Thus, the geographical dispersion of R&D should be analyzed in relation to that of production.

The Global Production Network

"Global production network," a concept proposed by Ernst both individually and in collaboration with Kim, refers to a form of production that first appeared at the end of the twentieth century. Ernst and Kim (2002: 1417) defined it as "concentrated dispersion of the value chain across the boundaries of the firm and national borders, with a parallel process of integrating hierarchical layers of network participants." As Henderson *et al.* (2002: 445) note, this is "a conceptual framework that is capable of grasping the global, regional, and local economic and social dimensions of the processes involved in many (though by no means all) forms of economic globalization."

Summarizing the preceding studies, the GPN can be defined as follows. It is totally different from conventional vertical integration in which all the steps of the production process of one product are located within one company. The GPN divides the whole process of production into several steps — marketing, product planning, development, logistics, production, and customer support — and locates each step in geographically dispersed places, crossing national and company boundaries. It is most often seen in the personal computer industry from the late 1980s. Figure 14.1 illustrates a GPN in the early 1990s.

As for the developing countries which are integrated into the GPN, Ernst (2002) refers to the potential benefits that they could reap from international linkages. Ernst and Kim (2002) also refer to the diffusion of both explicit and tacit knowledge to local suppliers through formal and informal

1. Marketing (United States)	2. Product planning (United States)	3. Product development (United States or Taiwan)	4. Logistics (Taiwan and China)	5. Mass production (China)	6. Sales (any part of the world)	7. Customer support (any part of the world)

Figure 14.1.   The global production network in the personal computer industry in the early 1990s.

Note: The locations noted in the parentheses are examples based on the interview at Company A.

Source: Personal interview at an American personal computer company, "Company A" in May, 2006.

mechanisms. Ernst (2000) cites Taiwanese (ODM) suppliers in the personal computer industry as an example of knowledge outsourcing through the GPN.[1]

However, there have been no studies that analyze the issue of R&D networks that include developing countries within the GPN. But even though the GPN framework does not assume that the development procedures themselves will be further dispersed geographically, recently they have been (Figure 14.2).

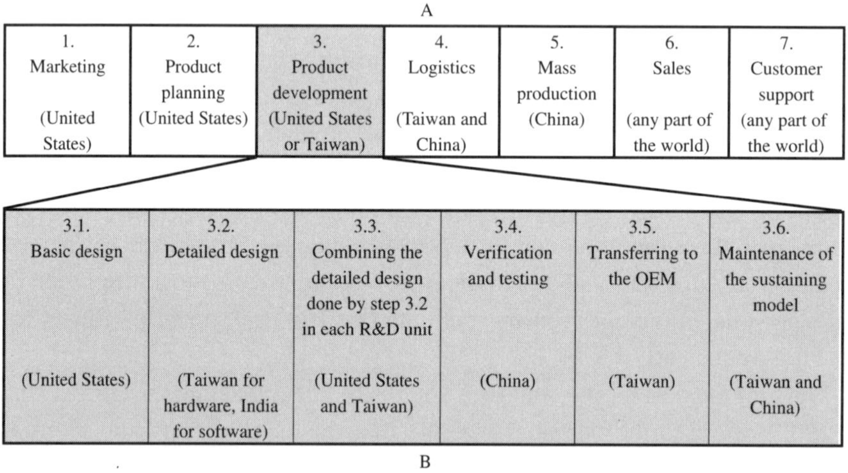

A

1. Marketing (United States)	2. Product planning (United States)	3. Product development (United States or Taiwan)	4. Logistics (Taiwan and China)	5. Mass production (China)	6. Sales (any part of the world)	7. Customer support (any part of the world)

3.1. Basic design (United States)	3.2. Detailed design (Taiwan for hardware, India for software)	3.3. Combining the detailed design done by step 3.2 in each R&D unit (United States and Taiwan)	3.4. Verification and testing (China)	3.5. Transferring to the OEM (Taiwan)	3.6. Maintenance of the sustaining model (Taiwan and China)

B

Figure 14.2. Geographically dispersed development in the GPN of the personal computer industry. A: The GPN in the early 1990s. B: Geographically dispersed development in the GPN after 2000.
Note: The locations noted in parentheses are examples based on the interview at Company A.
Source: Personal interview at an American personal computer company, "Company A" in May, 2006.

---

[1] "Ernst notes a pre-occupation with formal R&D and technology transfers, which may preclude an appreciation of the importance of diffusion of less codified forms of knowledge. Indeed, Ernst's research under the GPN banner has been concerned with the potential for different forms of knowledge (which he variously terms 'embrained', 'embedded', 'encultured') to be diffused from GPNs in developing country locations and thereby stimulate local industrial upgrading." (Henderson *et al.* 2002: 443–444).

So, a new framework to conceptualize the phenomenon should be developed by studying the relationship or coordination of each R&D unit in the GPN. I attempt this in the following sections.

Changes in the Globalization of R&D Activities

In this section, we will see how the globalization of R&D has changed since 2000. Traditionally, R&D activities are among the least internationalized functions of multinational companies. When the globalization of R&D started, both the home and host countries were in the developed world. If we divide R&D activities into (a) basic and applied research, (b) product development, (c) localization, and (d) process development, only the last two used to be located in developing countries. But recently, this has begun to change in two ways.

Locating R&D in developing countries — notably in Asia

First, multinationals have begun to locate R&D in developing countries, notably in Asia. Table 14.1 shows R&D expenditure abroad by majority-owned foreign affiliates of United States parent companies, by selected regions/countries. The proportion of R&D expenditure allocated to developing countries increased from 5.5 percent in 1995 to 13.5 percent in 2002. Expenditure in Asia increased from US$283 million to US$2,113

Table 14.1. R&D expenditure abroad by majority-owned foreign affiliates of United States parent companies, by selected regions/countries (unit = US$ millions, percentages in parentheses).

Year	R&D expenditure to developed countries (share of total)	R&D expenditure in developing countries (share of total)	Asia	China	India
1995	11,891 (94.5)	691 (5.5)	283	13	5
2002	17,844 (84.4)	2,855 (13.5)	2,113	646	80

Source: UNCTAD (2005:129).

million. Expenditure in China increased dramatically from US$13 million to US$646 million, and expenditure in India also increased, from US$5 million to US$80 million. As we have seen above, the establishment of R&D in developing countries is rising.[2]

In the personal computer industry, from the early 2000s, R&D began to be located in the developing economies in Asia, such as Taiwan, India, and China. Further details will be given in the next section.

Product development

Second, R&D activities located in developing countries have begun to expand their functions to include product development. As mentioned above, if we divide R&D activities into (a) basic and applied research, (b) product development, (c) localization, and (d) process development, off-shore R&D has recently expanded to include product development.

This phenomenon has also appeared in the personal computer industry. From the early 2000s, R&D within the personal computer industry located in the newly industrializing economies of Asia, such as Taiwan, India, and China, increasingly began to take on product development. Table 14.2 shows the role of each phase in the development of a personal computer, in this case by an American Company A in May, 2006. It shows that the whole product development procedure for one model is divided into several steps and these steps are assigned to several R&D units located all over the world.

Table 14.3 describes the roles of each geographically dispersed R&D facility as shown in Table 14.2, based on my interviews at Company A. It shows that each R&D unit has a specific role in the product development process for each model.

Reasons behind Changes in the Globalization of R&D Activities

The following section will analyze the reasons behind two aspects of the globalization of development activities: the expansion of locations to include developing countries, and the expansion of functions to include

---

[2]In the survey of the most attractive prospective R&D locations, done by EIU and UNCTAD, respectively, China won 1st place and India won 3rd place (EIU, 2004: 9; UNCTAD, 2005: 153).

Table 14.2. Dispersal of R&D in the product development of a personal computer (Company A, May, 2006).

Product development procedure	Step 1. Basic design	Step 2. Detailed design — Software BIOS/Utility	Step 2. Detailed design — Software Communication function LAN/wireless LAN/modem	Step 2. Detailed design — Hardware	Step 3. Combining the detailed design done in Step 2 in each R&D unit	Step 4. Test Verification and testing	Step 5. Transferring to the OEMs, solving problems on the manufacturing line	Step 6. Transferring to China (only for desktops)	Step 6. Minor changes and maintenance
A. High-end and mid-priced notebook models									
United States	○	□	□	□	○				
Taiwan				○	○	□	○		○
India		○		○					
Ireland			○						
China						○			
B. Low-end notebook models									
United States	○	□			○				
Taiwan				○	○	□	○		○
India				○					
Ireland			○						
China						○			

Symbols: ○ indicates main role; □ indicates supporting role and blank indicates no role assigned.

(*Continued*)

Table 14.2. (*Continued*)

| Product development procedure | Step 1. Basic design | Step 2. Detailed design | | | | Step 3. Combining the detailed design done in Step 2 in each R&D unit | Step 4. Test | Step 5. Transferring to the OEMs | Step 6. Maintenance of the self-sustaining model | |
| | | Software | | | Hardware | | Verification and testing | Transferring to the OEMs, solving problems on the manufacturing line | Transferring to China (only for desktops) | Minor changes and maintenance |
		BIOS/Utility	Communication function LAN/wireless	Communication function LAN/modem						
C. High-end and mid-priced desktop models										
United States	○	□	□		□	○				
Taiwan					○	○	□	○	○	□
India		○								
Ireland				○						
China							○			○
D. Low-end desktop models										
United States	○									
Taiwan					○	○	□	○	○	□
India		○								
Ireland				○						
China							○			○

Symbols: ○ indicates main role; □ indicates supporting role and blank indicates no role assigned.

Notes: "Verification" refers to a test from the designer's viewpoint, to verify if the computer runs successfully according to the original design. On the other hand, "testing" refers to a test from the end-user's viewpoint, asking the question, "If the user happens to operate the computer this way, how would the computer react?" "Self-sustaining model" refers to a model which has been marketed for over three months.

Source: Personal interviews at Company A, May, 2006.

Table 14.3. Detailed roles of each R&D unit (Company A, May 2006).

Location	Item	Details
United States	Location and scale	• 2 places in Texas. • About 25,000 workers (including about 10,000 engineers).
	Role in product development	• The basic design of the architecture. • Combining the detailed design work by each R&D unit all over the world.
Taiwan	Location and scale	• Taipei. • About 200 workers.
	Purpose	• Reducing costs. • Facilitating communication between headquarters in the United States and the Taiwanese OEM. • Facilitating communication between headquarters and the R&D in China. • Training engineers and giving technical support for R&D in China.
	Role in product development	• Designing hardware based on the basic design created by R&D at US headquarters • Combining detailed designs by each R&D unit all over the world. • Transferring the agreed design to OEM companies, and solving problems occurring in mass production. • Transferring self-sustaining models to R&D in China. • Maintenance of self-sustaining models of notebook computer.

(Continued)

Table 14.3. (*Continued*)

Location	Item	Details
	Other roles	• Negotiating with Taiwanese OEMs. • Mediating between R&D units at US headquarters and in China. • Giving technical instructions to R&D in China. • Training R&D engineers from Shanghai in Taipei
India	Location and scale	• Bangalore. • About 200–300 workers.
	Purpose	• Cost reduction. • Training engineers in software development, including BIOS.
	Role in product development	• Developing BIOS and utilities software from basic designs from the R&D unit at headquarters in the United States
Ireland	Location and scale	• Dublin. • About 150 workers.
	Purpose	• Enabling better communication with chip suppliers for communication functions located in Ireland.
	Role in product development	• Developing LAN, wireless LAN, and modem software from basic designs from the R&D unit at headquarters in the United States
China	Location and scale	• Shanghai and Amoy. • More than 1,000 workers.
	Purpose	• Cost reduction.
	Role in product development	• Maintenance and minor changes to self-sustaining models of desktop computer. • Verification and testing.

Source: Personal interview at an American personal computer company, "Company A" in May, 2006.

product development. We will consider the reasons for this from the point of view of both the multinationals and the developing countries, as well the technical background to the expansion.

The multinationals' side — seeking lower development costs

For the multinationals, the main reason for the change is to lower development costs. As competition in the personal computer industry intensifies, the need to seek lower cost grows — not only in production, but also in development. So, companies seek lower cost locations for product development.

Table 14.4 compares the costs of R&D at each location for Company A. The destinations are selected from those listed in Tables 14.2 and 14.3.

Table 14.4.   Comparison of R&D costs in selected countries.

Place	Monthly salary of middle-level engineer (US$)	Bonus	Rate of corporation tax (%)
Houston (United States)	4,047	Varies depending on the company	Country tax: 31.91% State tax: 0%
Bangalore (India)	339–648	N.A.	33.66%
Dublin (Ireland)	5,110–7,310	None	10–12.5%
Taipei (Taiwan)	958–2,575	4.79–5.41 months' salary	Depends on the amount of investment: • NT$50,000 or less: 0% • NT$100,000 or less: 15% • More than NT$100,000: 25%
Shanghai (China)	334–593	1–3 months	33%

Notes: (1) "N.A." indicates figures were not available in the documents. (2) There may be additional costs other than those listed in the table, and locating R&D in each location may be affected by other factors. See Table 14.3 for the role of each R&D site. (3) US$1 = NT$33.048 (Oct. 3, 2006).
Sources: http://www3.jetro.go.jp/; http://www.mof.go.jp/singikai/zeicho/top.htm.

The monthly salary of a middle-level engineer is US$4,047 in Houston, compared with US$339–US$648 in Bangalore, US$958–US$2,575 in Taipei, and US$334–US$593 in Shanghai. It appears that locating the R&D in developing countries allows a dramatic saving.

The developing countries' side — increasing the endowment of skilled R&D personnel

For the developing countries, the main reason for the change is the increasing availability of skilled R&D personnel in these countries. According to a survey by the Economist Intelligence Unit (EIU), 71 percent of respondents cited the ability to exploit pools of skilled labor as a main benefit from globalizing R&D (EIU 2004: 7). Table 14.5 shows changes in the numbers of R&D personnel in Taiwan and China. It can be seen that the numbers are growing in both countries.

Now, a further question arises. Is the increasing availability of skilled R&D personnel in developing countries in Asia such as Taiwan, India, and China partly a result of brain circulation?[3] The answer seems to be "yes." For these countries, brain circulation has been an effective source of technology development. For example, in Taiwan, the skilled personnel returning from the United States have played a leading role in technology development (*Tienxia Zazhi* 1994: 34; see Chapter 1 of this volume). Some of them worked at the Industrial Technology Research Institute (ITRI) founded by the Taiwanese government, and developed product technologies to be transferred from ITRI to external companies. According to Saxenian (2002), the returnees have played important roles in high technology industries in China and India as well.

Figure 14.3 shows the changing number of returnees from overseas in Taiwan and China. The number of returnees has generally increased year by year, except for Taiwan in the late 1990s.

---

[3]"Brain circulation" is described by the National Science Foundation (1998) as follows: "Several decades ago, the emigration of such highly skilled personnel to the United States was considered one-way mobility, a permanent brain drain depriving the countries of origin of the 'best and the brightest.' More recently, however, the mobility of highly talented workers is referred to as 'brain circulation,' since a cycle of study and work abroad may be followed by a return to the home country to take advantage of high-level opportunities"(1998: 1).

Table 14.5. Changes in the number of R&D personnel in Taiwan and China, 1995–2001.

Year	Taiwan	China
1995	105,800	4,178,600
1996	116,900	4,591,000
1997	129,200	4,553,500
1998	129,300	4,304,600
1999	134,800	4,500,200
2000	137,600	5,269,400
2001	138,400	5,212,600

Sources: Taiwan: Directorate General of Budget, *Accounting and Statistics*, Executive Yuan, Republic of China (2003: 66); China: China Science and Technology Statistics (2003).

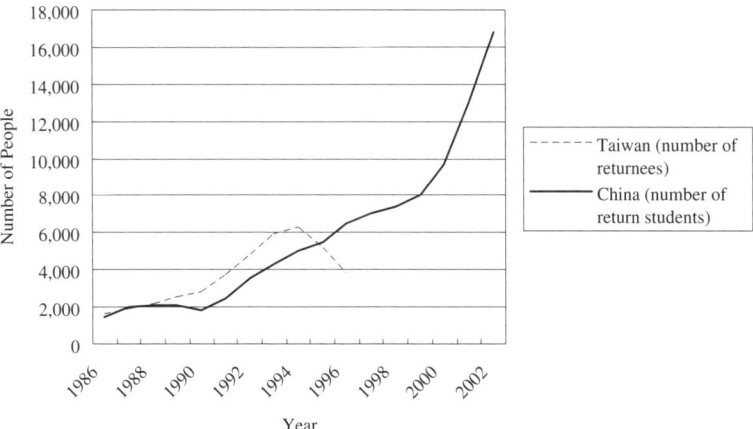

Figure 14.3. Changes in the number of returnees from overseas in Taiwan and China.
Notes: (1) Figures are 3 years moving average. (2) In Taiwan, these statistics stopped being collected in 1998.
Source: Taiwan: Ministry of Education, Republic of China 1999: 54; China: National Bureau of Statistics of China (2004: 781).

So, it can be concluded that some part of the increasing endowment of skilled R&D personnel in Asian developing countries such as Taiwan, India, and China is the result of brain circulation.

The technical background — ICT development and the modularity of computer architecture

Finally, we will examine the technical background which allows the whole process of product development to be divided into several steps and assigned to geographically dispersed places. We can identify two background factors: (1) the development of Information Communication Technology (ICT) and the codification of information and (2) the increasing modularity of the architecture of the personal computer.

The first factor, the development of ICT, has reduced the transaction costs of managing geographically dispersed R&D units. In addition, new methods allow the greater codification of scientific knowledge and the standardization of some R&D work, which facilitates the dispersal of R&D units (UNCTAD 2005: 158).

The second factor, the increasing modularity of the architecture of the personal computer, has enabled the whole product development procedure to be divided into several steps. Here, the term "architecture" refers to "the basic design structure of how to divide the product, and by that basic design structure, how to design the interface between each component" (Fujimoto 2001: 4).

Figure 14.4 shows the transition in computer architecture. The relationship between each component and its function can be categorized as modular or integral, while collaboration between companies can be categorized as open or closed, producing a diagram with four cells.

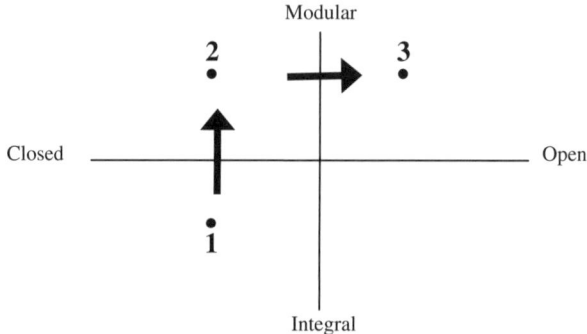

Figure 14.4. The transition in computer architecture.
Source: Author.

The transition from cell 1 to cell 2 happened when IBM developed System/360 in 1964. System/360 was of the closed-modular type, because IBM did not reveal details of the interface outside the company. Then, the transition from cell 2 to cell 3 took place dramatically, when IBM developed the IBM PC in 1981. The IBM PC was based on the open-modular type, as IBM made public the specifications of the operating system (OS), components and peripherals, allowing them to be developed by external companies. From then on, "IBM compatiblity" became the industry standard which allowed integration between products made by different companies. As the architectural modularity of the personal computer has increased, it has become possible to divide the whole product development procedure of the PC into several steps, and to locate these steps in geographically dispersed places all over the world.

The Emergence of the Global Development Network

So far, we have seen how the globalization of R&D activities has changed in the 2000s, and the reasons for these changes. This allows the development of a conceptual framework to describe the globalization of R&D in the GPN of the personal computer industry.

The global development network

How can we describe this new phenomenon, that of dividing up the whole process of product development for one model of personal computer and locating the parts in geographically dispersed R&D units all over the world? I would like to describe it as the formation of a "global development network" within the GPN of the industry. I define the "global development network" as follows: "geographically dispersed R&D units, each of which is located in a different country as the most suitable for carrying out the assigned task, forming a network to complete the whole process of product development for one model."

Figure 14.2 above shows the relationship of the global development network to the GPN in the personal computer industry. As explained earlier, the upper part (A) of Figure 14.2 shows the GPN in the early 1990s, and the lower part (B) shows the geographically dispersed development activities in the GPN in the 2000s. The lower part (B) of the figure can be identified as the "global development network," and the figure shows how the global development network divides up the functions of product development within the GPN, which were conventionally concentrated in one place in the 1990s, and how it assigns each function to several R&D units which are geographically dispersed all over the world.

The globalization of R&D activities which took place in the 2000s in the personal computer industry, with the locations expanding to include developing countries and with the functions expanding to include product development, implies that the conventional GPN now contains a new form of subnetwork, namely the global development network.

The rising presence of Taiwan

The following section will consider how the emergence of the global development network in the computer industry has changed the GPN, through strengthening the position of Taiwan in the following ways. Table 14.2 shows that all the R&D tasks carried out in China are administered or supported by R&D in Taiwan. For example, R&D in Taiwan is in charge of transferring self-sustaining models to the R&D unit in China; mediating between R&D units in the United States and China; giving technical instructions to China and training China-based engineers by periodically inviting them from Shanghai to Taipei. In addition to the above, my interviews at the company revealed that the role of R&D in Taiwan of administering, supporting, and training the R&D unit in China was much larger in 2006 than in 2004.[4]

In the global development network, as the presence of R&D in China has grown, the presence of R&D in Taiwan which administers and supports it has also increased: without the R&D in Taiwan, the R&D in China could not function. Moreover, R&D in Taiwan is in charge of combining the detailed design work carried out by R&D units all over the world, in cooperation with R&D in the US headquarters. This is because the R&D unit in Taiwan is located near the original equipment manufacturer (OEM) in Taiwan and is in charge of transferring the product to that company. It is also in charge of solving problems which occur in mass production at the OEMs. As we

---

[4]Interview with an engineer from the American personal computer company, "Company A" (May, 2006).

have seen above, it can be said that the emergence of the global development network within the GPN of the personal computer has made the presence of Taiwan in the industry larger than before.

The effects on the mobility of skilled R&D personnel and technology

How does the emergence of the global development network affect the mobility of skilled R&D personnel and technology? I assume that it increases the mobility of both. Although daily communication between geographically dispersed R&D units is carried out through the Internet, in practice the R&D personnel move between R&D units when any critical problem occurs, for example, from R&D in Taiwan to R&D in the United States or from R&D in China to R&D in Taiwan. The mobility is short-term in many cases, but it can be long-term in others. For example, the American Company A sometimes sends engineers from China to Taiwan for training lasting several weeks.[5]

In the global development network, technology also moves from one R&D unit to another. This is because all geographically dispersed R&D units often communicate with each other and exchange technical information to complete the whole product development process for one model. As a result, technology moves from one R&D unit to another, especially from units located in more developed countries, such as the United States or Taiwan, to less developed countries, such as China. So, it can be concluded that the emergence of the global development network increases the mobility of skilled R&D personnel and technology within the GPN of the personal computer industry.

Conclusion

In this chapter, I have proposed a conceptual framework to identify current aspects of the globalization of R&D activities in the 2000s, using the GPN of the personal computer industry as a case study.

In analyzing the globalization of R&D activities in the 2000s, it is possible to identify the expansion of locations to developing countries, and the

---

[5]Interview with an engineer from the American personal computer company, "Company A" (May, 2006).

expansion of their functions to product development. There are three main sets of factors lying behind the globalization of R&D: the multinationals' search for lower development costs, the availability of greater numbers of skilled personnel in the developing countries and the increasing modularity of the architecture of the personal computer.

Finally, I have suggested the concept of "global development network" to describe the globalization of R&D activities within the GPN of the personal computer industry. We have also seen how the GPN has itself been transformed since the emergence of the global development network. This has increased the importance of Taiwan in the personal computer industry, and has increased the mobility of skilled R&D personnel and technology within these global networks.

References

China Science and Technology Statistics (2003). *Quanguo Keji Jingfei he Keji Huodong Renyuan*. Beijing.

Development Bank of Japan (1988). "Ugoki hajimeru wagakuni kigyô no kaigaikenkyû: Takokuseki kigyôka e no shindankai." *Chôsa* 115.

Directorate General of Budget, Accounting and Statistics, Executive Yuan, Republic of China (2003). *Shehui Zhibiao Tongji 2003*. Taipei: Directorate General of Budget, Accounting and Statistics.

EIU (Economist Intelligence Unit) (2004). *Scattering the Seeds of Innovation: The Globalization of Research and Development*. London: Economics Intelligence Unit.

Ernst, Dieter (2000). "Inter-organizational Knowledge Outsourcing: What Permits Small Taiwanese Firms to Compete in the Computer Industry?" *Asia Pacific Journal of Management* 17: 223–255.

Ernst, Dieter (2002). "Global Production Networks and the Changing Geography of Innovation Systems: Implications for Developing Countries." *Journal of Economics of Innovation and New Technologies,* 11(6): 497–523.

Ernst, Dieter (2005). "Complexity and Internationalization of Innovation — Why is Chip Design Moving to Asia?" *International Journal of Innovation Management* 9(1): 47–73.

Ernst, Dieter and Linsu Kim (2002). "Global Production Networks, Knowledge Diffusion, and Local Capability Formation." *Research Policy* 31(8–9): 1417–1429.

Fujimoto, Takahiro (2001). "Architecture no sangyôron." In *Business Architecture — Seihin, Soshiki, Process no Senryakuteki Sekkei*, edited by Takahiro Fujimoto, Akira Takeishi, and Yaichi Aoshima, 3–26. Tokyo: Yuhikaku.

Gassman, Oliver and Maximilian Von Zedtwitz (1999). "New Concepts and Trends in International R&D Organization." *Research Policy* 28(2–3): 231–250.

Hayashi, Takabumi (2004). "Globalization and Networking of R&D Activities by 19 Electronics MNCs." In *Internationalization of Research and Development and the Emergence of Global R&D Networks*, edited by Manuel G. Serapio and Takabumi Hayashi, 85–112, Oxford: Elsevier.

Henderson, Jefferey, Peter Dicken, Martin Hess, Neil Coe and Henry Wai-Chung Yeung (2002). "Global Production Networks and the Analysis of Economic Development." *Review of International Political Economy* 9(3): 436–464.

Ministry of Education (1999). *Zhonghua Minguo Jiaoyu Tongji*, Republic of China. Taipei: Ministry of Education.

National Bureau of Statistics of China (2004). *Zhongguo Tongji Nianjian 2004*. Beijing: National Bureau of Statistics.

National Science Foundation (1998). "International Mobility of Scientists and Engineers to the United States — Brain Drain or Brain Circulation?" *Issue Brief* NSF98-316, June 22, 1998. Revised November 10, 1998.

Ronstadt, Robert C. (1978). "International R&D: The Establishment and Evolution of Research and Development Abroad by Seven U.S. Multinationals." *Journal of International Business Studies* 9: 7–24.

Saxenian, AnnaLee (2002). "Transnational Communities and the Evolution of Global Production Networks: The Cases of Taiwan, China, and India." *Industry and Innovation* (Special Issue on Global Production Network) 9(3): 183–202.

Tienxia Zazhi (1994) No. 160. September 1, 1994 (in Chinese).

UNCTAD (2005). *World Investment Report 2005*. New York, Geneva: United Nations.

Von Zedtwitz, Maximilian and Oliver Gassmann (2002). "Market versus Technology Drive in R&D Internationalization: Four Different Patterns of Managing Research and Development." *Research Policy* 31(4): 569–588.

Westney, D. Eleanor (1998). "Research on the Global Management of Technology Development." *Hitotsubashi Business Review* 46(1): 1–21.

CHAPTER 15

THE CHANGING GLOBAL ENVIRONMENT OF LOGISTICS: THE CASES OF HAKATA AND KITAKYUSHU IN JAPAN

Hiroshi Hoshino

Introduction

In the globalization of business activities, container transport has played a vital role in ensuring reliable supply chain management for manufacturers: to purchase raw material and parts, to produce the merchandise, and finally to deliver the finished goods to any part of the world at a reasonable cost.

The ports of Kitakyushu and Hakata are two core ports in the northern part of the Kyushu Region and are essential infrastructure for the promotion of trade and industry in Kyushu where the automobile and semi-conductor industries have formed clusters. However, it is often pointed out that these two ports have lost competitive advantage in comparison with neighboring foreign ports and other major domestic ports, for various reasons. First, rapidly growing ports located within a 1,000 km radius such as Busan and Shanghai are expanding their facilities as regional hubs. Second, neither Kitakyushu nor Hakata was selected under the Ministry of Land, Infrastructure and Transport's "Super-Hub Port Initiative" proposed in 2005. This decision indicates that the Japanese Government will not prioritize investment in the development of these two ports. Third, there has been a significant trend of cargo shifting away from Japan to other Asian countries, mainly China, in the last 20 years. Since the trade between Japan, the United States, and Europe is no longer central, shipping services to and from China have become the major routes, bypassing Japanese ports. Fourth, the size and capacity of container carriers deployed in the liner service are increasingly subject to economies of scale in their operations. Most shipping companies are carefully selecting a limited number of ports of call in order to reduce costs.

Judging from the above conditions, these two ports are facing various levels of threat. On the other hand, these trends could also provide them with new opportunities for survival as mini-hubs in western Japan. Through analysis of recent developments affecting the ports of Kitakyushu and Hakata and the changing global logistics environment, this chapter examines how these two ports could survive the increasingly fierce competition and become regional nodes, linking various forms of transport to assist the growth of businesses in the Kyushu region.

Port Competitiveness

In the discussion of port developments and the competitiveness of container ports in Asia, a number of researchers have focused on various aspects of the problem, such as geographical locational advantage, the productivity and performance of port operations, the state of regional industry in the hinterland, and choice of shipping lines.

Fleming and Hayuth (1994) emphasized the importance of a good geographical location for success in competition between ports. There has been a worldwide tendency to concentrate container traffic in large hub ports connecting with their hinterlands through the road and rail infrastructure. Besides traditional gateway ports at the centers of major regional markets, Singapore, Rotterdam, Dubai, and other ports located on major shipping lanes have attracted shipping companies through their strategic location and the feeder networks connecting them with other ports in the region.

Rimmer (1998: 193–208) analyzed port selection and competition among shipping companies within the Asia-Pacific Economic Region, especially in relation to the development of the global alliances forged in 1996. He pointed out that global alliances and further mergers would lead to rationalization of port facilities and more competition, because of increasing reliance on strategically located megahubs and feeder networks. While individual shipping companies had a tendency to serve ports in their home countries, an alliance of shipping companies would consider decisions about ports of call more carefully.

The ports of Hong Kong and Kaohsiung have long dominated container shipping both in relation to the start of the supply chain and also as final destinations for customers in East Asia. However, the emergence of new transshipment and gateway hubs means that ports such as Shanghai, Shenzhen and Qingdao in China, and Kwangyang in South Korea are vying with these established ports for a greater share of container traffic (Yap *et al.*, 2006: 167–188). These findings concerning shipping services on major trade routes suggest that shipping companies have reorganized their services, including ports of call, assignments of slot capacity, and rotation of vessels. They now focus more on mainland Chinese ports located in close proximity to each other that share their hinterlands.

From empirical studies of major shipping lines based in Singapore and Malaysia, key factors in the selection of a port are strategic location, port efficiency, port charges, adequate infrastructure, cargo size, connectivity, and a wide range of port services such as "one-stop shopping" services (Tongzon and Lavina, 2007: 477–492). Tongzon and Lavina suggest that shipping lines are restructuring their operations in response to competitive pressures in the industry, and are concentrating more on the maritime routes that best serve their interests through faster and cheaper transit rather than on a particular hinterland.

The location of shipping hubs is basically determined by the economics of shipping. Consequently, larger container ships call at fewer ports on any given route and transshipment has become more common, while the size of the average container ship has increased considerably over the last 10 years (Cullinane *et al.*, 2004: 33–36).

Existing publications show that geographical location close to their hinterlands is an important factor in shipping lines' choice of ports of call. Additionally, other factors including connection to various feeder networks can also be considered in their port selections.

Although the ports of Kitakyushu and Hakata are not located in the center of a manufacturing region, their locations on major trade routes between East Asia and North America may make them attractive as ports of call for shipping lines.

Port Development in Asia

The growth of trade from newly industrialized countries, including South Korea, Taiwan, Hong Kong and Singapore in the 1970s and from the ASEAN countries in the 1980s and 1990s, demanded rapid development and establishment of efficient container ports in Asia. Hong Kong, Singapore, and Kaohsiung were the three major ports in this region in the 1990s and are still ranked in the top 10 globally in terms of the number of container handlings in the 2000s (Table 15.1). Although Hong Kong has long been a major gateway for China as the world's factory, the rapid growth of China's economy required port facilities closer to the main economic activities. Consequently, new ports were developed in the industrial centers in areas such as Shanghai, Shenzen, and Quingdao.

Japan was the single largest exporting country in Asia from the beginning of containerization in the late 1960s up to 1990, when its share of cargo movement in the Asia–North America was still 27 percent (Table 15.2). However, as a result of the drastic changes resulting from the growth of China, exports from China combined with those from Hong Kong increased from only 23 percent of the Asia/North America trade in 1990 to nearly 70 percent in 2004. Also in 1990, container handling in Shanghai as the leading mainland Chinese port was only 452,000 TEUs, which was less

Table 15.1.   The 10 leading container ports in the world (2005).

Rank	Port	Throughput (in thousand tons)
1	Singapore	23,192
2	Hong Kong	22,427
3	Shanghai	18,084
4	Shenzhen	16,197
5	Busan	11,840
6	Kaohsiung	9,470
7	Rotterdam	9,300
8	Hamburg	8,050
9	Dubai	7,619
10	Los Angeles	7,485

Source: *Containerisation International*, March 2006.

Table 15.2. Cargo movement from Asia to North America, 1990–2004 (10k TEU).

	1990	%	2000	%	2004	%
Japan	78.3	27	81.8	11.7	81.3	7.7
Korea	34.3	11.8	46.2	6.6	53.7	5.1
China	22.5	7.8	294.1	42.0	622.4	58.7
Hong Kong	42.5	14.7	101.3	14.5	116.5	11.0
Taiwan	69	23.8	65.0	9.3	61.4	5.8
Others	43.5	15.0	112.5	16.1	124.2	11.7
Total	290.1		700.9		1059.5	

Source: Journal of Commerce, Japan Maritime PR Center, 2005.

than one-tenth of that in Hong Kong. China's container ports, especially Shanghai, are showing a significant increase in the number of container terminals and handling capability, even though Shanghai originally was not ideal as a port for large container ships due to its shallow waters and large tidal range. Table 15.1 shows that container handling in Shanghai in 2006 is over 18 million TEU, an increase by a factor of 50 in 15 years. If it maintains the current pace of development, Shanghai's container throughput is expected to surpass Hong Kong's by 2010.

The Korean Government has also invested in the development of new container terminals in preparation for a further increase in throughput, especially transshipping cargoes via Busan. Since the current terminal facility in the center of Busan city cannot be further enlarged due to limited land resources, Busan Port Authority started building a new container terminal 20 km west of Busan which will have 30 container berths by the year 2015.

Shuttle services connecting North America directly with Chinese ports have become quite common since the 1990s and shipping companies now operate more loops using Chinese ports of call as Table 15.3 indicates. Asia/North America Liner Services added 20 additional calls at Shanghai, 10 at Shenzhen, and 6 at Qingdao while it decreased the number of calls at Taiwanese and Japanese ports during 2002 and 2005.

When Japan was still the major exporting nation in Asia in the 1980s, container ships on either the Asia–North America service or the Asia–Europe service regularly called at Tokyo, Nagoya, Kobe and other

Table 15.3. Calling ports of Asia/North America liner services (number of callings).

Year	2002	2003	2004	2005	2002–2005
Port	(58 loops)	(68 loops)	(76 loops)	(80 loops)	change
Busan	26	30	34	38	+12
Kaohsiung	28	27	26	25	−3
Shenzhen	25	31	31	35	+10
Shanghai	18	30	35	38	+20
Qingdao	7	10	11	13	+6
Hong Kong	45	51	52	49	+4
Japan	33	31	34	31	−2

ports including Osaka, Yokohama, Moji and sometimes Shimizu for loading motorcycles, and Hakata for loading rubber tires. As Table 15.3 shows, the average number of ports of call for 59 round trips or loops in 2002 was 3.1 while it decreased to 2.8 for 80 loops in 2005. Only half of the loops between Asia and North America included Japanese ports. This indicates that groups of shipping companies in alliance require that ports of call should not only have advantages in terms of their hinterlands, but also as hubs of feeder networks allowing the integration of cargoes within the region.

Since alliance groups try to realize economies of scale in their operations and rationalization of port coverage, they tend to deploy larger container ships on the trunk lines. A Post-Panamax or Over-Panamax container ship with loading capacity of over 4,000 TEUs was first introduced by the Maersk Line at the end of the 1980s. According to the statistics of the Nippon Yusen Kaisha (NYK) Line[1] shown in Table 15.4, the average size of container ships now operated by the world's five megacarriers and alliances was 4,790 TEU in 2006 compared with 4,535 TEU in 2003.

After the world's largest container ship, the M/V Emma Maersk, with a loading capacity of 11,000 TEU, was launched in September 2006 and deployed on the Asia–Europe service, and with her sister ships gradually coming into service, the majority of the container fleet on trunk lines will

---

[1] NYK Line Research Group (2006).

Table 15.4.   Container fleets of mega-carriers/alliances (TEU) as of January 2003?

Alliances (as of January 2003)	Member companies	No. of ships	Total capacity	Average capacity
Maersk Sealand		84	425,234	5,062.30
Evergreen	EMC, LT, Hatsu	69	288,678	4,183.70
Grand Alliance	NYK, P&O, NED, OOCL, HL, MISC	119	550,518	4,626.20
New World Alliance	APL, MOL, HMM	73	355,592	4,871.10
CKYH	COSCO, KL, YML, Hanjin, Senator	155	647,393	4,176.70
Total		500	2,267,415	4,534.80
(as of January 2006)				
Maersk Sealand		148	734,974	4,966.00
Evergreen	EMC, LT, Hatsu	76	338,200	4,450.00
Grand Alliance	NYK, OOCL, HL, MISC	111	579,995	5,225.20
New World Alliance	APL, MOL, HMM	91	457,599	5,028.60
CKYH	COSCO, KL, YML, Hanjin, Senator	187	825,283	4,413.30
Total		613	2,936,051	4,789.60

Source: NYK Line, World Container Fleet, 2003/2006.

eventually consist of Post-Panamax ships. Consequently, container ports now require piers of at least 15 meters in depth and a high standard of terminal services, including advanced loading equipment and extensive container stowage space.

Strategy of Ports in the Kyushu Region

Positioning the ports of Hakata and Kitakyushu

The ports of Kitakyushu and Hakata are major gateways from Kyushu to other Asian countries. The number of containers handled at the port of Hakata[2] was 668,848 TEU in 2005, more than twice the figure for 1995 of 296,413 TEU, compared with 483,799 TEU for 2005 in Kitakyushu. As exports to the four Asian countries of China, South Korea, Taiwan, and

---

[2]Statistics of Port and Harbor Bureau, Fukuoka City.

Hong Kong make up 54.0 percent of all exports from Kyushu, as well as 40.2 percent of imports, Kyushu's economy is dependent on trade with other Asian countries. According to the statistics of the Ministry of Land, Infrastructure and Transport,[3] 40.6 percent of merchandise produced in Kyushu was exported through Hakata compared with 40.7 percent through Kitakyushu in terms of the weight of cargo, while 46.4 percent of the merchandise consumed in Kyushu was imported through Hakata compared with 33.6 percent through Kitakyushu. Since the number of direct callings to Kitakyushu and Hakata by major container services is limited, imports and exports in the western part of Japan except Kyushu are mainly handled by Osaka and Kobe, which in the past were the largest container ports in Japan. Regional cargoes between local cities in Japan and Asia are carried directly by small container ships, bypassing these major ports. In 2005, there were 17 sailings per week from Kitakyushu and 14 sailings from Hakata to China, compared with 47.3 sailings from Osaka and 40.2 sailings from Kobe. Even though Kitakyushu and Hakata are playing a major role in connecting Kyushu with major ports in Asia and worldwide, the impact is small in terms of container throughput, not only within the Asian region as a whole, but also within Japan.

In 2004, the Super-Hub Port Initiative was introduced for the first time by the Ministry of Land, Infrastructure, and Transport for the purpose of strengthening the comparative advantage of Japanese container ports over neighboring Asian competitors. Six major ports, namely Tokyo, Yokohama, Nagoya, Yokkaichi, Osaka, and Kobe. were selected as "Super-Hub Ports",[4] in pursuit of three core targets: (1) cost reduction of container handling by 30 percent; (2) a one-day shortening of the lead time from discharge of cargo to its release from the port and (3) creation of a one-stop administrative service. However, applications from the ports of Kitakyushu and Hakata were rejected because of the limited container throughput. This failed to reach a million TEU in either port, and thus their potential as hub ports was not rated very highly.

---

[3] *Statistics on Export/Import Container Movement in Japan, 2003*, Ministry of Land, Infrastructure and Transport.

[4] Maritime Bureau, 2006, *Report on Maritime Affairs*, Ministry of Land Infrastructure and Transport.

As far as the number of containers handled in the Kyushu region is concerned, no dynamic expansion of trade is expected in comparison with other Asian ports. However, a number of manufacturing firms have started to set up plants in Kyushu, and clusters in industries such as semiconductors and automobiles have formed since the late 1960s and early 1970s. Kyushu is thus widely recognized as Japan's "Silicon" or "Automobile" Island.

In the case of the automobile industry, major manufacturers including Toyota, Nissan, and Daihatsu have established plants in the northern part of Kyushu, and they produced over 1 million vehicle units in 2006. As for auto parts suppliers, as of October 2006, approximately 700 first- and second-tier suppliers[5] were located in Kyushu, which enabled 51 percent of auto-parts to be supplied locally from within the island. With support from the Fukuoka prefectural government, the automobile industry has set targets for the production of 1.5 million vehicle units with over 70 percent of local content in parts by 2009. Honda Motor Co. has set up a separate plant for motorcycle production in Kumamoto Prefecture in central Kyushu, and has positioned it as a mother plant for their global operations.

Because of the growing automobile industry in the hinterland, the direct export of vehicles to China and other Asian countries and the import of auto-parts from the southern part of China through Kitakyushu and Hakata have been increasing. It can also be pointed out that the number of automobiles produced in Kyushu and South Korea combined is 4 million in total, and that the number of parts supplied within the region is expected to increase in the near future. As the case of the automobile industry indicates, Kyushu is part of a supply chain linked to other Asian production platforms. Besides automobiles and semiconductors, the supply of agricultural products, machinery, and other goods produced in Kyushu for other Asian markets is gradually increasing.

Strategy for growth

As mentioned above, the operations of the shipping companies have changed drastically in the last 20 years. They now put an emphasis on limiting the number of ports of call and shortening the transit times between China and

---

[5] *Economic Survey of Kyushu, 2006*, Kyushu Economic Research Center.

North America or Europe. Consequently, the Sea of Japan surrounded by China, Korea, and Japan is now widely recognized as the major route by alliance groups and mega-carriers, especially for the Asia–North America trade. These new routes bypass the traditional Japanese ports facing the Pacific Ocean where the Japanese government established its industrial platforms and gateway ports. As all six of the current Japanese super-hub ports along the Pacific Coast are located in deep bays, so that calling at these ports requires a detour from the main routes, and slows progress.

On the other hand, the cities facing the Sea of Japan used to be called "the backside of Japan" because they were less developed, with no super-hub ports in the area. The ports of Kitakyushu and Hakata are located on the Sea of Japan side, close to the new main Asia–North American trade route. Container ships sailing to North America from major Asian hub ports such as Singapore, Hong Kong, Busan, Kaohsiung and the mainland Chinese ports operate in the Sea of Japan, just north of these two ports.

While shipping companies would rather select a route through the Sea of Japan than on the Pacific Coast side to shorten the transit time to North American destinations by between a day and a day-and-a-half, it might be an advantage for them to be able to load and discharge Japanese cargo without any deviation by calling at Japan Sea ports. This suggests that ships deployed on the Asia–European services may also be in a position to take advantage of calling at Hakata or Kitakyushu for loading additional cargo.

The ports of Kitakyushu and Hakata are in an ideal location to integrate domestic cargo through feeder networks. For example, it takes four days by container ship to get from Shanghai to Tokyo. On the other hand, combined sea and rail services could offer a shorter transit service to Tokyo, allowing a two-day container service from Shanghai to Kitakyushu, and less than 16 hours by rail freight from Kitakyushu to Tokyo. Also, any destination in the western part of Japan can be approached by truck, rail or coastal ship by way of Kitakyushu or Hakata.

In the last five years, both ports have successfully expanded their transport systems, including freight rail facilities set up by the Japan Freight Railway Co. in the freight terminals, motorways with junctions nearby, and an upgrading of airport facilities. Although the Japanese share of cargo in the Asian trade has gradually been shrinking, it is still an essential part of business for shipping companies. These ports have the advantage of potentially allowing Over-Panamax type container ships to sail through the Sea of Japan, calling at Hakata and Kitakyushu, and collecting local cargo both originating in Kyushu and carried through feeder networks from all over Japan.

Summary of Findings

As the global trend in shipping is for larger container ships to call at fewer ports, it has been observed that Japanese ports are being bypassed by many major liner services. Moreover, neither of the ports of Kitakyushu and Hakata qualified as super-hub ports in 2004, which could have secured investment for further development from the Ministry of Land, Infrastructure, and Transport. However, their locations in the northern Kyushu region facing the Sea of Japan could give them some opportunities for a new type of operation. The ships of the Mediterranean Shipping Company on the Asia–Europe services actually do dock at Hakata as their last port of call in Asia, and a few other shipping companies are showing interest in an additional calls at Hakata for the same reason.

As empirical studies indicate, strategic location is the key factor in choices of ports by shipping companies. As a port of call in a good location on a trunk route is often selected by shipping companies as a base for transshipment, it can be said that the advantages of Hakata and Kitakyushu are their locations on the Asia–North America routes sailing through the Sea of Japan. These ports could enhance their attractiveness for shipping companies by exploiting their hinterlands, with their growing automobile and semi-conductor industries, together with the high level of integration of the internal transport road and rail systems within Japan.

References

Cullinane, Kevin, Wang Teng Fei, Wang Teng and Sharon Cullinane (2004). "Container Terminal Development in Mainland China and Its Impact on the Competitiveness of the Port of Hong Kong." *Transport Reviews* 24(1): 33–56.
Fleming, Douglas and Yehuda Hayuth (1994). "Special Characteristics of Transportation Hubs: Centrality and Intermediacy." *Journal of Transport Geography* 2(1): 1–8.

Kyushu Economic Research Center (2006). *Economic Survey of Kyushu. 2006.* Fukuoka: Kyushu Economic Research Center.

Maritime Bureau (2006). *Report on Maritime Affairs.* Japan's Ministry of Land Infrastructure and Transport.

NYK Line Research Group (2003, 2006). *World Container Fleet.* Japan Chamber of Shipping.

NYK Line Research Group (2006). *Fact Book I.* Tokyo: NYK Line Research Group, available at www.nyk.com/english/ir/library/factbook/2006/2006factbook-1.pdf.

Rimmer, Peter J. (1998). "Ocean Liner Shipping Service: Corporate Restructuring and Port Selection/Competition." *Asia Pacific Viewpoint* 39(2): 193–208.

Shibata, Etsuko (1996). "A Study of International Logistics and Ports in East Asia." *Study of Shipping Economy* 30: 143–160.

Statistics of Kita-Kyushu Seaport and Airport Bureau. Various years. Kita-Kyushu City: Port Promotion Section.

Statistics of Port and Harbor Bureau, Fukuoka City. Various years. Fukuoka: Port and Harbor Bureau.

Statistics on Export/Import Container Movement in Japan (2003). Tokyo: Ministry of Land, Infrastructure and Transport.

Tan, Lumin (2001). "Development of Japanese and Korean Ports: Centering on the Lines of Asia/North America." *Study of Shipping Economy* 35: 129–147.

Tongzon, Jose L. and Lavina Sawant (2007). "Port Choice in a Competitive Environment? From the Shipping Lines' Perspective." *Applied Economics* 39(4): 477–492.

Yap, Wei Yim, Jasmine S.L. Lam and Theo Notteboom (2006). "Developments in Container Port Competition in East Asia." *Transport Review* 26(2): 167–188.

CHAPTER 16

THE DEVELOPMENT OF CHINA'S INTERNATIONAL SHIPPING INDUSTRIES

Meilong Le

China — The Most Rapidly Developing Area in the World

China's economy has been developing rapidly since its opening up to the outside world in 1979, especially after entering the World Trade Organization (WTO). Its Gross Domestic Product (GDP) in 2007 was 68 times as large as it was in 1978, increasing by 10 percent on average annually. In 2007, the GDP reached US$3.245 trillion, up 18.3 percent year-on-year. It now ranks fourth in the world, just after that of Germany at US$3.593 trillion (Table 16.1).

China's fast GDP growth largely depends on its economic reforms. China's economic structure has been changing rapidly. Nowadays, various private-owned enterprises account for more than 70 percent of China's economy. State-owned enterprises have been shrinking very quickly. The government has given up control of all except a few fundamental industries. To a large extent, the government's role has changed from controlling to servicing the economy.

Another characteristic of China's economy is its pervasive links to the outside world. China has become the largest manufacturing country in the world, and many of the world's largest manufacturing companies have joint factories in China. The "Made in China" sign can be seen on a vast variety of commodities.

Due to its close ties to the world economy, China's import and export trades have increased more quickly than its GDP (Table 16.2). The total amounts of imports and exports in 2007 were 105 times as large as in 1978.

Table 16.1. The growth of China's GDP, 1978–2007.

Year	GDP (RMB bn)	Growth rate (%)	GDP (US$ bn)	Year	GDP (RMB bn)	Growth rate (%)	GDP (US$ bn)
1978	362.4		43.8	1993	3,463.4	30	418.8
1979	403.8	11	48.8	1994	4,675.9	35	565.4
1980	451.8	12	54.6	1995	5,847.8	25	707.1
1981	486.2	8	58.8	1996	6,788.5	16	820.9
1982	529.5	9	64.0	1997	7,446.3	10	900.4
1983	593.5	12	71.8	1998	7,834.5	5	947.3
1984	717.1	21	86.7	1999	8,206.8	5	992.4
1985	896.4	25	108.4	2000	8,946.8	9	1,081.8
1986	1,020.2	14	123.4	2001	10,965.5	23	1,325.9
1987	1,196.3	17	144.7	2002	12,033.3	10	1,455.1
1988	1,492.8	25	180.5	2003	13,582.3	13	1,642.4
1989	1,690.9	13	204.5	2004	15,987.8	18	1,933.2
1990	1,854.8	10	224.3	2005	18,232.1	14	2,226.1
1991	2,161.8	17	261.4	2006	20,840.7	14	2,628.1
1992	2,663.8	23	322.1	2007	24,661.9	18	3,245.0

Source: *National Economy and Social Development Statistical Bulletin*, 1978–2007.

In 2007, they reached US$2.17 trillion, up 23.5 percent year-on-year. The "China Factor" has already become a frequently used phrase when people discuss the world economy.

Meanwhile, regional movements of peoples have also increased. In 2007, 345 million people entered and exit the mainland, China. The top 10 destinations were Hong Kong, Macau, Japan, Korea, Vietnam, Russia, Thailand, the United States, Singapore and Malaysia, and the top 10 countries of origin of inbound travelers were Korea, Japan, Russia, the United States, Malaysia, Singapore, Philippines, Mongolia, Vietnam and Thailand.

Logistics in China

China's modern logistics industry developed very fast during the 1990s and now is entering a period of rational, practical, and rapid development because of the following factors.

Table 16.2.   Trends in Chinese imports and exports, 1978–2007.

Year	Import and export (US$ bn)	Growth rate (%)	Import (US$ bn)	Export (US$ bn)
1978	20.6	—	9.75	10.89
1980	38.1	—	18.12	20.02
1985	69.6	—	27.35	42.25
1989	111.7	—	52.54	59.14
1990	115.4	3	62.09	53.35
1991	135.7	18	71.91	63.79
1992	165.5	22	84.94	80.59
1993	195.7	18	91.74	103.96
1994	236.6	21	121.01	115.61
1995	280.9	19	148.78	132.08
1996	289.9	3	151.05	138.83
1997	325.2	12	182.79	142.37
1998	324.0	0	183.71	140.24
1999	360.6	11	194.93	165.7
2000	474.3	32	249.2	225.09
2001	509.7	7	266.1	243.55
2002	620.8	22	325.6	295.17
2003	851.0	37	438.23	412.76
2004	1,154.7	36	561.38	593.36
2005	1,422.1	23	660.1	762.0
2006	1,760.7	24	791.6	969.1
2007	2,173.8	23	955.8	1,218.0

Source: *National Economy and Social Development Statistical Bulletin*, 1978–2007.

First, infrastructure construction is emphasized by all levels of governments. The transport conditions have been greatly improved. By 2007, the total length of railways was 75,000 km. Of these, 6,227 km were high speed lines of more than 200 km per hour, surpassing the EU. The total length of highways by 2007 was 3,573,000 km. Among them, 53,600 km were expressways, ranking second in the world. The national expressway framework, which consists of five North-South corridors and seven East-West corridors, was finished by 2007. In the Yangtze River Delta or Pearl River Delta, the advanced road network can guarantee transit times of less than four hours between any two cities. Meanwhile, transport capacity has also improved greatly. In 2007, goods transported by truck surpassed 16 billion tons (1.1 trillion kilometer tons), while the number of people traveling by coach reached 20.3 billion. By the end of 2007, China had 147 civil airports. Shanghai, Beijing, and Guangzhou Airports have become international hubs, and Shenzhen, Shenyang, Chengdu, Xi'an, and Xiamen Airports have become regional hubs. With 174 airplanes, Air China ranks seventh in the world according to passenger mileage, and China Southern and China Eastern ranks tenth and twelvth, respectively. In addition, there were eight other local airlines and nine private airlines by the end of 2007. Most airlines have cargo transport services, while three giant companies have exclusively cargo transport fleets.

Meanwhile, the information infrastructure has also greatly been upgraded. People can do businesses through the Internet and/or electronic data interchange (EDI). They can complete customs, commodities inspection and quarantine declarations, book shipping space, and send or receive business documents. Various management information systems have become widely applied in the logistics industry.

Second, various logistics companies have developed quickly and the management and service of logistics have entered a new phase. Logistics enterprises formed from those that were originally state-owned have become the backbones of China's logistics market. Such companies include the China Ocean Shipping Company Group (COSCO), China Shipping Company Group (CSC), and China Railway Express (CRE). Privately owned businesses which specialized in certain service fields such as P.L.G., TRANSFAR, and JCtrans have also developed very quickly. Large numbers of foreign and overseas logistics companies, including world famous transnational enterprises such as Maersk (Denmark), FedEx (US), UPS (US), Nippon Express (Japan), and Schneider National (US) have entered China's market. These foreign and overseas companies have brought China's logistics industry new ideas, technologies, and management patterns.

China's Ports

China's port construction has been highly emphasized by both central and local governments since the 1990s. By 2007, China had 1,400 ports and 35,242 production berths. Of these, nine had 200,000+ tons berths; 1,200 had 10,000+ tons berths, and 170 had container berths. Obviously, the construction of coastal ports has been the main focus. Between 2000 and 2005, China constructed 340 10,000+ tons berths, which increased throughput ability by a billion tons. The total throughput capacity and container handling capacity in coastal ports reached 3.438 billion tons and 61.5 million TEUs, respectively in 2007. In 2007, the total cargo throughput was 6.3 billion tons, which was nearly double that in 2005. In 2004 and 2005, the figure was 2.8 and 3.4 billion tons, respectively. In 2007, the throughput of 14 ports surpasses 100 million tons. The increase in the transport of imported ore and crude oil and domestic coal has played a very important role in this increase in throughput. Another area of growth has been container transportation. In 2007, the total container throughput was 114 million TEUs. The figures in 2004 and 2005 stood at 61.5 and 75.8 million TEUs, respectively.

Chinese ports now occupy half of the top 10 places in the ranking of world container ports, and three of them are in mainland China (Table 16.3). Obviously, the focus of the shipping industry has moved to the western Pacific Ocean rim, and China has become the leading country in terms of volume handled.

China's Shipping Companies

The largest shipping companies in mainland China are COSCO and CSC. The container service divisions of the two group companies are named COSCON (COSCO Container Lines) and CSCL (China Shipping Container Lines), which rank six and seventh in the world, respectively (Table 16.4).

Both COSCO and CSC have a long history. After 40 years of development, COSCO owns 550 vessels, including 13 fifth-generation container ships, three VLCC (Very Large Crude Carriers), 17 capsize bulks (of over 100,000 tons) and some heavy equipment carriers. The total deadweight is 30 million tons.

CSC has a much longer history than COSCO. By January 2006, CSC owned 410 vessels of various kinds. Within the group of companies, China Shipping Cargo Transport Company owns 140 vessels and CSCL owns 129 vessels, which include 52 container ships with capacities of over

Table 16.3. Top 10 container ports in the world.

2003	million TEU	2004	million TEU	2005	million TEU	2006	million TEU	2007	million TEU
Hong Kong	20.1	Hong Kong	21.93	Singapore	23.2	Singapore	24.8	Singapore	27.93
Singapore	18.1	Singapore	21.31	Hong Kong	22.42	Hong Kong	23.23	Shanghai	26.15
Shanghai	11.28	Shanghai	14.55	Shanghai	18.08	Shanghai	21.72	Hong Kong	23.88
Shenzhen	10.61	Shenzhen	13.65	Shenzhen	16.21	Shenzhen	18.47	Shenzhen	21.10
Busan	10.37	Busan	11.4	Busan	11.84	Busan	12.03	Busan	13.27
Kaohsiung	8.84	Kaohsiung	9.71	Kaohsiung	9.47	Kaohsiung	9.77	Rotterdam	10.79
Rotterdam	7.18	Rotterdam	8.41	Rotterdam	9.3	Rotterdam	9.60	Dubai	10.70
Los Angeles	7.1	Los Angeles	7.24	Hamburg	8.1	Dubai	8.92	Kaohsiung	10.25
Hamburg	6.14	Hamburg	7	Dubai	7.62	Hamburg	8.86	Hamburg	9.90
Antwerp	5.45	Antwerp	6	Los Angeles	7.48	Los Angeles	8.47	Qingdao	9.46

Source: Statistics of China Ports and Harbours Association, 2003–2007.

Table 16.4.   Top 10 container liners in the world (February 1st, 2007).

Company	Vessels	Total TEU	Capacity share (%)	Self-own vessels	Chartered vessels
Maersk Line	545	1,758,004	16.6	168	377
MSC	327	1,052,524	9.9	205	122
CMA	303	733,447	6.9	88	215
Evergreen	163	554,902	5.2	101	62
Hapag-Lloyd-CP	137	457,096	4.3	64	73
CSCL	132	396,437	3.7	80	52
COSCON	128	389,606	3.7	91	37
Hanjin-DSR	89	349,805	3.3	22	67
APL	108	344,147	3.2	36	72
NYK	124	333,652	3.1	43	81

Source: Alphaliner.

4,000 TEUs. There are many other major shipping companies in China, such as Sinotrans, JJ Shipping, and TMC.

Meanwhile, almost all the global shipping giants, such as Maersk, APL, Hyundai, Mitsui (MOL), Kawasaki (K Line), Yang Ming (YML), ZIM, Nippon Yusen (NYK), Hapag-Lloyd-CP, Mediterranean (MSC), Orient Overseas (OOCL), Hanjin, Evergreen, Lloyd Triestino, and Connecticut Maritime (CMA) have entered the Chinese maritime market. Most of them have developed these links very quickly. Some of them have market shares similar to those China's own shipping companies. Most of them have now established headquarters and branches in China, especially in Shanghai.

The Most Ambitious Port — Shanghai Port

Shanghai Port is the biggest port in terms of total cargo throughput and second largest port in terms of container throughput in the world. In 2007, the total cargo throughput and container throughput were 561.5 million tons and 26.15 million TEUs, respectively. With its emphasis on container transport, Shanghai Port will also become the biggest container port in the world in the near future (Table 16.5).

Table 16.5. Container throughput of Shanghai port.

Year	million TEUs	Year	million TEUs
1993	93.5	2001	634
1994	119.9	2002	861
1995	152.7	2003	1,128
1996	197.1	2004	1,455
1997	252.7	2005	1,808
1998	306.6	2006	2,172
1999	421.6	2007	2,615
2000	561		

Source: Shanghai International Port Group (SIPG).

Shanghai Port is becoming the world's largest port based on its developed hinterland and advantageous position. The hinterland includes the Yangtze River Delta, which accounts for one-third of the country's imports and exports, and the upper reaches of the river. The port is located at the country's economic center, the mouth of Yangtze River and the intersection of the East-West transport corridor with the North-South maritime route. Meanwhile, after its organizational reform of its operations, the port now has an ambitious port operator leading its internationalization, the Shanghai International Port Group (SIPG).

SIPG, a stock-holding company established in June 2005 with a registered capital of US$2.44 billion, is the main business body for international shipping. It has 15 affiliated companies, 7 subsidiary companies, 3 branches, 7 major share-holding companies and 13 minor share-holding companies. It accounts for nearly 60 percent of the total handling volume (SIPG, 2006).

By 2007, SIPG owned 9 container terminals with 35 berths on a total quay length of 10,096 meters, covering an area of 4.47 million square meters with 113 quay cranes. The container terminals are mainly located in three areas, Wusongkou downstream on the Huangpu River, Waigaoqiao on the southern bank of the Yangtze River estuary, and Yangshan deepwater port area (see Table 16.6, Figure 16.1).

The Yangshan Deepwater Port Project is a milestone in the Shanghai Port development history. When all the berths are constructed, the new port area will add handling capacity of 25 million TEUs.

Table 16.6.   An overview of SPIG container terminals.

Terminal	Quay length (m)	Berth	Quay cranes	Yard area (m²)
SCT	2,281	10	20	550,932
Waogaoqiao I	900	3	11	238,014
Waogaoqiao II, III	1,565	5	22	750,000
Waogaoqiao IV	1,250	4	14	687,000
Waogaoqiao V	1,100	4	14	687,000
Yangshan I, II	3,000	9	32	1,560,000
Total	10,096	35	113	4,472,946

Source: Shanghai International Port Group.

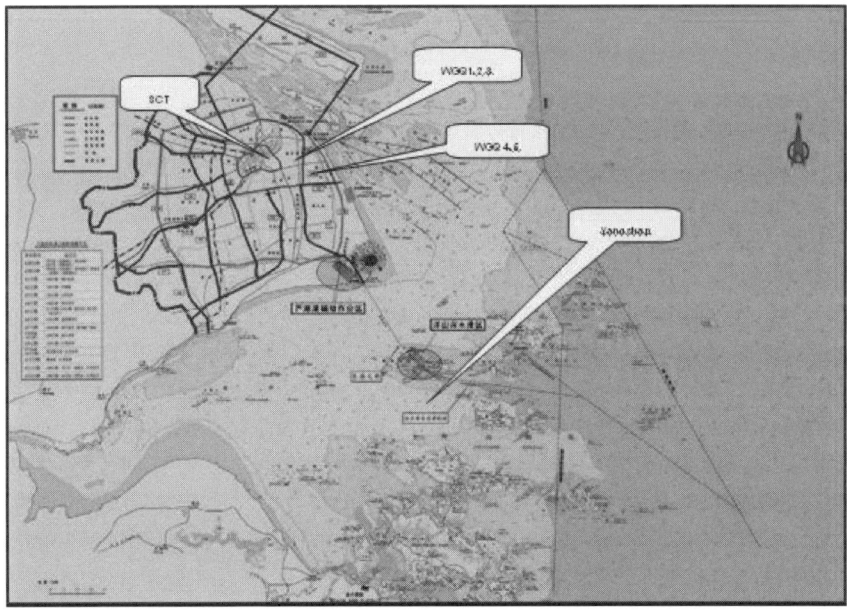

Figure 16.1.   Locations of terminals of Shanghai port.
Source: Abridged from the Chart — Hangzhou Bay.

Phase I of the Project includes the Phase I terminal, Luchao Logistics Park and the East China Sea Bridge. The terminal is located on Xiao Yang Shan Island. It has five berths, with a total quay length of 1,600 m and quayside water depth of 16 m (Figure 16.2). It has a sea-side area of 3,167,000 m², a land-side area of 1,340,000 m², and a container yard

Figure 16.2. Phase I terminal of Yang Shan deepwater port.
Source: Photo by Meilong Le.

area of $860,000 \, \text{m}^2$, which adds handling capacity of 2.2 million TEUs, allowing it to handle 3 million TEUs in practice. The Logistics Park situated at Luchao Harbor Area provides auxiliary services such as container stuffing and stripping, storage, transferring, repairing; customs clearance and inspection. The bridge is 32.5 kilometers long, 31.5 meters wide with six lane dual direction traffic. It has an annual capacity of 5 million TEUs. Phase I was put into operation in December 10, 2005.

Phase II is located just next to Phase I. It has a 1,400 m length quay with four berths, designed capacity for 2.1 m TEUs. It started operation in December 2006.

Now, container liner services from Shanghai Port serve all major ports around the world. Each month on average, 2,100 container ships depart from the port, en route to North America, Europe, the Mediterranean, Persian Gulf, Red Sea, Black Sea, Africa, Australia, South-east Asia, Northeast Asia, and other regions.

In the coming years, Shanghai Port will focus its business on containers, bulkbreaking, port logistics, and related services. In the container service field, it will achieve a breakthrough in transshipment by the upgrading of mother port functions and development of feeder services, consolidating local cargo supplies, and by rationalizing business. In the bulkbreaking service field, it will complete reorganization, optimize its industrial structure, improve efficiency, and upgrade its capabilities and function. In the port logistics field, it will integrate resources, establish logistics platforms, strengthen international cooperation and build up a strong brand.

With these core business aspirations, Shanghai Port will grow into an international hub with support from the vast hinterlands of Northeast Asia. SIPG will change into a transnational terminal operator through the absorption of foreign investment and establishment of transnational and transregional terminal investment companies. By building up a global brand, and by exporting management, capital and technology, SIPG is expected to become a leading international terminal operator.

Economic globalization necessitates development of logistics industries. Development of logistics industries further propels economic globalization. Today, we are in the era of extended and rapid global movements.

Acknowledgments

As a Deputy Dean of Sino-US Global Logistics Institute and Chairman of International Shipping Department of Shanghai Jiao Tong University, I have had many opportunities to attend seminars, workshops, discussions, conferences, forums and summits. Of all these meetings, this conference made a particularly deep impression, and I would like to thank APU for inviting me to attend such a forward looking event. I would also like to thank China Communications and Transportation Association, Shanghai Shipping Exchange, SIPG, Ningbo Port Group, Shantou Port, Nantong Port, Guangzhou Port Group and Pusan Port of Korea and CSCL for supplying me with material, and those others who have contributed in other ways to this chapter.

References

Alphaliner. http://www1.axsmarine.com/public/axs-alphaliner.php.

China Shipping Weekly (2004–2006). Beijing: China Communications and Transportation Association.

National Economy and Social Development Statistical Bulletin (1978–2007). Beijing: National Statistic Bureau.

SIPG (2006). *SIPG with Sound Development — A Bridge between Global Trade and China.* Shanghai: Shanghai International Port (Group).

CHAPTER 17

THE FUTURE OF THE WORLD'S
NUMBER ONE PORT — HONG KONG:
A CASE STUDY

Sunny Ho

Under the 'One Country, Two Systems' principle, the motherland has included Hong Kong in the Five-Year Plan and it says clearly that it will support Hong Kong's financial, logistics, tourism and IT industries. It will preserve Hong Kong's status as an international financial, trade and shipping centre.

Mr. Donald Tsang, Chief Executive of Hong Kong, made this statement during the Economic Summit on China's 11th Five-Year Plan and Development of Hong Kong on 11 September 2006. It reflects the common wish of China's central government, the government of the Hong Kong Special Administrative Region, the logistics industry and even the general public in Hong Kong that Hong Kong's position as a world leading logistics center should be maintained. The challenges are whether we can succeed in achieving this goal, and how.

In terms of policies and measures and co-ordination between the central and Hong Kong governments and between the public and private sectors, what is required to preserve Hong Kong's leading status?

One may query why there is such a concern. Is it not Hong Kong airport the world's busiest for international air cargo? Are not recent growth rates still very impressive? (Table 17.1)

On the seaport front, although Hong Kong was overtaken by Singapore in terms of container throughput in 2005, it still holds firmly to the world's

Table 17.1. World top 10 airports, 2003–2006.

Rank	2003	2004	2005	2006
1	Hong Kong 2.64 (+6.6%)	Hong Kong 3.1 (+17.4%)	Hong Kong 3.41 (+9.8%)	Hong Kong 1.69 (+6.7%)
2	Narita 2.09 (+7.6%)	Narita 2.31 (+10.6%)	Narita 2.23 (−3.4%)	Seoul 1.09 (+6.2%)
3	Seoul 1.81 (+8.3%)	Seoul 2.1 (+16.0%)	Seoul 2.12 (+0.8%)	Narita 1.08 (+1.1%)
4	Anchorage 1.71 (+1.6%)	Anchorage 1.86 (+1.9%)	Anchorage 2.02 (+8.3%)	Anchorage 1.01 (+3.8%)
5	Changi 1.61 (+1.6%)	Changi 1.78 (10.2%)	Frankfurt 1.84 (+8.3%)	Frankfurt 0.97 (+10.6%)
6	Frankfurt 1.5 (+2.8%)	Frankfurt 1.7 (+13.1%)	Changi 1.83 (+3.3%)	Changi 0.93 (+6.9%)
7	Taipei 1.49 (+8.7%)	Taipei 1.69 (+13.5%)	Taipei 1.69 (+0.2%)	Taipei 0.82 (+0.8%)
8	Miami 1.31 (+4.9%)	Miami 1.45 (+10.8%)	Pudong 1.6 (+16.7%)	Pudong 0.82 (+11.8%)
9	Amsterdam 1.31 (+5.3%)	Amsterdam 1.42 (+8.8%)	Amsterdam 1.45 (+2.0%)	Miami 1.44 (−0.6%)
10	Heathrow 1.22 (−0.8%)	Pudong 1.37 (+47.4%)	Miami 1.44 (−0.6%)	Amsterdam 0.74 (+5.2%)

Source: ACI (Airports Council International) www.airports.org.

Table 17.2.   The world's top 10 container ports, 2004–2005.

Ports	2005			2004		
	Rank	TEUs	% Change	Rank	TEUs	% Change
Singapore	1	23,192,000	8.70	2	21,329,100	15.90
Hong Kong	2	22,601,630	2.80	1	21,983,952	7.50
Shanghai	3	18,084,000	24.30	3	14,554,000	29.00
Shenzhen	4	16,197,000	18.60	4	13,659,000	28.20
Busan	5	11,843,151	3.10	5	11,491,968	10.40
Kaoshiung	6	9,471,056	−2.50	6	9,714,115	9.80
Rotterdam	7	9,286,756	12.00	7	8,291,994	16.10
Hamburg	8	8,047,545	15.50	9	7,003,479	14.10
Dubai	9	7,619,219	18.50	10	6,428,883	24.80
Los Angeles	10	7,484,624	2.20	8	7,321,440	2.00

Compiled by Transport & Housing Bureau, Transport Branch, PMLDU.

second position with a throughput that is envied by many of its major world counterparts (Table 17.2).

So, why the concern? Ted Kawamura, Managing Director of the Japan Shippers' Council and a veteran in the international trade and shipping industry, in his speech at the opening of the Asian Shippers' Meeting held June 17–19, 2002 in Shanghai, said, "The Hong Kong port is like the Japanese ports some 20 years ago. Because of its high cost, it is likely to lose out in competition."

The main challenge for Hong Kong to sustain its position as the leading logistics center in the region relates to its competitiveness with its rivals just across the boundary, namely Shenzhen and Guangzhou. These two ports at present have substantial cost advantages over Hong Kong (Table 17.3). Nevertheless, I am still optimistic about Hong Kong's future as a leading

Table 17.3.   Distribution South China cargo (ocean trade).

Years	2000–2005	2005–2010	2010–2015	2015–2020
Shenzhen Ports	33%	45%	54%	62%
Hong Kong Port	67%	55%	46%	38%

Source: Hong Kong Port Cargo Forecasts 2000/01, Hong Kong Port & Maritime Board.

global logistics hub, provided that we do the right things, and do them right now. I must also emphasize that there is a basic difference between the present Hong Kong and Japan two decades ago, in that Hong Kong is centered in the world's most important manufacturing area — the Pearl River Delta (PRD), which will continue to be the "factory of the world" for the foreseeable future. The area will continue to attract investment and reinvestment to sustain growth. Factories in the PRD will move further inland in the future, but they will not move away from the region.

Actually, as far as the share of the PRD cargo is concerned, it is already firmly expected that Shenzhen port will eventually overtake the Hong Kong port. The Port Cargo Forecast published by the Hong Kong government in 2000 predicted that by 2010, Hong Kong's share of PRD cargo would fall to 45 percent, against Shenzhen's 55 percent. There is no illusion that Hong Kong will maintain its number one position forever.

What is alarming, however, is that the timetable seems to be speeding up. The most important cargo source for Hong Kong comes from boundary crossing road transport, followed by waterway transport. However, we started experiencing a decline in the actual movement of containers carried by road since 2005. Boundary truck movements dropped 6.4 percent in 2005, and further 4.8 percent in the first 8 months of 2006 (Table 17.4).

Table 17.4. Cross-boundary container truck movement from Hong Kong (ingoing and outgoing vehicles with containers).

Year	Total
2002	4,679,225
2003	4,601,953
% growth over 2002	−1.7%
2004	4,608,196
% growth over 2003	0.1%
2005	4,421,300
% growth over 2004	−6.4%
2006 (Jan–Aug)	2,714,884
% growth over 2005 (Jan–Aug)	−4.8%

Source: Hong Kong Customs and Excise Department.

The decline is against the background of a general increase in imports and exports in the PRD.

Hong Kong container terminals are still reporting positive growth in throughput. In the first nine months of 2006, Hong Kong container terminal throughput increased by 10.4 percent year on year. However, according to the terminal operators, the increase is mainly due to their efforts to capture more international ship-to-ship transshipment business and transshipment by feeders from the Western part of the PRD only. In relation to the important source of export containers coming by road, however, the decrease is severe.

Hong Kong has an advantage in capturing containers that come from the western PRD by barges or small motor vessels. This is similar to many places in Japan where water transport is used because road haulage is excessively expensive. A container from Zhongshan to Hong Kong by barge is US$125 cheaper than to Yantian by truck. For this reason, Hong Kong has so far been able to capture the majority of cargo to and from the western PRD.

Nevertheless, if we became complacent with the thought that this advantage could generate cargo for Hong Kong forever, then inevitably Hong Kong would soon be in deep trouble. There are several reasons for Hong Kong being able to capture the bulk of imports and exports from the western PRD. First, let us look at the geography of Shenzhen. Shenzhen port is divided into an eastern port (Yantian) and a western port. All waterway transportation from the western PRD to Yantian has to go through Hong Kong. Therefore, it makes economic sense to transship containers in Hong Kong rather than go further away to Yantian by water transport. For historical reasons, the western Shenzhen port consisting of Shekou, Chiwan, and Ma Wan terminals, has been able to attract non trans-Pacific services only. Henceforth, its coverage, in terms of the trade routes served, is restrictive.

Secondly, local governments in the western PRD are known to practice a "One-Town, One Port" policy. Almost every town, large or small, has its own dedicated port. The regulatory regime of Chinese Customs, however, means that once a craft has completed customs clearance procedures, it would not be allowed to call at another port in the western PRD. Therefore, feeder vessels are forbidden to make multiple calls in the western PRD before they set sail to the eastern Shenzhen port.

The third reason, which is also very important, is that western PRD ports are all inland ports. These ports are classified as Class II ports in China and exporters exporting from Class II ports are not allowed to claim export tax refund if the container is to be transshipped at another Chinese port. This is because Chinese customs regulations do not regard the export process as completed before the mainline vessel has sailed from the port. However, because Hong Kong is a separate customs territory from mainland China, once the feeder vessels have left western PRD ports for Hong Kong, the export process is regarded as completed and exporters can claim an export tax refund immediately. These are the three main reasons why containers from the western PRD are transshipped at Hong Kong instead of western Shenzhen.

Things will change in due course, nonetheless. The increase in the number of sailings calling at the western Shenzhen port and the general increase in imports and exports to and from the western PRD are improving load factors for the feeders and hence allowing scheduled services to develop. The availability of regular services in turn attracts more shippers to use them. Western Shenzhen terminal operators have also made a lot of effort to introduce regulatory reforms (Figure 17.1).

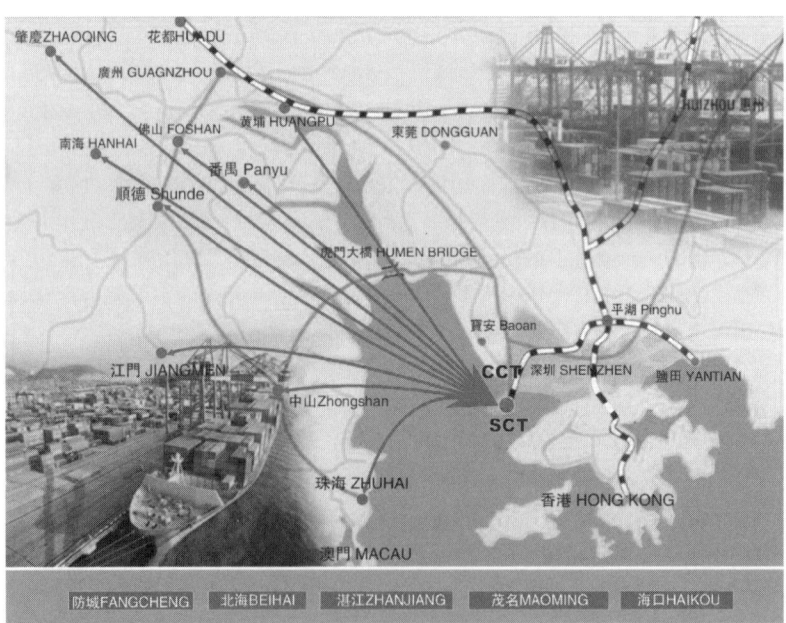

Figure 17.1.   Regular feeder services now available, Western Shenzhen.

Chinese customs changed its regulations in 2005 and shippers are now allowed to claim the export tax refund once the feeder vessels have left the western PRD ports. In 2005, 2.8 million twenty-foot equivalent unit (TEUs) were carried to western Shenzhen port by feeders, registering a hefty increase of 86% over 2004. The forecast for 2006 was over 4.3 million TEUs, representing another 54 percent increase.

The danger of ships switching away from Hong Kong is also reflected in the changes in the numbers of sailings calling only either at Hong Kong or Shenzhen. In 2000, nearly all sailings calling at Shenzhen would also call at Hong Kong. Five years later, half the sailings called at Shenzhen only and not at Hong Kong — the shipping lines calling only at Hong Kong had been reduced by half during this period.

While the debate rages on whether or not Hong Kong really needs new container terminals, we are seeing tremendous expansion in Shenzhen and the Guangdong port. Expansion projects include Yantian Phase IIIb (eight berths), Shekou Phase III (one berth), Chiwan Phase III (one berth), Mawan's two multipurpose berths, Daichang Bay Phase I (five berths) and Nansha Phase II (five berths). There will be ample excess capacity and fierce competition among the terminals in Shenzhen and Guangzhou. They are bound to go after the international transshipment containers that are currently Hong Kong port's main source of growth.

On the air side, meanwhile, Hong Kong airport's position looks more secure. Although there are altogether five international airports in the region, namely Hong Kong International Airport, Macau Airport, Zhuhai Airport, Shenzhen Bo An Airport, and Guangzhou Bai Yun Airport, Hong Kong's share of international air cargo is overwhelming. Hong Kong draws its advantage from its free port status, simple customs system, sophisticated and flexible operations, and large number of highly experienced personnel in the industry that guarantee speedy and reliable air freight services.

How has this changed since 20 years ago? At that time, almost all China cargo was transshipped via Hong Kong. However, what is the situation now?

Hong Kong airport certainly has many advantages over its competitors in the region. However, the prime reason for its current dominant position, in my opinion, is that in the past, there was no real and meaningful competition.

A major distinction between Asian, American, and European air freight industries is that, in Asia, a very high percentage of air freight cargo is carried in the belly of passenger flights. In Europe and the United States, cargo is mainly carried by special air cargo freighters. The prime consideration of passenger flights in their choice of airport is landing rights and passenger revenue. Cargo revenue is always secondary.

In China, with the exception of Beijing and Shanghai, no other cities have sufficient passengers to build up a comprehensive international network. Guangzhou and Shenzhen are too near Hong Kong, and Hong Kong has already captured most of the passenger and cargo sources.

Nevertheless, the market situation is changing. In order to foster economic growth, the Chinese airports authority has substantially relaxed its landing rights control, and foreign airlines have responded positively by adding new services to China.

In addition, because of China's continuous economic growth in the past decades, both passenger and cargo movements have grown significantly. Local governments have also made substantial investments in related infrastructure. In the PRD, Guangzhou Bai Yun Airport has added a lot of international services. The Shenzhen Bo An Airport has positioned itself to be a regional airport to serve international freighters. Hong Kong will be facing greatly intensified competition in the near future.

Development in the industry might help these newly developed airports to secure more business. The percentage of cargo carried by freighters is on the increase. The market share of integrators such as FedEx, UPS and DHL, is increasing at the expense of the traditional airlines. In Hong Kong, freighters carry over 54 percent of total cargo volume, up from 50 percent a few years ago and this trend is going to continue. Among these three integrators, at least one operator has said openly that it is seeking an alternative hub to Hong Kong. These integrators have full control over their operations including aircraft operation, terminal services, information technology, and customer services. They are also less dependent on freight forwarders. This has weakened the attractiveness of Hong Kong which draws a major strength form the clustering of freight forwarders and operators which makes convenient and successful co-loading and consolidation of cargo possible. It is not too difficult for these integrators to move their operation hubs away from Hong Kong.

In the face of these challenges, how could Hong Kong maintain its leading position as a logistics hub? The answers are "cut costs" and "add value."

Some experts may have the opinion that Hong Kong should concentrate on the high value niche market only, because as far as operating cost is concerned, Hong Kong could never compete with the operators across the boundary. Land is much more expensive in Hong Kong and the wage level is almost 10 times higher than on the mainland. Although there is some truth in this view, it is also not entirely true.

Hong Kong has its own strengths and these are not easily replicated by its closest competitors. We may include its free port status, simple customs clearance system and a well-defined legal system, among others. There must be some reason why cargo still goes through Hong Kong. However, it has become necessary for Hong Kong to narrow the differences in costs with the PRD and to further enhance productivity if it is to sustain growth. For example, shippers have to pay about US$160 more to carry a container from Dongguan to Hong Kong, than to the Shenzhen port of Yantian. The cost difference has been narrowing, however, by about 10 percent, with relaxation in the cross boundary trucking regulations known as the "4up, 4-down" and the agreement by the mainland government to allow spare drivers. The cost gap could only be eliminated if the existing boundary trucks could perform more than one round trip a day (Table 17.5).

Table 17.5. Relative costs of transport from Dongguan to the US West Coast via Hong Kong and Yantian (US$).

Route	Via Hong Kong (by truck)		Via Yantian (by truck)	
	TEU	FEU	TEU	FEU
Haulage	320	335	160	170
Documentation fee	14	14	—	—
Terminal handling charge	274	366	141	269
Ocean freight arbitrary	—	—	50	50
Ocean freight	1,300	1,800	1,300	1,800
Total	1,908	2,515	1,651	2,289
(Savings)	—	—	258	226

Compiled by the Hong Kong Shippers' Council.

Dongguan, the main production area in the PRD, is almost equidistant from Yantian and Hong Kong. The loss of sea cargo to Yantian in recent years is mainly due to the difference in trucking costs and the terminal handling charges (THC) of the shipping lines.

There are a number of limitations at present preventing the trucks from achieving this objective, the objective of more than one trip a day. The first obstacle stems from the fact that most of the manufacturers in PRD are small- to medium-sized enterprises (SME) and are scattered all over the PRD. The main investor groups in PRD are Hong Kong and Taiwan investors who engage in traditional consumer goods manufacturing. The small sizes of their manufacturing facilities mean that there are not enough haulage orders from most of them to allow trucking operators to make multiple trips a day. The second obstacle is that time required to clear customs fluctuates widely which makes job planning difficult.

The final obstacle is that most shipping lines have different offices looking after their Hong Kong operations and PRD operations. They maintain different pools of empty containers for Hong Kong and the PRD. Henceforth, even if a truck secured a second order, it is required to go back to Hong Kong to pick up empty containers for the second job. This requirement not only substantially inflates costs but it also makes scheduling difficult because a lot more uncertainties are involved. Consequently, we have seen only marginal reductions in the costs of boundary crossing trucking.

Hong Kong needs a "PRD Haulage Order Booking Platform." If there were sufficient numbers of importers and exporters using this platform, then trucking companies could choose orders from the same or nearby locations, so that each truck could handle more than one round trip a day. Trucking costs would come down with improved asset utilization and enhanced productivity. The way to build up the critical mass of users would be the greatest challenge for this project to succeed.

The industry has repeatedly called for cancellation or reduction of the business license fee for the boundary crossing trucks. The mainland authority should not set limits on the number of licenses and should not charge high fees for them. In addition, the Hong Kong and the PRD governments should work together to find out solutions for eliminating the double requirements of annual vehicle inspections, double insurance, and so forth.

There is also the idea of "freight villages + green lanes" which if successfully implemented, would substantially lower carriage costs to Hong Kong. The concept is that shippers could make use of PRD domestic trucks to deliver export full-container-load (FCL) cargo or less-than-container-load (LCL) cargo to these freight villages. LCL cargo could be consolidated there. Then the cargoes, both FCL and LCL, would be carried to Hong Kong container terminals or air cargo terminals by boundary crossing trucks. The concept is indeed quite simple. However, it will have to utilize technologies like Global Positioning Systems (GPS), Electronic Seal and Radio-Frequency Identification (RFID) to monitor cargoes while en route from local customs stations to freight villages, freight villages to the border, and from the border to the Hong Kong terminals. It requires the governments and the industry to agree on the procedures, the technology used, the operators and contractors, and the establishment of a proper legal framework. Cross boundary trucks could provide 24-hour shuttle services in the green lanes. Because assets would be used to the full, operators could quote much lower rates. Moreover, the further away from the factories from Hong Kong, the greater the savings would be. With the trend of factories moving further out in the PRD, freight villages and green lanes would be needed. However, we must emphasis that there should be several freight villages and green lanes to ensure sufficient competition among them.

Indeed it is worthwhile to look into total deregulation of the cross boundary operations. Mainland trucks should be allowed to carry containers between the mainland and Hong Kong. This is just like the present trucking operations between Eastern Europe and the EU. Fully opening up the boundary crossing trucking business would bring boundary crossing trucking rate to the mainland domestic level. There are bound to be objections from the labor side. However, one has to consider that if cargoes are not coming to Hong Kong, boundary trucking will not be coming either.

The second most important factor affecting Hong Kong port's competitiveness is the high THC levied by shipping lines. Hong Kong shippers are paying the world's highest THC. Hong Kong container terminal operators have in the past few years repeatedly stated that they have reduced their charges by as much as 30 percent. However, shipping lines have refused to adjust the THC levels, even though shipping lines still claim that THC is merely a "cost recovery" exercise. Shipping lines are profiting hugely from THC, the high level of which is eroding Hong Kong port's competitiveness.

On the air cargo front, the biggest challenge is also high operating costs. A study made by the Airport Authority in Hong Kong in 2003 indicates that the total cost of shipping via Hong Kong is lower than via other airports in the PRD. This is because of the tremendous volume of cargo through Hong Kong, so freight forwarders are able to carry out successful co-loading and consolidation of cargo. As we all know, actual freight rates depend on whether there is an optimal mix of weight and volume cargo, so that the aircrafts' space and weight capacities can be used to their full. This requires substantial cargo throughput, a large cluster of freight forwarders and operators, a flexible regulatory regime, and efficient and flexible operations. These are exactly the strengths of Hong Kong and they also explain why Hong Kong freight forwarders are able to offer very competitive freight rates. On many occasions, freight forwarders are quoting rates to their clients even lower that the nominal rates they obtain from the airlines. However, the report also clearly points out the threat of high operating costs. At present, the PRC customs regulations require shippers to hire exclusive trucks to carry goods to Hong Kong. In the case of small volume shipments, unit costs will be very high. This is why the industry has repeatedly asked for relaxation of the regulations, to allow consolidation of trucking services. Shippers need to work together with the industry and with support from the Hong Kong Special Autonomous Region government to request the mainland authority to change its regulatory regime to allow consolidation of trucking services from major towns and cities in the PRD and further out.

In addition, facilities that suit the needs of the air freight industry are also far from adequate in Hong Kong. A very large portion of air cargo is handled at the Asia Terminal Ltd (ATL) and Hong Kong Distribution Centre (HIDC). Rental is exceedingly high in these two purpose built cargo facilities. This causes the freight forwarders and their contractors, the CFS operators, to levy a large number of unjustifiable charges that may include handling fees, gate charges, registration fees, documentation fees, etc. The long list of charges and surcharges will certainly work against the sustainability of growth of the Hong Kong air cargo hub.

I support the proposal for building a logistics park near the Hong Kong CLK Airport. However, the government must treat it as an infrastructure project. If the logistics park operator is required to undertake all costs including road links, bridge links, land reclamation, and other development costs, the project is not going to work. While Hong Kong is holding onto its status as the world's busiest airport for international air cargo, action must be taken now to tackle the issue of high operating cost before it is too late.

In addition to actions that aim to reduce operating costs, we must also add value to the industry. Hong Kong has no chance to compete with the mainland merely on cost. I would like to stress two points here: (a) introduction of high value-added services and (b) modernization of the current operations.

In relation to value-added services, Hong Kong is really the center of Asia, linking North, East, and South Asia, and the whole of China. We have the best sea and air connectivity, the simplest customs system, and the most efficient operators in the region. We should target those industries in which time is critical and which require demand efficient and flexible operations, such as pharmaceuticals, electronic instruments, cut flowers, and seafood, to provide tailor-made facilities for them. The government should provide assistance to these industries, even down to the company level, given that the presence of these businesses would be beneficial to the whole of Hong Kong.

In modernizing operations, I would especially like to highlight the Digital Trade and Transport Network (DTTN) project, which is currently being undertaken in Hong Kong. When the US Government introduced the 24-Hour Rule in 2004, the backwardness of the Hong Kong logistics industry in handling data was fully exposed. Far larger than the direct costs such as advance manifest fees and data amendment fees, Hong Kong exporters were losing virtually two whole days of productive time at tremendous expense through data handling. Following the 24-Hour Rule, there were other security initiatives such as the Air Cargo Manifest Rule, E-Manifest (E-Man), Advance Cargo Information (ACI), among others. Every one of these initiatives put more pressure on the industry. Fortunately, these new requirements awakened the government and the industry to the fact that immediate action was needed. Consultants were employed to look into the modernization of data and document flows for the whole industry, and this led to the creation of the DTTN. This will provide the industry-wide IT infrastructure to allow all parties in the supply chain to transmit their data and documents to other parties with minimum or no changes in their current IT systems. We look forward to the success of the DTTN and the enhancement of productivity that it is supposed to bring about.

The Hong Kong port will be facing multiple challenges in the future. However, the port has advantages that competitors will not be able to replicate easily. Taking the proper action today will help sustain Hong Kong port's leading global position tomorrow.

CHAPTER 18

IMPACT OF PORT SECURITY ON LIQUEFIED
NATURAL GAS AND CONTAINER CARGO
MOVEMENTS

Paul T.-W. Lee and Young-Tae Chang

Introduction

After the 9/11 terrorist attacks on the United States on September 11, 2001, it was widely recognized that a container carrying a "dirty bomb," an explosive device carrying highly dispersible radioactive material, could be exploded at a major marine terminal and that potential targets, such as liquefied natural gas (LNG) facilities or bridges are vulnerable and open to threat from terrorist attacks. Supply chain security is therefore not only a complex challenge involving energy and container cargo movements but is also critical to global economies.

This chapter aims to answer the following question: what is the impact of port security on LNG and container cargo movements? The reason why energy and container cargoes are considered in this chapter is that, first of all, oil and LNG are not only reliable and affordable sources of energy for national economies, but allow both countries and their militaries to move.[1]

---

[1] Then US President George Bush admitted during his 2006 State of the Union speech that: "Keeping America competitive requires affordable energy. And here we have a serious problem: America is addicted to oil, which is often imported from unstable parts of the world. The best way to break this addiction is through technology." In addition, Secretary of Energy Spencer Abraham addressed the importance of energy on March 20, 2003: "Failure to meet increasing energy demand with increased energy supplies, and vulnerability to disruptions from natural or malevolent causes, could threaten our nation's economic prosperity, alter the way we live our lives, and threaten our national security."

Second, container cargoes which enter US seaports from all over the world are now scanned for radiation under the Security and Accountability for Every (SAFE) Port Act, also known as the Port Security Bill, signed by former President George W. Bush on October 13, 2006.[2] In searching for answers to the question above, this chapter is concerned with the implications of new US security initiatives on container cargoes and the challenges these initiatives present, particularly in terms of port selection, competition, performance, and charges.

Energy and National Economic Security in Asia

Energy issues are not only critical to the United States but also to Japan, Korea, and Taiwan, countries which are largely dependent upon imported energy. Such dependence means that a nation's economy is highly vulnerable to wild swings in the price, transportation, and supply chain management of imported energy. To make matters worse, since the September 11 terrorist attacks, conflicts in the Middle East and political instability in East Asia have been threatening energy security for these countries. Therefore, they regard the supply of energy as a national security issue. Major oil importing countries in Asia from the Middle East are China, Japan, Korea, and Taiwan. A striking point to note is that China's oil import-dependence grows most rapidly from — 16 percent in 1990 to 46 percent in 2004 (IEA, 2006).

LNG is a steadily increasing energy source in Asian economies. It is rapidly becoming the fuel of choice for regional markets as the need for ever-longer pipelines improves the comparative advantages of LNG over gas transported by pipeline. Korea, China, Japan, and Taiwan have increased imports of LNG from various sources to meet current energy requirements and maintain stable economic growth. Since 2002, China's imports of LNG have also been higher than those of other countries above in Asia.

Following the trends in LNG and oil imports, the dependence of East Asia on energy imports is rapidly increasing. This, together with the increase in international container transport, means that maritime traffic in the Malacca and Singapore Straits has been expanding. Ship movements in excess of 70,000 vessels per annum are now expected. As the Straits offer

---

[2]The SAFE Port Act will be further discussed in a later section.

the best option for ships plying between the Indian Ocean and the Pacific Ocean, these vessels carry one-third of global trade and four-fifths of East Asia's imports of crude oil. The key user states of Japan, Korea, and more recently China, are concerned about keeping this vital artery open as it is not only the shortest route but also the most secure in terms of navigational aids. However, the strategic and economic importance of the Straits of Malacca also makes it one of the world's major sea routes most vulnerable to a terrorist attack.

The prospect of maritime terrorism in the Malacca Straits has resulted in strategic and defence analysts considering a range of possible scenarios as to how this could come about (Akimoto, 2001a, 2001b, 2002; Coulter, 2002; Bergin and Bateman, 2005). A recent study by Teo (2007) looks at how the three states located on the Straits — Singapore, Malaysia, and Indonesia — have developed effective but divergent policies on combating maritime terrorism. Given the heightened post-September 11 security concerns, maritime terrorism and piracy problems have alarmed the waterway's major users. In particular, the sheer number of possibilities has prompted Raymond (2006) to sift through the various scenarios (see Table 18.3) and declare most to be extremely unlikely and impractical. Rimmer and Lee (2006) raise two critical issues about the Straits of Malacca and Singapore: (a) how would bulk shipping react to any impedance to vessel movements and (b) would container shipping react any differently? They examine the distances, time, and costs involved for tanker shipping in the event of any diversion from the Straits of Malacca and Singapore. A similar analysis has been conducted for container shipping, but there is a major difference because, unlike bulk shipping, the ship itself is the major unit of analysis. Consequently, Rimmer and Lee's 2006 study has been augmented by information drawn from a series of case studies of shipping companies operating tankers and container ships, either singly or in tandem.

Why does the US Government Regard Sea-Going Container Cargoes as Risky?

Table 18.1 indicates estimated container cargoes bound for the United States. The sum of Asian plus European container cargoes bound for the United States was estimated at 17.2 million TEU in 2005.

Table 18.1. Estimated container cargoes bound for United States.

Year	Trans-Pacific route		Trans-Atlantic route		Total bound for USA
	Asia → USA	USA → Asia	Europe → USA	USA → Europe	(Asia + Europe) → USA
2004	12.4	4.2	3.2	1.7	15.6
2005	13.9	4.3	3.3	1.8	17.2
% change	12.1	2.4	3.1	5.9	10.3

Source: UNCTAD (2006).

Table 18.2. Major Asian container ports exporting to the United States, March 2003.

World rank	Port	% of US container imports
1	Hong Kong	9.8
2	Shanghai	5.8
3	Singapore	5.8
4	Kaohsiung	5.6
6	Busan	5.0
7	Tokyo	2.8
10	Yantian	2.0
12	Nagoya	1.9
13	Kobe	1.6
19	Yokohama	1.5
20	Laem Chabang	1.4
	Total	43.2

Source: OECD Maritime Transport Committee (2003).

Table 18.2 shows the major Asian container ports which exported container cargoes to the United States as of March 2003. Among the top 20 container ports exporting to the United States, 11 ports are located in Asia, accounting for 43.2 percent of total US container imports. The top five US containerized cargo trading partners overall in 2005 were all Asian countries: China, Japan, Hong Kong, Taiwan, and Korea (US Department of Transportation, 2007).

Many experts on terrorism, including those at the Federal Bureau of Investigation and in academic think tanks and business organizations, have concluded that oceangoing cargo containers are vulnerable to some form of terrorist action. Their conclusions can be summarized as follows:

- Approximately 90 percent of the world's cargo moves by container and the global economy depends upon it.
- Each year, 108 million cargo containers move between major seaports in the world. In 2004, more than 9.6 million maritime containers arrived at US seaports, an average of 26,000 a day (US Customs and Board Protection, 2006).
- In 2005, 7,500 ships under foreign flags made 51,000 calls in US ports (Chaffee, 2006).
- In many nations, such as the United Kingdom, Korea, and Japan, over 90 percent of trade volume arrives or leaves by ship.
- Since the terrorist attacks of September 11, 361 seaports in the United States have been increasingly viewed as potential targets for future terrorist attacks.
- Ports are vulnerable because they are sprawling, interwoven with complex transportation networks, close to crowded metropolitan areas, and easily accessible.

Major research institutes and government agencies in the United States suggest a range of scenarios that demonstrate the diversity of threats, vulnerabilities, and potential consequences of terrorist attacks on container shipping: sinking ships in port channels, hijacking ships, and detonating a nuclear, dirty or conventional bomb. Potential scenarios for piracy and terrorism in the Malacca and Singapore Straits are illustrated in Table 18.3.

Table 18.3. Maritime terrorism in the straits of Malacca and Singapore: Potential scenarios.

Action	Impact	Comment
Straits of Malacca blocked by mines	Straits blocked to traffic due to actual mining or threat to mine seaways.	Vessels, especially those on international voyages, would be rerouted via Sunda Strait and Lombok Strait.

(Continued)

Table 18.3. (*Continued*)

Action	Impact	Comment
Tanker as floating bomb to strike ports	The hijacking of a LNG tanker and blowing it up in Singapore harbor would devastate Singapore; the Singapore Government considers the impact on global trade would be severe and incalculable. Potential threat from ships carrying high-risk cargoes intensified by the high number of pirate attacks.	The potential to cause damage will vary with the differing capacity of each vessel and its cargo, the means of triggering the explosion, and the actual impact on the port facility. Effects of an LNG tanker explosion would be limited by its location; an oil tanker would cause a localized fire; and a chemical tanker would have a toxicity risk.
Surface-to-air (SAM) missile launched at aircraft from vessel	Impact on Singapore would be massive, not only due to loss of life, closure of the airport and immediate effect on the Singaporean economy but because there is no guarantee that a similar attack would not be carried out in future.	Short of inspecting every ship, there is little law enforcement agencies could do to mitigate the effects.
Sinking vessels to disrupt shipping routes	Impact on global trade and Europe and Asia would be tremendous, due to disruption of sea transportation. Sinking a large commercial cargo ship in a major shipping channel could thereby block all traffic to and from the port.	Reroutes via Sunda Strait and Lombok Strait would be considered for ships carrying seaborne trade cargoes. The long time disruption would threaten major Asian economies such as Korea, Japan, Taiwan, and Japan heavily dependent on imported energy; and it would disrupt the world oil trade and cause large-scale environmental damage.

Source: Frittelli (2005), Raymond (2006), Rimmer and Lee (2006), and Lee and Chang (2007).

The possibilities listed here range from traffic being blocked by mines to the sinking of vessels, but in all cases, the impacts on the global economy would be quite significant. Any forms of disruption in the shipping routes, such as mines or sunken vessels, may lead to rerouting of cargoes, increasing both logistics costs and the time consumed, with a severe impact on global trade. There is also the potential for LNG and crude oil tankers being hijacked or bombed. The impact varies depending on the vessels themselves, their cargoes, and locations, but over and above the impact on global trade, there are possibilities of toxicity and other environmental risks from chemical and crude oil tankers. The use of surface-to-air missiles is another tactic which could potentially be used by terrorists, disrupting Asian and European economies in addition to possibly severe loss of life.

Ports play an important role in international trade, in particular in the United States. Ports are used to import and export cargoes worth hundreds of billions of dollars, and to generate jobs, both directly and indirectly, for countries and their trading partners. In the United States, ports are also seen as important to national security by hosting naval bases and vessels and facilitating the movement of military equipment and supplying troops deployed overseas, particularly after the attacks of 9/11.

Literature Survey

This section reviews the literature on the impact of security on maritime transport and supply chains.[3] Since the 9/11 terrorist attacks in the United States, there have been various studies conducted on the economic impact of increased security. As Table 18.4 shows, the estimated costs differ between researchers due to their different methodologies, but estimated costs range from US$47 billion to US$168.8 billion. Leaving aside arguments about the methodology of such calculations, it is evident that the economic impact of 9/11 has been huge.

The United States Congressional Budget Office (CBO) published a report on the estimated economic costs in the case of disruptions in container shipments at the ports of Los Angeles and Long Beach due to both

---

[3]On the impact of 9/11 on risk and returns of marine firms, see Homan (2006).

Table 18.4.   The economic impact of security.

Source	Estimated cost	Remark
Navarro and Spencer (2001)	$47 billion	In the immediate aftermath of 9/11, economic output loss in the United States
Walkenhorst and Dihel (2002)	$75 billion	Global welfare losses caused by terrorist attacks
OECD (2003)	$58 billion	For USA alone, direct and indirect costs caused by terrorist attack at maritime transport
Ward (2004)	$146.8–168.8 billion	Overall estimated costs borne by, among others, individuals and families, wage losses in NY, insurance costs, increased security costs, infrastructure costs, losses tax revenues and tourism, government bailout spending on airlines

Source: WTO (2006).

an unexpected one-week halt triggering a one-month backlog, and an unexpected three-year halt with precautionary one-week stoppages in all other US ports (CBO, 2006). More briefly, the report also considered the possibility of an unexpected forced shutdown of Hong Kong, the largest single source of container shipments to the United States worth over US$43 billion in 2004 (CBO, 2006).[4]

Contrary to the above studies, the 2006 WTO Trade Report argues that the impact of natural disasters and terrorists on international trade flows and growth is short-term and generally minimal. The impact of disasters on international trade also tends to be localized. If terrorist risks persist, however, transaction costs of international trade will increase, mainly via higher insurance premiums, tightened security measures at borders, ports and airports, longer delivery times for container cargoes, and additional

---

[4]A brief summary of the report is contained in Rimmer and Lee (2006).

costs caused by specific security measures in the airline industry and in maritime transport. Clark *et al.* (2004) also argue that port efficiency, affected by increased security measures, has an important impact on maritime transport costs, while Crist (2003) highlights the fact that that most of these additional security costs are charged to shipping companies.

Lewis *et al.* (2003, 2004) also focused on different aspects of port security in terms of supply chain productivity. They addressed the issue of the quantitative impact on productivity of new security measures, such as the Container Security Initiative (CSI), the Customs Trade Partnership Against Terrorism (C-TPAT), and the US Customs 24-hour advanced manifest reporting rule on megaports such as Singapore and Shanghai; and on supply chains from the perspectives of users, providers, and regulators, and at the levels of operations and policy. They employed optimization approaches to identify efficient container security operations at transshipment seaports. Erera *et al.* (2003) have estimated the cost of security for sea cargo transport and discussed challenges in supply chain management and design from the viewpoint of maritime transport. Barnes and Oloruntoba (2005) have explored the issue of how to assure security in maritime supply chains. Crist (2003) has discussed risk factors and economic impacts related to maritime transport, while Palac-McMicken (2005) has carried out cost and benefit analysis in the transport sector with regard to combating terrorism. As briefly discussed above, Rimmer and Lee (2006) sought to identify the costs if tankers or container ships were denied access to the Malacca and Singapore Straits.

Having reviewed the above literature, it can be seen that no studies of the impact of the SAFE Port Act on stakeholders in port and shipping fields are available. The next section is a brief overview of a series of security measures launched by the United States followed by a discussion of their impact and implications.

Chronological Review of US Security Measures for Container Cargoes

Since September 11, 2001, the United States has introduced a series of measures in the fields of aviation and port security. This section will focus on the measures for container cargoes and port security.

C-TPAT: Customs-Trade Partnership Against Terrorism (November 2001)

Since 9/11, container cargo and security are inseparable issues which must be tackled together by port authorities. As an immediate consequence of 9/11, the US government introduced the Customs-Trade Partnership against terrorism in November 2001. It is an innovative, voluntary government/private sector partnership program to strengthen supply chain security. But in order to obtain certification as a secure container cargo from US Customs, it is necessary to submit cargo information to the Customs Office 24 hours before the cargo is loaded on a vessel at a foreign seaport (the 24-Hour Rule).

Container Security Initiative (CSI) (January 17, 2002)

In January 2002, the United States launched the CSI which consists of four core elements: (1) using intelligence and automated information to identify and target high-risk containers; (2) pre-screening those containers identified as high-risk at the port of departure, before they arrive at US ports; (3) using detection technology to quickly pre-screen high-risk containers and (4) using smarter containers where any tampering becomes evident. The host country determines who pays the direct costs of screening and unloading containers. However, the importers in the United States pay the costs associated with moving, inspecting, and unloading containers.[5] Allen (2006) argues that there are benefits to be gained from joining, especially for developing countries; this is because, apart from leading to more secure ports, the spill-over effects of this initiative would most likely lead to improved security for all ships and carriers, regardless of their routes, due to system improvements at major international ports. In addition, ports that do not have certain measures in place may be unable to export goods to the United States.

There were 50 CSI ports operating in the world as of September 30, 2006. Those operating in Asia include Busan in Korea; Tokyo, Kobe, Yokohama, and Nagoya in Japan; Shanghai, Shenzen, and Yantian in China; Port Kelang

---

[5]The issue of who will pay for security costs will be later discussed in this chapter.

and Tanjung Pelepas in Malaysia; Hong Kong; Singapore and Kaohsiung and Chi-Lung in Taiwan.

Establishment of administrative organization

As a legal body, the US Customs Services became the US Customs and Border Protection (CBP) under the new Department of Homeland Security on March 1, 2003. The CSI framework continues to secure the safety of container cargoes bound for the United States.

Coast Guard regulations for ships and facilities

In addition to the above, the US Coast Guards adopted the following international measures:

- The Maritime Security Act, which requires compliance with International Maritime Organization (IMO) rules;
- The International Ship and Port Facility Security Code (ISPS), introduced by the International Maritime Organization;
- Ship and Facility Security Plans to be approved by port, state and
- Non-compliant vessels or vessels calling at non-compliant facilities may be denied entry into the United States.

Although the United States had introduced several security measures by 2005, many US congressmen together with the Bush government, felt such measures were not enough to protect their homeland against possible terrorist attacks by way of maritime container cargoes.

SAFE Port Act (October 2006)

After many arguments among the American politicians, at last on Friday 13 October, 2006, the "Security and Accountability for Every Port" Act (also known as the SAFE Port Act or Port Security Bill) was signed by President George W. Bush. Its major contents are as follows:

- It is a bipartisan bill to overhaul maritime security and strengthen cargo inspections at foreign and US Ports.

- Installation of radiation detectors were required by the end of 2007 in 22 of the largest ports in the United States, which handle 98 percent of all cargo entering the country.
- The Department of Homeland Security (DHS) aimed to increase the number of container cargoes scanned to 80 percent by the end of 2006 and to almost 100 percent by the end of 2007.
- The Act envisaged selecting three foreign ports as pilot programs in order to test the technology for non-intrusive cargo inspections.
- About US$800 million was to be set aside annually for setting new requirements that the DHS had to meet in order to strengthen maritime and cargo security.

The Act aimed to prevent terrorists from sneaking a nuclear, chemical or biological weapon into the United States inside 1 of the 11 million shipping containers that enter the nation each year — many without inspection. The Act authorized the development of high-tech inspection equipment so that customs agents can check cargo containers for dangerous materials without having to open them. It required radiation-detection technology to be installed in 22 of the nation's busiest ports by the end of 2007.

Impact and Implications of the SAFE Port Act for Discussion and Further Research

The SAFE Port Act has influenced many areas of trade, including maritime transportation and supply chain management. In this section, the following questions are discussed.

- Who will pay for the security costs resulting from the Act?
- What is the impact of the SAFE Port Act on the productivity and competitiveness of the users and providers of the global supply chain?
- Assuming that a container port has not been designated by the US authorities, what will happen to that port?
- How will the Act influence the distribution of transshipment container cargoes between designated and undesignated ports?

Before reviewing the costs associated with the SAFE Port Act, it is necessary to identify the various stakeholders affected. This Act will arguably result in increased costs to everyone involved in international trade: exporters, port authorities, carriers, US manufacturers who rely on foreign imports, retailers who sell goods with imported components, and finally US consumers.[6] The initial costs will fall on port authorities because of the capital investments required and the deterioration in port performance caused by security procedures. They will most likely pass these costs onto carriers, who in turn will recover them by increasing charges for exporters. Most stakeholders concerned with security agreed about the necessity of the Act to improve port security. However, they disagree on the issue of who should pay the costs incurred by the Act. In the United States, there has been a debate over whether port security should be paid for with federal revenues, by state and local governments, by the maritime industry, or by a cost-sharing arrangement between all of the stakeholders.[7]

On one hand, some argue for more federal funding on the grounds that port security is a national concern and therefore the federal government should finance it through general revenues. On the other hand, skeptics of additional spending maintain the "user-pays principle,"[8] pointing out taxpayers' resistance to providing funds to large and profitable corporations to secure infrastructure that is in their own financial interests. In other words, it is logical that the maritime industry should finance port security through fees to the users of the services because improved security is a direct benefit to them as it reduces cargo theft and other economic damages.

A system of user charges on container cargoes can be designed to create a means of generating funds for improving port security as required in the series of security legislation. Advocates of user surcharges maintain that they are an effective means of ensuring improved security because they

---

[6]Allen (2006) focuses on three stakeholders that will experience the most observable CSI-related cost increases: port authorities, carriers, and exporters.

[7]The Coast Guard roughly estimated the cost of implementing the new IMO security code and the security provisions in MTSA to be approximately $1.5 billion for the first year and $7.3 billion over the succeeding decade. Congress has provided over $650 million through FY2005 in direct federal grants to ports to improve their physical and operational security. This is in addition to the budgets of the Coast Guard, Bureau of Customs and Border Protection, TSA, and other federal agencies involved in port security.

[8]Some economists argue that a user fee system is also more efficient than direct subsidies because the users of the port service being provided (in this case port security) are likely to demand that policymakers spend the funds in the most productive manner.

would provide a more secure and predictable source of funding than annual appropriations.[9] But they could be criticized on the grounds that the user fees are a tax. The way of funding or charging for port security may influence the evaluation of ports, and is consequently closely interrelated with port competitiveness. This is a major concern of port authorities about the impact of the SAFE Port Act on port performance and efficiency. Future research is required to take into account the methods of funding and charging for security, and in measuring the performance in terms of both productivity and efficiency.

Both "just-in-time" deliveries of goods and the expeditious flow of commerce through ports are essential elements in supply chain management in maritime transportation. According to the series of security measures reviewed previously, containers bound for the United States should be scanned. Assuming that a port has not installed the radiation detectors required by the Act, it is doubtful whether it can attract transshipment container cargoes. This is related to port selection and competition issues caused by the Act. Previous studies of port choice models based on differences in time, trade routes, cargo, methodologies, sampled data and subjects surveyed do not reflect these security issues. In other words, the majority of the studies that have focused on port choice models involving decisions by shippers rather than by other stakeholders have not considered new variables in relation to port security like the SAFE Act. The following question may therefore warrant further investigation: how will the issue of port security influence port efficiency and competitiveness?

Concluding Remarks

The goals of global cargo movements from the point of view of users and providers of international supply chains are the efficiency and productivity of these supply chains, "just-in-time" deliveries, competitive transaction, and logistics costs, safety, and welfare. After the 9/11 terrorist attacks in 2001, the United States introduced a series of security measures for airports and seaports. The SAFE Port Act has influenced port and container cargo

---

[9]Advocates of user surcharges also propose that a port security trust fund be created in a manner that prevents the user fees from being spent on anything other than port security. If such a port security trust fund were created, they argue, port security would not have to compete with other funding priorities in the annual appropriations process.

movements in many ways. Users and providers of maritime transportation must tackle new issues, including minimizing the negative impact of the security measures initiated by the United States in relation to international supply chains.

This chapter has discussed the issues of who will pay the security costs caused by the Act, how to interpret the implications of the Act in relation to port selection by shippers and shipowners, and the distribution of trans-shipment container cargoes between the ports. Empirical studies of these issues are required to identify the concrete impact of the Act.

In conclusion, the SAFE Port Act should reflect the following elements suggested by its name, to promote global cargo movements and efficient and effective international supply chains: safety, advantage, fast service, and efficiency (i.e. "SAFE"); prosperity, opportunity, reward and trust (i.e. "Port"), and "act now" (i.e. "Act").

This work was supported by Jungseok Research Institute of International Logistics and Trade, INHA University Research Grant (INHA-JRI-2009).

References

Akimoto, Kazumine (2001a). "Re-routing Options and Consequences." Paper presented at the 13th international conference on Sea Lines of Communication, "The Strategic Importance of Seaborne Trade and Shipping: A Common Interest of Asia Pacific," The Chifley Hotel, 3–4 April 2001, Canberra.

Akimoto, Kazumine (2001b). "The Current State of Maritime Security: Structural Weaknesses and Threats in the Sea Lanes." Unpublished paper, conference on Maritime Security in Southeast Asia and Southwest Asia, Institute for Policy Studies, 3 December, Tokyo.

Allen, Nicholas Hughes (2006). "The Container Security Initiative Costs, Implications and Relevance to Developing Countries." *Public Administration and Development* 26: 439–447.

Barnes, Paul H. and Richard Oloruntoba (2005). "Assurance of Security in Maritime Supply Chains: Conceptual Issues of vulnerability and Crisis Management." *Journal of International Management* 11(4): 519–540.

Bergin, Anthony and Sam Bateman (2005). "*Future Unknown: The Terrorist Threat to Australian Maritime Security.*" Canberra: The Australian Strategic Policy Institute.

Chafee, Senator Lincoln (2006). "Home Security and Transportation." International Conference on National Security, Natural Disasters, Logistics & Transportation: Assessing the Risks & the Responses, University of Rhode Island, September 25–26, 2006.

Clark, X., D. Dollar and A. Micco (2004). *"Port Efficiency, Maritime Transport Costs and Bilateral Trade."* Working Papers 10353, Cambridge, MA: National Bureau of Economic Research.

Congressional Budget Office (2006). *"The Economic Costs of Disruptions in Container Shipments."* Washington, D.C.: Congressional Budget Office, US Congress.

Coulter, Daniel Y. (2002). "Globalization of Maritime Commerce: The Rise of Hub Ports." In *Globalization and Maritime Power*, edited by Sam J. Tangredi, 133–142. Washington, D.C.: Institute for National Strategic Studies, National Defense University.

Crist, Philippe (2003). *"Security in Maritime Transport: Risk Factors and Economic Impact."* Paris: OECD.

Erera, Alan *et al.* (2003). "Cost of Security for Sea Cargo Transport." Singapore: The Logistics Institute — Asia Pacific.

Firttelli, John F. (2005). "Port and Maritime Security: Background and Issues for Congress." CRS Report for Congress, USA. http://www.fas.org/sgp/crs/homesec/RL31733.pdf.

Homan, Anthony C. (2006). "The Impact of 9/11 on Financial Risk, Volatility and Returns of Marine Firms." *Maritime Economics and Logistics* 8: 387–401.

IEA (International Energy Agency) (2006). *World Energy Outlook 2006.* Paris: OECD/IEA.

Lee, P.T.-W. and Y.T. Chang (2007). "Impact of Port Security on LNG and Container Cargo Movements." Paper presented at the 2008 International Association of Maritime Economists Conference, Athens, Greece, July 4–6, 2007.

Lewis, B. *et al.* (2003). "Optimization Approaches for Efficient Container Security Operations at Transshipment Seaports." *Transportation Research Record* 1822: 1–8.

Lewis, B. *et al.* (2004). "Supply Chain Inventory Impacts of Transportation Security Measures and Disruptions." Working Paper, The Logistics Institute, Georgia Institute of Technology.

Navarro, Peter and Aron Spencer (2001). "September 11, 2001: Assessing the Costs of Terrorism." *The Milken Institute Review* 4: 17–31.

Palac-McMicken, Evanor (2005). "Economic Costs and Benefits of Combating Terrorism in the Transport Sector. " *Asian-Pacific Economic Literature* 19(1): 60–71.

Raymond, Catherine Zara (2006). "Maritime Terrorism in Southeast Asia: Potential Scenario." *Global Terrorism Analysis* (The Jamestown Foundation), 4(7), http://www.jamestown.org/single/?no_cache=1&tx_ttnews%5btt_news%5D=725.

Rimmer, Peter J. and Paul T.-W. Lee (2006). "Repercussions of Impeding Shipping in the Malacca and Singapore Straits." International Conference on National Security, Natural Disasters, Logistics & Transportation: Assessing the Risks & the Responses, University of Rhode Island, September 25–26, 2006.

Teo, Yun Yun (2007). "Target Malacca Straits: Maritime Terrorism in South East Asia." *Studies in Conflict & Terrorism* 30(6): 541–561.

UNCTAD (2006). *"Maritime Review of Transport."* Geneva: UNCTAD.

US Customs and Board Protection (2006). *"Fact Sheet."* www.cbp.gov.

US Department of Transportation (2007). *"America's Container Ports: Delivering the Goods."* Washington, D.C.: US Department of Transportation.

Walkenhorst, P. and N. Dihel (2002). "Trade Impacts of the Terrorist Attacks of 11 September 2001: A Quantitative Assessment." Paper presented to the Workshop on The Economic Consequences of Global Terrorism, Berlin, 14–15 June, 2002.

World Trade Organization (2006). *"World Trade Report 2006: Exploring the Links Between Subsidies, Trade and the WTO."* Geneva: World Trade Organization.

CHAPTER 19

TRANSNATIONAL ARCHITECTURAL PRODUCTION IN DOWNTOWN BEIJING

Xuefei Ren

Introduction

In June 2001, a large machinery factory located in the newly designated central business district (CBD) of Beijing was demolished. The land was leased to a private development company, SoHo China Inc., which announced that Jianwai SoHo, an urban megaproject with 18 high-rise apartment towers, two office skyscrapers, and 300 retail shops, would be built on this site within the next three years.[1] In terms of investment, Jianwai SoHo is not the largest project planned in the CBD. However, it has become the most publicized project in the local and national media because of its minimalist and futuristic architectural design. The property prices at Jianwai SoHo rocketed to the highest level in Beijing. All residential, office, and retail space was sold out before the project was completed. Following the success of Jianwai SoHo, SoHo China Inc. has gone on to use avant-garde design from international architects as a branding tool to market its projects. The development company has commissioned a dozen well-established architects from around the world to design them.

Local developers in Beijing are not alone in the growing trend to commission international "starchitects" for branding and marketing of their megaprojects. During the past decade, a small number of elite architectural design firms, mostly based in Europe and the United States, have delivered

---

[1] Jianwai is the district name where the project is located. SoHo refers to "Small Office, Home Office."

a large number of high-profile architectural projects in a variety of locations world-wide. These signature projects represent a fundamental change in the way that urban space is used today. In the age of globalization, urban space is produced more and more through transnational processes — through increasingly global flows of investment capital, design professionals, and images. The change has had significant consequences for the built environment, and presents new challenges for urban studies.

Previous studies have examined the role of urban megaprojects and trophy buildings in the process of inter-urban competition and place-marketing (Sudjic, 1992; Fainstein, 2001; Olds, 2001; King, 2002, 2004; Sklair, 2005, 2006; McNeill, 2005). However, compared to foreign direct investments, public-private partnerships and the economic impact of megaprojects, the role of transnational architectural production in megaproject developments has not been given sufficient attention. Building on previous research regarding urban megaprojects, this chapter examines the role of spatial articulation of urban design in megaproject developments in the new CBD in Beijing.

This chapter intends to address the following questions: Why do local developers in Beijing aspire to international architectural design in their megaproject developments? How are connections forged between local clients and elite international architects? How are the flows of architectural design deterritorialized from their original local and national settings and interpreted in the new urban environment in China? Based on ethnographic data, fieldwork interviews, and media reports, as well as statistics from both public and private sources, this study shows that the articulation of spatial design has become a major force of capital accumulation in megaproject developments. Transnational architectural production functions as symbolic capital — defined as capital that can be derived from signs and symbols. The symbolic capital of signature design is transformed into economic and cultural capital by various actors in the process of urban megaproject developments. Local political and economic elites in Beijing have used signature design from international architects as a branding tool to market their properties and to promote Beijing as a global city. By adopting a non-Chinese architectural language, local elites have created a transnational urban space that caters to the needs of new city users.

Global Economic Restructuring: Urban Entrepreneurialism and Megaprojects

This study is situated within the ongoing debate about globalization and the production of new urban spaces. In response to the global economic restructuring in the 1970s and 1980s, local entrepreneurial governments in the West have increasingly adopted growth-oriented economic development policies. Key components of such policies include the investment in and promotion of high-profile megaprojects. These projects include cultural and business districts, up-scale housing complexes, museums, convention centers and state-of-the-art transportation and telecommunication infrastructure. Local governments attempt to use megaprojects to create a new global image for urban regeneration, to re-brand and re-position their cities in the global economic competition.

Contemporary urban megaprojects are characterized by their diverse investment sources, internationalization strategies, and their goal of projecting a global city image. As megaprojects require huge capital investment, they are usually financed with diverse capital sources that might change over time (Olds, 2001). In order to attract investors, it is common for local governments to provide substantial tax cuts and promise large-scale infrastructure construction. Private-public partnerships can be found in most megaproject developments. In terms of strategy planning, megaprojects are developed with internationalization strategies in mind (Olds, 2001). They tend to target the transnational capitalist class with purchasing power (Sklair, 2001). Many projects include high-profile buildings which can symbolize a global image for their host cities. Projecting the image of being global is just as important as actually being global in the competitive global economy (Marshall, 2003: 4). By possessing these characteristics, megaprojects can provide a particular urban site with an environment where the work of globalization can be done.

Past research on urban megaprojects has been carried out around three major themes. First, there are studies focusing on broader structural forces that have given rise to megaproject developments. These forces include economic restructuring in both developed and developing countries, the emerging global financial system, the weakening of the nation state, and the rise of urban scale as a meaningful articulator, as well as intensifying inter-urban competitions (Douglass, 1998; Harvey, 1990; Jessop, 1998; Olds, 2001; Sassen, 2001; Marshall, 2003). In general, megaproject construction is seen as a developmental strategy adopted by local governments to cope with the challenges brought about by deindustrialization, to enhance local strength, and to better compete with other cities. The interaction and combination of these structural forces drive local growth coalitions to use flagship megaproject developments to enhance urban competitiveness.

Most studies originating from this structural political economy perspective have assumed an unproblematic relationship between broader socio-economic forces and spatial outcomes. However, there is no direct one-to-one relationship between general social forces and specific spatial outcomes (Knox, 1991; Hubbard, 1996; Beauregard and Haila, 1997). Old and new broader socio-economic forces are sifted through local particularities and have a differentiated impact on the built environment. To better understand the impact of global economic restructuring on urban built-up environments, we need to pay more attention to the role of the spatial articulation of urban design in the processes of place-making.

The second strand of studies, mainly among urban governance scholars, focuses on the role of entrepreneurial local governments in planning and developing megaprojects. This literature suggests that along with the shift to a post-industrial economy, the form of urban governance has also changed from managerialism to entrepreneurialism (Harvey, 1989). To attract mobile capital, local governments have increasingly adopted risk-taking entrepreneurial approaches such as tax abatements, subsidies, and megaproject construction to create an attractive business environment. Empirical case studies of urban entrepreneurialism and megaproject construction have been carried out concerning cities in the United Kingdom (Loftman and Nevin, 1996), Australia (McGuirk *et al.*, 1998), North America (Althubaity and Jonas, 1998), Germany (Herrschel, 1998; Lehrer, 2006), as well as in China (Cartier, 2002; Wu, 2000a, 2000b; Xu and Yeh, 2005). The research focus here is on the changing form of urban governance. Local entrepreneurial politicians, together with private business, are seen as the power brokers in making decisions on developing megaprojects. The role of architecture and urban design is seen at most as cosmetic.

Lastly, there are also studies that examine the socio-economic impact of megaproject developments. Most studies have shown that the economic impact of megaprojects is either uncertain or hard to evaluate (Altshuler and Luberoff, 2003; Flyvbjerg *et al.*, 2003). In many cases, the intended profit-making developments became loss-making projects. As the strategy of megaproject construction can be easily copied from city to city, it is unlikely that a locality can achieve a boost in overall structural competitiveness from such building efforts (Jessop, 1998). In terms of impact on political mobilization, past studies have found that the multiple meanings derived from megaprojects can be both legitimating tools for popular support (Hubbard, 1996), and potential sources for social conflict and protest (Frantz, 2005), depending on the specific local contexts of political culture. Culturally speaking, the cost of flagship developments is shown in terms of reduced cultural diversity, as increasingly similar-looking projects have been built in different urban contexts (Evans, 2003; Marshall, 2003). Overall, the exclusion of urban residents from the decision-making process is widely observed in megaproject developments.

In the literature above, the role of the spatial articulation of architecture and urban design in megaproject developments has not been given sufficient attention. This study explores the linkage between the spatial form of global cities and the underlying urban political economy by determining the extent to which the spatial articulation of architecture and urban design has played an independent role in capital accumulation processes in these urban megaproject developments. If urban space is a venue for the mobilization, extraction, and geographic concentration of surplus value in capitalist societies (Harvey, 1990; Lefebvre, 1991; Gottdiener, 1994), then in the process, spatial design has become a major productive force in differentiating, branding, and marketing urban spaces to attract investment and capture consumption dollars. Zukin (1982) calls the process the "artistic mode of production." This artistic mode of production is evident in the transitional economy in urban China as well. Using the development of the CBD in Beijing as a case study, we examine how the symbolic capital of architectural design is transformed into economic and cultural capital by local elites in the process of marketing their megaprojects and promoting Beijing as a new global city.

The Hybrid Chinese Urban Megaprojects

Unlike in the West, megaproject construction in China is not a response to the pressure of de-industrialization processes. Rather, it is China's extraordinary economic growth since the 1990s that has brought about the frenzied construction boom in the country. Chinese megaprojects are a hybrid product of local investment capital, strong government intervention, and international architectural design.

Compared to global cities in the West, the real estate market in major Chinese cities has not yet been penetrated by global investment capital, due to the country's relatively strict regulations regarding the entry of foreign investment firms in the sector of property development. Real estate development in China is still largely a local practice. Much of the real estate development in Chinese cities is financed by domestic investment capital, rather than foreign capital. Table 19.1 shows that in both Beijing and China as a whole, foreign investment only occupies a very small percentage of the total investment in the real estate sector (1.4 percent and 1.8 percent, respectively). Pre-sales and domestic bank loans constitute the majority of capital resources for real estate developments. After more than a decade of tremendous economic growth, a large amount of surplus capital has accumulated in the primary circuit of production, such as the mining, manufacturing and export sectors. Domestic banks are swollen with savings and desperate to find new investment opportunities. As land prices started soaring in the 1990s, real estate sectors became an ideal outlet in which to

Table 19.1.   Sources of real estate investment: Beijing and China in 2003.

	Beijing (in %)	China (in %)
Domestic loans	31.4	23.8
Foreign investment	1.8	1.4
Self-fundraising by developers	20.1	28.6
Pre-sales	46.8	46.1
Total (in billion RMB)	1,203	13,128

Note: US$1 dollar is roughly 8 RMB.
Source: *Beijing Real Estate Yearbook* (2004) and *China Real Estate Yearbook* (2004).

invest. The large surplus of domestic investment capital, facilitated by loose regulations of financial institutions, has been channeled from the primary circuit of production into the secondary circuit of production of built-up environments (Harvey, 1990).

Similar to those in other East Asian countries such as Singapore (Haila, 1999), urban megaproject developments in China are characterized by strong government intervention. The strong incentives for government intervention can be explained by two major factors: political career advancement of public officials by building "image projects," and revenue return by land leasing. Many key officials at municipal levels are directly appointed from central governments. They are rewarded for outstanding economic performance and physical achievement within their terms of office. They attach great importance to visual growth, both in economic and physical terms, to show their capabilities (Xu and Yeh, 2005). Building flagship megaprojects is seen as a direct way for political elites to advance their personal careers. Moreover, governments can also obtain revenue sources from leasing land to private developers for megaproject developments. The Chinese Constitution guarantees the right of the state to take away land from current land users in the name of the "public interest," which is similar to the power of "eminent domain" in the United States.[2] In the course of the 1990s, millions of urban homes in Beijing were confiscated by local governments, and the land was transferred later to private developers. The land leasing fee obtained in the process has become the major revenue for city and district governments.

Another feature characterizing Chinese urban megaprojects is the high degree of involvement of international architectural firms in the planning processes. Although the same group of international architectural firms such as Skidmore, Owings & Merrill (SOM), Kohn Pederson Fox Associates (KPF), and Foster & Partners, have delivered urban megaprojects in many world cities, their presence is especially visible in China. This is due to the strong political and financial support from local and central governments for the megaprojects for which international firms are commissioned, as well as to the lag in development of local indigenous Chinese architectural firms. In 1998, the central government commissioned the French architect

---

[2]Article 10 of Chapter 1 of the Constitution.

Paul Andreu to design the National Theatre. Located in Tiananmen Square in Beijing, the National Theater is the highest-profile state project ever commissioned from a non-Chinese architectural firm, and it generated heated debates among local architects and planners (Ren, 2006). In the following few years, two other major projects in Beijing, the National Stadium for the 2008 Olympics and the Chinese Central Television headquarters, were assigned to Herzog & de Meuron from Switzerland and Rem Koolhaas from Holland, respectively. These signature megaprojects require huge budgets, and would be difficult to actualize without strong political and financial support from local government.

The central government's move to use international architectural firms has been followed quickly by local governments and private developers. Local decision makers see a brand-name design by a well-known architect as an effective tool to promote their projects to a wider audience of international investors and tourists, and to reorient the image of Beijing from a dusty post-socialist city to an international metropolis with a vibrant architectural scene. Numerous international architectural design competitions are organized across the country, and visually bold design proposals from international architectural firms are frequently chosen by local clients. Since China joined the World Trade Organization in 2001, a large number of international architectural firms have flocked to China. These international built environment professionals were among the first to introduce globalization to the form of Chinese cities. Table 19.2 lists major urban megaprojects designed by international firms in Beijing. Most of them will be completed before the 2008 Beijing Olympics.

Case Studies

Based on case studies of two megaproject developments in downtown Beijing, the rest of this chapter examines empirically how local political and economic elites have employed international architectural firms as a marketing tool to brand their megaprojects and to promote Beijing as a new global city. The first case is the planning of Beijing's new CBD through international design competitions. From 2001 to 2003, Beijing's municipal and district governments organized two international design competitions for master plans for the new CBD. These competitions marked the first time

Table 19.2. Major megaprojects in Beijing designed by international architectural firms: 1998–2005.

	Megaprojects	Architectural firms	Nationality
Airports	Beijing Capital International Airport, Terminal 3	Foster & Partners	England
Masterplans	SoHo City Masterplan	Zaha Hadid with Patrik Schumacher	England
	CBD Masterplan	Johnson Fain & Partners	USA
	Masterplan for the Core Area of CBD	Pei Cobb Freed & Partners	USA
	Huamao Center Masterplan	Kohn Pederson Fox Associates	USA
	Central Axis Masterplan of Olympics	Albert Speer & Partners	Germany
Corporate/ Mixed developments	Jianwai SoHo	Riken Yamamoto & Fieldshop	Japan
	Shangdu SoHo	Peter Davidson	Australia
	Wealth Center	GMP	Germany
	Zhongguancun West, BSTP Lot 21	Kohn Pedersen Fox Associates	USA
State organizations	Chinese Central Television Headquarter	Office for Metropolitan Architecture	Holland
	Bank of China Head Office	Pei Partnership Architects	USA
	China Natural Offshore Oil Corporation Headquarters	Kohn Pederson Fox Associates	USA
	China Petro Headquarters	Henn Architekten	Germany
Exhibition centers	International Automotive Expo	Henn Architekten	Germany
	Beijing International Sports and Exhibition Center	RTKL	USA

(*Continued*)

Table 19.2. (*Continued*)

	Megaprojects	Architectural firms	Nationality
Cultural institutions	Chinese Museum of Film	RTKL	USA
	National Theatre	Paul Andreu	France
	National Museum	GMP	Germany
	National Library	Office for Metropolitan Architecture	Holland
	Beijing Book City	Office for Metropolitan Architecture	Holland
	National Art Museum of China	RTKL	USA
	Capital Museum	RTKL	USA
Sports Stadiums	Olympic Green	Sasaki Associates Inc.	USA
	2008 Olympics Wukesong Cultural and Sports Center	Burckhardt + Partners	Switzerland
	National Stadium	Herzog & de Meuron	Switzerland
	National Swimming Center	PTW and ARUP	Australia

the Beijing municipal government invited non-Chinese planning firms to participate in the redevelopment of the central city. In the design competitions, the top concern of city officials was to create a cityscape suitable for an emerging global city. Design proposals and documents published by the local governments are used in the analysis that follows.

The second case is the development of Jianwai SoHo, a large-scale mixed-use private development project in the center of the new CBD. Riken Yamamoto, a Japanese architect known for innovative housing design, was commissioned to design Jianwai SoHo. Its minimalist modern design is a successful advertising tool for the developers. The total sales reached US$1 billion by 2004. Since its completion, Jianwai SoHo has become a fashionable new address in downtown Beijing. Following the commercial success of Jianwai SoHo, the development company has gone on to invite other architects from Europe, Australia, and Asia to design its projects. Its practice of using architecture as an advertisement is widely followed by many other private developers across the country.

In the period of 2004–2005, we conducted over 60 interviews with the developers, architects, marketing staff, and sales personnel working at Jianwai SoHo, as well as with journalists, artists, and academics who were involved in the project as consultants. These interviews lasted between 30 minutes and one hour. Some interviews were conducted in the offices of the developers and architects, and in the company sales lounges. Others took place at the sites of promotional events organized by the development companies, such as gala evenings for the opening of sales of other projects and panel discussions featuring developers and real estate analysts. In addition to interviews, we also conducted participant observation at a few cultural festivals organized by the development company to examine how the space is used and interpreted on an everyday basis by a variety of city users.

Building the Central Business District in Beijing

Beijing, the capital city of China, is usually framed as the political and cultural center of the country. Only recently, as inter-city competition intensifies, has the Beijing city government decided to develop the city into a major financial center. In achieving this goal, Beijing needs to compete with its primary rival, Shanghai. In the early 1990s, Shanghai developed its own financial district, Pudong (Olds, 2001). The Beijing city government decided to build its own CBD, as the first step in competing with Shanghai as the financial capital of China.[3]

The plan of building a CBD was first proposed in the Beijing General City Plan, which was approved by the State Council in 1993. It was stated that "a modern central business district with multi-functions of finance, insurance, trade, information, commerce, culture and entertainment should

---

[3]In the early 1990s, the Financial Street (*Jinrongjie*) was developed in Xicheng District in the west part of Beijing. However, due to insufficient infrastructure construction, it has not succeeded in attracting many multinational firms. Building a CBD in Chaoyang District shows the intensifying inter-district competition in Beijing.

Figure 19.1.   The central business district in Beijing.

be built in Beijing."[4] In 1998, the Beijing city government issued the "Specific Controlling Plan," indicating that the CBD was to be located in Chaoyang district in the eastern part of Beijing.[5] The CBD Administration Committee was established to supervise the overall development activities. In 1999, Wang Qishan, a former executive of China Construction Bank, was appointed by the central government as the mayor of Beijing. Since then, it has become one of the primary goals for the new administration to build a financial district that can lure multinational firms to Beijing (Figure 19.1).

The area allocated for the CBD is approximately four square kilometers at the crossing of the Third East Ring Road and Jianguomenwai Boulevard. The site used to be an industrial area with a number of large manufacturing facilities, for machinery, automobile repairs, tools, electric wire, and cables. Approximately 54,000 households worked and lived in the area.[6] However, the city government envisioned the emergence of a new modern

---

[4]*Beijing General City Plan*, Beijing city government, 1993.

[5]*Specific Controlling Plan of Beijing*, Beijing city government, 1998.

[6]From the CBD Administration Committee, http://www.bjcbd.gov.cn.

business district, which could integrate businesses, exhibition sites, hotels, residences, and entertainment functions, and become a new headquarters and management center for financial, insurance, telecom, and information companies. Therefore, the existing manufacturing facilities had to be relocated elsewhere, old residential buildings had to be demolished, and residents had to be evicted.

The first step to turn the area into a modern business district was to draft a master plan accommodating global business functions. In the process of preparing a master plan, Beijing followed Shanghai's practice of inviting international architectural design firms as a promotional tool (Gaubatz, 2005). In 2000, with the help of the Beijing Municipal Institute of City Planning and Design (BMICPD), the Chaoyang district government organized the first international design competition for master plan proposals. Eight international firms were selected and invited to submit design proposals. Among them were firms from the USA (Skidmore, Owing & Merrill, Johnson Fain & Partners, NBBJ), Germany (GMP Architects-LA), Japan (Urban Environment and Research Institute), and Holland (Kuipercom & Pangnons). Only two entries among the eight were Chinese firms (Beijing Planning and Design Institute, and Shanghai Urban Planning and Design Institute). The participation of international design firms was widely publicized in local and national media.

To reflect the "international" nature of the design process of the CBD, the organizers also put together a jury committee composed not only of Chinese but also of international experts in architecture and planning. The committee selected the design by Johnson Fain & Partners (US) for the first prize. In 2003, the second international design competition was held to select a detailed plan for a smaller core area of the CBD. The design proposal from Pei Cobb Freed & Partners (US) was chosen.

Similar to the design process for the financial district in Shanghai, in which local design institutes drafted a final master plan for Pudong, none of the winning designs from the two competitions were actually used as the final master plans. Beijing Planning and Design Institute, a *de facto* government-owned design institute, combined features from different design proposals and finalized the master plan. The participation of international architectural and planning firms in the design competitions was seen as a great success in itself. For local governments, it matters less that the final master plans are eclectic selections by local design institutes from different proposals, and that the implementation of master plans will probably not be strictly followed. What matters more is that the final master plans resulted from international design competitions, and therefore they are a "global" product. The participation of international firms in the design process was used as a marketing tool to promote the new CBD.

In the documents accompanying the master plan, the city government clearly emphasized the significance of creating a modern cityscape symbolizing a financial district:

> The core area of [the] CBD is designed to be a skyscraper concentrat[ed] area. It is to be occupied by large architecture such as [the] CCTV building, World Trade Tower, Silktie Center, and Jianwai SoHo. Major buildings are allowed to exceed 300 meters in height and form the symbolic building block of [the] CBD … [the] CBD is to build a perfect urban image with concentrat[ed] skyscrapers and outstanding symbol buildings, and thus form a spatial layout with [a] glaring focal point in picturesque disorder.[7]

As seen in the above quote, the municipal government intended to use the new CBD as a display window to highlight Beijing's modernization and progress. A vertical "financescape" with concentrating skyscrapers exceeding 300 meters was seen as the right urban form to symbolize the rise of Beijing as a global city. The new landscape of the CBD could not be just like another downtown. It had to shock and impress. The visual impact is achieved by densely concentrating dozens of skyscrapers in the narrow area on both sides of major highways cutting across the CBD (Figure 19.1). City and district government officials used international design competitions as the first marketing campaign to promote Beijing's new CBD. After the master plan was passed, the Beijing municipal government issued a series of favorable policies to attract multinationals and Fortune 500 companies to set up their regional headquarters there. These policies aimed to reduce the operation costs for business service firms by providing tax cuts, subsidies, and other benefits. By 2004, a large number of business service firms had moved into the new CBD (see Table 19.3).

---

[7]http://www.bjcbd.gov.cn.

Table 19.3. The concentration of financial institutions in the CBD, Beijing, by 2004.

	CBD	Beijing	Concentration of business firms in CBD (in %)
Branch offices of foreign banks	17	24	70.8
Foreign banks	68	92	73.9
Investment firms	88	133	66.2
Headquarters of multinational enterprises	21	25	84.0
Foreign representative offices	4,189	8,485	49.4
Fortune 500 enterprises branch offices	293	91	31.2
Foreign direct investment in billion USD	0.563	3.08	18.3

Source: CBD Administration Committee, http://www.bjcbd.gov.cn.

Architecture as Advertising: Jianwai SoHo in Beijing

Jianwai SoHo is not the largest urban megaproject constructed in Beijing, nor is SoHo China Inc. the largest developer in the country. However, the project has been in the media spotlight for its minimalist, high-tech, and futuristic architectural design. The sales of property at Jianwai SoHo far exceeded other similar projects in the CBD area. The developers have become celebrities and, along with property development, have ventured into cultural industries such as publishing and movie production. This section examines how the symbolic capital of transnational architectural production is employed and turned into economic and cultural capital by local developers.

From factory workshops to SoHo apartments

The development of Jianwai SoHo is part of the larger process of replacing manufacturing facilities in inner city Beijing with service industries. The site for development was originally Beijing No.1 Machinery Factory, which was the largest machine production facility in the country, with dozens of workshop buildings and employing thousands of workers. Like many other state-owned enterprises, Beijing No. 1 Machinery Factory was in serious financial deficit. Workers were laid off, or their salaries went unpaid. In the course of the 1990s, as the government ordered manufacturing facilities to be moved out of the city to make space for the financial sector, the factory gave up its land to the city government and relocated to the suburbs. In 1995, SoHo China Inc. acquired the land from Beijing Land Reserve Center. In June 2001, Beijing No. 1 Machinery Factory was demolished, and the construction of Jianwai SoHo started on the site immediately.

Jianwai SoHo is a large-scale mixed development with a site area of 169,000 square meters and a floor area of 700,000 square meters. The name "SoHo" refers to "Small Office, Home Office." It is partly inspired by the loft-style apartments in the SoHo district of New York. The individual apartment units, many of which are as large as 250 square meters, combine dwelling and work areas and have few fixed partitions, so that tenants can divide the space as they see fit. In less than four years, a forest of SoHo apartments, up-scale shops, and sleek office towers replaced old factory workshops in downtown Beijing.

Developers as architecture patrons

The founders of SoHo China Inc. are distinguished from other developers by portraying themselves as patrons of avant-garde architecture. The company was founded in 1995 by an entrepreneurial couple. The CEO of the company, Pan Shiyi, established himself as a private developer with his property development work in southern China in the early 1990s, when the country liberated the property market and real estate speculation started. His wife, Zhang Xin, studied economics at the University of Cambridge and worked as a banker in Wall Street before coming back to China. The entrepreneurial couple have used innovative architecture and urban design extensively to market their properties.

Their first major project in Beijing is SoHo Newtown, a high-end residential project of 2,200 apartment units located at the border of the CBD. In this project, the developers worked with architects from Hsinghua Design Institute, one of the most prestigious local design firms (Figure 19.2). In a personal interview, however, Pan Shiyi expressed frustration with Chinese architects: "Chinese architects tend to think of architectural design only as paper drawings and engineering, and they don't see it also as art. What I want is something different from the others, something that will surprise people, and something people will talk about" (personal interview).

Figure 19.2. The Commune by the Great Wall.

To achieve a bold visual effect, the developers reached out to international architects. In 2000, the company finished their second project, named "The Commune by the Great Wall." Although the name was borrowed from the "People's Commune," the collective farming system established during the socialist period in rural China, the place evokes no memories of socialist communes. It is a cluster of 12 ultra-modern luxury villas built in the rolling mountains near the Great Wall. With each house designed by a prominent architect, the Commune by the Great Wall is the most up-scale boutique hotel in China. It is regularly booked for weekend parties by image-savvy multinational companies such as Mercedes-Benz and Shisedo (Figure 19.2). In 2002, the developer Zhang Xin was awarded a "special prize to an individual patron of architectural works" at the 8th Venice Biennale in Italy for this project. In 2004, she was selected by an international jury as the first winner from mainland China of the Mont Blanc de la Culture Arts Patronage Award.[8]

---

[8] www.sohochina.com.

This international recognition helped the developers accumulate personal cultural capital and build further networks with international architects, curators, artists, and academics. In a short period, the couple have become celebrity developers, have frequently appeared on TV talk shows, and been interviewed by international media such as the *New Yorker* magazine (Zha, 2005).

Jianwai SoHo is the third major project by SoHo China. From the very beginning, the developers intended to build the project into a new landmark in Beijing's CBD through the use of daring architectural design. The developers got to know architect Riken Yamamoto at a lecture organized by Chang Yung-ho, the leader of the new generation of overseas-educated Chinese architects working in China. It was at this event that Chang Yung-ho introduced Riken Yamamoto and a few other established architects to the developers. In Oct 2000, SoHo China invited three architects to submit design proposals for Jianwai SoHo: Arata Isozaki, Riken Yamamoto, and Rocco Yim.

The developers were looking for a design that would be both modern and non-Chinese looking, and at the same time marketable to wealthy upper middle-class Chinese consumers. Among the three proposals submitted, Isozaki's design was full of Chinese metaphors in abstract forms, such as features of animals including phoenixes, turtles, and cranes. It is ironic that such a design, full of Chinese references, was actually proposed by a foreign architect. However, the developer was looking for a completely modern design, and was not impressed by Isozaki's China-inspired proposal. As the developer Pan Shiyi commented, "Chinese elements don't have to be expressed in specific architectural languages" (personal interview). Rocco Yim's design was rejected as well, because it was too experimental and impractical. As Pan Shiyi commented, "this is a very interesting design, but it's too experimental, and nobody would buy a house like this in Beijing" (personal interview). There are therefore limits to the patronage for avant-garde architecture; experimentalism has to be practiced within marketability. Finally, Riken Yamamoto's ultra-modern design was selected among the three. Yamamoto's design stressed high-tech minimalism and was modern-looking with strong visual appeal, both of which the developers were looking for.

Minimalist and fragmented architecture

Minimalism is a striking feature of Jianwai SoHo's architectural style. All buildings at Jianwai SoHo are white, square, and completely lacking any architectural decoration. In its sales brochure, it states that "Jianwai SoHo follows the principle of simple and concise." "Less is More," a famous saying by Mies van der Rohe, is cited many times in the brochures. In an interview, the chief architect Keiichiro Sako commented on the choice of minimalist design:

> Our design was chosen because the developer wanted something with impact, something different from surrounding buildings, and something that can be a new landmark ... I have seen the buildings in the area. Many buildings have excessive decorations on the top or façade. Each building wants to become a landmark. We attempted to make Jianwai SoHo stand out [from] other high-rise buildings, by employing minimalism and keeping the design as simple as possible.

The preference for minimalism by the developers is not a coincidence. During the massive construction boom in China, Chinese developers and architects copied architectural styles from different countries and historical periods. It is not unusual to see a neo-classical building standing next to an international style building, and not far from that, Chinese-style pagodas. Most buildings are heavily decorated in order to catch attention and to become new landmarks. In this jungle of different architectural styles, a minimalist building can provide a great contrast from surrounding buildings, and therefore have a strong visual appeal. Moreover, a minimalist approach can totally break free from traditional Chinese architectural style, and thus can be perceived as modern, foreign, and futuristic. The developers believe that such minimalist design will appeal to wealthy Chinese who are eager to use non-Chinese cultural symbols to express their rising status (Figure 19.3).

Another characteristic of Jianwai SoHo's architectural style is its emphasis on fragmentation and diversity. Architect Riken Yamamoto used 16 small streets to connect different residential and office buildings. He put many piazzas, gardens, and benches on the streets. There are no fences or walls. The 16 streets are part of the bigger city. Yamamoto claims that his

Figure 19.3.   Jianwai SoHo in Beijing.

design of narrow winding streets connecting different buildings was inspired by traditional Chinese courtyard styles. However, the completed towers and squares at Jianwai SoHo scarcely remind people of low-rise Chinese courtyards. Architect Keiichiro Sako commented that the land values in the CBD are too high for any developer to afford to build low-rise courtyard-style structures.

The real motivation behind adopting human-scale small streets might be found in the developers' admiration of other global cities. As the developer Zhang Xin wrote in a company publication:

> There are restaurants, shops, offices and people living here at Jianwai SoHo. It is like the center of New York, Paris, and London … Beijing needs this cosmopolitan lifestyle. We hope that Jianwai SoHo can partly meet this need … Beijingers took off their gray people's suits, gave up their bicycles. With confidence, they have started to live a lifestyle of that of New Yorkers, Parisians and Londoners in their newly built city.[9]

---

[9]Pan, S. *SoHo Newtown Files*, p. 89, 2000.

Throughout the planning of Jianwai SoHo, the developers constantly had other global cities as reference points. The particular spatial articulation has isolated Jianwai SoHo from its immediate urban context of Beijing, and the place more closely resembles other established global cities, such as New York, Paris, and London. In building and marketing Jianwai SoHo, the developers are projecting a new cosmopolitan lifestyle that they believe is attractive to wealthy upper middle-class Chinese. They are suggesting to potential investors that, by living and consuming here at Jianwai SoHo, people can experience the lifestyle of cosmopolitans in other global cities.

The money talk: Who are the buyers?

Jianwai SoHo targets the group of people in China at the top of the income pyramid. The sales at Jianwai SoHo were the highest among all major CBD megaprojects released onto the market in the same time period. The total sales of the properties at Jianwai SoHo reached more than US$1 billion in 2004. The price of an apartment at Jianwai SoHo is more than US$2,000 per square meter. A two-bedroom apartment of about 140 square meters costs roughly US$280,000, while the annual salary of a well-paid white collar worker in Beijing is only around US$7,000.

The project also targets a wide range of investors beyond Beijing. Local Beijing residents only represent a small percentage of the investors. According to a report released by SoHo China on the 2004 sales of Jianwai SoHo, 54 percent of the purchases were made by wealthy Chinese from other provinces, 18 percent by foreigners, and only 28 percent by local Beijing residents. There were 180 people who purchased more than US$10 million worth per person.[10] The wealthy Chinese property owners at Jianwai SoHo can be roughly divided into two groups: business owners in sectors such as mining, manufacturing, and trade, and high-income urban professionals such as lawyers, accountants, and business executives.

Coal mine owners from nearby Shanxi province represent a distinctive group of property owners at Jianwai SoHo. According to local newspapers as well as a company release, in the last quarter of 2005, SoHo China achieved total sales of US$1.2 billion, more than half of which was purchased by coal mine owners from Shanxi province. Due to China's increasing demand for

---

[10] *Soho Xiaobao* (April), SoHo China Inc., 2004.

energy and its soaring prices, many coal mine owners have quickly amassed a fortune and invested heavily in big city real estate. In a personal interview a saleswoman described one of her clients from Shanxi Province:

> When I met him for the first time, I wonder[ed] if he can afford to buy anything at our place. He didn't even take a flight to Beijing. He arrived by train! And I had to pick him up at the dirty train station. He has a mining company in Shanxi province. He's interested in buying a commercial space on lower floors for investment. We had many long talks negotiating the price. In the end, he didn't say anything and left. A few days later, I got a phone call from him saying he would come to Beijing again. This time, he brought with him his older brother. After a final check, they bought a large shop front worth [···] more than US$10 million.

This case is an example of how the huge amounts of surplus capital, accumulated in the primary circuit of production such as mining, are channeled into the real estate sector. During interviews with the sales personnel, many recounted that although the investors may not understand and appreciate the minimalist architecture design *per se*, the branding effect achieved by the architectural design is a major factor in their decision making for investment purposes. Many of them saw properties at Jianwai SoHo as having higher potential for investment return, because the project "looked" different from other commercial projects and appeared more eye-catching.

Along with coal mine owners, there is another distinctive group of property owners: high-income urban professionals working for international firms. In August 2005, the Jianwai SoHo Property Owners Committee was established, and four members were elected as representatives. A quick glance at their profiles shows the new class of younger and highly educated urban professionals whom they represent.

1. Mr Du: 39 years old; graduate degree; he is currently working as a lawyer for King & Wood (USA), Beijing office;
2. Ms Wang: 36 years old; graduate degree; she has worked for an American International Satellite Company, and AT&T; she is currently working for UTStarccom (USA);
3. Mr Zhang: 52 years old; college degree; he is currently working for China International Trade Consulting; and

4. Mr Han: 45 years old; graduate degree; he has six years of study and work experience in Japan; he is currently working as the executive representative of Saike Café (a national coffee shop chain).[11]

A highly educated corporate lawyer might share little with a coal mine owner in terms of cultural and consumption tastes. However, what this small group of extremely wealthy Chinese consumers has in common is their eagerness to acquire a symbol to exemplify their newly achieved and privileged socio-economic status. And here enter the trend-setting international architects hired by local developers. By creating a never-seen-before urban space in Beijing, local developers and international architects have provided a rare commodity, the consumption of which can symbolize the consumers' rising economic power. As Zukin argues, "shifts in a 'dominant class' accumulation strategy generally invoke new cultural norms in order to justify and facilitate the exercise of unaccustomed forms of social control" (Zukin, 1982: 147). This applies well to the practice by local Beijing developers of employing international architects to promote their properties. In the case of Jianwai SoHo, the articulation of spatial design has become a major force in the process of capital accumulation. The symbolic capital of international architectural design is transformed into economic capital and cultural capital in the process of megaproject development and marketing. Minimalist and futuristic architectural design has helped to differentiate Jianwai SoHo from other similar commercial developments in Beijing, and has promised investors a higher return on investment through the branding effect. In the meantime, the investors also made their decisions on the basis of the sense of cultural privilege associated with consuming this transnationally produced space; a place that is so different from the rest of the city as to show their newly acquired and privileged socio-economic status in the market reforms in China.

Conclusion

This chapter has examined the role of transnational architectural production in the process of urban megaproject developments in the CBD of Beijing.

---

[11] http://yeweihui.sohoxiaobao.com.

Based on empirical case studies, we have explored how city officials have used international design competitions to promote the new CBD, as well as how connections are forged between local elites and international architectural firms in the development of Jianwai SoHo. We argue that the spatial articulation of urban design has become a major force of capital accumulation in the process of building Beijing into a new global city. Signature design from international architects functions as symbolic capital. It is transformed into economic, political, and cultural capital by various actors in the process of development and marketing of urban megaprojects. International architects are sought after by local elites to be used as branding tools to market their properties, and to re-orient the image of Beijing from that of a dusty post-socialist city into that of an emerging global city.

Local elites in Beijing are not alone in the growing trend of using international "starchitects" to put their city on the map. The use of signature projects for place marketing has become a frequently used strategy among urban governments for urban regeneration. A small number of elite architectural design firms, mostly based in Europe and North America, have delivered a large number of iconic architectural projects in a variety of locations (Sklair, 2005, 2006). These projects represent a new phase of spatial production: the transnational production of urban space. It is characterized by the increasing participation of transnational agencies, such as multinationals, international architects, the global media network, and globalizing state bureaucrats, in the processes of placemaking.

The transnational production of urban space has to be understood in the broader context of global economic restructuring. It is brought about by larger structural changes, such as the integration of the global economy, the shifting territorial scales in which things can get done, the ascending importance of a symbolic economy in post-industrial cities, as well as the development of a global telecommunication network. The international investment capital roaming around the globe has provided financial resources for numerous high-profile architectural projects in global or globalizing cities, where the investment return is the highest. The inter-city competition for investment capital has increased its intensity to such a degree that state power has to be redirected to the urban scale, to act as an agent actively facilitating inter-urban competition for investment. The nature of the post-industrial economy has turned symbols and signs into a distinct economic variable (Zukin, 1982). Similar to other forms of cultural production, architectural design from leading design firms has become a hot commodity sought after to help create a positive image for a place, and to facilitate urban regeneration and attract investment. Finally, the formation of the global telecommunication network has made it possible to transfer large-size design drawings instantly across the globe, and therefore has provided a technical infrastructure to make transnational architectural production possible.

The new phase of transnationally produced urban space has significant consequences for the urban political economy and built-up environment. In Beijing, local developers and international architects have created a type of urban landscape never seen before in the central business district, catering to affluent new city users. By adopting a non-Chinese architectural language, local elites in Beijing are projecting the city and themselves as more cosmopolitan and international, and thus acquiring a new transnational identity in the symbolic production of urban space. The new urban landscape can only be understood as the product of intersecting transnational flows of design professionals, image, and investment capital, as well as the mediation of these global and local processes through the built environment.

References

Althubaity, Amer and Andy Jonas (1998). "Suburban Entrepreneurialism: Redevelopment Regimes and Co-ordinating Metropolitan Development in Southern California." In *The Entrepreneurial City: Geographies of Politics, Regime and Representation*, edited by T. Hill and P. Hubbard. New York: Wiley.

Altshuler, Alan and David Luberoff (2003). *Megaprojects: The Changing Politics of Urban Public Investment.* Washington, DC: The Brookings Institute.

Beijing Real Estate Yearbook (2004). Beijing: Beijing Statistics Bureau.

Beijing General City Plan (1993). Beijing: Beijing City Government.

Beauregard, Robert A. and Anne Haila (1997). "The Unavoidable Incompleteness of the City." *American Behavioral Scientist* 41: 327–341.

Cartier, Carolyn (2002). "Transnational Urbanism in the Reform-era Chinese City: Landscape from Shenzhen." *Urban Studies* 39: 1513–1532.

China Real Estate Yearbook (2004). China Statistics Bureau.

Douglass, Mike (1998). "World City Formation on the Asia Pacific Rim." In *Cities for Citizens*, edited by J. Friedmann and M. Douglass. New York: John Wiley & Sons.

Evans, Graeme (2003). "Hard-branding the Cultural City: From Prado to Prada." *International Journal of Urban and Regional Research* 27: 417–440.

Fainstein, Susan S. (2001). *The City Builders: Property Development in New York and London, 1980-2000.* Lawrence: University Press of Kansas.

Flyvbjerg, Bent, Nils Bruzelius and Werner Rothengatter (2003). *Megaprojects and Risks: An Anatomy of Ambition.* Cambridge: Cambridge University Press.

Frantz, Monika (2005). "From Cultural Regeneration to Discursive Governance: Constructing the Flagship of the 'Museumsquartier Vienna' as a Plural Symbol of Change." *International Journal of Urban and Regional Research* 29: 50–66.

Gaubatz, P. (2005). "Globalization and the Development of New Central Business Districts in Beijing, Shanghai and Guangzhou." In *Restructuring the Chinese City*, edited by L.J.C. Ma and Filiua Wu. New York: Routledge.

Gottdeiner, M. (1994). *The Social Production of Urban Space.* Austin: University of Texas Press.

Haila, Anne (1999). "The Singapore and Hong Kong Property Markets: Lessons for the West from Successful Global Cities." *European Planning Studies* 7: 175–187.

Harvey, David (1989). "From Managerialism to Entrepreneurialism: The Transformation of Governance in Late Capitalism." *Geografiska Annaler* 71(B): 3–17.

Harvey, David (1990). *The Condition of Post Modernity.* Cambridge: Blackwell.

Herrschel, Tassilo (1998). "From Socialism to Post-Fordism: The Local State and Economic Policies in Eastern Germany." In *The Entrepreneurial City: Geographies of Politics, Regime and Representation*, edited by T. Hill and P. Hubbard. New York: Wiley.

Hubbard, Phil (1996). "Urban Design and City Regeneration: Social Representation of Entrepreneurial Landscapes." *Urban Studies* 33: 1441–1461.

Jessop, Bof (1998). "The Narrative of Enterprise and the Enterprise of Narrative: Place Marketing and the Entrepreneurial City." In *The Entrepreneurial City: Geographies of Politics, Regime and Representation,* edited by T. Hill and P. Hubbard. New York: Wiley.

King, Anthony Douglas (2002). "Speaking from the Margins: Postmodernism, Transnationalism, and the Imagining of Contemporary Indian Urbanity." In *Globalization and the Margins*, edited by Richard Grant and J. R. Short. New York: Palgrave Macmillan.

King, Anthony Douglas (2004). *Spaces of Global Cultures: Architecture, Urbanism, Identity.* New York: Routledge.

Knox, Paul L. (1991). "The Restless Urban Landscape." *Annals of the Association of American Geographers* 81: 181–209.

Lefebvre, Henri (1991). *The Production of Space.* Cambridge, Mass: Blackwell.

Lehrer, Ule (2006). "Willing the Global City: Berlin's Cultural Strategies of Inter-urban Competition." In *The Global Cities Reader*, edited by N. Brenner and R. Keil. New York: Routledge.

Loftman, Patrick and Brendan Nevin (1996). "Going for Growth: Prestige Projects in Three British Cities." *Urban Studies* 33: 991–1019.

Marshall, R. (2003). *Emerging Urbanity: Global Urban Projects in the Asia Pacific Rim.* New York: Spon Press.

McGuirk, Pauline, Hilary Winchester and Kevin Dunn (1998). "On Losing the Local in Responding to Urban Decline: The Honeysuckle Redevelopment, New South Wales." In *The Entrepreneurial City: Geographies of Politics, Regime and Representation*, edited by T. Hill and P. Hubbard. New York: Wiley.

McNeill, David (2005). "In Search of the Global Architect: The case of Norman Foster (and Partners)." *International Journal of Urban and Regional Research* 29: 501–515.

Olds, Kris (2001). *Globalization and Urban Change: Capital, Culture, and Pacific Rim Megaprojects.* New York: Oxford University Press.

Pan, Shiyi (2000). *SoHo Newtown Files.* Tianjin: Tianjin Academy of Social Science.

Ren, X. (2006). "The Chinese Debate about Grand Projects and International Architects." *Perspectives* 7: 189–191.

Sassen, Saskia (2001). *The Global City: New York, London, Tokyo.* Princeton NJ: Princeton University Press.

Sklair, Leslie (2001). *The Transnational Capitalist Class.* Malden MA: Blackwell.

Sklair, Leslie (2005). "The Transnational Capitalist Class and Contemporary Architecture in Globalizing Cities." *International Journal of Urban and Regional Research* 29: 485–500.

Sklair, Leslie (2006). "Iconic Architecture and Capitalist Globalization." *City* 10: 21–47.

Specific Controlling Plan of Beijing (1998). Beijing: Beijing City Government.

Sudjic, Deyan (1992). *The 100 Mile City.* London: A. Deutsch.

Wu, Felicia (2000a). "Place Promotion in Shanghai, PRC." *Cities* 17: 349–361.

Wu, Felicia (2000b). "The Global and Local Dimensions of Place-Making: Remaking Shanghai as a Global City." *Urban Studies* 37: 1359–1377.

Xu, Jun and Anthony G. Yeh (2005). "City Repositioning and Competitiveness Building in Regional Development: New Development Strategies in Guangzhou, China." *International Journal of Urban and Regional Research* 29: 283–308.

Zha, J. (2005). "The Turtles: The Star Couple of Chinese Real Estate." *The New Yorker* (July 2005), 72–81.

Zukin, Sharon (1982). *Loft living.* Baltimore, MD: Johns Hopkins University Press.

INDEX

9/11, 74, 329, 332

Adachi, 150, 151, 158–168, 174–176
adaptation, 125
adoption, 49, 52, 62
Advance Cargo Information, 321
Africa, 14, 15, 70, 89, 128, 183, 256, 257, 259, 306, 307
aging, 31, 39, 46, 48, 49, 90, 182, 187–189, 191, 192, 197, 237, 238
Agreement on Textiles and Clothing (ATC), 249, 250
agriculture, 90, 102, 207
AIDS prevention, 156
air cargo, 320, 321
Air Cargo Manifest Rule, 321
Air China, 300
airlines, 331
airports, 300
Albania, 84
Algeria, 89
America, Latin, 90, 95, 119, 128
America, North, 69–71, 82, 83, 130, 232, 288–290, 294, 306, 307
America, South, 97, 100
Americans, 113, 159
Andreu, P., 348
APEC, 194, 195
APL, 303, 304
Arabs, 9
architects, 351, 356, 364, 365
architecture, 336, 341–345, 348
ASEAN, 14–17, 288

Asia, 12, 30, 41, 43–45, 49, 52, 53, 60, 61, 73, 89, 95, 125, 183, 232, 270, 276, 286, 288, 290
Asia, East, 10, 16, 18, 21, 39, 42, 46, 56, 59, 60, 62, 63, 69, 91, 166, 257
Asia, economy of, 12
Asia, Northeast, 306, 307, 321
Asia, South, 28, 30, 100, 108, 115, 321
Asia, Southeast, 9, 11, 14, 16, 28, 56, 100, 115, 306
Asia, Southeast retirement, 59
Asia, West, 9
Asia Development, 205
Asia-Pacific region, 6, 10, 17, 18, 27, 28, 30, 34, 47, 48, 50, 53, 54, 225, 286
Asia Terminal Ltd., 320
Association for Overseas Technical Training, 164
asylum, 73, 74, 76, 78–82, 88
Asylum and Immigration Act (UK), 81
Australia, 4, 28, 53, 69, 72, 85, 101, 128, 129, 232, 306, 351
Austria, 218
automobiles, 293, 295
automotive industry, 185

Bangkok, 59
Bangladesh, 28, 100, 251, 252, 258, 259
banks, 346
Beijing, 11–13, 18, 300, 316, 336, 341, 342, 350–355, 358, 363–365
Beijing General City Plan, 351, 352
Beijing Land Reserve Center, 356
Beijing Municipal Institute of City Planning and Design, 354

Beijing No. 1 Machinery Factory, 355, 356
Beijing Planning and Design Institute, 354
Belgium, 35, 84
Berkeley, 2
birth rates, 46, 52, 73
Black Sea, 306, 307
blue collar workers, 102
boatpeople, 83
Bombay, 9
brain drain, 2–6, 21, 202, 209, 212, 218–220
Brazilians, 90, 101, 111–113, 115, 159
Brunei Darussalam, 28
Brussels, 81
bubble economy, 97
Bulgaria, 86
bulk breaking, 307
Busan, 285, 289, 332
Busan Port Authority, 289
Bush, G.W., 324
business process outsourcing, 204

California, 2, 125
call centers, 204
Cambodia, 251, 252, 254, 256, 259
Canada, 4, 28, 71, 86, 101, 191, 192, 194, 218
capital, human, 22
capital, symbolic, 355, 363
capitalism, 37
career tracks, 140
caregivers, 190–195
cargo, 319
Caribbean, 128
Carlyle Group, 13
Catholic Church, 210, 211
Central Business District (CBD), 341, 345, 348, 350, 351, 353, 355, 358, 360, 361, 363, 364
Chang, Y., 358
Chaoyang, 354
Cheju Island, 103
Chengdu, 300
Chiang Mai, 57–59
Chiang Rai, 59
Chiba, 107

children, 33, 39, 43, 46, 47, 49–53, 55, 57, 58, 62, 78, 95, 163, 227, 236–238
Chi-Lung, 333
China, 9, 12–14, 16–18, 28, 32, 43, 45, 50, 52–54, 82, 95, 96, 100, 104, 128–130, 134, 137–141, 159, 249–251, 254, 257–259, 261, 269, 270, 276, 277, 280, 281, 287–289, 291–294, 297–301, 309, 316, 321, 326, 346, 347
China Construction Bank, 352
China Eastern Air, 300
China Ocean Shipping Company, 300
China Railway Express, 300
China Shipping Cargo Transport Company, 301
China Shipping Company, 300
China Southern Air, 300
Chinese Central Television, 348
Chinese, in Japan, 105, 123–142
Chiwan, 313, 315
churches, 127, 155
cities, 44, 45, 51, 102, 236
citizenship, 45, 60, 61, 139
Clark, H., 3
coal, 301, 361–363
coast guard regulations, 333
Cold War, 11
colonialism, 69
Commission for Immigration Reform (US), 76
Commission on Overseas Filipinos, 184
commodification, 38
Commonwealth of Independent States (CIS), 45
competitiveness, 286
components, 111
computers, personal, 265, 266, 278, 279, 281
Congo, Democratic Republic of, 84
Congress, 13
Congressional Budget Office (CBO), 329
Connecticut Maritime, 303, 304
Constitution, Chinese, 347
construction, 90
consumption, 239

Container Security Initiative (CSI), 331, 332
containers, 285, 287, 289, 290, 293, 294, 301, 303, 304, 306, 307, 309, 312, 313, 315, 323, 325–327, 330, 335, 337
Cornelius, W., 89
corporations, 45
COSCO, 301
criminal behavior, 61
culture, Japanese, 173, 174
currencies, 14
customs, 313–315, 320
Customs-Trade Partnership against Terrorism (C-TPAT), 332

daburu, 149
Daichang, 315
Daihatsu, 293
deindustrialization, 102
Denmark, 71, 72, 149
Department of Homeland Security, 333, 334
Department of Labor (US), 75
developers, 336, 341
development, 7, 219
DHL, 316
Digital Trade and Transport Network, 321
diplomacy, 10, 14, 15
disaster training, 154 155
disasters, 49, 73, 330
discrimination, 61, 196
divorce, 38, 51
doctorates, 129
Doha Round, 15
doi moi, 252
domestic workers, 28, 30, 39, 41, 42, 44, 54, 55, 57–59, 183, 185, 186
Dongguan, 317, 318
drugs, 15
Dubai, 286

East, the, 12
East China Sea Bridge, 304
Economic Partnership Agreement (Japan), 90
Economist, The, 11, 12

education, 1, 2, 5, 6, 21, 26, 39, 53, 57, 58, 62, 95, 97, 128, 139, 162–164, 167–174, 176, 177, 195, 214, 215, 217, 218, 239
elderly, 31, 38, 48, 55, 57–59, 187, 194–196, 227, 245, 246
elections, 96
electronic data interchange (EDI), 300
E-Manifest, 321
emigration, 93
employees, categories of, 136, 137
employer sanctions, 76
employers, 75, 76, 136, 137
employment, 203, 207, 209–212
energy, 324
engineers, 123, 129, 132
entertainers, 78, 181, 183, 184, 186
entrepreneurship, 139, 140
etiquette, 132
Europe, 11, 17, 46, 69–71, 75, 76, 79, 82, 83, 86–90, 98, 130, 183, 232, 255, 285, 294, 306, 316, 341, 351
European Community, 79
European Union (EU), 12, 15, 71, 77, 80–83, 86, 89, 101, 249, 253, 256, 258, 259, 262, 299
Evergreen, 303, 304
exploitation, 31, 47, 70, 77

families, 32, 33, 39, 40, 42, 43, 45, 46, 48, 50, 54, 55, 60, 71, 228–231
family reunification, 72, 88
farm subsidies, 15
fashion, 256
fathers, 53
Federal Bureau of Investigation (FBI), 327
FedEx, 300, 316
feminization, 70
fertility, 42, 46, 47, 52, 74, 85, 90, 186
festivals, 118
financial crisis, 10
fishing, 102
footware, 257
foreign direct investment (FDI), 32, 56, 88, 203, 225, 251
Foreign Registration Act (Japan), 177

foreign residents, 148–153, 156–157, 168, 169, 171–177
Foreign Students' Career Support Center (Japan), 129
foreign workers, 148, 187
foreigners, 23–25, 62, 100, 119, 160
forestry, 102
Foster & Partners, 347
France, 17, 71, 72, 79, 83, 86, 149
free trade agreement (FTA), 91, 166, 181, 198, 262
Fudan University, 132

G-8, 69
gaikokujin mondai, 149, 150
Gallagher, A., 77
gambling, 102
gender, 49, 140, 185
General Agreement on Tariffs and Trade (GATT), 10, 15, 249
German, 72
Germany, 17, 55, 78–81, 85–87, 99, 128, 189, 297, 353
Ghana, 228
Global Commission on International Migration (GCIM), 34
global development network, 279, 281
Global Forum on International Migration and Development, 35
global householding, 40, 43, 45, 47–49, 51, 60, 62
global production network (GPN), 265, 267–269, 279–281
global value chain (GVC), 254, 255
globalization, 5, 6, 9, 10, 12, 14, 26, 44, 45, 49, 51, 61, 69, 142, 147, 225, 265–267, 269, 270, 282, 342–345
GMP Architects-LA, 354
Great Wall, 357
Greece, 84
green card, 75
grounded theory, 127
Guangdong, 261, 315
Guangzhou, 300, 315, 316
Guatamala, 228
guest workers, 75, 88

Gunma, 117
Gunma prefecture, 108

Haenam, 50
Hakata, 285–287, 290–292, 295
Hanjin, 303, 304
Hanoi, 17
Hanshin Earthquake, 154
Hapag-Lloyd-CP, 303, 304
Hawaii, 95, 209
health, 182, 183, 196
health care, 188, 189
health workers, 181, 183, 190, 195, 197, 212, 218, 219
Heian period, 93
Herzog & de Meuron, 348
High-Level Dialogue on International Migration and Development, 34, 35
highways, 299
Ho Chi Minh City, 226, 233, 245
Holland, 354
Honda, 293
Hong Kong, 10, 28, 39, 42, 46, 47, 54, 56, 183, 209, 212, 255, 257, 261, 287, 288, 292, 298, 309, 312–315, 317–320, 326, 330, 333
Hong Kong Airport, 309, 315, 321
Hong Kong Airport Authority, 320
Hong Kong Distribution Center, 320
Hong Kong Port, 311, 322
hospitals, 219
hostesses, 78, 97
hot springs, 106
households, 37–39, 41, 44, 46, 47, 49, 53, 54, 57–62, 225, 226, 228–233, 236–239, 245, 246, 352
Hsinchu Science-Based Industrial Park (HISP), 23, 24
Hsinghua Design Institute, 356
Hu Jintao, 13
Huangpu River, 304
Hu-Dehart, E., 89
Human Development Index, 202
human resources, 202
human rights, 33, 73, 156
Human Rights Watch, 55

human trafficking, 31, 47, 61, 70, 74, 77, 78, 83
Humanitarian Action (Switzerland), 84
Huntington, S., 6, 149, 150
Hyundai, 303, 304

Ibaraki, 107
IBM, 12, 126, 279
identity, 45
illegal migrants, 72, 73, 75–78, 82–85, 88, 89, 148
illegal migration, 74, 75
illegal workers, 184
image projects, 347
immigrants, 96, 125, 126
immigration, 24, 26, 74, 93, 100, 123, 150, 197, 209
Immigration Act (US), 75
Immigration Ad Hoc Council (European Community), 80
Immigration Control and Refugee Recognition Act (Japan), 78
Immigration Reform and Control Act (US), 83
imperialism, 45
imports, 251
incomes, 27, 39, 42, 226, 228, 240, 244–246
India, 2, 11, 12, 14, 21, 28, 30, 32, 128, 129, 270, 276, 277
Indian Ocean, 9, 325
Indo-China, 82
Indonesia, 10, 31, 33, 45, 54, 56, 100, 325
Industrial Revolution, 9, 11
Industrial Technology Research Institute (ITRI), 276
industry, 3, 9, 108, 111
inequality, 226, 228–231, 240, 244–246
information technology (IT), 10, 24, 73, 125, 133, 136–139, 202, 204, 278
infrastructure, 299, 300, 316
innovation, 22
intellectual property, 13
international exchange, 152, 153, 172
International Labor Organization (ILO), 33

International Maritime Organization (IMO), 333
International Organization for Migration (IOM), 70, 72, 73, 77, 78, 89, 147
international relations, 14
International Ship and Port Facility Security Code, 333
internationalization, 158, 161, 162
internet, 300
investment, 14, 246, 346
Iran, 2, 100
Ireland, 71
Isozaki, A., 358
Italy, 71, 83, 84

Jakarta, 34
Japan, 2, 9, 10, 13, 16–18, 24, 25, 28, 39, 42, 46, 47, 50, 52, 55, 56, 59, 62, 69, 71, 72, 74, 76, 78, 81–83, 85–87, 89–91, 93, 95–100, 102, 103, 116, 118, 119, 123–142, 148, 150, 181–187, 189, 191, 195–198, 212, 218, 249, 253, 285, 288–290, 298, 312, 324–326, 353
Japanese, 104, 112
Japanese Language Institute of the Philippines (JPIL), 194, 195
Japan Freight Railway Co., 294
Japan Immigration Associations, 127
Japan Nursing Association, 196
Japan, Sea of, 294
Japan Shippers' Council, 311
Japan Student Services Organization (JASSO), 129, 132
Japan-Philippine Economic Partnership Agreement (JPEPA), 181
Japan-Philippines Free Trade Agreement (FTA), 193
J.C. Penney, 255
JCtrans, 300
Jianguomenwai, 352
Jianwai SoHo, 341, 350, 351, 355, 358–364
JJ Shipping, 303, 304
Johnson Fain & Partners, 354

Jordan, 262
juche, 96

kamikaze, 94
Kanagawa prefecture, 62
Kansai, 103, 108, 111, 115, 117
Kanto, 106
Kaohsiung, 287, 288, 333
Kawamura, T., 311
Kawasaki, 174
Kawasaki Line, 303, 304
kikajin, 93
Kim Il Sung, 96
Kitakyushu, 285–287, 291, 292, 295
knowledge, economy, 21, 22
Kobe, 103, 114, 289, 292, 332
Kohn Pederson Fox Associates, 347
Korea, 2, 10, 16, 17, 28, 39, 42, 45–47,
    49–53, 56, 58, 71, 72, 85, 93, 95, 96,
    212, 255, 287–289, 291, 293, 294,
    298, 324–326
Korea, North, 82, 96
Koreans, 86, 102–104, 108, 115, 119
Koreans, in Adachi, 159, 166
Koreans, in Japan, 96, 101, 155
Kuipercom & Pangnons, 354
Kumamoto, 293
Kuwait, 212
Kwangyang, 287
Kyoto, 103
Kyushu, 285, 286, 291–293, 295

labor, 48, 60
labor, circulation, 44, 45
labor, demand for, 117
labor force, 39
labor, non-wage, 38
labor shortage, 85, 86, 90, 99, 100, 108,
    116, 147
language, 126, 132, 133, 142, 151–154,
    157, 162, 163, 171, 175, 176, 194, 198
Lebanon, 212
Legal Immigration and Family Equity Act
    (US), 84
Lenovo, 11, 12
Lesotho, 254, 256, 259
Levi Strauss, 255

liberalization, 11
licensing, 26
lifestyles, 151, 156
liner services, 289, 295
liquefied natural gas (LNG), 323, 329
Liz Claiborne, 255
Lloyd Triestino, 303, 304
loans, 227
local government, 62
location, 286, 287, 295, 298, 300, 307
London, 361
Luchao Logistics Park, 304, 305
Luxembourg, 12

Ma Wan, 313
Maastricht Treaty, 80
Macau, 298, 315
Madrid, 87
Maersk Line, 290, 300, 303
maids, 55, 57, 58
mail order brides, 50, 97
Malacca, Straits of, 325, 327, 331
Malaysia, 10, 28, 31, 54, 56, 100, 184,
    287, 298, 325
managers, 102
Manchester, 9
Manila, 17, 45
Mansha, 315
manual workers, 104, 197
Marcos, F., 209–211
Maritime Security Act, 333
marriage, 38, 39, 41–43, 48–51, 57, 58,
    60–62, 106, 142
master plans, 353, 355
mathematics, 22–24, 215, 217, 221
Mattel, 12
Mawan, 315
medical services, 59
Mediterranean, 306, 307
Mediterranean Line, 303, 304
Mediterranean Shipping Co., 295
megaprojects, 336, 341–347, 355
Meiji period, 9
Mercedes-Benz, 357
Mexico, 88, 89, 256, 259
middle class, 44, 54, 55, 115, 118, 361

Middle East, 28, 30, 148, 183, 190, 209, 212
Middle East China, 324
migration, 1–3, 14, 23, 24, 27, 28, 30, 32, 33, 35, 39, 42–45, 47, 49, 60, 63, 69–71, 73, 85, 88, 95, 99, 100, 116, 147, 148, 181–183, 196, 201, 202, 209, 214, 219, 220, 298
military, in Okinawa, 114
military service, 53
military spending, 12
Mindinao, 219
minimalism, 359, 363, 364
Ministry of Internal Affairs and Communications (Japan), 151
Ministry of Justice (Japan), 82, 85, 89, 127, 131, 148
Ministry of Land, Infrastructure and Transport (Japan), 292, 295
minorities, 118, 119
MIT, 53
Mitsubishi, 133
Mitsui, 303, 304
mobility, 125, 135–137, 142
Moji, 290
Mongolia, 298
Mongols, 94
Mont Blanc Award, 357
Morocco, 73, 84, 89
multicultural coexistence, 150, 151, 155, 158, 160–177
Multi-Fibre Arrangements (MFAs), 249–251, 255–259
multinationals, 269, 275
Muslims, 100, 149
Mutual Recognition Agreement, 195
Myanmar, 31

Nagano, 107
Nagasaki, 95
Nagoya, 104, 108, 289, 292, 332
National Academy of Sciences, 6
National Police Agency (Japan), 89
National Stadium (Beijing), 348
National Theatre (Beijing), 348
nation-state, 5, 44, 46, 62
Netherlands, 88, 95

networking, 22, 24, 151, 164, 172, 266, 267, 269, 282
new immigration model, 98–100, 101, 108, 116
New York, 11, 13, 361
New Zealand, 3, 4, 28, 85, 101
newcomers, 96, 97, 104, 105, 149
nihonjinron, 95
nikkeijin, 97, 100, 105, 111, 112, 115, 119
Nippon Care Services Craft Union, 197
Nippon Yusen Kaisha (NYK) Line, 290, 303
Nissan, 293
Non-Governmental Organizations (NGO), 78
North, the, 12, 45, 70, 71
North American Free Trade Association (NAFTA), 88
Norway, 72, 86, 218
NTT, 133
nurses, 55, 59, 90, 190, 193–195, 212, 217–220

Oceania, 183
OECD, 1, 21, 22, 69–72, 74, 83, 85, 88
official development aid (ODA), 32
offshore production, 128, 140
off-shoring, 13, 123, 124
oil, 28, 30, 75, 79, 209, 301, 323–325, 329
Okinawa, 114
oldcomers, 96, 104, 159
Oracular, 12
ore, 301
Orient Overseas, 303, 304
Osaka, 103, 112, 290, 292
Overseas Development Assistance (ODA), 225
Overseas Filipino Workers (OFW), 186, 210, 211, 219, 220
overseas representatives, 137
overstayers, 89, 90
Owings & Merrill, 347, 354

pachinko, 96
Pacific Ocean, 325
Pacific Rim Immigration Information Group, 77

Pakistan, 28, 30, 100, 228, 250
Pakistanis, 159
Pan, S., 356, 358
Papua New Guinea, 55
Paris, 361
passports, 75, 87
Pearl Harbor, 13
Pearl River, 299
Pearl River Delta (PRD), 312–315, 317–320
Pei Cobb Freed & Partners, 354
pensions, 48, 188, 189
Persian Gulf, 306, 307
personal services, 102, 105
Peru, 112
Peruvians, 101, 112, 115
petty bourgeoisie, 103
Philippine Overseas and Employment Administration (POEA), 183, 210–212
Philippines, 2, 10, 11, 15, 28, 30, 32, 45, 48, 50, 54–56, 90, 100, 105–108, 115, 155, 159, 181–186, 190–192, 195, 197, 198, 201–205, 207, 209–212, 214, 215, 217, 219, 298
Phuket, 59
placemaking, 364
Plaza Accord, 148
P.L.G. TRANSFAR, 300
population, 5, 27, 28, 31, 38, 42, 46–48, 58, 70, 73, 85, 93, 98, 99, 151, 159, 182, 186–189, 205, 220, 237, 238, 261
Port Kelang, 332
Port Security, 335, 337
ports, 285–289, 294, 295, 300, 301, 329, 331
poverty, 48, 71, 73, 113, 207, 209, 228
prejudice, 143
production, 11
professionals, 30, 70, 86, 101, 104, 106, 107, 114, 116, 125, 183, 195, 197, 209, 212, 218, 365
profitability, 99
prostitution, 15, 31, 97, 197
protectionism, 14

Protocol to Prevent, Suppress and Punish Trafficking in Persons, 78
public-private partnerships, 342–345
Pudong, 351

Qatar, 212
Qingdao, 287, 288
qualifications, 194, 195, 198, 218
quotas, 259

race, 119
railways, 299
raw materials, 13
real estate market, 346
Red Sea, 306, 307
referendum, 165
refugees, 48, 73, 79, 82, 83
Rem Koolhaas, 348
remittances, 32, 39, 49, 56–58, 62, 186, 202, 212, 225–233, 236–240, 244–246
reproduction, of labor, 37, 38
reproduction, social, 37, 38, 42, 60
research, 4
research and development (R&D), 24, 265–270, 275, 276, 278, 280–282
residence status, 86
retirement, 48, 59, 62, 63, 189
road transport, 300
Rohe, M. van der, 359
Romania, 81, 86
Rotterdam, 286
rural areas, 226
Russia, 11, 298

Sadruddin Aga Khan, 73
SAFE Port Act, 333–335, 337
Saigon, 59
sakoku (national seclusion), 95
Sako, K., 359, 360
salaries, 139, 276
salaryman, 95
Sara Lee, 255
Saudi Arabia, 28, 183, 190, 212, 218
Schneider National, 300
scholarships, 24

science, 215, 217, 221
sciences, natural, 23, 24
Second World War, 1, 82
security, 74, 87, 149, 150, 323, 331
Security and Accountability for Every
    (SAFE) Port Act, 324
security services, 102
segregation, 112–114, 119
semi-conductor industry, 185, 295
semi-conductors, 293
semi-skilled jobs, 197
Seville, 89
sex industry, 105–107, 197
Shanghai, 132, 133, 138, 140, 261, 280,
    285, 287–289, 300, 303, 304, 316,
    331, 332, 351, 353
Shanghai Port, 303, 304, 306, 307
Shanghai Urban Planning and Design
    Institute, 354
Shanxi Province, 361–363
Shekou, 313, 315
Shenyang, 300
Shenzhen, 287, 288, 300, 312–317, 332
Shimizu, 290
Shinjuku, 150–153, 155, 156, 158, 167,
    171, 175, 176
Shinjuku Foundation for Culture and
    International Exchange, 152, 153
Shinjuku Multicultural Center, 157
Shinjuku Multicultural Coexistence Plaza,
    151
Shinjuku News, 154
shipping, 287, 294, 295, 301
Shisedo, 357
Shizuoka, 117
Silicon Valley, 125
Singapore, 10, 28, 39, 42, 46, 47, 52, 54,
    55, 56, 184, 286, 288, 298, 309, 325,
    327, 331, 333, 347
Sino Trans, 303, 304
Skidmore, 347, 354
skiing, 106
skills, and migration, 1, 3–5, 11, 21, 22,
    24, 28, 30, 85, 86, 90, 124, 129, 181,
    197, 202, 212, 221, 276
social class, 105, 111–113

social mobility, 103
socialization, 37, 38
soft power, 14
software, 133, 134, 137, 204
SoHo China, 336, 341, 356, 358, 359, 361
SoHo Newtown, 356
SOPEMI Report, 71, 81, 83, 85
South Africa, 252, 256
South, the, 12, 45, 71
Soviet Union, 82, 252
Spain, 73, 83, 89, 98
Special Targeted Enforcement Program
    (STEP), 75
spouses, 50, 51, 60, 61, 124, 139, 237, 238
Sri Lanka, 28, 30, 84
starchitects, 336, 341
State Department (US), 77
State Owned Enterprise (SOE), 254, 261,
    297
students, 4, 22, 24, 86, 104, 125, 128,
    130–133, 217
Sudan, 12
Super-Hub Port Initiative, 285, 292
Super-hub ports, 294
supermarkets, 255
surplus, trade, 13
Switzerland, 71, 84

Tachikawa, 150, 151, 168–176
Taipei, 2, 45, 140, 280
Taiwan, 2–4, 6, 10, 23–25, 28, 39, 42, 46,
    47, 50, 52–55, 59, 86, 212, 255, 270,
    276, 277, 280, 281, 288, 291, 318,
    324, 326
Taiwan National University, 2
Tanjung Pelepas, 333
teachers, 214, 215, 217, 219–221
Technical Education and Skills
    Development Authority (TESDA),
    192, 194, 195
technology, 11, 21–26, 74, 134
terrorism, 75, 87, 323, 325, 327, 329, 330,
    334
Tesco, 255
textiles and clothing (T&C), 9, 249, 250,
    251, 254, 256, 261, 262

Thai, 159
Thailand, 10, 17, 28, 31, 33, 50, 54,
    57–59, 90, 100, 298
Thais, 115
The Gap, 255
third world, 95
Thomas, P.S., 210, 211
Tiananmen Square, 348
Time Magazine, 13
TMC, 303, 304
Tochigi, 107
Tokaido, 108
Tokugawa period, 94
Tokyo, 13, 16, 18, 106–108, 111, 112,
    114, 115, 117, 127, 134, 289, 294
Tokyo Metropolitan Area (TMA), 149–
    151, 155, 167–169, 171, 174–177
Tokyo Metropolitan Government, 165
Tokyo, prefecture, 105
Toyota, 133, 293
trade, 9, 11, 14–17, 25, 44, 182, 183, 297,
    329, 330
trainees, 131, 185
training, 192–195
transnationalism, 125, 126
Tsang, D., 309
Tunisia, 84, 89
Turkey, 89, 256
Twenty-Four Hour Rule, 321

UN Population Bureau, 70
undocumented workers, 31
unemployment, 74, 99, 100
uniforms, 141
United Arab Emirates, 212
United Kingdom, 72, 74, 79, 81, 85, 87,
    101, 128, 189, 190, 218, 249
United Nations, 10, 14, 27, 28, 33–35
United Nations Development Program, 202
United Nations Economic and Social
    Commission for Asia and the Pacific
    (UNESCAP), 34, 184
United Nations High Commissioner for
    Human Rights (UNHCHR), 33
United Nations High Commissioner for
    Refugees (UNHCR), 33, 73, 79

United States, 1, 2, 4, 6, 10, 12, 13, 16–18,
    22, 24, 28, 52, 53, 71, 72, 74 75, 79,
    83, 87–89, 99, 101, 104, 114, 125,
    128, 129, 150, 183, 189, 190, 209,
    215, 218, 222, 232, 245, 249,
    251–253, 255, 256, 258, 259, 262,
    269, 280, 285, 298, 316, 324, 326,
    329, 330, 332, 335–337, 341, 354
United States Bilateral Trade Agreement
    (USBTA), 253, 254
universities, 6, 102
UNOCAL, 12, 13
unskilled jobs, 197
UPS, 316
UPS Nippon Express, 300
Urban Environment and Research
    Institute, 354
urban space, 342–345, 364, 365
Uruguay Round, 249
US Africa Growth and Opportunity Act
    (AGOA), 256
US Customs and Border Protection
    (CBP), 333
US Customs Service, 333

Vaile, M., 15
Venice Biennale, 357
Very Large Crude Carrier (VLCC), 301
Vietnam, 17, 50, 52, 54, 56–57, 83,
    225–233, 236–240, 244–246, 250,
    252–254, 256, 259, 261, 262, 298
Vietnam Household Living Standards
    Survey (VLSS), 225–228
Vietnamese, 159
Virginia, 11
visas, 123, 128, 131–133, 157
voting, 156, 169

wages, 75, 100, 190, 222
Waigaoqiao, 304
Walmart, 255, 262
Wang, Q., 352
war, 49
Washington, 12, 13, 16
welfare, 47–49, 196
West, the, 12, 52, 82

westerners, in Japan, 114
women, 30, 31, 46, 47, 50, 52, 54, 58, 70,
    77, 78, 95, 105, 115, 124, 140–142,
    183–186, 188, 196, 197, 212, 219
working class, 116
working conditions, 197
Working Group on Organized Crime, 77
World Bank, 70
World Trade Organization (WTO), 15,
    249, 253, 254, 258, 297, 348
World War I, 9
World War II, 9, 95
Wusongkou, 304

xenophobia, 86, 95
Xiamen, 300
Xian, 300
Xiao Yang Shan Island, 304

Yamaguchi, 103
Yamamoto, R., 350, 358
Yamanashi, 107
Yang Ming Line, 303, 304
Yangshan, 304
Yangtian, 317, 318
Yangtze River, 299, 304
Yantian, 313, 315, 332
Yim, R., 358
Yokkaichi, 292
Yokohama, 114, 290, 292, 332

Zhang, X., 356, 357
Zhongshan, 313
Zhuhai, 315
ZIM, 303